DATE DUE

JUN 28 2011

JUN 28 2011

MAR 0 8 2018

MAR 2 1 2018

NOV 2 6 2018

Our Bodies, Our Crimes

Our Bodies, Our Crimes

The Policing of Women's Reproduction in America

Jeanne Flavin

NEW YORK UNIVERSITY PRESS

New York and London

NEW YORK UNIVERSITY PRESS
New York and London
www.nyupress.org

Library of Congress Cataloging-in-Publication Data
Flavin, Jeanne, 1965–
Our bodies, our crimes : the policing of women's
reproduction in America / Jeanne Flavin.
p. cm. — (Alternative criminology series)
Includes bibliographical references and index.
ISBN-13: 978-0-8147-2754-6 (cl : alk. paper)
ISBN-10: 0-8147-2754-9 (cl : alk. paper)
1. Women's rights—United States. 2. Abortion--United States.
3. Women prisoners—Family relationships—United States.
4. Children of women prisoners—United States. 5. Women
prisoners—Health and hygiene—United States. 6. Women—
United States—Social conditions. I. Title.
HQ1236.5.U6F532   2008
323.3'40973—dc22   2008023038

New York University Press books are printed on acid-free paper,
and their binding materials are chosen for strength and durability.
We strive to use environmentally responsible suppliers and materials
to the greatest extent possible in publishing our books.

Manufactured in the United States of America

10 9 8 7 6 5 4 3 2 1

To my friends and my sisters

Contents

Introduction

I do know that it's true that if you wanted to reduce crime, you
could—if that were your sole purpose—you could abort every black
baby in this country, and your crime rate would go down.
> —William Bennett, former Secretary of Education,
> responding to a caller on his radio show, September 29, 2005[1]

The blind conviction that we have to do something about other
people's reproductive behaviour, and that we may have to do it
whether they like it or not, derives from the assumption that the
world belongs to us, who have so expertly depleted its resources,
rather than to them, who have not.
> —Germaine Greer, *Sex and Destiny*, 1984

Like many people, I was slow to recognize reproductive rights
as such. When I was about 8 years old, I sat down at the kitchen table in my
working-class home in rural Kansas and wrote a letter to my state senator,
Bob Dole, urging him to oppose abortion because it involved killing an
unborn baby. I wrote with the moral certainty that a lot of children have at
that age, supported by loving and devout Catholic parents and catechism
teachers who reminded me at regular intervals that "Abortion is murder"
and "Women who don't take responsibility for their mistakes are just looking for an easy way out."

A few years later, I discovered that a local teenager was pregnant—and
defiant. She did not marry her baby's father, and she insisted on attending
high school in spite of objections from some of the locals.[2] I could imagine
that raising a baby as a single teenage mother wasn't easy, but I wondered,
even then, whether it needed to be so hard. After I left home, and went off
to college, I had friends who faced tough decisions about whether or not to

have or rear a child. They were not self-centered or irresponsible. Typically, they were all too aware of others' judgments and the financial and social consequences their decisions would have, not only for themselves but also for any child they might bring into the world.

My politics began to shift to the left in the 1980s as I met women who navigated life encumbered by limited resources and bleak prospects. As an intern at a county juvenile court, I encountered a 15-year-old girl who carted her two children in a red wagon nearly two miles to the courthouse where she was to answer charges of shoplifting chocolate chip cookies and a package of bologna. She felt bad for stealing the cookies, but she was not in the least remorseful for stealing the bologna to feed her kids. In graduate school in the early 1990s, I became aware of the women ensnared in the criminal justice system, including thousands of women with histories of substance abuse. I met a woman who was sentenced to 10 years for becoming pregnant while using cocaine even though she gave birth to a healthy son. Later, I came to know a woman who served a 20-year sentence during which she tried to sustain a relationship with her child. Her son, a toddler when she was arrested, was being raised a thousand miles away.[3]

Over the years, I saw more clearly how restricted a woman's "choices" can be, particularly when she is isolated economically, socially, or geographically. These women exposed me to the influence of public institutions like schools, clinics, and the courts on women's personal and reproductive lives. They also highlighted the problem of reducing reproductive rights to just the single right of a safe and legal abortion. As law professor Dorothy Roberts pointed out in her celebrated work *Killing the Black Body,* for women who are poor and black, reproductive rights are as often about the right to conceive, to be pregnant, to access good-quality reproductive health care, and to rear one's children without unwarranted or harmful official interference as they are about the right to end a pregnancy.[4]

As I use the term here, "reproductive rights" include the basic rights of all women to have sex according to their own thoughts and feelings, free of discrimination, coercion, violence, fear, or shame. Reproductive rights include the right to enjoy freedom of movement (without being limited by the threat of violence) and to be free from illnesses or other conditions that might interfere with sex and reproduction. Women also have the right to decide whether or not to have children—and, if so, how many—and to determine the spacing and timing of children. Finally, in my view, reproductive rights encompass the right to mother and the right to provide for healthy children by meeting not only their physical needs but also their educational, emotional, and social needs.[5]

Being able to reproduce is so closely identified with being a woman (and vice versa) that, for many, it is almost impossible to think about what it means to be a woman without thinking in terms of the ability to bear and rear children. Respect for a woman's reproductive rights, then, is also inextricably connected to respect for a woman's rights as a human being, independent of whether or not she adheres to societal norms of how a woman should be. Not all women's reproductive capacity, and thus not all women's worth as women, is equally valued.

Simone de Beauvoir's famous observation "One is not born, but rather becomes, a woman" reminds us that we are born biologically male or female but learn what it is to be a man or a woman.[6] Our gender is not a fixed characteristic; it is a social process, something that is negotiated and accomplished through routine interactions with other people and social structures. Both men and women "do gender"—that is, handle situations in such a way that the outcomes are considered gender appropriate. For women, the culturally and socially dominant standards of femininity against which they are measured are strongly tied to sexuality. Evidence of this permeates daily life, for example, in the emphasis on women and girls managing their bodies through make-up, fashion, and weight. Hegemonic ideals about femininity not only dictate how women should look but also how they should behave. We expect women to marry, procreate, give birth, and parent, and we expect these experiences to happen in specific ways.

Some women (i.e., those who are white, middle class, and heterosexual) are more likely to be seen as "real" women because their performance of gender is considered closer to the ideal than "other" women. The ability of women of color, poor women, and lesbians to reproduce becomes particularly problematic for the state, given their higher rates of female-headed households and children born "out of wedlock." Correspondingly, society blames poor women of color for a huge range of social problems, including crime, drug use, poor schools, and poverty.[7] As the blame has mounted, so has the regulation of their reproduction.

The potential of women to reproduce is distinct from the institution of motherhood. It is the latter, feminist writer Adrienne Rich charges, which "aims at ensuring that that potential—and all women—shall remain under male control."[8] The patriarchal regulation of motherhood, and women's reproduction more broadly, are the focus of this book. In *Our Bodies, Our Crimes,* I consider how the criminal justice system disciplines women's reproductive behavior and how it maintains the patriarchal notion that women's value derives mainly from their sexuality and reproductive capacity.[9]

Importantly, because women's gender is tied up in reproduction in a way that men's gender is not, the consequences of official attempts to restrict reproductive freedom have a much more profound effect on women than they do on men. Women's reproduction is more likely to be targeted than men's is, and with far more devastating consequences. My concern here is with how the criminal justice system responds when a woman's gender performance falls short as when, for example, a teenager abandons her newborn or a woman uses cocaine while she is pregnant.

As an official agent of social control, the criminal justice system responds not only to crime but also to transgressions against gender norms. By restricting some women's access to abortion and obstetric and gynecologic care, by telling some women not to procreate and pressuring them to be sterilized, by prosecuting some women who use drugs and become pregnant, and by failing to support the efforts of incarcerated women and battered women to rear their children, the law and the criminal justice system establish what a "good woman" or a "fit mother" should look like and how conception, pregnancy, birth, and child care and socialization are regulated.

This regulation of reproduction reinforces limited biological definitions of maleness and femaleness. It promotes a view of gender as a fixed, individual trait rather than a more fluid understanding, one rooted in historical and institutional contexts. And, as we see in the insufficiency of the criminal justice system's responses to marital rape, domestic violence, and child abduction, it helps sustain the family as a site of male dominance over women.

Sometimes the state's intervention into women's reproductive lives is obvious, as when judges order women not to procreate or correctional staff refer women who use illicit drugs to a program that pays the women to be sterilized. Other times, as with incarceration, it is less obvious. Prison not only incapacitates women and prevents them from committing crimes while they are locked up, it also prevents them from accessing their reproductive rights. By denying incarcerated women good-quality reproductive health care, by imprisoning many of them for the duration of their reproductive years, and by interfering with their ability to see (much less rear) their children, incarceration punishes women not just for their crimes but for their perceived shortcomings as women and mothers.

Women do possess and exercise agency, of course, and have the capacity to resist or reject dominant definitions of femininity and womanhood.[10]
But many women's capacity is constrained by their social conditions, including poverty and limited employment and housing options, as well as
restricted access to abortion and contraceptives, gynecologic care, and
drug treatment. The judgments women face, for example, when they pro-
ceed with a pregnancy while addicted to drugs or remain with an abusive
partner, also restricts their options. Workers in the criminal justice system,
including judges, prosecutors and defense attorneys, and correctional staff
and administrators, often ignore the context in which women's actions take
place in favor of assuming it is completely within a woman's power to enter
drug treatment or set up a new household.

Overview of the Book

I have not written an exhaustive account of how the criminal justice system
responds to the threat that women's sexuality and reproductive behaviors
pose to the dominant order. There are simply too many examples to give
each one its due here. Subjects such as violence among same-sex couples,
sexual assault, and incest receive far less attention in this book than they
deserve. I focus almost exclusively on women in this book, even though
men are also subjected to some reproductive regulation. For example, men
who owe child support have been issued "pay up or zip up" no-procreation
orders.[11] Young black men are locked up at rates that have undermined
families and entire communities.[12] By and large, however, I find that the efforts to restrict and control reproduction have been focused on poor racial
and ethnic minority women and therefore they receive the greatest consideration in this book.

Arguments that we need to restrict and even criminalize some women's
behaviors to ensure the healthy reproduction of the United States have been
around at least since the nineteenth century. In part I, chapter 1, I describe
how the eugenic criminology movement that dominated at the turn of the
century continues to structure our values and assumptions about who is
"good" or "bad." Today, the language is less overtly racist, but the underlying sentiment remains: some women should be prevented from exercising
their reproductive rights; other women's reproduction should be supported
and encouraged.[13]

As the control of women's bodies and reproductive lives has become
more intrusive and pervasive, I fear it has become invisible and taken for

granted. Abortion may be the most hotly debated reproductive right, but it is hardly the only one. To highlight the scope of these rights, the remainder of this book is divided into three parts that correspond roughly to the timing or site of the reproductive control: Begetting, Bearing, and Mothering.[14] In part II, I address policies aimed at limiting a woman's say over her fertility and fecundity. This section begins, fittingly, with conception. In chapter 2, I describe how some women have been subjected to institutional segregation and sterilization orders. For example, in recent years, a number of women have been ordered not to procreate or have undergone sterilization as part of their punishment.[15] In chapter 3, I focus on the renewed interest in criminalizing abortion by targeting abortion providers and imposing restrictions on women who seek abortions. Abortion has long been an option for those who can afford it while marginally available to those who cannot. Many women are trapped: disdained for being pregnant while they are poor, teenagers, incarcerated, or using illegal drugs yet similarly disparaged if they seek an abortion.

Even with the greater availability of contraceptives and the greater acceptance of children born outside of marriage, each year, untold numbers of women (many of them frightened teenagers) give birth to a child they are ill positioned to take care of. In chapter 4, I consider the extreme case of women and girls who abandon and, in some cases, kill their newborns. The highly variable criminal justice responses suggest a strange incertitude about whether the women who commit these acts deserve our scorn or our sympathy.

In part III, I move the discussion from conception and fecundity to pregnancy. In chapter 5, I examine the repercussions of recognizing claims of "fetal rights." Homicide is one of the leading causes of death among pregnant women.[16] Rather than offering enhanced penalties in cases where a person's criminal act hurts a woman who is pregnant, many states have passed fetal homicide laws that treat the fetus as an independent "victim" with distinct (and sometimes competing) legal rights from the woman herself. Here I also examine cases in which drug-using women have been arrested and prosecuted for becoming pregnant and continuing their pregnancies to term. The very fact of these prosecutions suggests that pregnant women are punished twice: once for violating our drug laws and again for transgressing against dominant notions of how a pregnant woman should behave. Both fetal homicide laws and prosecutions for maternal substance use render a woman subordinate to the interests of the fetus that she carries.

In chapter 6, I examine the quality of reproductive health care in prisons and jails. Every year, about 2,000 women give birth while incarcerated.[17] The quality of prenatal care available to incarcerated women is notoriously poor. Shoddy medical treatment also compromises the gynecologic health of women who are not pregnant and, in many cases, has effectively denied incarcerated women their right to sexual and reproductive health.

In part IV, I document the criminal justice system's impact on women's attempts to parent. In chapter 7, I continue the discussion of incarcerated women. Today, between 1.5 and 2 million children in the United States have at least one incarcerated parent. Incarcerated women face many parenting challenges, such as visiting and communication, as well as negotiating foster care and custody arrangements. These barriers interfere with incarcerated women's ability to mother their children and place many women at risk for having their parental rights permanently severed. In chapter 8, I show how battering affects a woman's ability to bear and raise her children in a safe environment. Since the 1970s, men's violence against women has come to be regarded as a crime. It has yet, however, to be widely recognized as a reproductive rights concern.

In the conclusion to this volume, called "Being," I consider what the criminal justice system's attempts at controlling women's reproduction say about how we define and value *all* women. Laissez-faire liberals argue that the state should not be involved in the reproductive arena. Social conservatives argue that the state must be involved in it, as a matter of protecting the state's interest in a healthy pregnancy outcome.[18] Concerned about how this involvement has played out to date, I support a third view, one that encourages us to ask "not *whether* the state should be involved in these decisions, but *to what extent* and *how?*"[19] I conclude that we need policies that both respect women's reproductive rights and ensure that women across the spectra of age, race, ethnicity, social class, and sexuality are situated such that they can exercise their rights.[20]

Our Bodies, Our Crimes is mainly about state-imposed restrictions on women's reproduction. As a single woman who has never wanted to conceive, bear, or raise a child of her own, I am acutely aware that reproductive justice demands the freedom *not* to reproduce. Women who choose not to procreate or to marry pose a serious threat to patriarchy and conventional social structures. At its heart, then, this book is about the freedom to be a healthy woman and a valued member of society independent of one's reproductive contribution or perceived lack thereof.

PART I

Beginning

1

"Race Criminals"
Reproductive Rights in America

The man or woman who deliberately foregoes [the supreme blessings of children] whether from viciousness, coldness, shallow-heartedness, self-indulgence, or mere failure to appreciate aright the difference between the all-important and the unimportant,—why, such a creature merits contempt as hearty as any visited upon the soldier who runs away in battle, or upon the man who refuses to work for the support of those dependent upon him, and who tho able-bodied is yet content to eat in idleness the bread which others provide. The existence of women of this type forms one of the most unpleasant and unwholesome features of modern life.
  —President Theodore Roosevelt, in a speech delivered before the National Congress of Mothers, March 13, 1905

What is the problem of women's freedom? It seems to me to be this: how to arrange the world so that women can be human beings, with a chance to exercise their infinitely varied gifts in infinitely varied ways, instead of being destined by the accident of their sex to one field of activity—housework and child-raising.
  —Crystal Eastman, "Now We Can Begin," December 1920

To illustrate more than 200 years of reproductive rights history in the United States, one might imagine drawing a line that begins when abortion was a widely deplored crime. Our line would then move steadily up and on to the 1960s when women's sexual liberation gained more attention and helped abortion become more widely accepted. Naturally, our line would culminate in the progressive present when abortion is legal and our laws and policies reflect widespread acceptance and respect for all women's reproductive rights.

One might imagine such a line, but one would be very, very wrong.

This book focuses mainly on the contemporary context of the struggle for reproductive justice; however, in this chapter I sketch a very broad historical overview of this struggle. The history of abortion and, indeed, the entire history of reproductive rights is not a straight line but one that is uneven and jagged, to say the least. In particular since the 1980s, reproductive rights have eroded steadily, and today is hardly a zenith, especially for low-income racial and ethnic minority women. We need more than one line to capture the erratic attitudes and actions of medical and legal professionals, not to mention politicians, activists, and the general public. Nor can a single line record all of the institutional sites where this control takes place. The regulation of women's reproduction has a long history, one that has always been tied up in larger societal concerns about the "right" people reproducing in the "right" ways. To that end, I look not only at the battle over abortion but also the eugenics campaigns of the twentieth century.

Abortion and the Crusade against Quack Doctors

Most people are aware that abortion used to be considered a crime in the United States. Far fewer realize that at the beginning of the nineteenth century, abortion was essentially legal in America and first-trimester abortions (and many second-trimester abortions) faced little regulation.[1] Abortion before quickening (or the point usually occurring during the fourth and the sixth months when a woman can feel fetal movement) was considered, at most, a misdemeanor. In the 1820s, a handful of state statutes were introduced that punished abortion after quickening.[2]

In the early nineteenth century, abortion was practiced mainly by unmarried and desperate women. By 1840, however, married, middle-class or upper-middle-class, native-born Protestant women were increasingly using abortion to control the spacing and number of their children.[3] By the middle of the century, abortion had become fairly common. Possibly as many as one-fifth to one-third of all pregnancies in the early and mid-nineteenth century ended in abortion.[4] Then, in the 1870s, the tenor shifted, and grisly accounts of botched abortions began to appear more and more frequently in newspapers.[5] By 1900, every state had passed a law criminalizing abortion at any stage of pregnancy, unless it was required to save a woman's life.

What accounts for the rapid change? Abortions had not suddenly become unsafe. Rather, the shift reflected in large part a campaign generated by elite or "regular" physicians who opposed abortion and birth control use among middle-class "native" Protestant women. These physicians preyed on growing fears of race suicide and the higher fertility rates of poor, foreign-born, and predominantly Catholic women.[6]

Regular physicians used abortion to suit their own ambitions—that is, they wanted to become recognized as professionals.[7] In nineteenth-century America, anyone who claimed medical talent could practice medicine. Physicians who had some formal training and subscribed to the medical model found themselves competing with midwives, healers, botanics, homeopaths, and out-and-out quacks who—in the absence of licensing laws—also could claim the title of "doctor." To address this problem, professional physicians launched what one headline heralded as a "Crusade against Quack Doctors." An 1876 *New York Times* article announced the New York County Medico Society's crusade against "the hundreds of quacks, abortionists, and all sorts of irregular medical practitioners whose names, prefixed by "Dr.," adorn the house-fronts on almost every street in the City."[8] The crusading doctors focused on abortion, successfully pressing to outlaw it unless it was necessary to save a woman's life and declaring that only doctors would decide when abortion was permitted.[9] Physicians presented themselves as being obligated to save women from the ignorance that led them to become inadvertent murderesses.[10]

Even after abortion was criminalized, most nineteenth-century laws included a therapeutic exception that allowed abortions when physicians deemed it necessary to save a woman's life. Doctors did not forbid abortions absolutely because a complete ban on abortions would not have advanced their own professional goals. Making a moral claim ("We are saving the lives of unborn embryos") based on technical expertise ("Only we can determine when a pregnant woman's life is in jeopardy") also prevented other interested parties, such as lawyers, clergy, and women, from challenging doctors' asserted right to control abortion.[11] At the time, feminists were more concerned about promoting voluntary motherhood (including the right of a woman to refuse to sexually submit to her husband) and reducing death in childbirth than with abortion.[12] Without an effective challenge to the medical profession's control of abortion, the public came to accept, and continues to do so, even today, the legitimacy of doctors' decision-making in the area of abortion (not to mention pregnancy and childbirth).[13] As a result, a personal decision has become a medical one.[14]

The laws at the time mainly criminalized abortion providers. As Rosalind Pollack Petchesky observes in *Abortion and Woman's Choice*, "Laws criminalizing abortion in the latter half of the nineteenth century did not suppress abortion as much as they revealed it, regulated it, certified it as a legitimate domain of public intervention and control."[15] Up until 1940, prosecutors focused specifically on abortion providers whose practices killed or seriously injured a woman patient. Relatively few people were ever charged under the abortion laws, and when they were charged, jurors were reluctant to convict them. When abortion providers were convicted, punishments were lenient and often included probation.[16] Some state laws did not specify any punishment at all for women who sought abortions. In 1934, the punishment for women who had abortions ranged from fines of $100 to $1,000, and periods of incarceration ranged from 30 days to 10 years.[17] The lack of consistency in enforcing the existing laws or pursuing prosecution or serious punishment suggests an ambivalence toward the practice.[18] In spite of abortion's illegality, large numbers of early-twentieth-century women were still able to obtain abortions from physicians and midwives.

The Depression, Physicians, and "Back-Alley Butchers"

Over time, proportionally fewer abortions were performed out of medical necessity. Between World War I and World War II, medical advances meant that fewer conditions (such as tuberculosis or cardiovascular disease) could be considered as indications that an abortion was necessary to save a woman's life. Also, as physicians became more comfortable with their professional status, they relaxed their standards about performing abortions. They performed abortions not only when a woman's life was in danger but also when her offspring might be deformed or when they sympathized with her plight—for example, if she was poor or the victim of rape or incest.

The Great Depression of the 1930s brought the relationship between economics and reproduction into stark relief. Unable to afford to have children, women sought abortions on a massive scale.[19] Legal and illegal abortion practices expanded as women appealed to doctors for help. Increasingly, physicians considered social conditions in making medical decisions about which abortions were "therapeutic," that is, necessary to preserve a woman's life or health.[20]

During the same period, the site of medical care (including minor surgical procedures such as early abortions) was shifting from midwives' practices and private physicians' offices to hospitals.[21] This trend accelerated after World War II. Accompanying this shift was greater public awareness and oversight of the medical processes taking place in hospitals.[22] Hospital administrators feared that their facilities would develop reputations as abortion mills. In the 1940s and 1950s, they began to introduce therapeutic abortion boards to determine whether an abortion was justified.[23] Typically, these boards encouraged doctors to keep the incidence of abortion low. The institutional support that these boards provided took the pressure off individual physicians whose abortion decisions might be challenged.[24]

Physicians and hospital boards were more likely to accommodate white middle-class women's requests for a therapeutic abortion.[25] Poor and minority women and women in rural areas were much more likely than their white, middle-class, and urban counterparts to patronize more dangerous and inexpensive illegal abortion providers.[26] Many poor women's lack of ties to an informal network prevented them from finding a provider. They were compelled to either give birth or attempt self-abortion, at times with fatal or life-threatening consequences.[27] Fear led many women to defer seeking help, which made illegal abortions even riskier.[28] Those poor and minority patients who did receive a therapeutic abortion were more likely to be involuntarily sterilized. Basically, a few therapeutic abortions became legal, while poor women's access to abortion was restricted further. Nontherapeutic abortions became criminalized and harder to procure, even through physicians operating a private practice.[29]

Within a section of the medical profession, however, doctors came to form a liberal consensus about the horrors of criminalized abortion and the importance of performing abortions for those patients who needed them. Hospitals were increasing the sites where abortions took place and where women sought treatment for medical complications from illegal abortions. Doctors' awareness of the disastrous consequences of abortion laws grew.[30] Eventually, their concern led them to form an uneasy alliance with a grassroots social movement led by women that contributed to abortion's legalization.[31]

"Race Criminals" and the Eugenics Movement

The eugenics movement of the first decades of the twentieth century underscored the notion that some women's reproductive capacity was more valuable than others. In the 1920s, many (though not all) Progressives in America promoted a eugenics agenda that they claimed would ensure the health of the "native" white European Protestant population.[32] African Americans, immigrants, and the working class were perceived to be present in growing numbers. So, too, were what President Theodore Roosevelt called "race criminals"—white middle-class women of "good stock" who chose not to have children.[33] Women were reproducing, but it was the "wrong" women, those deemed unworthy of reproduction who came from dubious genetic origins.

Eugenics advocates played into fears of "race suicide" by advancing the notion that not only were immigrant women intellectually and morally inferior but they also could pass on deviant traits to their many offspring. At the same time as physicians encouraged native women to reproduce, they launched a program designed to limit the propagation of the poor, the foreign-born, and the so-called unfit.[34] Toward those ends, eugenicists encouraged white Protestant women to have children and steer clear of birth control and abortion (i.e., "positive eugenics"). While abortions were discouraged among white Protestant women, eugenics advocates promoted a campaign to limit the fertility of poor and immigrant women (i.e., "negative eugenics"). As discussed in greater detail in the next chapter, this campaign labeled women and girls as "sexually delinquent" and "feeble-minded" and then either sterilized them or segregated them in institutions, or both.[35]

After World War II and the growing awareness of the eugenic horrors of the Holocaust, institutional sterilizations declined, but coercive or involuntary sterilizations continued outside of institutional settings. For example, by 1965, some 28 states had laws permitting involuntary sterilization. Over time, the idea that poverty, delinquency, feeble-mindedness, and promiscuity were inherited characteristics fell out of vogue. Replacing it, however, was the equally damaging notion that poverty was caused by poor women having too many children, rather than dropping wages or a lack of social support. To this way of thinking—and one that persists today—reducing the number of children born to poor women would alleviate poverty.

In the 1960s and 1970s, tens of thousands of sterilizations were disproportionately performed on Native American, black, and Hispanic women; many, though not all, were coerced or involuntary.[36] Instead of citing a desire for racial purity, doctors (who were overwhelmingly white and middle class) often suggested that by limiting the number of births in low-income, minority families, government spending on Medicaid and welfare programs could be reduced and the families could achieve financial security.[37] Also, many of these doctors believed that minority women could not or would not use other methods of birth control effectively. Therefore, many doctors encouraged sterilization.

Race and Reproductive Rights

Decided in 1973, the *Roe v. Wade* ruling held that in the first trimester, the abortion decision should be limited to a woman and her doctor. After the first trimester, the state may regulate abortions when necessary to promote women's health (as defined in *Doe v. Bolton* to include physical, emotional, psychological, and familial factors).[38] After fetal viability (usually defined as somewhere between 22 and 26 weeks of gestation), the state can prohibit abortions except those needed to preserve a woman's life or health.[39]

In the years leading up to *Roe v. Wade,* most white, middle-class feminists were fighting for the right to abortion and birth control. The radical feminists focused on the pursuit of sexual pleasure without fear of being forced into a marriage or getting pregnant. They fought for sexual liberation and voluntary motherhood.

As a campaign strategy, emphasizing the need for safe and legal abortions was effective.[40] But then, as now, voluntary fertility control through abortion and contraception was never the driving force behind black and Puerto Rican women's quest for reproductive rights.[41] While they shared white women's desire to limit their own fertility on their own terms, their experiences and political agenda were quite different. Sexual liberation and voluntary motherhood were less pressing goals. They already suffered under persistent stereotypes that they were not only sexually liberated but "hypersexual." Also, because of the legacy of widespread sterilization abuse, many activists of color associated abortion rights with population control, racial genocide, and coercion.

Black and Puerto Rican women activists supported safe and legal abortion, but more than white women activists of the time, they recognized that reproductive rights extended to the need for state-supported child-care services, decent wages and benefits, safe and affordable housing, and good medical care that would permit them to bear and raise healthy children.[42] Sadly, their advocacy was only of limited success and has proven to be a missed opportunity for women to gain access to the full range of reproductive rights.

In the early 1970s, poor women, on their own initiative and without needing the government to remind them how difficult and expensive it can be to rear a child, sought and obtained abortions at a substantially higher rate than white middle-class women did.[43] But even after *Roe v. Wade* was decided, the federal government continued their efforts to reduce poor and minority women's childbearing. By the middle 1970s, the public was taking its cues from the federal government's lead. Powerful and negative attitudes toward poor, childbearing women of color—aka "ghetto matriarchs," "Jezebels," and "welfare queens"—developed that did not take into account factual information about how many children or abortions poor women actually had. Black and Hispanic women on welfare were cast as cheating prostitutes. They became, as historian Rickie Solinger describes, "the symbol of dependent women making bad choices. The figure of the [Welfare] Queen stood for a woman who made the kind of choices that caused other women, working people, the oppressed middle class, and all good Americans to resent her and even hate her and to see her as the member of a reviled caste."[44]

Meanwhile, Catholics and Protestant fundamentalists undertook anti-abortion campaigns to advance their own tactical agendas. Their campaigns emphasized motherhood, claims of fetal rights, and a view of the traditional family unit as an endangered species, threatened not only by abortion but also by homosexuality, divorce, and nonmarital sexuality.[45] In the 1970s and early 1980s, the New Right readily saw the connections among sexuality, work, and family; poor women were the ripest targets for their agenda.[46] The combination of these "strains of hostility" resulted in a "political program that fatally attacked the idea of abortion rights and seriously diminished the citizenship status of poor women in the United States."[47] Almost immediately after the *Roe v. Wade* decision in 1973, efforts got under way to limit the use of public funds to pay for poor women's abortions.

At first, most federal courts acknowledged that it was not fair for the state to refuse to pay for a woman's elective abortion while paying for other pregnancy-related treatment through Medicaid. But a group of 1976 Supreme Court cases upheld state regulations that denied Medicaid funding for all elective abortions. This, combined with Congress's adoption of the Hyde Amendment in 1976, struck a devastating blow to poor women's reproductive rights. The Hyde Amendment banned Medicaid funding for all abortions except where the woman's life was endangered, when a pregnancy resulted from incest or a rape that had been reported promptly to law enforcement or the public health service, or when two physicians determined that the woman would sustain severe or long-lasting harm to her physical health. The ban had to be reenacted every year. The fierce debates about the Hyde Amendment that took place in the late 1970s were over what one critic described as "how abused or sick or endangered a Medicaid recipient had to be if she were to receive funding for an abortion."[48]

A number of factors worked against abortion rights supporters of the time.[49] The public viewed welfare recipients in an increasingly dim light and were reluctant to see poor women get another "freebie" in the form of a federally funded abortion. It was hard to convince the public that measures like the Hyde Amendment, that most directly affected poor women, threatened the reproductive rights of *all* women. As noted earlier, black and Hispanic activists tried to counter this assault, but they were engaged in a battle to defend their right to experience a pregnancy, not to terminate one.

In 1980, the majority of the Supreme Court ruled in *Harris v. McRae* that *Roe* had promised women freedom from undue interference in their decision to terminate a pregnancy and had *not* provided a constitutional right to an abortion. Even when it was medically necessary, the federal government was no longer obliged to fund a poor woman's abortion.[50] As Solinger observes, "the government would not criminalize abortion, but neither would the government pay for it, no matter where that left a poor woman."[51] Another blow was dealt to the abortion rights movement in 1989 when the George H. W. Bush administration urged the Supreme Court to revisit the *Roe* decision by hearing the case of *Webster v. Reproductive Health Services.* *Webster* questioned whether it was constitutional to prohibit public facilities or employees from performing abortions except to save a woman's life. The Court upheld the restrictions; only four Justices voted to uphold *Roe* in its entirety.[52]

Webster has been described as "an open invitation to state legislators to see just how strictly they can regulate abortion without Justice O'Connor's [the swing vote] finding the burden on the abortion right 'undue.'"[53] Since *Roe,* a series of court rulings have undermined the principle of abortion as a woman's right. The trimester framework laid out in *Roe* has been replaced by a standard that upholds abortion counseling, waiting periods, and parental involvement requirements provided they do not impose an "undue burden."[54] Emerging guidelines suggest that only medically necessary abortions are permitted (and even then, the state is not obligated to pay for them). Abortion is now often treated as a religious and moral issue rather than a health issue. Women, particularly if they are unmarried teenagers, are treated as incompetent to choose between abortion and childbirth.[55] Anticipation of these developments is no doubt what prompted Supreme Court Justice Blackmun to write in his 1989 *Webster* dissent, "For today, the women of this Nation shall retain the liberty to control their destinies. But the signs are evident and very ominous, and a chill wind blows."[56] As discussed in a later chapter, the chill wind continues to blow into the twenty-first century, with the 2007 Supreme Court *Carhart* ruling to uphold the ban on the so-called Partial Birth Abortion Act despite—for the first time since *Roe v. Wade*—the absence of an exception to preserve a woman's health.

Reproductive Rights after Roe v. Wade: *The Limits of Choice*

Emphasizing Choice

It bears asking why the hypothetical line of reproductive rights drawn earlier in this chapter has taken such a sharp nosedive since *Roe v. Wade* was decided in 1973. For starters, valuable ground was lost when, in the battle to attract more mainstream support for abortion, advocates focused narrowly on abortion and framed the issue in terms of choice, privacy, and states' rights, while backing off claims of reproductive rights and women's bodily sovereignty. The language of choice that has become so widely accepted fails to acknowledge that women's choices are often severely circumscribed by social and material conditions. "Then and now, many Americans have glossed over this," Rickie Solinger argues in *Beggars and Choosers:*

> Poor and/or culturally oppressed women in the United States and abroad may lack the money to "choose" abortion. They may live where abortion is inaccessible, illegal, or life-threatening. They may lack the resources to feed the children they have, much less a new baby. They may want to be mothers but lack the resources to escape stigma, punishment, or death for having a baby under the wrong conditions. They may lack the resources to avoid pregnancy from sexual violence. Can women in any of these circumstances be described as in a position to make a choice, a private, personal choice in the way that middle-class Americans generally use that term?[57]

Too often, we have focused narrowly on individual women's reproductive choices and abortion while ignoring the larger context that restricts many women's choices to the point of obliterating them. One does not "choose" to pay for contraceptives or reproductive technologies that are not covered by insurance.[58] In fact, many women still do not have contraceptives covered by their insurance plan, even though these same plans may cover male impotence drugs like Viagra and Cialis.[59] Not many of us would choose to live in an area where a pharmacist can refuse to dispense contraceptives or a health care provider can refuse to provide sterilization or abortion services.[60] And few would claim in good conscience that a teenager who has been raped chooses to face delays or obstacles in obtaining emergency contraception after her assault.

Emphasizing Victimization and Women's Incompetence

In seeking the legalization of abortion, nineteenth- and early-twentieth-century feminists tended to emphasize women's victimization, a strategy that continues to haunt feminism and abortion rights activists today. Feminists had difficulty acknowledging that young, single women sought abortions for reasons other than having been done wrong by their lovers or sexually exploited by their employers.[61] Feminists and other activists were less willing to acknowledge the possibility of female sexual pleasure, much less female sexual independence. It was not until the early twentieth century that birth control advocates helped transform feminism by declaring the legitimacy of these goals.[62] Women were challenging older heterosexual dating and sexual norms; some women's wage-earning ability gave them more freedom to refuse undesirable marriages. By the end of the twentieth century, it was no longer possible to assume that all unmarried women who got pregnant "were victims, that their boyfriends were villains, and that abortions were evidence of victimization."[63]

Even now, abortion rights activists frequently cite rape and incest in their appeals to keep abortion legal and challenge parental notification laws. For example, in 1989, President George H. W. Bush vetoed a federal spending bill that provided for Medicaid-covered abortions in case of rape or incest. In an ultimately unsuccessful effort to secure a congressional override of the veto, pro-abortion lobbyists and lawmakers did not argue that the veto undermined women's reproductive rights. Rather, they contrasted the evilness of rapists with the innocence of rape victims. Pro-choice lawmakers "smothered questions about women's rights and fetal life under a gravy of breast-beating about crime and punishment, innocence and guilt," mentioning victims 135 times and crime 46 times in an hour's worth of speeches from the House floor.[64] In 1993, an exemption for rape or incest was granted only after Sen. Henry Hyde and his supporters realized that they probably did not have the votes they needed if they continued to ban abortion funding without such exemptions.[65]

The appeal of arguments that play on fears of rape and incest, of course, is that they gain the support of those who would be alienated by more radical arguments based on women's right to bodily sovereignty and sexual pleasure or socialist arguments seeking recognition of poor people's humanity. While victimization was used successfully to secure support for the Hyde Amendment's rape and incest exemption, the campaign left millions of poor women without federal coverage for their abortions. It also further stigmatized women who seek abortions who are *not* victims of rape or incest by reinforcing the false distinction between those women who "deserve" the right to an abortion, because they became pregnant through no fault of their own or ignorance, and other women who are characterized as being irresponsible and careless. As part of the effort to garner public recognition of women's reproductive rights, depicting women as incompetent and helpless victims rather than as fully capable, sexual actors was (and remains) problematic. In the process, reproductive rights have become defended, and to some extent defined, as a victim's right rather than a woman's right.[66]

Furthermore, claiming that abortion should be legal to spare women botched back-alley abortions has turned out to be a double-edged sword. While this argument marshalled support for the *Roe* decision, it also reduced *Roe v. Wade* to what one critic deemed "a consumer protection ruling" designed to save desperate, helpless women from being victimized from the evil, uncaring abortionist rather than a necessary measure to assure women's sovereignty over their own bodies.[67] Even today, many feminists and other liberals characterize abortion as a tragic outcome of an unwanted pregnancy. Staunch, elected Democrats such as Hillary Clinton nonetheless adopt the stance that abortion should be "safe, legal and rare."[68] Many abortion advocates prefer to steer clear of messier discussions of late-term abortions and head for less controversial ground, such as ensuring access to abortion in case of rape or incest or when a woman's life is in danger, and promoting contraceptive use. While this cautious approach is understandable in a conservative climate, it also undermines the idea that abortion is a legitimate and effective means of preventing an unwanted birth. Fundamentally, it implies that a woman's decision to terminate a pregnancy is a bad idea.

Emphasizing Responsibility and Self-Control

Discussions of reproductive rights also frequently use the language of personal responsibility and self-control. Here, too, we find a double-edged sword buried in the rhetoric. While on the surface it sounds empowering to assert women's control over their own lives, this language fails to take into account that biology and social circumstance often produce a gap between a woman's personal reproductive ideal and her reality. "Contemporary discussions of fertility control emphasize not the *wish* to plan one's births, to intervene in an inherently ungovernable process," political scientist Lealle Ruhl observes, "but rather the *obligation* to do so."[69] This emphasis on willed pregnancies and the assumption that responsible women can and should control their reproductive functions extends to all women. It has led to the unintended consequence that women increasingly are held accountable for their pregnancy losses or other adverse pregnancy outcomes.[70]

Moreover, poor women, and especially those who are black or Hispanic, are more likely than others to be perceived as representing more and different reproductive threats to the social order. Their "irresponsibility" is targeted differently and often comes under the regulation of the criminal justice and family court systems.[71] A strong national identity that emphasizes America as the land of opportunity and the importance of people pulling themselves up by the proverbial bootstraps contributes to the problem. The pervasive American dream mythology informs even as it harms an entire array of social policy and services. It creates a context in which it is okay to blame poor people for being poor because they are simply not working or trying hard enough. If poor people only have themselves to blame for being poor, then not only is it permissible for state actors to direct them to get a job and not have children but also it is a short hop to seeing the government as being obliged to direct ("help") poor women in how to live their lives. The criminal justice system's involvement in women's reproduction is only one arena where this view seems to hold true, and with damaging effects. It also plays out in the interconnected arenas of public housing, welfare policy, child protective services, access to medical care, and so on. Increasingly, the climate has become one of surveillance, regulation, and enforcement rather than one of support and collaboration.

Conclusion

The vision of early activists remains to be realized. Laudable exceptions notwithstanding, reproductive rights have remained narrowly associated with abortion, and abortion has come to be accompanied by assumptions that women possess either near-complete agency and choice or evince a total absence of autonomy that is associated with victimization and oppression. A concern for reproductive justice has never been allowed to occupy the center stage. While the abortion movement succeeded in using the law and medical authority to achieve legitimacy for abortion, such a strategy still involved institutional control being exercised over women.

Paradoxically, sociologist Nanette J. Davis notes, "the more the abortion movement succeeded as a one-issue campaign, the more women would lose in terms of acquiring ultimate control over their bodies and their lives."[72] And, as subsequent chapters suggest, the legacy of this one-issue campaign continues to be felt most keenly—though not solely—among the most socially and economically vulnerable women in society. While feminists have tried to link abortion to the larger need for reproductive justice, these efforts have not received mainstream support. In the absence of a farther-reaching social movement to call attention to this, the legal and criminal justice systems have managed to quietly undermine reproductive freedom. Many if not most of the gains made during the struggle to legalize abortion and keep it legal have been offset by a larger failure to fully recognize a range of reproductive rights for all women.

Our Bodies, Our Crimes is written against this backdrop of abortion debates that continue to dominate the discussion of reproductive rights. By contrast, I focus on a range of ways in which the legal and criminal justice systems regulate feminine gender ideals and limit access to full citizenship by influencing reproduction. This tension between who should or should not conceive and who should or should not be able to make reproductive decisions manifests itself throughout the criminal justice system (e.g., through law enforcement, the courts, and the correctional system) and throughout the reproductive cycle. *Our Bodies, Our Crimes* considers which reproductive actions are criminalized, as well as how the reproduction of "criminal" women is controlled.

Throughout that struggle for reproductive justice in the United States—a struggle to overcome not only dangerous and illegal abortions but also the incarceration of women and girls for moral offenses and the sterilization of women and girls labeled feeble-minded or delinquent— the criminal justice system has been used to enforce standards regarding which women are fit to have control over their own reproduction and, as well, who may become and remain mothers. Today, some women are actively prevented from reproducing (e.g., through "no-procreation" court orders or incarceration), are coerced into reproducing the "right" way (e.g., by state intervention in their pregnancies and assertions of fetal protectionism), or are punished for reproducing the "wrong" way (e.g., being denied custody of their children if they are battered or being prevented from parenting while incarcerated). Sometimes these actions are justified as being "for the woman's own good," while at other times they are claimed to be "in the best interests of the (preborn) child." But make no mistake, as the chapters that follow seek to demonstrate, individually and collectively, these policies have a devastating impact on a woman's autonomy and her right to privacy, not to mention her physical, socioeconomic, and emotional well-being. Whether a policy stems from a retributivist or paternalist ideology, whether we view women as unwilling or unable to control their reproductive capacities, such extremes fail to respect women's individual and bodily sovereignty. And these policies define what it means to be a woman in very narrow and harmful ways.

PART II

Begetting

2

"Breeders"
The Right to Procreate

A Georgia judge ordered a mother of seven who pleaded guilty to killing her 5-week-old daughter to have a medical procedure to prevent her from having more children. . . . Medicaid is covering the cost of the operation.

—Associated Press, February 9, 2005

Call our offices for flyers to distribute to your local hospitals, police departments, probation department, drug treatment programs and social workers.

—From the website of Project Prevention, an organization that pays women who use drugs $300 or more to use permanent or long-term birth control, 2008

In 2004, Monroe County (NY) Family Court Judge Marilyn O'Connor singled out a woman, Stephanie Pendleton, for having "neglected her responsibilities as a mother" by using cocaine while she was pregnant.[1] At the trial, a representative of Monroe County Department of Health and Human Services presented a permanency plan for reuniting the youngest child, Bobbijean, with her parents. Judge O'Connor, however, modified this plan and ordered that Stephanie was no longer legally allowed to get pregnant and Rodney was no longer legally allowed to father any more children until they had "obtained custody and care of Bobbijean P. and every other child of [Stephanie's] who is in foster care and has not been adopted or institutionalized." The judge went on to order them to attend county-sponsored family planning sessions and reminded them that they could be sterilized at public expense. Later that same year, Judge O'Connor ordered another woman, Judgette W., to have no more children until she regained custody of the seven she already had.[2] In 2007, the no-procreation order issued to Stephanie was vacated.[3]

The judge's concern about children being born to parents who might mistreat them is understandable. Child maltreatment is not uncommon in the United States, and parental failures are all too real. Approximately 73.5 million children live in the United States.[4] Each year, an estimated 850,000–900,000 children are victims of some form of child maltreatment, usually neglect; about 1,500 children will die as a result, most of them under the age of 4. Between 30 and 40 percent of the perpetrators will be mothers acting alone.[5]

Given their extensive previous involvement with family court, one would be hard-pressed to assert that Rodney, Stephanie, and Judgette are model parents, or even necessarily that they are good or "fit" parents. What *is* questioned here is the notion that a judge has the right to order them, or anyone, to be sterilized or not to reproduce. This is arguably one of the most difficult premises for the general public to accept: that a woman's reproductive rights—including her right to procreate—are distinct from whether or not she is or might be a "good" pregnant woman or a "good" mother. These rights reside in her existence as a human being, along with the rights to control her body. A judge may conclude that a woman should not rear her child (a conclusion laden with its own value judgments, as discussed in chapter 7). That, however, is a decision distinct from whether a woman has a right to have sex, to become pregnant, or to give birth.

Reproductive rights scholar Rachel Roth observes that "the history of reproductive politics makes clear that women bear the brunt of scorn heaped on parents deemed too poor to have children, and women have borne the brunt of coercive measures directed at discouraging both sexes from reproducing, including unwilling and unwitting sterilization."[6]

The idea that some people (those who are too poor or too addicted or too feebleminded or too irresponsible or too crazy, etc.) simply shouldn't reproduce has been around for quite some time. So, too, has the corresponding idea that the government should do something to ensure the "right" people reproduce and the "wrong" people don't. These notions sustained the positive and negative eugenics campaigns at the turn of the century which sought to encourage the reproduction of the "fit" and discourage that of the "unfit."[7] It is to this period of history that we now turn and explore the historical criminalization of female sexuality in greater detail.

In so doing, we can better appreciate the cause for concern presented today by state intrusion into the procreation of poor women and other socially vulnerable populations.

The Female Sexual Delinquent

When the first institutions for retarded women were opened in the 1800s, they were governed by a "curative" philosophy that emphasized education and care, protecting these women and girls from being abused by others, and possibly releasing them at some point to be useful members of the community.[8] By the late nineteenth century, however, institutions' concern about protecting individual residents had morphed into a concern about protecting society against the so-called feebleminded, who had been recast as criminalistic degenerates.[9] Not coincidentally, a similar shift occurred in the response to sexually active young women.

This shift from a curative to a custodial philosophy took place in a context of growing concern that feeblemindedness was inherited and linked to moral transgressions and criminality.[10] Right after the anti-abortion campaign in the 1860s and 1870s, hereditarian and biological determinist theories sprang up that laid the foundation for the eugenics movement.[11] In the 1880s, Zebulon Brockway's Elmira Reformatory in New York represented the first systematic attempt at rehabilitating inmates. Because some inmates continued to commit crimes, Brockway concluded that such prisoners must be mental and physical degenerates.[12]

As Wendy Kline explains in *Building a Better Race,* changing the definition of feeblemindedness to refer to a fundamental genetic flaw rather than a slight mental impairment

> had enormous implications both for those already housed in institutions for the feebleminded and for those whose attitude, behavior, or appearance would target them for incarceration and sterilization in the future. The person labeled mentally deficient was no longer deemed an object of curiosity or sympathy but a threat to the genetic health and stability of the race. According to this new definition, nothing in the environment—no amount of education, training, or nurturing—could alter the destructive potential stored within a feeble mind. And because "feeblemindedness" had not been a precise diagnostic term to begin with, it was easily transformed into a catchall term for any type of behavior considered inappropriate or threatening.[13]

As a view that feeblemindedness was hereditary and tied to moral degeneracy emerged, so did concern about the "girl problem" and female sexuality. In the 1900s, young women's and girls' expanded opportunities for employment and recreation were accompanied by a host of social problems, including "prostitution and vice, venereal disease, family breakdown, and out-of-wedlock pregnancies" that provoked considerable public anxiety.[14]

This concern escalated dramatically in the first two decades of the twentieth century. A new generation of Progressive reformers and social workers redefined the problem as one of female immorality. Over time, there was a shift from treating young, sexually active women as hapless victims of male seducers to focusing on the perils of female sexuality and the need to protect society from young women's moral transgressions. Rather than blaming "evil men" for seducing young women (as the moral reformers did), Progressives acknowledged the sexual agency of young, working-class women and girls. Progressives shifted their concern away from controlling the behavior of men (e.g., by prosecuting statutory rape) toward monitoring and controlling young women and the social conditions that were considered to be the cause of their behavior.[15] During this era, Progressive reformers joined up with public officials, physicians, business leaders, and social scientists to launch a crusade against vice and prostitution. They established juvenile courts and reformatories to monitor and correct female sexual delinquents.[16]

Thus, female sexual delinquency and feeblemindedness came to be linked. "Beginning in the 1910s, then," Kline notes, "feeblemindedness and, in particular, the 'moron' category became almost synonymous with the illicit sexual behavior of the woman adrift. Eugenic ideology provided a language and rationale for linking the sexual and reproductive behavior of women with the deterioration of the race."[17] As poor women's economic and sexual autonomy increased, purity crusaders such as Josephine Shaw Lowell, founder of the Newark (NY) Custodial Asylum, argued that young women's bodies posed a moral, social, and medical danger to society.[18] Young women were presumed to be inherently promiscuous; their sexual delinquency in itself was a crime problem. Left unchecked, they would fornicate for pleasure and have sex indiscriminately without regard for the suitability of their partner. Such women posed a "menace to the gene pool" because of their supposed genetic capacity for producing crime-prone offspring.[19] Something needed to be done to extend state control over these women who were destined to be the "weak-minded mother[s] of criminals."[20] Two solutions emerged, both of which involved the criminal justice system to some degree: segregation and sterilization.

At the turn of the century, many experts believed that crime and insanity could be eradicated if the procreation of feebleminded people was stopped. Initially, eugenicists advocated segregating or quarantining the female "high-grade moron" as a means of preventing sexually promiscuous women from infecting the white Protestant race. Progressive Era eugenicists and other moral reformers reasoned that if sexually promiscuous working-class women were quarantined in institutions, then female sexuality would remain "pure" and associated with marriage and family.[21]

Segregation was not without its problems: namely, the expense of maintaining an institution, crowding, and poor management. But the main reason segregation became less popular is that, by the 1910s, it already was apparent that "promiscuous" sexual behavior had spread into the middle classes. Reformers realized that poor and working-class women were not alone in resisting the idea that sexuality should be limited to marriage and motherhood.[22]

It was one thing to institutionalize poor people; in many cases, parents placed children in institutions because they were not financially equipped to care for their child, especially if the child could not be counted on as a wage earner. But middle-class citizens were reluctant to institutionalize their own. Birth control was ruled out due to fears that should it "catch on" among the white Protestant middle classes, their birth rates would be even further reduced.[23] So it came to pass that sterilization emerged as a eugenics strategy.

Eugenicists at the turn of the century were ambitious: by some accounts, they aspired to sterilize nearly 11 million Americans (more than 10 percent of the population at the time), giving priority to those million or so who were institutionalized in poorhouses, mental hospitals, and prisons.[24] At first, compulsory sterilization programs (which attempted to force people to undergo surgical sterilization) were aimed at "feebleminded" and "genetically inferior" women. These programs tended to be motivated by eugenic concerns about heredity, a belief that a "therapeutic" sterilization could lead to vitality, a desire to punish criminals, or some combination thereof.

Upon the founding of the Newark Custodial Asylum for Feeble-minded Women in 1878, eugenics doctrine became the basis for public policy.[25] In Indiana, beginning in 1899, H. C. Sharp devised the vasectomy and carried out hundreds of them on young men at the Indiana State Reformatory.[26] Word of the "Indiana Movement" spread, and physicians were joined by members of the legal profession. In 1911, the American Breeder's

Association formed a committee to examine the best means for "cutting off the defective germ-plasm of the American population."[27]

Other states followed suit, most notably California, which accounted for one-third of all sterilizations of feebleminded and insane people that took place nationwide.[28] During his 26-year tenure (which began in 1918), F. O. Butler, superintendent of the Sonoma State Home for the retarded, performed 1,000 sterilizations and oversaw another 5,400. Between 1931 and 1941, Butler identified nearly 1,500 of the admissions as defective delinquents, sterilizing more than 74 percent of the boys and 86 percent of the girls.[29]

California's policy focused more on female sexuality than on racial minorities or immigrants, but that is not to say that race was irrelevant. The concern about the sexual behavior of white female patients stemmed from a belief that they were primarily responsible for racial degeneration.[30] California statutes also provided for the "asexualization" of state prisoners (including castration and the removal of ovaries) who had been convicted at least two times for sexual offenses and three times for any other crime, provided evidence was given that the prisoner was "a moral or sexual degenerate or pervert."[31]

California was by no means alone in its sterilization efforts. Both North Carolina and Virginia performed more than 8,000 eugenic sterilizations between the late 1920s and the mid-1970s. For instance, from 1924 through 1972, Virginia sterilized more than 8,300 persons, some of whom were described as "'high functioning' retardates who were prostitutes, truants, and petty criminals, not sterilized for their offenses but simply sent to the hospital by local authorities and diagnosed as retarded."[32]

In the 1920s, New Jersey's Reformatory for Women at Clinton Farms transferred feebleminded prisoners of childbearing age to the Vineland institution for the mentally retarded and arranged for inmates who seemed low in intelligence or who had illegitimate or biracial children to be sterilized.[33] West Virginian juvenile court judge Morgan Owen sought support for a new law to sterilize "mental defectives" at three state hospitals, the industrial school for boys, and the industrial home for girls, noting that "a large percentage of the girls brought into court were for sex offenses and a great many of them were found to be feeble-minded."[34] Nationally, many women appear to have been labeled "feebleminded" or delinquent because of a combination of their class and their sexuality rather than their mental aptitude.[35] Most of the girls committed to institutions for delinquency were sexually active rather than guilty of serious sexual or criminal misconduct.[36]

People held in institutions were at the greatest risk for compulsory sterilization; they also tended to be disproportionately black. The fact that certain racial and ethnic groups were overrepresented in prisons and institutions for delinquents was touted as evidence of these groups' inherent inferiority rather than reflective of selective law enforcement or economic disadvantages.[37]

Though sterilization was cheaper and more efficient than segregation and permitted feebleminded women to be released from institutions, eugenicists recognized that it was far from an ideal solution. In particular, there was concern that once sterilized and without the fear of a possible pregnancy hanging over their heads, feebleminded women would become even more promiscuous.[38]

In 1927, the Supreme Court decided *Buck v. Bell,* which upheld the constitutionality of Virginia's sterilization law. The Court rejected the idea that people had a fundamental right to procreate and concluded that it was okay for the state of Virginia to involuntarily sterilize mentally retarded persons. This case ushered in an era where women became the primary candidates for sterilization. At the end of 1927, most sterilization recipients in the United States were men; five years later, only one-third of those sterilized were men.[39] By 1932, some 30 states had enacted statutes that legislated sterilizations.[40] In almost all of these states, eugenics boards were established to decide whether a doctor could sterilize an individual (usually a prisoner or a hospital patient, but sometimes a member of the general public) with a real or imagined physical or developmental disability.[41] The *Buck v. Bell* decision was followed by a surge of interest in the negative eugenic strategies of sterilization and segregation.

Public interest in negative eugenics began to decline in the 1940s.[42] In 1942, *Skinner v. Oklahoma* outlawed the use of sterilization as a punishment for a crime. *Skinner* was a landmark decision that established a protected fundamental right to procreate. An Oklahoma law, the Oklahoma Habitual Criminal Sterilization Act, permitted involuntary sexual sterilization for repeat criminals. Jack Skinner was first convicted of stealing chickens when he was 19 and later on two occasions of armed robbery. In ruling to outlaw sterilization as a punishment, Justice William O. Douglas cited concern for equal protection, noting that it was unconstitutional for the law to sterilize the three-time chicken thief while letting the three-time embezzler procreate. But he was also clearly concerned about broader issues, observing, "We are dealing here with legislation which involves one of the basic civil rights of man. Marriage and procreation are fundamental to the very

existence and survival of the race."[43] Mindful of Nazi policies that led to the
sterilization and murder of several hundred thousand "defective" criminals
and mentally retarded people, Douglas cautioned that the power of a state
to sterilize "can cause races or types which are inimical to the dominant
group to wither and disappear."[44]

After the Holocaust and World War II, institutional sterilizations declined, although compulsory sterilizations continued outside of institutional settings well into the 1970s.[45] The effort to connect public assistance
to sterilization occurred throughout the United States, but it was particularly vigorous in the South.[46] Poor black women were among those whose
reproductive integrity was most jeopardized.

By the mid-1960s, the term "welfare" had become narrowly associated
with public assistance provided mainly to single minority mothers. Previously, the term had encompassed social insurance programs that provided
benefits to widows and their dependents, along with elderly and disabled
people. Public assistance for poor women now became what social historian Michael Katz calls a "despised program of last resort primarily for the
'undeserving' poor—unmarried mothers, many of them black and Hispanic."[47] This shift coincided with a further erosion in respect for the reproductive rights of poor women. Public assistance became linked to compulsory sterilization programs.[48]

Black and mainly Puerto Rican activists struggled with mixed success
to call attention to sterilization abuse.[49] Then, in 1973, the sterilization of
a 12-year-old black girl, Minnie Lee Relf, and her 14-year-old sister Mary
Alice sparked wider awareness of the abuses that were taking place. In 1973,
Minnie and her sister were sterilized in a federally funded health clinic in
Montgomery, Alabama, under a state eugenics statute that authorized the
procedure for the "mentally incompetent" without requiring the consent
of either the girl or her family.[50] Minnie's mother, who could neither read
nor write, had thought that she was consenting to her daughters' getting a
contraceptive. The *Relf* case went to federal court, where it established that
not only was sterilization abuse taking place but also the abuse was being
subsidized by the federal government.[51] In response to the public's growing outrage, the U.S. Department of Health, Education and Welfare (HEW,
and the forerunner of today's Department of Health and Human Services)
created guidelines to eliminate sterilization abuse. After the *Relf* decision,
HEW declared a moratorium on the sterilization of women under the age
of 21 or anyone whom doctors had found to be mentally incompetent.[52] The
most flagrant and widespread abuses—the forced sterilizations of women

on welfare and those receiving care in government facilities—were halted. The movement to end involuntary sterilizations had been largely successful, but not before an estimated 60,000–100,000 women had been sterilized nationwide.[53]

The paternalistic beliefs that poor people, especially poor women of color, are not competent to control their own fertility and that the government is empowered to intervene still influences reproductive policy today.[54] And, though on a much reduced scale, we continue to see evidence that the fundamental right to procreate recognized in *Skinner* has yet to be universally respected by judges, prosecutors, and other state actors.

Sterilization and No-Procreation Orders

The actions of Judge O'Connor, described at the beginning of this chapter, problematic though they are, are not unique. "No-procreation" orders and sterilization bans are still being issued or informally arranged in today's criminal courts. In 2005, a Georgia judge ordered Carisa Ashe, a mother of seven, to undergo a tubal ligation as part of her agreement to plead guilty to voluntary manslaughter for the 1998 death of her infant daughter, even though there was disagreement over whether the death of the premature infant stemmed from "shaken baby syndrome."[55] If convicted of murder, Carisa faced life in prison. After agreeing to be sterilized, she was sentenced to five years' probation. In November 2004, a Louisiana woman, Brenda Shaffer, faced prosecution for first-degree murder in the death of her newborn daughter, even though the district attorney admitted he was unable to prove that the baby had been born alive.[56] Brenda agreed to the prosecutor's offer requiring her to plead guilty to negligent homicide and undergo a tubal ligation within 30 days. In 2000, a 22-year-old Florida woman, Kelsey Ard Smith, pleaded no contest to attempted first-degree murder of her baby and four counts of felony child abuse. She agreed to undergo a tubal ligation and was sentenced to more than 12 years in state prison to be followed by 14 years of probation.[57]

Judges' concerns about the unconstitutionality of ordering a woman not to procreate may prevent them from ordering a sterilization or procreation ban. It has not, however, kept some of them from making their wishes known. James R. Eddins Jr., 27, and Christie Kennedy, 23, were held responsible for their toddler's dehydration death. In 2002, North Carolina Superior Court Judge Kim Taylor ordered them to attend a variety of drug, grief, education, and vocational programs. She also forbade them from having custody of any children—including the three others they have together—and encouraged them to be sterilized.[58] A federal judge in New Mexico sentenced Corrina McCray to three years and 10 months in prison for the beating death of her child. The judge seemed sympathetic to Corrina's case, acknowledging her "horrible childhood" and commenting that she "never had a chance." "I hate to see this, and I hate to see what you did to your kid," Conway said. Yet sterilization clearly crossed the judge's mind as he also commented that "I'd sterilize [Corrina] if I had the authority to do it, but I don't."[59]

A Baltimore prosecutor saw incarceration as a means of reproductive control, similar to the way institutional segregation was used in the past. Denise Lechner was developmentally disabled and had been raped by her father for years. In 2006, at the age of 26, she was convicted of child abuse in the death of her toddler son. Baltimore County state's attorney Susan Hazlett favored incarceration as a means of ensuring Denise would not be able to have any more children. "I'd like her to be in prison until she is no longer able to reproduce," she observed. "If she gets out of jail while she's still fertile, I think there's a good chance she would have another child, and I would fear for that child's life."[60]

Because cases like these are not consistently publicized or routinely tracked, we do not know how many of them exist or how often women are pressured to be sterilized by judges, prosecutors, and possibly their own attorneys. Seeking to prevent a woman's procreation may be an extreme step for a judge or a prosecutor to take (not to mention an unconstitutional one), but such actions are not unheard of. While actual bans or orders may be a relatively rare occurrence in a given year, it should not surprise us if judicial actors weigh in on individual women's reproductive decisions with some regularity.

Fundamental Rights to Privacy and Bodily Integrity

I recognize that a woman's right to rear her child may be restricted in the interest of protecting a child's right to live. To be sure, no one has a right to abuse a child. To understand why mothers like Stephanie and Judgette (mentioned at the beginning of this chapter) have the right to procreate, we need to consider the idea of "fundamental rights." Fundamental rights receive the highest constitutional protection, and it is this protection that justifies the existence of our government. The Bill of Rights was drafted from the perspective that some rights are so vital, so essential, that to deprive a citizen of these rights would diminish her civil standing and, in fact, her humanity.[61] In other words, in the United States, "we the people" do not exist to serve the government (as under a tyranny). Rather, our government exists to protect us and our fundamental rights.

The Bill of Rights limits the federal government's ability to intrude on our freedoms. Later, Congress adopted the Fourteenth Amendment to extend the protections provided by the Fifth Amendment of the Bill of Rights and to limit *states'* abuse of power. These two amendments, the Fifth and the Fourteenth, prohibit the federal and state governments from depriving a person "of life, liberty, or property without due process of law." The due process clause provides for both procedural due process (that is, the government must follow certain procedures before it deprives a person of life, liberty, or property) and substantive due process (the government must have an adequate reason for taking away a person's life, liberty, or property).

The U.S. Supreme Court consistently has held that most of the protections outlined in the Bill of Rights (such as the freedom of religion and expression and the right to privacy) are encompassed under the Fourteenth Amendment's use of the word "liberty." The Bill of Rights and the Constitution specifically lay out a small number of fundamental rights, including the right to be alive, the right to marry, the right to freedom of thought and expression, the right to pursue happiness, the right to vote, and the right to fair legal procedures. Other rights are not explicitly stated in the Bill of Rights but nonetheless are implicit in the concept of liberty, and thus there is no need to enumerate them. These rights have been recognized by Supreme Court rulings, and they include not only the right to travel across state lines but also, and more relevant to the present discussion, the right to bodily integrity, the right to privacy (including the right to an abortion), and the right to procreate.

"The right to control one's body, free of state intrusion," Cynthia R. Daniels asserts in *At Women's Expense,* "is one of the most fundamental rights of liberal citizenship."[62] It is more fundamental than the right to vote and the right to work. Daniels compares the compromise of the right to bodily integrity to slavery and the literal taking of a body against its will. In one powerful passage, she articulates how central this right is by identifying conditions under which intrusion on a person's physical being has *not* been permitted by the courts, namely:

Robbery suspects cannot be forced to undergo surgery in order to remove critical evidence, such as a bullet, from their bodies. Persons suspected of drug dealing cannot be forced to have their stomachs pumped if they swallow evidence. Suspected rapists cannot be forced to undergo involuntary blood tests for [HIV]. Parents cannot be forced to donate organs to their children, even if the child's life is at stake and the parent is the only appropriate donor. One may not be forced to donate bone marrow to a cousin who is dying of bone cancer. Organs cannot even be taken from a cadaver without the prior consent of the dying.[63]

If a person cannot be forced to have criminal evidence removed from his body, or a father cannot be compelled to donate an organ to his child, then it follows that forcing a woman to be sterilized or to take contraceptives similarly violates her right to bodily integrity.

Bodily integrity is not the only right at stake when one is threatened with the imposition of sterilization or an order not to procreate. The right to privacy recognizes that a person has the "right to be let alone"—that is, there is a personal sphere where the state cannot intrude and cannot regulate.[64] The right to choose whether or not to have children is one of the places within this sphere. In rulings such as *Skinner v. Oklahoma, Roe v. Wade,* and *Planned Parenthood of Southeastern Pennsylvania v. Casey,* the Supreme Court has consistently recognized that state regulation of such private and intimate decisions threatens a woman's very personhood.[65] Every woman should have the opportunity to develop and pursue her own goals, roles, identities, and morals independent of state orthodoxy, otherwise women will be treated by the state as what one legal scholar referred to as "diffuse subjects without boundaries" rather than people.[66]

As we saw in *Skinner,* the U.S. Supreme Court has held that the right to decide whether to conceive a child is an essential part of the fundamental right to privacy. More recently, in the 1972 case of *Eisenstadt v. Baird,* the court ruled that "if the right of privacy means anything, it is the right of the individual . . . to be free from unwarranted government intrusion into matters so fundamentally affecting a person as the decision whether to bear or beget a child."[67]

A case like *Bobbijean,* where a judge tells someone not to procreate, also raises Fourteenth Amendment due process and equal protection issues. Due process protections prohibit prosecutors, judges, and courts from applying or interpreting an existing law or policy in an unforeseeable or unintended way. Due process requires that a woman in Stephanie's situation be given fair notice, not only of what alleged actions may subject her to punishment but also the severity of the punishment that may be imposed.

Stephanie was called to court on charges of neglect involving her new-born, Bobbijean. She had no notice that Judge O'Connor might impose an unprecedented "no-procreation" or "no-pregnancy" condition as part of her reunification plan. Most of the evidence of unfitness in the *Bobbijean* case appears to have been presented by a caseworker who had known Stephanie for only seven months.[68] Even so, neither the petition nor the caseworker's disposition plan asked for a prohibition on her right to procreate. Rodney and Stephanie did not appear at the court proceedings to rebut the charges of child neglect. No attorney represented their interests. But then again, while Stephanie and Rodney may have been aware that the court date would affect their parental rights to their daughter, they had no reason to believe the judge planned to strip them of their right to procreate. In this way, their rights to due process were violated.

No-procreation cases also raise questions of equal protection, insofar as the fundamental right to procreate is denied to some individuals but not to others. Specifically, women may be more likely than men to have the state's will imposed over their reproduction. Rachel Roth searched legal and news databases and other sources for such cases.[69] She found that women ordered not to procreate tended to be charged with abuse, neglect, or criminal activity such as theft or check fraud not related directly to their children. Judges, she concluded, appear to be more likely to restrict women's reproduction than men's, and more likely to do so in cases where the crime was not directly related to children.[70]

Coercive sterilization is much less common now than it used to be. When it does take place, it seems to result from the actions and beliefs of individual judges and prosecutors rather than a national public campaign. It is worth considering, then, what justifications are offered for pressuring a woman not to procreate, given that such actions lack a constitutional basis. In contrast to earlier eugenics advocates, we find that contemporary proponents of sterilization and no-procreation orders are much more circumspect about their goals, preferring to couch them in terms of "personal responsibility" and cost savings. The sentiments underlying ideas about who should reproduce and the purported need for state involvement, however, are similar. Coercive sterilization and no-procreation orders serve a form of old eugenic wine in new bottles. In general, defenders of sterilization and no-procreation policies tend to rely on three rationalizations: desire to promote responsibility, economic concerns, and concern for children. Each of these rationalizations is evaluated in the next section.

Rationalizations

Promoting Responsibility

Nowadays, it is unusual to hear a judge or other advocate of sterilizing women convicted of crimes directly accuse them of being "immoral" or "feebleminded." Instead, discussions emphasize the need for poor women to assume personal responsibility for their actions.[71] Judges and prosecutors appear to take their cues from larger society's emphasis on the ideals of individualism, independence, and personal accountability. As but one example of this, the 1996 welfare legislation that, in the words of President Bill Clinton, "ended welfare as we know it" is called "The Personal Responsibility and Work Opportunity Reconciliation Act of 1996."[72]

Poor women's presumed immorality and promiscuity are rarely mentioned outright, though they are often implied. "Irresponsibility" seems to have become a less inflammatory code word for immorality. For example, a woman (such as the aforementioned Judgette W.) who has seven children with more than one father while living on public assistance is widely considered irresponsible for (a) having children she cannot financially support, (b) being in a relationship with a man who is an inadequate economic provider, and (c) procreating with more than one man. This irresponsibility is treated as immoral in a country that projects an image that self-sufficiency and independence are expected, valued, and rewarded. Many people are of the opinion that responsible reproductive citizens do not use drugs (at least not illicit ones) and their children do not have multiple fathers. Furthermore, responsible citizens are not dependent on the state. This last assertion is especially hypocritical.

Even if we all were to agree that a woman having a child she cannot provide for is irresponsible, the reality is that people act irresponsibly all the time. In fact, only around one-half of baby boomer households are saving enough to retire when they now plan to.[73] At least one in four likely will depend heavily on government benefits for the bulk of their income in retirement.[74] This group includes parents of all socioeconomic backgrounds who took family vacations, bought new cars, threw weddings they could not afford, and otherwise amassed debt that will prevent them from having adequate retirement savings. Moreover, many, if not most, of them will depend on public assistance and entitlement programs at some point in their lives due to old age, disability, or unemployment. So why does the state single out poor women for blame and attempt to impose restrictions on their fertility?

Perhaps because blaming poor mothers allows us Americans to maintain an ethos and collective identity as being highly individualistic and self-sufficient without having to hold ourselves to that standard. Many of the women subjected to state intrusions on their right to procreate have backgrounds of family violence, drug addiction, developmental disability, and mental illness. By insisting that the responsibility is the women's alone (and can be handled through sterilization or not procreating), society is absolved of its obligation to provide at least a modicum of support with health benefits (including drug treatment and treatment for mental illness), housing, and other social necessities. "Women are assigned responsibility for taking care of fetuses," Rachel Roth observes in *Making Women Pay*, "without being given the resources they need to do so, and then penalized for falling short."[75]

A tendency also exists to treat women as being irresponsible decision makers. But women do not "choose" to be mentally ill, abused, or addicted to drugs. Nor is the ability to address the conditions completely (or sometimes, even remotely) within their power. From a practical standpoint, this reality, accompanied by the often grim social circumstances of their present lives, makes it unlikely that women will be deterred by the prospect of sterilization from using drugs or abusing or neglecting their children. Instead, as noted above, it seems clear that we need to offer women more social support before the point at which child abuse or neglect takes place. Sterilization and no-procreation orders, once implemented, do nothing to improve the objective economic and social reality of women's lives. The purpose of these orders thus seems more expressive than instrumental, serving as a vehicle to communicate our collective displeasure and resentment rather than a meaningful way of addressing child abuse and neglect.

Economic Justifications

Another common theme is the desire to save money. The rationale for no-procreation and sterilization policies is often discussed in economic terms: Who is going to pay for the children poor women bring into the world? As Germaine Greer notes, the middle class resents "having to shell out for the maintenance of the children of others, however paltry and meager it can be shown to be."[76] Judge Marilyn O'Connor flatly stated that Stephanie, the mother of Bobbijean in the no-procreation case mentioned at the beginning of this chapter, "should not have yet another child which must be cared for at public expense before she has proven herself able to care for other children. The same is true for the father and his children. As to both parents, providing care for the children includes providing financial support."[77] In justifying the no-procreation order in *Bobbijean*, Judge O'Connor cited the "immense burden" that this "neglected existence" places on a child and on society and, in particular, its schools, jails, the Department of Health and Human Services, and the family court system itself.

The burden Judge O'Connor identifies seems to be primarily economic rather than moral or social in nature, as her ruling discusses at length the various costs associated with foster care. For example, a child with "purchased family care" costs nearly $28,000 per year. The court record also notes that children in residential care, infected with HIV, with symptoms of cocaine addiction, and with other special needs, incur even more expenses. This argument is not new. Citing economic grounds to justify no-procreation orders is part of a legacy of concern about the intergenerational transmission of pauperism. Margaret Sanger infamously asked nearly a century ago, "The offspring of one feebleminded man named Jukes has cost the public in one way or another $1,300,000 in seventy-five years. Do we want more such families?"[78]

Economic arguments ignore the fact that welfare programs do not drain government budgets. Temporary Assistance for Needy Families (TANF) welfare programs constitute less than 1 percent of the federal budget.[79] TANF/welfare benefits are limited to a maximum of five years in a lifetime and are quite stingy. For example, food stamp benefits average about $80 per person per month (in 2003 dollars). Cash benefits in the Aid for Dependent Children (AFDC)/TANF program in 2003 averaged only about $140/month.[80]

To put the cost of TANF in perspective, consider that in 2006, federal TANF outlays totaled $17 billion.[81] By contrast, the Congressional Budget Office estimated that more than five times that amount—$95 billion—had been spent on operations in Iraq and the war on terrorism in fiscal year 2006.[82] Consider, too, that taxpayers cover the costs of public subsidies to corporations. From 2001 to 2003, loopholes and other tax subsidies gave 275 Fortune 500 companies (who earned almost $1.1 trillion dollars in pre-tax profits in the United States) a total of $175.2 billion in tax breaks;[83] 82 of these companies paid no taxes in at least one of the years examined.

Setting aside social justice arguments, from an economic point of view, investing in mothers and their children makes good sense. Providing meaningful social support would strengthen their long-term ability to contribute to society or at least would reduce any burden they present. Economists have found that investing in high-quality early-childhood development, education, and childcare would strengthen the economy and benefits tax-payers in several ways.[84] Public expenses are lower because children will fail fewer grades and are less likely to require special education. Children and their families will have markedly lower crime and delinquency rates along with higher incomes and will pay more taxes than those who do not participate in early childhood development. Moreover, these children will be less likely to go on welfare. Studies suggest that every dollar invested in childcare and education yields a savings or a return of between $4 and $17, mostly because of money that does not have to be spent on incarceration.[85] Similarly, given the cost of long-term foster care and incarceration, investing financial resources in helping parents find housing and treatment for their substance use and mental health problems would be more economical.

As it is, no-procreation orders impose a financial means test or what one judge called a "'credit check' on the right to bear and beget children."[86] The New York Civil Liberties Union asked, in responding to *Bobbijean*, "Who is next? A family of four, all currently on welfare? Parents with one child in foster care for neglect? A family of eight children, all of whom in their senior years will draw Social Security and two of whom may end up on Medicaid?"[87]

"Think of the Children"

A third rationalization for limiting some women's reproduction is captured in the hackneyed expression "Think of the children." Proponents of no-procreation orders, sterilization, and other state intrusions on women's bodies and reproductive rights often claim their actions are necessary to protect a fetus or a child from harm. In July 2003, a Michigan family court judge ordered a woman to submit to a medically verifiable method of birth control in an abuse and neglect proceeding regarding her two children. The judge asserted that Renee Gamez's drug use made it likely that she would bear a child with special needs.[88] The state argued that it had a compelling interest in ordering her to be placed on birth control as part of the child protective services agency plan to reunify Renee with her children. In a Florida case, the defendant accepted the suggestion of a tubal ligation procedure. The prosecutor, David Fleet, later commented that "we believe she is a danger to infants, and the only way to protect a future infant would be to keep her from having that infant."[89] In *Bobbijean*, the court singled out Stephanie for having "neglected her responsibilities as a mother" by using cocaine during her pregnancies. "It is painfully obvious," Judge O'Connor noted in her ruling, "that a parent who has already lost to foster care all four of her children born over a six-year period, with the last one having been taken from her even before she could leave the hospital, should not get pregnant again soon, if ever."

Even a cursory examination of the claim that sterilization protects children reveals the flawed assumptions on which it is based. Recall that a parent cannot be compelled to donate an organ to save a born child. It follows, then, that a woman cannot be sterilized to save a child not yet conceived. Furthermore, and as discussed in chapter 5, many of these claims are based on an exaggerated sense of the risks associated with maternal drug use.[90] Along similar lines, there is a tendency to forget that most child maltreatment takes the form of neglect, not abuse. Evidence suggests racial prejudice may motivate the actions of some judges and prosecutors, as much as concern for children's futures. After reviewing the prosecution of a woman who had used cocaine while pregnant, a South Carolina state court judge observed: "Now this little baby's born with crack. When he is seven years old . . . they can't run. They just run around in class like a little rat. Not just black ones. White ones too."[91] We also find that black children who are abused or neglected are more likely than abused and neglected white children to be removed from their parents' care and placed under state supervision.[92]

Removing a child from the home out of a genuine, justifiable concern for the child's own safety or personally wishing that a woman would not get pregnant again "soon, if ever" is one thing. But to follow up that action or that opinion with an official order that a woman *will* not get pregnant is another matter. In effect, it is declaring a separate interest: not just in protecting children but in regulating who gets to become pregnant and doing so in such a way that devalues the humanity of poor and homeless women (who are disproportionately likely to be racial minority women) and women who are addicted to drugs, while privileging others. The consequence of this extends beyond the biological question of "Who procreates?" It speaks to the question of "Who matters?" It speaks to the relationship existing between the right to procreate and the need to recognize the humanity of individuals, as well as groups of individuals. "When the state creates conditions for maternal legitimacy that give special treatment to white, middle-class women and threaten almost all other women," Rickie Solinger concludes in *Pregnancy and Power,* "then reproductive capacity becomes a vehicle for institutionalizing racism and other forms of oppression."[93]

Project Prevention

The direct interference of criminal justice or family court officials with women's procreation and sex lives is not routine, but it is not a rare occurrence, either. For instance, Jennifer Reich's study of the child welfare system found that judges often demand that women seeking reuinification with their children avoid or abandon any intimate relationships with men to demonstrate that they value their bond with their children above all others.[94] State officials also may be involved indirectly with sterilization efforts.

Project Prevention is a national organization based in Harrisburg, North Carolina, which claims chapters in 27 states and the District of Columbia. Between its founding in 1997 and December 2007, Project Prevention paid $200–$300 or more to 854 women (and 27 men) who use drugs to be permanently sterilized, and to over 1,400 women to use forms of long-term birth control such as an IUD or Depo-Provera.[95] One year's campaign slogan announced the goal of achieving a total of "2006 in 2006!"—a goal that was met and surpassed.[96]

Although pitched as a sincere effort to improve the quality of women and children's lives, in reality it is a heavily racialized program; more than half of Project Prevention's clients are racial or ethnic minorities.[97] The organization was first named Children Requiring a Caring Kommunity or C.R.A.C.K. The original name reflected founder Barbara Harris's focus on crack cocaine rather than substances like alcohol or tobacco or prescription medicines that pose a threat to fetal health but are more commonly used by white and middle-class women. The organization's outreach efforts target communities of color. Project Prevention's 2005 "road show" plans featured a trip from Harrisburg to Southern California with a mobile billboard. Planned stops included disproportionately black cities such as Norfolk and Richmond, Virginia, which are 44 and 57 percent black, respectively. Yet, Harris insists that Project Prevention "doesn't target any particular race. . . . We target drug addicts, and that's it. Skin color doesn't matter, and we believe all babies matter, even black babies."[98]

Project Prevention's recruitment strategies depend upon maintaining a relationship with the criminal justice system. Project Prevention relies on referrals from probation offices, jails, drug treatment programs, methadone clinics, and law enforcement agencies; staff receive $50 for referring people to Project Prevention.[99] For example, an Albuquerque detention center permits the project to host information sessions for its women inmates.

"Project Prevention is growing and even making inroads into state institutions," Harris boasted in 2003:

> Just over the past year, we've had many organizations, county and state agencies come on board and start referring women to us. We have jails that allow our volunteers in to tell inmates about our program. We have drug treatment programs that are referring women to us. We have methadone clinics that have our information posted on the walls, and probation departments—just many, many agencies, in a lot of states, that are learning about us and making referrals to us."[100]

The proactive involvement of criminal justice workers in controlling a woman's fertility is troubling, tying as it does the notion of rehabilitation to compliance and reproduction. A woman probationer or parolee must not procreate if she wishes to be seen as cooperative and reformed by her probation officer, parole officer, and others. Moreover, by paying people who work in jails, probation departments, and drug treatment programs to refer women to their organization, Project Prevention supplies a financial incentive for state agents to encourage women to forego their reproductive rights.

Conclusion

Sterilization programs like Project Prevention and no-procreation orders target the reproductive capacity of poor women rather than the oppressive conditions under which women often live. Such approaches fail to address women's need for effective drug treatment programs, mental health services, and social, economic, and educational support.

Regardless of the seriousness of the charges against a woman, forced sterilization or no-procreation orders are never justifiable. If women's interest in privacy and bodily integrity is always defined in reference to the state interest in, say, healthy pregnancies or good parenting or the well-being of yet-to-be-conceived children, then the state interest will always win out. Arguing—as the judge did in *Gamez*—that a prohibition on procreation is justified if the child might be born with "special needs," raises the question of whether the state may limit the procreation of parents who have a family history of genetic disorders or of mothers who are on prescription medicine (e.g., for seizures) that may also pose risks to a fetus.[101] Theoretically, the regulation of virtually *any* action (e.g., walking on an icy sidewalk, getting into a car with a reckless driver, getting cash from an ATM after dark) could be justified by citing the state interest, and, ultimately, the state would have nearly absolute power over all of us.[102]

There is also a challenge to be leveled against no-procreation or sterilization orders on philosophical grounds in terms of how the rights of some human beings are valued more than others. Nicole Hahn Rafter, author of *Creating Born Criminals,* points out that part of the legacy of eugenic criminology has been its influence on our value judgments of who or what is good or bad: "We define beauty in terms of whiteness and refinement, and we associate 'welfare mothers' with stupidity, hyperfecundity, illegitimacy, and criminalistic offspring."[103] We see this value judgment when we contrast the lack of support for the procreation of poor women, especially those who use drugs, with the growing trend toward white middle-class women giving birth later in life.

More women are choosing to become pregnant after the age of 35, and doing so with the tacit support of society, even though these women are also at higher risk of giving birth to a low birthweight or premature infant.[104] Further, many of these women are now taking fertility drugs and undergoing artificial insemination procedures, which greatly increase the chances of multiple births. In 2004, one out of 18 births to women aged 35 years and over (and one in five births to women aged 45–49 years) was a multiple delivery, compared with only one out of 33 such births among younger women. From 1980 to 2004, the twin birth rate climbed 70 percent.[105] Multiple births, in turn, are associated with negative pregnancy outcomes such as low birthweight, preterm delivery, and overall higher rates of infant morbidity and mortality.[106] Premature births impose a significant financial and social burden on the health care system in the United States, with the cost of preventing or treating these complications estimated at more than $2 billion a year.[107]

Many of the same people who object to a poor woman who uses illegal drugs getting pregnant are nonetheless fully supportive of the procreation of other women who delay childbirth. The latter group tends to be wealthier and better educated than other women and therefore are perceived as better reproducers, despite their heightened risk of birth abnormalities. The point is not that women should be forbidden from delaying childbearing. Rather, we should acknowledge the hypocrisy in deciding to recognize and support some women's right to procreate while denying that recognition and support to others.

The right to privacy (which encompasses the decision of whether to have a child, the right to bodily integrity, and the right to be let alone) is strongly implicated in both the right to become pregnant and, as discussed in the following chapter, the right to terminate a pregnancy. The Constitution protects a woman's right to make reproductive decisions and exist in her own body free from unwarranted government intrusion. A woman always retains her status as a human being and as a citizen, not an object who can be acted upon.[108] The "private sphere" and one's right to be free of state intrusion into one's physical person do not simply evaporate when a woman abuses or neglects her children, uses illicit drugs, or commits a crime.

3

"Back-Alley Butchers"
Terminating Pregnancies

A real life description, to me, would be a rape victim. Brutally raped; savaged. The girl was a virgin; she was religious; she planned on saving her virginity until she was married. She was brutalized and raped, sodomized as bad as you can possibly make it, and is impregnated. I mean, that girl could be so messed up, physically and psychologically, that carrying that child could very well threaten her life.

> —Bill Napoli, Republican state senator, responding to
> being asked what, in his mind, would constitute a valid
> exception to South Dakota's 2006 abortion ban

Few decisions are more personal and intimate, more properly private, or more basic to individual dignity and autonomy, than a woman's decision . . . whether to end her pregnancy.

> —Supreme Court Justice Harry A. Blackmun, writing in
> *Thornburgh v. American College of Obstetricians*[1]

On January 28, 2000, Barbara Gaddy was admitted to a New York county jail on drug charges; she was about eight weeks pregnant.[2] Barbara wanted to terminate her pregnancy. For four weeks, county jail officials refused her request for an abortion and repeatedly harassed and threatened her.[3] Barbara was finally able to schedule an abortion for March 2nd. In the meantime, anti-abortion activist Karen Jackson filed a lawsuit asking the court to block Barbara from having an abortion because taxpayers should not have to pay for an elective medical procedure. A New York State Supreme Court justice barred Barbara from having the abortion (scheduled for the next day) until a hearing took place on whether county corrections officials should pay for the procedure.[4] Barbara's appointment was cancelled.[5]

As we saw in the previous chapter, respect for a woman's right to bodily sovereignty requires that the state does not prohibit a woman from becoming pregnant. Nor should the state require that a woman *remain* pregnant and have a child against her own interests, either. These basic principles have been upheld by courts since *Roe v. Wade* was decided in 1973. However, while abortion has remained legal, available, and safe, since 1980 a woman's ability to decide to terminate her pregnancy has been seriously undermined.[6] The lengths that some legislators, prison and jail administrators, judges, and sheriffs (and in some cases, even a woman's own attorney) will go to prevent a woman or girl from exercising her right to terminate a pregnancy speak to the precarious status of women's reproductive rights.[7]

Each year, over 6 million women in the United States will become pregnant.[8] About one-half of all pregnancies are unintended.[9] Around one-fifth of all pregnancies (and around 40 percent of all unintended pregnancies) will result in an induced abortion.[10] Around one-third of the women who obtain legal abortions are 20–24 years old, around 55 percent are white (though abortion rates are highest among black women), over 80 percent are unmarried, and around 60 percent have had at least one live birth before.[11] Nearly 90 percent of abortions are performed in the first trimester; about 6 percent are performed after 15 weeks gestation.[12] Abortion is one of the safest medical procedures performed today. In the United States, the proportion of maternal deaths due to abortion (legal or illegal) is essentially zero; the risk of death associated with childbirth is 11 times higher than that associated with a first-trimester abortion.[13]

Our abortion policies reflect a view that a woman should not be permitted to make decisions about her body solely and on her own behalf. The public's conflicted feelings about abortion are manifested in government policies that recognize the formal legality of abortions but impose many obstacles that obstruct women's access to the right.[14] It is not enough for a woman to decide that she needs or wants an abortion. If she is young or poor or incarcerated or advanced in her pregnancy, she very likely will have to convince others, including doctors, judges, parents, and correctional authorities of the correctness of her decision. This effectively abrogates pregnant women's decision-making power by privileging the interests of her physician, the state, and the fetus over her own. This has a significant impact, not only on women's access to abortion but also on women's ability to achieve economic, political, and social equality.

Opposition to abortion often emerges from deeply rooted beliefs that abortion involves the taking of a human life. Resistance or objection to abortion is also seated in traditional attitudes regarding women's roles as wives and mothers and the belief that a pregnant woman is not entitled to the same recognition of her citizenship and her rights to privacy and equality as others.[15] As political scientist Rosemary Nossiff observed, when it comes to abortion policy in the United States, a pregnant woman is treated as "a patient and a future mother first, and an individual with constitutional rights second."[16]

Justice Anthony Kennedy's opinion in *Gonzales v. Carhart* both reflects and perpetuates this troubling and sexist approach to women's reproductive decision making.[17] In justifying the federal ban on so-called partial-birth abortion, Kennedy asserted that the Court "has confirmed the validity of drawing boundaries to prevent practices that extinguish life and are close to actions that are condemned" and noted that the Partial Birth Abortion Ban Act "recognizes that respect for human life finds an ultimate expression in a mother's love for her child." Moreover, he went on to assert, some women may regret having abortions and some doctors may not tell women all the details of the abortion procedure being used. Therefore, a ban of the procedure that "perverts a process during which life is brought into the world" was in order.

In her dissent, Justice Ruth Bader Ginsburg took Kennedy to task for relying on "antique notions about women's place in the family and under the Constitution." She cited other court cases that were premised on similarly sexist assumptions about women's "maternal functions" and "the paramount destiny and mission of woman . . . to fulfil[l] the noble and benign offices of wives and mothers" that force women into a second-class status.[18] Moreover, by banning the procedure in the name of protecting women from making a decision they may later regret (instead of requiring that abortion providers accurately and adequately inform them of the risk), "the Court deprives women of the right to make an autonomous choice, even at the expense of their safety."[19]

Laws and social policies that value women's roles as mothers and wives more than their rights as individuals are one of the main causes of persistent gender inequality and contribute heavily to gendered citizenship.[20] Women have obtained the legal right to vote, to own property, to pursue professional careers as doctors, lawyers, and legislators. Nevertheless, women have yet to become wholly incorporated as full citizens in public life. For instance, according to Rutgers University's Center for American Women in Politics in 2007, only around one in six seats in the 110th U.S. Congress was held by a woman, and only one in four state legislators was a woman. In the entire history of the United States, only 32 women have been appointed to presidential cabinet or cabinet-level positions.[21]

Policies that grant women reproductive rights only to the extent that the state's interest in fetal health is protected are part of the problem. The maternalist policies of the early twentieth century were intended to help impoverished widows, allow single mothers to stay home with their young children, and otherwise provide support to women (white women, at least). But instead of leading to full citizenship for all women, such policies have reinforced women's status as dependents on the state rather than citizens with full rights.[22]

More to the point of this chapter, abortion is not simply a matter of securing the civil right to individual freedom and privacy.[23] If the right to an abortion, or any reproductive right for that matter, is not enforced or protected, then it is a right in name only. Simply having the civil right to an abortion is not enough. Abortion also must be recognized as a social right; that is, we must make sure surrounding social conditions make it possible to actually obtain an abortion.[24]

Many abortion opponents argue that adoption is a reasonable alternative to abortion for those pregnant women who do not want to rear a child. For instance, in March 2007, a Texas state senator proposed a bill that would pay pregnant women $500 for giving a baby up for adoption rather than having an abortion. But this reasoning blurs an important distinction. The decision to terminate a pregnancy is quite different from the decision about whether to terminate one's parental rights, and to suggest otherwise is naive. Besides presenting adoption as an abortion alternative fails to take into account that women are, in effect, being asked to make a decision about adoption *while they are still pregnant.* Also, it seriously downplays the physical impact and implications of being pregnant, as well as the social consequences of being seen, treated, and defined as a pregnant woman.

In this chapter, I focus on how the criminal justice and the legal systems undercut women's access to abortion. Some measures discourage physicians from providing abortions by permitting them to be harassed or intimidated by anti-abortion activists or by singling them out for prosecution. Other measures are aimed at women themselves, such as making it a crime for minors to obtain an abortion without parental consent or obstructing incarcerated women and girls' access to abortion services. A third category of anti-abortion activity includes direct attempts to re-criminalize the procedure itself through bans or "trigger" legislation. It is to the availability of abortion services in the United States that we now address our attention.

Discouraging Abortion Providers

The stigma of being labeled an "abortionist," the fear of being sued or prosecuted, and the continuing threat of clinic violence and harassment have contributed to a shortage of doctors willing to provide abortions. Some 87 percent of all counties in the country (in which about 35 percent of all women live) do not have an abortion provider.[25] In 2005, South Dakota, North Dakota, and Mississippi had only one legal abortion provider serving each state.[26] In South Dakota, for example, area doctors stopped performing abortions around 1997; doctors from Minnesota fly in once a week on a rotating basis.[27] Nearly 1 in 10 women obtaining an abortion in the United States must travel more than 100 miles to reach an abortion provider.[28]

Fewer than 10 percent of abortions are now performed in a doctor's office or a hospital.[29] At the same time as abortion laws were liberalized in the late 1960s and early 1970s, technological innovations such as the vacuum suction method and developments in administering local anesthesia made abortions less risky, less painful, and less expensive.[30] It also made it possible for freestanding clinics to deliver medical services, including abortions. Sociologist and abortion scholar Carole Joffe describes the development of freestanding clinics as "a mixed blessing."[31] For while clinics continue to provide effective, less expensive, and possibly more supportive service, their success has contributed to the further isolation of abortion service providers from mainstream medicine. Today, 43 states allow health care institutions to refuse to provide abortion services; 15 of these states limit the exemption to private facilities; 1 state exempts only religious health care facilities.[32] If physicians in hospitals do not perform abortions, then they cannot train medical residents to do so.

While the growing assault on abortion rights has reinvigorated many individual and group efforts to defend abortion, prosecution and harassment, violence, and other restrictions can drain the energy and resources not only of the abortion service providers but also of pro-abortion grassroots organizations.[33] The "culture of fear and aversion" which has developed around abortion makes even advocates hesitate before contentious cases.[34]

Anti-Abortion Violence

Violence and other disruptive actions taken against abortion providers may discourage women and girls from seeking an abortion or delay their procedures. Violence may also deter people from taking jobs in facilities that perform abortions, contributing to the shortage of abortion providers. Anti-abortion violence and disruptions have declined since the Freedom of Access to Clinic Entrances (FACE) Act was passed in 1994. The FACE Act makes it a federal crime to use force or the threat of force to prevent people from receiving or providing reproductive health services, including abortion. Behavior prohibited under the FACE Act includes obstructing the entrance or the exit of a facility (including clinic doors and parking lots), trespassing, vandalism, threats, and acts of physical violence.

Although clinic violence has declined since 1994, it has not disappeared entirely, as recent examples illustrate. In May 2006, in Iowa City, William Dennis Owens-Holst grabbed a clinic employee by the neck and arm and threw her against a car before trying to break into the clinic.[35] Owens-Holst said he wanted to "break the fingers of the abortion doctors so they couldn't kill babies." Owens-Holst plead guilty to third-degree burglary and simple assault. He was sentenced to five years probation, fined $750, and ordered to pay $435 restitution to the clinic. In June 2006, a Maryland man was arrested after his father called the police because he feared his son planned to bomb an abortion clinic. Police found a pipe bomb filled with nails in the son's house and a gun in the glove compartment of his car. According to a Bureau of Alcohol, Firearms, and Explosives spokesperson, Robert F. Weiler admitted that he intended to use the gun to shoot doctors who performed abortions. A federal grand jury indicted him on charges of possessing and making an unregistered destructive device, illegally possessing a firearm, and possessing a stolen firearm.[36] In December 2005, a young couple tried to firebomb a Louisiana abortion clinic. Patricia Hughes pleaded guilty to manufacturing and possessing a delayed incendiary device (a Molotov cocktail) and was sentenced to six years in prison. Jeremy Dunahoe pleaded guilty to being an accessory after the fact and was sentenced to one year in jail.[37]

According to the 2005 annual survey produced by the Feminist Majority Foundation (FMF), the most commonly reported types of severe violence are blockades, bomb threats, stalking of physicians or clinic staff, and death threats.[38] While overall, severe violence declined 20 percent from 2000 to 2005, and has been cut in half since it peaked in 1994, the number of clinics experiencing at least moderate levels of violence (e.g., vandalism, picketing providers' homes, break-ins), however, has increased to about one-third of all clinics.[39]

Singling out Abortion Providers for Prosecution

Nationally, much physician misconduct goes unrecognized and unpunished.[40] Relatively few doctors lose their licenses, in part because physicians are reluctant to report their colleagues' misconduct.[41] Abortion doctors seem to be the rare exception. Because of pressure from the anti-abortion movement, doctors who perform abortions are more likely to face criminal charges than others. As is the case with abortion clinic violence, fear of legal harassment and a desire to avoid having to launch an expensive defense effort may discourage physicians from performing abortions.

In the years immediately preceding *Roe v. Wade,* many women witnessed firsthand the dangers of illegal abortion.[42] Tragically, some women *did* die at the hands of unskilled people. Some abortion providers did sexually harass, demean, and exploit their clients.[43] Some demanded sex in exchange for an abortion. Some were drunks. Some performed abortions in filthy rooms under unsafe conditions. Yet most abortion providers were not murderers or villains; the back-alley butcher icon did not accurately depict underground abortion providers.[44] When abortion was illegal, the law arguably posed a greater source of danger to women than the abortion providers did.[45] "The varying prices and the sexual harassment of patients, the unsafe and unsure conditions, could flourish in the black market," Leslie Reagan writes in *When Abortion Was a Crime.* "Without regulation to ensure competence, all abortion patients were vulnerable."[46] The increasingly secretive context created by abortion's illegality also gave women little recourse to address any bad and potentially life-threatening experiences.

Today, around 70 percent of abortions are performed in abortion clinics.[47] Abortion is one of the safest medical procedures, and most abortion providers are competent, ethical professionals. Still, mistakes do happen, and some abortion doctors do engage in reprehensible misconduct. In 2005, a Florida doctor was arrested and charged with performing abortions after his license had been revoked for botching a procedure, failing to perform necessary preoperative procedures, not treating a severe uterine perforation, and not returning calls from patients who were bleeding and in extreme pain.[48] In 2003, Arizona abortion provider Brian Finkel was convicted of 22 counts of sexually abusing patients over a 17-year period.[49] Ten years earlier, Dr. Abu Hayat was sentenced to up to 29 years in prison for a botched abortion on a woman who was around eight months pregnant that resulted in a child being born with a severed arm. He also refused to complete an abortion procedure because the patient—who nearly died—would not pay him an additional $500.[50] The secrecy and stigma that continue to be associated with abortion clinics are part of what allow abuses to continue. If something does go wrong at an abortion clinic, a woman may be less likely to report it than if it had happened during a visit to her family practitioner or in a hospital.

Evidence also suggests, however, that abortion doctors may be targeted for prosecution. Dr. Bruce Steir was a California abortion provider who had performed over 40,000 abortions in his career. In 1996, Steir performed an abortion on a 27-year-old woman, Sharon Hamptlon, who was 20 weeks pregnant. During the procedure, he accidentally (and unknowingly) perforated her uterus. This led Sharon to hemorrhage and eventually to die after she left the clinic. At the time of Sharon's death, Steir had five other charges of negligence in abortion cases pending against him, all cases in which a woman's uterus had been perforated. The district attorney charged him with second-degree murder for the death of Sharon Hamptlon.[51]

In response to these charges, in 2000 the ACLU of Northern California (ACLU-NC) investigated the possibility of political bias by the Medical Board of California.[52] The ACLU-NC concluded that while Steir deserved to lose his license, he did not deserve to be singled out for criminal prosecution. The ACLU-NC argued that Steir was chosen for prosecution due to anti-abortion politics rather than because his case was exceptionally rank. ACLU-NC found that an anti-abortion activist was inappropriately involved in the Medical Board's case against Steir. Most California doctors whose negligence contributed to a patient's death did not have their licenses taken away, much less face criminal prosecution.[53] Moreover, in some cases, doctors had committed more egregious acts or had more serious prior records but were not referred for criminal prosecution or were criminally prosecuted on a less serious charge.

In another high-profile prosecution, a Republican abortion foe in Kansas used his political office to pursue a campaign to close down an abortion provider. In 2004, Phill Kline, then the Kansas attorney general, began his efforts to subpoena the records of a well-known abortion provider, Dr. George Tiller.[54] Kline was eventually successful in obtaining the redacted records in 2006. Kline initially claimed that he wanted the records so that he could prosecute statutory rape cases, but later admitted he was actually interested in seeing if Tiller had been performing illegal late-term abortions.[55] Shortly after Kline obtained the records, he was voted out of office. Before he left, however, he charged Tiller with 15 counts of unlawful late-term abortion and 15 counts of failure to report the justification of a late-term abortion. Among the cases in question were those of several young teenagers and a 10-year-old, all of whom were in their late second or early third trimester.[56] The charges were later dismissed on jurisdictional grounds. In February 2007, the Kansas Supreme Court ruled against reinstating the charges.[57] But the challenges are far from over.[58] In October of the same year, Kline (who became the district attorney for Johnson County, Kansas) filed dozens of charges against a Planned Parenthood clinic. The state attorney general's office indicated that it had already reviewed the accusations on which Kline's criminal charges were based and found no wrongdoing.[59]

Prosecuting Women for Illegal Abortions

Violence, legal harassment, and a hostile climate contribute to the overall shortage of abortion services. As a result, self-administered abortions may be on the rise, particularly among poor immigrant women who come from countries with abortion laws that are more restrictive than those in the United States.[60] Many women take misoprostol, also known as Cytotec, or the "star pill," a prescription ulcer medication that can cause miscarriages. In many Latin American countries, women can buy Cytotec directly from a pharmacist. In the United States, women seeking to use it as an abortifacient may procure it through underground channels, such as from friends and relatives living abroad or buying it at some local bodegas. A 2000 study of misprostol knowledge and use among a primarily Dominican female population in three New York City obstetrics/gynecology clinics found that over one-third of the women knew about misoprostol's off-label use as an abortifacient.[61] About 5 percent reported having personally used it, mainly for reasons of ease and the cost.[62] The study also found that women who had taken misoprostol or knew about it had an incomplete understanding of the risks associated with its unsupervised use.[63]

Women without access to safe, legal, and affordable abortion services seek alternatives, including neonaticide and infant abandonment (discussed in the next chapter) and illegal self-administered abortion. Historically, prosecutors were more inclined to pursue charges against abortion providers than the women seeking an abortion. Today, although a relatively rare occurrence, women are sometimes prosecuted for getting or performing illegal abortions. In South Carolina, at least a half dozen women have been prosecuted for attempting to obtain or perform an illegal abortion between 2000 and 2005.[64]

Gabriela Flores was a 22-year-old immigrant farm worker and mother of three children. She got pregnant and could not afford an abortion. When she was four months pregnant, she took some pills her sister sent her from Mexico that contained misoprostol. After delivering a dead fetus the next morning, she and a friend buried the fetus in her backyard. Someone—thinking the fetus had been born alive—reported the incident to the police. Prosecutors wanted to charge Gabriela with murder but could not do so in the absence of evidence that the fetus could have survived on its own. Instead, in 2004, they charged her with illegal abortion and failure to notify a coroner. Gabriela spent four months in jail. In another case, Massachusetts teenager Amber Abreu, who came to the United States from the Dominican Republic, faced charges of procuring a miscarriage (a felony punishable by up to seven years in prison) by taking misoprostol in an attempt to induce an abortion. In Massachusetts, abortion is illegal after 24 weeks. Prosecutors, who believe that Amber was between 23 and 25 weeks pregnant, said they were considering charging her with homicide.[65] Also in 2007, Katrina Pierce was charged with a misdemeanor for attempting an "abortional act." Police records show that 10 days before someone reported that she had tried to abort her fetus by taking over-the-counter and prescription drugs, police had responded to a domestic violence call at her home.[66]

Impeding Women's Access to Abortions

Typically, a woman first suspects she is pregnant around a month after her last period. If she wants an abortion, she usually can act fairly quickly to obtain an abortion in the first trimester. The risk of complications increases with the length of pregnancy: from one death for every 1 million abortions at 8 or fewer weeks, to one death per 11,000 abortions at 21 weeks or more of gestation.[67] Some of the procedures associated with second-trimester abortions are far more involved than those used in first-trimester abortions. Throughout the country, laws have been implemented that may delay a woman's access to abortion and therefore make her abortion less safe, more expensive, and potentially more emotionally difficult.

Medicaid Restrictions, Waiting Periods, and Counseling Requirements

The cost of a surgical abortion or a medication abortion (e.g., one using a drug that induces abortion, like mifepristone or methotrexate) at 10 weeks gestation is highly variable and ranged between $90 and $1,800 in 2006.[68]

Most abortions are performed at reduced-cost clinics where women on average are charged around $400.[69] Financing an abortion proves to be a major obstacle for many women. Overall, poor women take longer than other women to secure an abortion because it takes them more time to raise money for the procedure.[70]

Medicaid offers poor women comprehensive reproductive health care, including family planning, prenatal care, and services related to childbirth at government expense. Yet the federal government, 32 states, and the District of Columbia restrict public funding for abortion to those cases where a woman's life is in danger or the pregnancy results from rape or incest.[71] In fewer than 20 states does the state cover (with its own funds) all or most medically necessary abortions for women on Medicaid; most of these states do so pursuant to a court order rather than voluntarily.[72] Even in these states, women may have to wait days or weeks to arrange such coverage.[73] The Supreme Court has ruled that it is not unconstitutional for a state to withhold funds for elective abortions, while at the same time paying for childbirth, even if this means, as Justice Brennan argued in his *Maher* dissent, that poor women are unique victims of the pressure to bear children they do not want to have or cannot afford.[74]

Waiting periods and other requirements also can increase the expense. Most states require a woman to be offered state-mandated information designed to discourage abortion, often in conjunction with a mandatory waiting period of at least 24 hours between the counseling and the abortion.[75] Some of these laws require women to make two trips to the provider (or stay overnight) to receive the information in person rather than via the phone, fax, the Internet or mail.[76] This can be a substantial burden to a woman who is a teenager, poor, or incarcerated; has a job; attends school; or lives miles away from an abortion provider.

The medical accuracy of counseling materials is also questionable. The American Medical Association opposes informed consent that is specific to a procedure. In the 1992 *Casey* decision, however, the U.S. Supreme Court ruled that laws requiring abortion-specific counseling were permissible as long as the information given to the women is "truthful and nonmisleading."[77] The Court also affirmed the states' authority to develop written materials for this purpose and to require providers to distribute them.

Today, more than 30 states have abortion counseling laws requiring providers to give specific information to women seeking abortions, describing the nature of the procedures and the associated risks, and the probable gestational age of the fetus.[78] A 2006 survey found that 22 state health departments had developed informational materials.[79] While most of the information presented in these materials was accurate, some content was either misleading or outright wrong. For example, some states assert a possible link between abortion and breast cancer, even though the American Cancer Society held in 2006 that "scientific evidence does not support a causal association between induced abortion and breast cancer" and the U.S. National Cancer Institute concluded that it was "well established" that abortion is not associated with an increased breast cancer risk.[80] A couple states' materials claimed that a fetus can feel pain, even though the sensory systems do not develop until at least 23 weeks gestation and the ability to interpret the information probably does not develop until the third trimester.[81]

Federally funded crisis pregnancy centers are another source of misinformation about abortion. These centers receive millions of dollars in federal funding and are supposed to provide counseling to pregnant teenagers and women. A report released by Rep. Henry A. Waxman (D-CA) in 2006 found that nearly 90 percent of federally funded crisis pregnancy centers provided false and misleading information about the physical and mental health effects of abortion.[82] The centers also grossly exaggerated the medical and psychological risks of abortions, falsely claiming that abortion causes an increased risk of breast cancer, infertility, and serious mental health problems. False information also infuses the Unborn Child Pain Awareness Act, which the U.S. Senate drafted in 2005. This particular act would require an abortion provider to deliver a 193-word script containing dubious information about the "pain-capable unborn child."

Mirroring Justice Kennedy's paternalistic view that women must be shielded from making a decision they may later regret, 10 states have passed "witness to the womb" legislation that requires that abortion clinics offer each woman an ultrasound image of her fetus or inform her of the availability of ultrasounds before the procedure is performed.[83] In my view, such measures, too, go beyond offering women accurate and pertinent information about abortion. They provide misleading and extraneous information under the guise of counseling and in the name of "protecting" a woman from her own decision-making power.[84]

Parental Notification and Consent Laws

Adolescents are more likely than older women to obtain abortions later in pregnancy. Teenaged women obtain one-third of all abortions performed at 13 or more weeks gestation.[85] One in four abortions among girls who are less than 15 years old will be performed after the first trimester.[86] Some of the delay is because many young women do not recognize specific signs of pregnancy and take significantly longer to realize they are pregnant.[87]

Minors' abortions also may be delayed by laws requiring either parental involvement in the decision or a judicial waiver to bypass this involvement.[88] Thirty-five states require some form of parental involvement in a minors' decision to have an abortion, either notifying a parent or securing parental consent.[89] Supporters of mandatory parental involvement assert that such measures protect the health and promote the best interests of young women, as they improve family communication. For most young women, though, notification and consent are one and the same.[90] It is understandable that many parents would want to know if their daughter was pregnant or undergoing any medical procedure that might have serious complications, no matter how unlikely.[91] However, parental consent and notification laws may actually jeopardize some young women's health rather than protect it.

Most parents of pregnant teens already know about their daughter's pregnancy.[92] When a young woman chooses not to involve a parent, it is often for a valid reason such as a desire or need to maintain a good relationship with her parents, fear of being thrown out or beaten, or because she has been the victim of family violence, including incest. Judicial waivers were meant to take into account these situations by waiving the parental notification requirement if the court decides that the minor is sufficiently mature and well informed to make her own decision or that an abortion is in her best interest.

Some girls may be afraid to request a judicial waiver in jurisdictions that require cases of rape or incest to be referred to social services. They may doubt that their confidentiality will be protected. Many young women are not aware of judicial waivers or encounter ignorance and misinformation when they seek information about the process.

Political scientist Helena Silverstein, whose study of mandatory parental involvement was the subject of her book, *Girls on the Stand,* found a "continuum of ignorance" of the judicial bypass process among court employees, court advocates, and judges.[93] Fully half of the courts in the three states she studied proved "absolutely or materially ignorant" of their responsibilities.[94] For instance, court workers told callers to hire an attorney though, in this particular state, court-appointed counsel was available to minors who pursue the bypass option. Some court employees made it known they were hostile to abortion or opposed parental consent being bypassed. Some rejected the possibility that the bypass option existed or that a judge would authorize a waiver of consent, stating, for example, "Without your parent's consent, there's no way you could do that."[95] Some judges use bypass hearings as an occasion to communicate their personal opposition to abortion or require that minors obtain counseling from a pro-life, religiously inspired pregnancy centers like Sav-A-Life (a requirement that also causes a further delay).[96]

Moreover, the minor who successfully navigates the hurdles of ignorance, misinformation, and proselytizing still may be denied the waiver. A young woman in Alabama was 17 years old and eight weeks pregnant.[97] She had three friends who had gotten pregnant, including one who had an abortion and two others who were struggling to raise a child while attending school. She did not want to jeopardize her chances at a college athletic scholarship and pursuing a career in medicine. She also wished to avoid waiting to have the procedure until she turned eighteen because by then she would be in her second trimester. After seeking the advice of her gynecologist, a school nurse, and health clinic staff, and after looking at an ultrasound, she decided she wanted an abortion.[98] In the past, her parents had threatened to cut off financial support if she got pregnant so, wishing to maintain her good relationship with them, she sought a judicial waiver. The trial judge decided not to grant the waiver. He concluded:

> The legislature, in its infinite wisdom, has determined that an unborn child who never has had even the ability to do any wrong, could be put to death so that his mother can play [sports]. . . . Ah, but this young woman has more ambition than to play [sports]. Her possible . . . scholarship is but the means to the end of her becoming a [health-care provider]. But what is the duty of a [health-care provider]? To save lives. Should her child die so that, possibly, she might later save other lives? . . . She said that she does not believe that abortion is wrong, so, apparently, in spite of her church attendance, there won't be spiritual consequences, at least for the present. . . . This is a capital case. It involves the question whether [the minor's] unborn child should live or die."[99]

The young woman had sought advice from a variety of sources and weighed a number of factors in making her decision. Yet despite the maturity she demonstrated, she was still subject to the prejudice of a judge. One can only speculate how a less tenacious adolescent would have fared. A court of appeals later reversed the decision of the trial court judge.

A push for parental consent laws is also taking place on the federal level. In July 2006, the Senate passed the Child Custody Protection Act (CCPA); the House passed a similar bill, the Child Interstate Abortion Notification Act (CIANA) in 2005 (that did not pass in the Senate) and again in September 2006.[100] CCPA/CIANA would make it a federal crime to bypass parental consent laws by knowingly taking a minor across state lines for an abortion, unless she has already fulfilled the parental consent or notification requirements in her home state. If passed, this measure would impose fines of up to $100,000, jail time, or both on people who help the young woman (including health care providers and supportive adults such as grandparents, siblings, and clergy) in most cases where minors were taken out of state for an abortion. The second section of CCPA/CIANA imposes what has been described as a "confusing maze of requirements" in the form of a complicated federal parental notification and mandatory delay law.[101]

Advocates for CCPA/CIANA claim that it will address the problem of a young woman being coerced by a boyfriend or a sexual predator into having an abortion she does not want and that does not have a parent's consent.[102] But this ignores the consequences of a young woman being coerced into *remaining* pregnant against her wishes. Even young women who do not involve a parent in their abortion decisions often seek support from other people in their lives who they do trust, such as grandparents and older siblings. CCPA/CIANA would discourage these people from providing such support and would contribute to the further isolation of those minors who already are in a precarious social circumstance. Moreover, it is not only teens who may find themselves being coerced into an abortion; women of any age can face strong pressure to terminate a pregnancy.[103] The problem of coerced abortions would be better addressed through efforts to ensure abortion providers verify that a woman's consent to the procedure is being freely given.

Abortion Policies in Prisons and Jails

Because of their circumstances, incarcerated women and girls are heavily dependent on correctional staff and administrators to ensure their reproductive rights are respected. Although not systematically documented, evidence strongly suggests that some incarcerated women and girls are pressured into having abortions or seek to abort pregnancies stemming from a sexual assault by a member of the correctional staff. Nine girls held at Alabama's only juvenile detention facility for girls in Chalkville filed a lawsuit claiming that they were pressured to have abortions after male correctional staff (including correctional officers) impregnated them.[104] After attorneys filed the lawsuit, women contacted them alleging the same types of treatment had taken place as much as two decades earlier. Memos, letters, and written complaints dating back to 1994 surfaced, charging correctional staff with physical abuse, rape, sexual harassment and consensual sex. The Alabama Department of Youth Services was granted immunity to nearly all claims (except those related to violations of the Title IX federal law that prohibits sex discrimination at schools that receive federal money) because it is a state agency. The claims against the director of youth services, the principal and the superintendent of the Chalkville campus were thrown out because they were leveled against state workers.[105]

At least as common as incarcerated women being pressured into obtaining abortions are incarcerated women facing obstacles to terminating their pregnancies. Abortion is sometimes treated or viewed as an "elective" surgery because, as is the case with other elective procedures like hip replacement, angioplasty, and cosmetic surgery, the woman's decision to have the procedure is rarely a life-threatening emergency situation and the procedure is planned in advance. In the case of incarcerated women, this characterization has been used to permit abortions only on the same basis as other elective medical care—namely, by completing required paperwork, paying for transportation and security to an outside medical provider, and paying for the procedure itself. But abortion differs from many elective surgeries in key ways. First, when a woman is pregnant, the medical treatment she needs—not merely "elects"—depends on whether she seeks to continue or terminate her pregnancy. Second, many elective surgeries do not need to be performed within a specific time frame. Abortion, by contrast, constitutes a "serious medical need" because denying or delaying the procedure renders the woman's condition irreparable. Third, denying a woman an abortion can have serious mental, emotional, and physical consequences for the woman herself, as well as any friend or family member who may be called on to care for the child. When a woman is incarcerated, these consequences are often exacerbated.[106]

In many prison and jail systems, women must first secure a court order in order to have an abortion, a process which can take weeks or possibly months and may require them to pay a lawyer's fees. Even with a court order, many counties have refused to transport pregnant inmates to abortion facilities or to cover the cost of the abortion. For example, until recently, several Arizona county jails had an unwritten policy of refusing to bring pregnant inmates to abortion facilities without a court order, even though they routinely transported prisoners for prenatal care, childbirth, and even various nonmedical reasons such as visiting a terminally ill family member or attending a relative's funeral. In Maricopa County (AZ) Jail, inmates seeking an abortion were not informed of the policy, nor were they provided assistance in finding an abortion clinic or scheduling an appointment. There were no rules or procedures to ensure an inmate's request for an abortion and motions for a court order were dealt with promptly. The case of "Jane Doe" illustrates the obstacles that can be thrown in the path of an incarcerated woman who seeks to terminate her pregnancy.[107]

In 2004, Jane found out that she was pregnant right before she was to be sentenced for driving under the influence.[108] Facing months of jail time and not prepared to have a child, she decided to terminate her pregnancy. She asked her attorney to try to delay her sentencing hearing so she could get an abortion. The prosecutor refused the extension and suggested that Jane Doe get an abortion while she was on work furlough. In her first week of incarceration, and awaiting transfer to the work furlough area, she told the nurse of her plans to terminate her pregnancy. The next week, she was scheduled for an ultrasound, and she again told medical staff that she wanted an abortion. She planned to obtain an abortion on her own, if necessary, since she had been cleared for work furlough. However, jail staff transferred her to another housing area where inmates are not allowed to participate in work furlough and in which telephone access is especially restricted.

Despite the obstacles the jail placed in her path, with the help of her family, Jane was able to prepay for an abortion at a local clinic, but the deputies refused to transport her without a court order. She was told that she would have to get an attorney to help her obtain the court order. She also would have to pay for transportation and security costs, as well as staff expenses. Even after she prepaid for an abortion at a local clinic, her request for a court order was denied twice. After a seven-week delay, a second judge finally granted the order in the 13th week of pregnancy; further delay would have required a more invasive, riskier two-day procedure. The jail's policy was finally struck down in 2005 by the Superior Court of Arizona in Maricopa County.[109] Joe Arpaio, Maricopa County sheriff, defended his policy, saying: "I do not run a taxi service from jail to an abortion clinic and back. Where do you draw the line?"[110]

The government is forbidden from placing a substantial burden in the path of a woman who seeks an abortion. In *Monmouth County Correctional*

Institutional Inmates v. Lanzaro, the majority ruled that when the decision to require a court order depends on the nature of the treatment or reason for transport (rather than the security risk posed by the individual inmate), then the court order serves no legitimate penological purpose.[111] The U.S. Court of Appeals for the Third Circuit found that requiring women to obtain a court order to get an abortion, but not for other forms of treatment or transport outside the facility (such as visiting a sick or dying relative), was unconstitutional. *Monmouth* established that requiring a court order before permitting a nontherapeutic abortion interferes with an incarcerated woman's right to have an abortion and constitutes deliberate indifference to a serious medical need. As the ruling in *Estelle v. Gamble* established, jail and prison administrators are legally obliged to provide medical care for inmates, because people who are incarcerated must rely on prison authorities to treat their medical needs.[112] This obligation is violated when officials know a need for medical care exists and either intentionally refuse that medical care or delay it for nonmedical reasons such as an inmate's willingness or ability to pay.

Despite the rulings in *Estelle* and *Monmouth,* incarcerated women and girls who seek to have an abortion continue to face obstacles. Rachel Roth, then a research fellow at Ibis Reproductive Health, conducted an extensive survey of relevant state statutes, administrative regulations, and attorney general opinions to assess incarcerated women's access to abortion.[113] According to Roth, at least one-third of all states have no official written policy governing incarcerated women's access to abortion. Two states' policies mention abortion counseling only. Nineteen states provide funding only for "lifesaving" abortions. Six states and the District of Columbia fund "therapeutic" or "medically necessary" abortions, and nine states provide access to abortions at least during the first trimester.

State policies vary widely, even within the same federal circuit. New Jersey, for example, has clearly articulated and readily available policies. New Jersey provides abortions for women who are up to 18 weeks pregnant and takes women to Planned Parenthood to discuss their options. By contrast, in Delaware, women not only must pay for abortions but also are charged $100 for transportation and security (provided by "moonlighting" correctional officers on Saturdays). Pennsylvania has no official written abortion policy for inmates and handles requests for abortion on a case-by-case basis. As Roth drily observes, "Women in the two state prisons would not be reassured to learn that if they wanted an abortion, they would have to wait for the staff . . . to formulate a process to handle their request."[114] Furthermore, if the local hospital is Catholic or a public facility in a state that prohibits nonlifesaving abortions at public facilities, the prisoner must try to convince the warden to authorize a trip to a different hospital or clinic.[115] Where women are incarcerated in remote areas, women's access to abortion is even further obstructed.

Federal and State Abortion Bans

Correctional policies, parental notification laws, and waiting period requirements reflect attempts to restrict or interfere with women's access to abortion. Other measures, such as the Partial-Birth Abortion Ban Act of 2003 aim to criminalize it entirely.

Many people are troubled by the prospect of a woman contemplating an abortion when the second trimester of her pregnancy is well under way. At 20 weeks, a pregnant woman feels the movement of the fetus. Her body has changed in visible ways. Not only is she more aware of the presence of the fetus (and others may be aware of her pregnancy as well), but also, with every passing week, it becomes less likely that the abortion will be a relatively brief appointment with a short recovery. Moreover, the abortion procedure is now more complicated. First-trimester abortions typically involve vacuum aspiration or dilation and extraction (procedures that each are usually completed within 10–20 minutes), or they use drugs that induce abortion, like mifepristone or methotrexate, and are effective within a week. Abortions in the second trimester or later are more involved and invasive. So while it is natural to wonder how a woman can consider terminating a pregnancy after the first trimester, the same question obliges us to recognize that the decision is probably quite significant to the pregnant woman herself. Conservative pundits' claims to the contrary, it is unlikely that a woman could approach the decision to terminate a pregnancy after the first trimester casually or indifferently even if she wanted to.

Women seek second-trimester abortions for a variety of reasons. A pregnant teenager might not realize she is pregnant right away, lack a nearby abortion provider, have no money, or have to comply with a parental consent law; she may be in her second trimester before she has successfully overcome these hurdles.[116] A woman in her 40s may have incorrectly assumed that she was menopausal, not pregnant. Pregnant women of all ages may not learn of fetal defects until the second trimester. A woman may find that a condition such as placenta previa now threatens her health or life. An incarcerated woman may be delayed by hurdles presented by prison staff or state-mandated policies.

As part of an effort to ban a procedure commonly used in the second trimester of pregnancy, in 2003, Congress passed the Partial-Birth Abortion Ban Act and President George W. Bush signed it into law.[117] The law specified penalties of a $250,000 fine and a maximum of two years' imprisonment for any doctor who performs a so-called partial-birth abortion.[118] Twenty-seven states have enacted similar bans, though most have been specifically blocked by a court.[119]

The term "partial-birth abortion" is not used in the medical or legal literature, nor is it used by doctors who routinely perform second-trimester abortions.[120] That it is a term with no legal or scientific basis does not stop politicians or the media from using it. During the Senate debate over the act, Sen. Rick Santorum, the bill's sponsor, said, "The term 'partial birth' comes from the fact that the baby is partially born, is in the process of being delivered." In his State of the Union address, President George W. Bush said the bill would "protect infants at the very hour of their birth." In the highly charged political context of abortion, the word "birth" is fraught with meaning. It is also important in a legal context, since rights of citizenship are bestowed at birth. To recognize the fetus as being born represents a move toward recognizing the fetus as a citizen with corresponding rights (see chapter 5). By implying that the procedure being banned is a birth interrupted by an abortion, proponents of the ban laid the groundwork for considering abortion to be a form of infanticide.

One problem with the Partial-Birth Abortion Ban Act and similar bans enacted at the state level is that they are too vague and broad in what they prohibit. Anti-abortion activists assert that the intent of the act was to ban intact dilation and evacuation (also known as intact dilation and extraction, IDX, intact D and E, D&X, and intact D&X) exclusively. This is a rarely used procedure. In 2000, only 2,200 (or less than two-tenths of 1 percent of all the abortions performed in the United States) were intact dilation and evacuations.[121] The language of the act, however, seems to apply to several different commonly used abortion procedures, including standard dilation and evacuation, which have been used safely for years.[122]

Following the passage of the act, the Center for Reproductive Rights, the American Civil Liberties Union, and Planned Parenthood Federation of America each immediately filed lawsuits in federal courts claiming that the act violated the right to due process.[123] Ultimately, all three trial courts declared the law unconstitutional because it lacked the necessary health exception for cases in which the banned procedures were necessary to preserve the health and safety of women.[124] Two of the courts also held that the law was so broad in its definition of "partial-birth abortion" that it would criminalize some common abortion procedures performed as early as 12 weeks into the pregnancy and therefore imposed an "undue burden" on a woman's right to an abortion.[125] Appellate courts affirmed the lower courts' rulings.

In June 2006, the Supreme Court agreed to review one of the appellate cases, *Gonzales v. Carhart.* In April 2007, in a 5–4 vote that included two new Bush appointees, the Supreme Court upheld the ban on the procedure.[126] The federal ban (and most of the state bans) permit an exception in order to save a woman's life but not to preserve her health. Even this, however, raises the question of what constitutes a genuine threat to a woman's life. As one obstetrician/gynecologist observed, "If someone has a 10 percent chance of dying, is that what [a threat to a woman's life] mean[s]? Or is it 30 percent or 50 percent or 80 percent? By the time you figure out somebody is at a high risk of dying, they're probably going to die."[127]

The act erroneously asserts that "a partial-birth abortion is never necessary to preserve the health of a woman." The Court asserted that because Congress had found that intact dilation and evacuation was never necessary, the health exception could be omitted. But the oral testimony before Congress had been heavily weighted in support of the ban.[128] According to the U.S. District Court for the Northern District of California (which had reviewed this testimony), over an eight-year period, Congress heard testimony from eight physicians, six of whom supported the ban and had never performed the procedure in question, and one of whom was not an obstetrician/gynecologist. The testimony was not only unbalanced but "intentionally polemic." For instance, one doctor testified that he personally would not perform an abortion to save the life of a woman unless he believed that there was at least a 50 percent chance that she would die without the abortion, even if the pregnancy was the result of rape or incest.[129]

The American College for Obstetricans and Gynecologists (ACOG) was among the many organizations that filed an amicus brief opposing the ban. The ACOG's 50,000 members represent around 90 percent of all board-certified obstetricians and gynecologists practicing in the United States. Contrary to the Supreme Court's majority opinion, the ACOG brief pointed out that intact dilation and evacuation may provide significant health and safety benefits to women with certain bleeding disorders, heart disease, and compromised immune systems or women carrying fetuses with certain abnormalities.[130] For instance, for some women with placenta previa (where the placenta partially or entirely covers the cervical opening) or placenta accreta (in which the placenta abnormally invades the wall of the uterus), intact dilation and evacuation minimizes the chance of a woman hemorrhaging. The banned procedure also reduces the risk of harm to a woman with chorioamnionitis (a bacterial infection of the fetal membranes), which spreads rapidly to the fetus, placenta, and uterine wall, and eventually to other pelvic organs, causing peritonitis and sepsis.

Intact dilation and evacuation is also safest for a woman whose fetus has certain fetal anomalies. Open spina bifida and severe hydrocephalus often are not detected until the second trimester when amniocentesis is performed, typically between the 15th and 18th weeks of pregnancy. Some of these conditions almost invariably result in fetal death.[131] A fetus with severe hydrocephalus has a greatly enlarged head that makes extraction difficult. The intact dilation and evacuation procedure allows a doctor to reduce the risk of injury to the woman's cervix. Also, women carrying fetuses with these conditions may prefer to terminate their pregnancies rather than undergo the anguish of delivering a stillborn or watching one's newborn infant suffer and die.

Efforts to criminalize abortion are not confined to the federal government nor to a rare second-trimester abortion procedure. The drive to criminalize all abortions continues on state fronts. In the early 1990s, Louisiana and Utah passed bans on all abortion procedures that were never enforced. They included some exceptions to the ban, but no broad protections for a woman's health. The laws were struck down by lower courts as unconstitutional, and the Supreme Court refused to hear appeals. In March 2006, South Dakota Governor Mike Rounds signed into law an outright abortion ban, the Women's Health and Human Life Protection Act (House Bill 1215), which provided no exceptions for rape or incest or to protect a woman's health; it did provide an exception to save a woman's life. Performing an abortion in violation of the law was categorized as a Class 5 felony, punishable by five years imprisonment and a fine of $10,000. A petition led to a referendum and the successful repeal of HB 1215 in November 2006. Over a dozen states already have abortion trigger laws or pre-*Roe* bans on the books. (As their name suggests, some of these laws and bills are written in such a way that they are "triggered" in the event that the U.S. Constitution no longer prohibits states from banning abortion.) As of spring 2007, a half-dozen states were considering similar legislation that would outlaw abortion in all or most circumstances.[132]

Conclusion

If abortion is technically a legally permissible procedure, but poor women, women in rural areas, incarcerated women, and teenaged women are blocked from accessing the procedure, then it can hardly be considered a realizable right. Too many women's choices are circumscribed by the structural barriers they face once they decide to have an abortion. A woman may want to have a child but knows that she won't be able to afford to raise her child. Or, she may decide to have an abortion but is prevented from doing so by the lack of affordable abortion providers in her area. Considering abortion an "elective" procedure or a matter of "choice" is simplistic in light of the barriers placed in women's ability to freely decide whether to have a baby or an abortion.

Opposition to abortion seems grounded less in a genuine concern for life and more in a need to control women's lives, including and especially their reproduction. Constitutional law scholar Laurence Tribe observes:

> It may become clear in the end that at a deep level the opposition to women's having the right to choose to end a pregnancy is more about the control of women than about the sanctity of life or of nature. If this is so, then opposition to a right to choose seeks to restrict the liberty of unwilling women in the name of something less than the "absolute" of the protection of human life. And if this is the case, then even the pro-life advocate may conclude that the objection to abortion rights ought to yield, as a matter of morality, to the claim of the woman to her liberty and equality. To conscript a woman to save a *life* might be one thing. To conscript her to save a *way* of life, one in which she is relegated to a second-class role, is another entirely.[133]

A paradox exists: On one hand, the state is sufficiently concerned about "irresponsible" or "unfit" reproducers that it is willing to intervene to discourage some women from procreating. On the other hand, the state is unconcerned about equal access to abortion and, in some cases, puts hurdles in place to make the procedure more difficult, if not impossible, to access. By selectively withholding benefits to a woman or girl who seeks to end her pregnancy, state actors are able to impose their will on women—and maintain women's subordinate position in society—irrespective of the legal status of abortion.[134] By criminalizing abortion, the state effectively forces a woman or girl to remain pregnant for nine months and to give birth to a child she may not want or may not be able to care for. The state simply should not have such sovereignty over a woman's body and her life.

4

"Baby-Killers"
Neonaticide and Infant Abandonment

The point here is not that infanticide is excusable, but rather that it is far from 'unthinkable.'
—Cheryl L. Meyer, Michelle Oberman, et al.,
Mothers Who Kill Their Children, 2001

I got to go to school, I got to go to school.
—A 17-year-old Harlem girl, who brought a dead baby girl
in a plastic bag to the hospital on her way to school,
speaking to hospital staff, quoted in *New York Times,* 2005

Of the 4 million women who give birth each year in the United States, a tiny fraction of a percent will abandon or kill their newborns. Though probably only a couple hundred in number, these cases are disturbing for a host of reasons. Many represent everything that is wrong with reproductive policy in the United States. A young woman becomes pregnant without meaning to. She experiences a pregnancy that nobody acknowledges, much less supports, and that she herself denies exists. She is terrified that others will notice her pregnancy, rather than being hopeful or proud. She gives birth without any intent or wish to become a mother. Her need for medical treatment often is what leads to the police being summoned. She perceives virtually everything about the reproductive experience as being beyond her control.[1]

The phenomena of neonaticide (the killing of a newborn) and infant abandonment map in sharp relief our society's discomfort with adolescent sexuality, our failure to address the problems of unintended pregnancies, sexual abuse, and statutory rape, and the stigma that continues to be attached to abortion and teenage pregnancies.[2] In this chapter, I am not arguing that a woman or girl has a right to kill or abandon her baby. Respecting women's reproductive rights does require, however, that we recognize not only the precarious psychological state of the woman or girl who commits neonaticide but also the precarious social context in which her actions take place. Instead of laying the blame squarely on the shoulders of the neonaticidal woman or girl, we should consider, too, society's role in ensuring that consent to sex is given freely and without coercion and that pregnancies are intended—and supported. The criminal justice system seems ill suited to this challenge.

Pregnancy Denial and Magical Thinking

Reliable estimates of the incidence of abandonment and neonaticide do not exist. What we know comes mainly from findings of small-scale studies that have gleaned information from a variety of sources, including news accounts and legal cases, psychiatrists' records, and police and prison records.[3] The total number of *known* neonaticide or abandonment cases probably does not exceed a few hundred a year at most.[4] The highly secretive circumstances surrounding these events mean that many (and quite possibly most) cases are never discovered and therefore are not reflected in official statistics.

Existing information suggests that neonaticide and abandonment take place across the spectrum of race, ethnicity, and socioeconomic class.[5] It also appears that a disproportionate number of cases involve young women in their teens and twenties. Like other teenagers who get pregnant, the young woman who abandons or kills her newborn typically is unmarried and physically healthy. She probably lives with her parents, guardians, or other relatives.[6] She is often deeply concerned about the reaction of her parents and those around her.[7] She may be mortified that she got pregnant in the first place. In other words, she experiences some of the normal reactions that often accompany an unintended and unwanted pregnancy.[8]

In other respects, young women who abandon or kill their newborns are unique. For one, they typically are in a state of profound denial that they are pregnant and are going to have a baby. Other women, upon realizing they are experiencing an unwanted pregnancy, consider an abortion, adoption, or how they are going to navigate motherhood.[9] By contrast, a woman or girl who kills her newborn often spends her pregnancy hoping the problem will resolve itself. She may lack the sense of personal efficacy or social ties that would lead her to seek help or advice. Her massive denial that she is even pregnant keeps her from seeking prenatal care or making plans for the birth and care of her child.

Michelle Oberman, a law professor and a leading authority on neonaticide, describes this state of perpetual delusion as "magical thinking." The woman or girl knows deep down that she is pregnant but is "unable to bring herself to imagine the birth of her baby or what might happen afterward."[10] One young woman described her state of denial as being "as if I was just going to stay pregnant forever."[11]

According to Oberman, for women who have gotten into a pattern of absolutely denying that this baby is going to be born, "the moment of labor and delivery comes as an absolute shock. The women move into a period of psychotic break to help them cope with the overwhelming pain. Suddenly, denial is no longer working as the coping strategy, and they begin to make very impulsive decisions."[12] These decisions may include deciding to suffocate or strangle the infant, or to leave the baby to drown in a toilet. For example, a 13-year-old Bronx girl wanted to hide her pregnancy from her strict mother. After giving birth, she threw her newborn baby out of a bedroom window when he started to cry.[13]

The period of disassociation and denial can persist for hours (and even days) after the birth. Later, when reality sets in, a woman may try to turn back time and cover up her actions by hiding the body of the baby or throwing it away. A 17-year-old Harlem girl delivered a live baby girl in a toilet. She washed the baby off, wrapped it in her pajamas, put it in the closet, and then went to bed. The next morning, concerned about her bleeding, she took the now dead baby girl's body to the hospital with, as one news account reported, "her school bag on one shoulder and a plastic bag in hand."[14] The girl seemed unaware of the gravity of her actions. When hospital staff questioned her, she became impatient, insisting, "I got to go to school, I got to go to school."

While part of the problem relates to the mental state of the woman or girl giving birth, we should be cautious about interpreting her actions as a form of psychopathology. Killing or abandoning an infant may be an extreme reaction, but it is not necessarily a reflection of mental illness. Research suggests that severe mental illness is unusual among those who commit neonaticide. Only a minority of cases of neonaticide result from postpartum psychosis or long-term mental disorders.[15]

One striking finding is the degree to which many of these woman and girls have spent their pregnancies living around people who did not notice they were pregnant.[16] News accounts often report that at some point a mother or neighbor asked the young woman if she was pregnant and were told "no." The failure of other adults to notice the pregnancy is troubling, given how difficult it would be to conceal a pregnancy for nine months.[17] Such a lack of adult awareness of the pregnancy suggests a lack of intimate (or at least close), safe, and open relationships with family members or friends. Perhaps, though, this obliviousness is not as remarkable as it seems. Family members, teachers, and other concerned parties may be experiencing some degree of denial, too.

The same cultural beliefs that make a young woman too ashamed to admit that she has had sex and gotten pregnant may affect parents and family members as well. The shame of having an unwed pregnant daughter may bring on its own level of denial. When combined with below-average weight gain during pregnancy, the camouflaging effects of baggy clothing, fleeting or spotty contact with savvy adults, and a conscious effort to conceal the pregnancy, successfully avoiding detection seems more plausible.[18]

As noted in chapter 3, most teenagers *will* inform a parent or other adult about their pregnancy. But there are circumstances under which this might not be the case. Many young women are afraid of getting kicked out of their homes if the pregnancy is discovered.[19] Some women are embarrassed that they did not know the father very well or fear their family's reaction to a biracial child. In some cases, women who are pregnant with another man's child wish to avoid the rejection of their partners or family members.

Deeply held religious convictions or cultural forces opposing extramarital sex can play an incredibly powerful role. The case of Shadia Muse illustrates how culture and gender may intersect to create additional difficulties in acknowledging an unwanted pregnancy.[20] Shadia was a Somali high school student living with her mother, brother, and sister in central Ohio. In Somali culture, premarital sex and having a child without being married bring much shame to one's family and community. An unwed pregnant woman is considered "a prostitute, a harlot," and the child is also shunned and often ridiculed. Somali women's advocate Saida Yassin reports that a pregnant Somali girl "hides, hides, hides, and when labor comes, she doesn't know what to do."[21] Abortion is also condemned. In Somalia, unwed pregnant women often abandon their infants in the capital city in hopes that the infant will be found and turned over to be raised by the government. Shadia had hidden her pregnancy from her family and denied she was pregnant when a neighbor inquired. After giving birth, Shadia went to the hospital for medical attention, where hospital personnel reported her to the police. Police later found the newborn dead in the trunk of a car. The police charged Shadia with murder and issued a warrant for her arrest. After she left the hospital, Shadia disappeared, and her family reported her missing. As of January 2008, she was still listed on the Central Ohio Crime Stoppers website as "wanted for the murder of her newborn baby."[22] Her photo (apparently a snapshot) reveals a smiling baby-faced teen wearing a varsity-type jacket, incongruous among the mug shots of four other men who are wanted for murder in the stabbing or shooting of their adult victims.

Sexual abuse and statutory rape also contribute to some cases of neonaticide and abandonment. Pregnancy that results from sexual abuse can be accompanied by profound shame and fear. Some women and girls deny the pregnancy as part of an attempt to hide the abuse that accompanied it. Around 5 percent of all women of reproductive age who are raped will become pregnant, and one in three will not realize they are pregnant until the second trimester. According to a 1996 study, an estimated 32,000 pregnancies result from rape each year.[23] Most rape-related pregnancies occur among adolescents and often involve a perpetrator who is related or known to the victim.[24] Typically, the pregnancy results from repeated acts of violence or abuse, such as incest, statutory rape, or forcible rape by an intimate partner.[25] Many of these crimes never come to the attention of the police.[26]

According to the National Longitudinal Study of Adolescent Health, 7 percent of adolescent women reported having been forced into sexual intercourse; 8 percent of these were re-victimized in the following year.[27] For example, in 2005, a newborn was found crying at the bottom of an air shaft in West New York, New Jersey.[28] A high school junior was charged with trying to kill the child. Investigators later found the remains of a second infant in the same air shaft. DNA tests confirmed that the father of both infants was the girl's own father, Jose Julio Ventura, who had sexually assaulted the girl since she was 14 years old. The father threatened to kill the girl and her mother if she told anyone about her pregnancies and the sexual assaults.[29] The young woman, who has an IQ of 72, waived her right to be charged as a juvenile, pleaded guilty to aggravated assault and reckless manslaughter, and faces up to seven years in prison.

One natural question is, why doesn't the woman or girl simply get an abortion rather than abandon or kill her newborn? First, and most obviously, such an action requires that a woman or girl accept the fact that she is indeed pregnant. Obtaining an abortion—particularly in light of the obstacles that exist (e.g., a lack of money, parental notification laws, a shortage of providers, and social stigma)—requires a degree of self-assurance and tenacity that can challenge even the most "together" of individuals, much less someone who has not come to grips with the reality of being pregnant. Also, a young woman who is afraid to tell her parents she is pregnant is probably afraid because a family member is implicated or she fears their disapproval of and opposition to not just premarital sex and contraceptive use but abortion. Too many young women's own moral objections to abortion prevent them from considering it as an option. A 2005 survey of high school seniors found that 70 percent of the female students said they would not consider having an abortion if they became pregnant in high school.[30] In a climate that is hostile to abortion rights, many young people have a dim view of termination as a possible response to an unintended pregnancy.

It is also natural to ask why a woman doesn't at least make sure the baby is okay after she gives birth. But again, this would require that she accept not only the reality of being pregnant but also the reality of having given birth. In the hours after she gives birth, she must be able to make the baby's need for survival figure more prominently than her own desperate fear of the consequences of someone finding out. And, for women who are struggling or not in a position to support themselves, the prospect of taking care of a child may be too overwhelming to face.

Preventing Unwanted Teen Pregnancy

Because it appears that a disproportionate number of the women who abandon or kill their newborns are young, the problem must be considered alongside the larger issues of teen pregnancy and adolescent sexuality.[31] Teenage pregnancy rates in the United States dropped almost 30 percent in the 1990s; the most recent data suggest that both teenage pregnancy and birthrates are at an all-time low. Still, teen pregnancy is not an uncommon occurrence. The United States has the highest rates of teen pregnancy and birth in the western industrialized world. Each year, around 750,000 women and girls between 15 and 19 years of age become pregnant; more than one-half will give birth, and nearly one-third will have an abortion.[32]

A major reason for the decline in teen pregnancy is that contraceptive use has increased.[33] Contraception and abortion became more readily available in the mid-1960s and 1970s, breaking the link between sex and reproduction. Now women, like men, could choose whether or not to become a parent and could engage in sex solely for pleasure without the looming fear of unwanted pregnancy. At around the same time, comprehensive sex education in schools began to shift away from preparing adolescents for marriage and parenthood and discouraging premarital sex.[34] Sex educators began to treat marriage as one context among many in which sex could take place. A focus emerged on teaching young people how to manage the "risks" of sex, driven in part by concern about HIV/AIDS and a perceived crisis in teenage pregnancy.[35]

Since the late 1980s, the religious right has pressed for a shift away from the basic principle that young people should be provided with information that will allow them to decide for themselves what is proper sexual behavior. Instead, moral conservatives have lobbied heavily to replace comprehensive sex education with a single message: No sex should take place outside of heterosexual marriage.[36] The resurgence of moral and religious conservatism has limited young people's access to affordable and effective means of birth control, as well as accurate and comprehensive sex education in public schools.

It was not always this way. In the 1970s, states began to expand minors' authority to consent to health care related to sexual activity, and U.S. Supreme Court rulings have extended the right to privacy to a minor's decision to obtain contraceptives. Confidentiality is very important to ensuring young women's access to contraceptive services. While parental involvement is desirable, many young women will still have sex but will not seek contraceptive services if they have to tell their parents. Yet only in 25 states and the District of Columbia are minors who are 12 years of age or older permitted to consent to contraceptive services. In another 21 states, only certain categories of minors can consent to such services (e.g., those who are high school graduates, married, pregnant, or who have been pregnant in the past).[37]

Federally funded abstinence-only-until-marriage programs contribute to a climate of fear and misinformation about adolescent sexuality and pregnancy. In the early 1980s, under President Ronald Reagan's administration, the federal government started to fund abstinence-only-until-marriage programs, increasingly treating them not only as the preferred approach but the only approach.[38] Between 1996 and 2005, over $1 billion in state and federal funds were allocated to abstinence-only/no-contraception education programs. In order for a state to qualify for federal support, its sex education program must conform to a definition of "abstinence education." The definition laid out in Title V of the Social Security Act includes teaching that "mutually faithful monogamous relationship in the context of marriage is the expected standard of sexual activity" and that "sexual activity outside of the context of marriage is likely to have harmful psychological and physical effects." Empirical research has challenged the veracity of the claim that virginity loss before marriage or during adolescence causes such harm.[39]

Furthermore, studies suggest that Health and Human Services (HHS) and the Administration for Children and Families have become a "flat earth society" by continuing to fund abstinence-only programs in the face of strong evidence that they don't work.[40] Authors of an HHS-contracted evaluation of abstinence-only-until-marriage programs reported that "youth in the program group were no more likely than control group youth to have abstained from sex and, among those who reported having had sex, they had similar numbers of sexual partners and had initiated sex at the same mean age."[41] Nor were differences found in the rate of unprotected sex.

According to the Sexuality Information and Education Council of the United States (SIECUS), some of the curricula used by abstinence-only programs that receive federal funds have been found to present distorted and inaccurate information about the effectiveness and health consequences of contraception and abortion, such as "the chances of getting pregnant with a condom are 1 out of 6," "Condoms provide no proven reduction in protection against Chlamydia," and "AIDS can be transmitted by skin-to-skin contact."[42] Some abstinence-only curricula promoted gender stereotypes ("guys are turned on by their senses and women by their hearts") and rely on fear and shame to motivate changes in behavior by, for instance, comparing having sex outside of marriage with jumping off a tall building.[43]

By contrast, studies have found that comprehensive sex education programs that include information about abstinence, contraception, and the prevention of sexually transmitted infections result in teens delaying sex, having fewer partners, and being more likely to use contraceptives.[44] In recent years, more information has emerged regarding the limited effectiveness of abstinence-only programming and the relative benefits of comprehensive education, suggesting that another shift may be in the works. A growing number of states have rejected the federal abstinence grants rather than be forced to use the money to fund abstinence-only programming.[45] Such a trend bodes well for efforts to prevent unwanted pregnancies.

Society's Response to Neonaticide and Abandonment

In the face of a critical social climate and the stigma of some pregnancies, some women and girls will respond to an unwanted pregnancy and birth by abandoning or killing their newborn. From time to time, these cases attract a flurry of media attention. When they come to light, public expressions of grief and concern for the newborn are not uncommon. If the baby has died, memorials and elaborate funerals may be organized. While much concern is extended to the newborn victim, far less is directed to the needs and well-being of the woman or girl who gives birth. Often, attention to the woman focuses on determining her identity or discussing whether she will be prosecuted.

Our responses to neonaticide or abandonment should instead consider the medical and psychological needs of the woman or girl who gives birth. In the first place, before they have even given birth, most of these women and girls who conceal their pregnancies have not had their health checked or attended to during the pregnancy and delivery. Typically, they have not sought or received any prenatal or postpartum care, which places them at greater risk of complications.[46] More generally, pregnant teenagers, compared with older pregnant women, face higher risks of some serious health problems including pregnancy-induced high blood pressure, anemia, and premature labor.[47]

Since there are no doctors, midwives, medical staff, or birth attendants present, sometimes, after giving birth, girls or women need medical attention as the result of complications such as infections or hemorrhaging. In many cases, women and girls who abandoned or killed their newborn sought medical care after delivery only to have medical personnel report them to the police. For instance, an eighth-grader in Minnesota, "Lillian," became pregnant by a 22-year-old family friend who lived in her home. Lillian gave birth in her bedroom, then strangled and hid the baby in a shoebox. Her parents noticed the excessive bleeding that followed her delivery and called paramedics. After Lillian admitted giving birth, the medical staff then called the police, and the eighth-grader was later charged with intentional second-degree murder.[48] In Washington state, a 24-year-old woman's actions were discovered a week after she gave birth. Her mother grew concerned about her chronic bleeding and called for medical help over her daughter's protests. The young woman subsequently was convicted of second-degree manslaughter.[49] A 15-year-old girl was reported to the police after taking an ambulance to a New Hampshire hospital because she was hemorrhaging.[50] Most of these young women and girls go to great lengths to deny their pregnancies and births out of concern for their own well-being and future; being turned into the police when they seek medical treatment only confirms their worst fears.

Criminal Justice Responses

Once a neonaticide or abandonment case has been identified, the response of the criminal justice system varies widely. In *Mothers Who Kill Their Children*, the authors report the results of their study that included 37 cases of neonaticide between 1990 and 1999.[51] Some teenagers were charged as juveniles, while others were prosecuted as adults. Some women were not charged with a crime at all; others were charged with first-degree murder. Women also were charged with other offenses, including "child abuse, negligent homicide, second-degree murder, felony child endangerment, involuntary manslaughter, negligent manslaughter, and abuse of a corpse."[52] Another study based on 34 cases identified through media accounts published from 1988 to 1998 found that over two-thirds of the women and girls were charged with murder.[53]

Sometimes prosecution for homicide is not possible because of the difficulty in determining whether or not the infant was born alive. In 2004, a Virginia state legislator, John Cosgrove, introduced a bill that would require the notification of law enforcement authorities when a baby has been delivered dead and the woman who gave birth has not been attended by a medical professional.[54] Cosgrove explained that he introduced House Bill 1677 in response to "instances of full term babies who were abandoned shortly after birth. These poor children died horrible deaths. If a coroner could not determine whether the child was born alive, the person responsible for abandoning the child could only be charged with the improper disposal of a human body."[55] In the outcry that followed the introduction of this bill, critics pointed out that such a measure would treat women as criminals until proven otherwise. Had the bill passed, a woman who delivered a stillborn not only would have to deal with having gone into labor, delivering a stillborn fetus, delivering the placenta, and experiencing the uterine contractions, she now would have had to call the police or risk being charged with a Class 1 misdemeanor.[56] The bill also assumed that determining whether an infant was born alive is a straightforward matter. In reality, it requires a fairly involved protocol, including examination of the infant, the umbilical cord, the amniotic fluid, the placenta, and membranes.

Cosgrove was concerned about women who had killed their newborn but claimed to have miscarried or delivered a stillbirth. He did not consider the distinct possibility that women might be falsely accused of committing neonaticide. In Louisiana, for instance, 27-year-old Michelle Greenup was accused of killing and disposing of her newborn baby.[57] Michelle had hidden her pregnancy from family, friends, and her incarcerated husband because she did not want them to know she was pregnant by another man. Michelle was originally charged with second-degree murder. Medical records were eventually introduced, however, which indicated that she had miscarried about 12 weeks after receiving a Depo-Provera injection.[58] (Michelle had tested negative for pregnancy before the injection.) Depo-Provera is known to cause miscarriages in women who become pregnant. Michelle was detained over a year in jail before the charges of second-degree murder were dropped.

Adjudication in cases of infanticide or abandonment ranges from outright acquittal to life imprisonment. Some offenders are required to participate in psychotherapy, and others are expected to perform community service.[59] A 2004 *Milwaukee Journal Sentinel* analysis found that the sentences of Wisconsin women convicted in the deaths of their newborns ranged from very light to very severe, with "virtually nothing in between."[60] Among 13 women convicted over a 10-year period, 7 were sentenced to probation or one year or less in jail. In the other 6 cases, the prison terms were long (an average of 21 years) and included a life sentence.[61] Another study found that of the 21 cases in which the sentences were identified, 18 resulted in a sentence of incarceration.[62]

States seem to have adopted more punitive responses to neonaticide in the early 1990s. For example, a 1998 news report indicated that the only Ohio women incarcerated for murdering or attempting to murder their newborns were convicted after 1993. This coincides with increasingly punitive responses to women who used illicit drugs during their pregnancies (a subject taken up in chapter 5). In some states, women convicted of killing their infant may even face the death penalty. Texas is known for imposing especially harsh sentences.[63] Texas's statute makes killing a child under the age of 6 a capital offense. Four of the nine women on Texas's death row in October 2006 were convicted of crimes involving children.[64]

In general, the two strongest determinants of the sentence for most criminal offenses are one's prior record and the seriousness of the offense. Most of the women and girls who commit neonaticide have no prior involvement with the criminal justice system.[65] In terms of the gravity of the offense, the vast majority of cases of neonaticide involve suffocation or drowning. Rarely do they involve overtly violent acts such as stabbing or cutting. Factors other than prior record and offense seriousness seem to influence the outcomes for neonaticide cases.[66]

Sympathetic juries may be reluctant to convict or impose harsh sentences on some offenders. Other women may benefit from the difficulty the prosecutor faces in trying to establish that the infant had been born alive. Most of the disparity in charges, prosecutions, and sentencing, though, seems to stem from society's mixed feelings about the crime. On some level, society appears to recognize that neonaticide is distinct from killing an adult, as manifested by the unwillingness to convict or sentence harshly many women who kill their newborns. Our legal system, however, has yet to develop a separate category of offenses that reflects this distinction.[67]

The lack of consensus with regard to how best to respond to this relatively rare and unique problem is borne out by the findings of a trio of Georgetown psychology professors. Norman Finkel, John Burke, and Leticia Chavez undertook a study designed to examine community sentiment with regard to infanticide (including neonaticide and filicide).[68] Their study looked at the impact of whether or not the case involved the killing of a newborn or an older infant, the severity and psychiatric support of the claims of depression, the age of the defendant, and the violence of the death on the verdict and outcome of the case. The researchers asked 75 college students to consider hypothetical infanticide cases, which differed on certain characteristics. The authors did not find any consistent pattern of results. They concluded that "a complex picture emerges in the verdict, sentencing, and dispositional patterns—a picture that does not look like either murder, manslaughter, or madness" but could be better described as "miscellaneous."[69] For instance, some subjects construed the abandonment death scenario as evidence of a lack of intent to kill, while others viewed it in a harsher light, pointing out that the woman had time to think about her actions during the walk to the site of the abandonment.[70] As one commentator observed, "The ambivalence results not only from society's desire to hold people accountable, but also from the conflict between traditional notions of motherhood and the tragedy of filicide."[71]

Because of the lack of public and legal consensus, the perspective of an individual judge can carry an inordinate amount of weight. "Some judges may tend to focus more on the outcome, this death of this defenseless human being," notes Scott Horne, the president of the Wisconsin District

Attorney's Association. "Others might focus more on the circumstances that the young parent is facing."[72] For example, a circuit judge sentenced one woman to life in prison after her newborn son's body was found at a garbage transfer station, saying, "Moms don't do these kinds of things. By your actions and inactions, you've destroyed a precious life."[73] In another case, a judge sentenced a 30-year-old mother to 30 years in prison, saying that her newborn son was "not an object that you toss, that you throw in the garbage because of some stressful reasons."[74]

One thing is clear: those who argue that a "certain and severe" response by the criminal justice system is needed to deter women from committing neonaticide are standing on shaky ground. If a woman knows she will be apprehended and punished severely, the argument goes, then she will be less likely to kill or abandon her newborn. Deterrence-based arguments assume a person is thinking clearly and rationally, is aware of the consequences of her actions, and is expecting her crime to be detected and punished. As we have learned, a woman who has given birth in secret often panics. She is more worried about avoiding detection than the consequences of her actions on the survival of the infant, much less possible legal consequences. She may not even consider that there *are* legal consequences. Moreover, deterrence assumes that most women's actions will be detected and brought to the attention of law enforcement; untold numbers of cases of abandonment and neonaticide never are and most likely never will be. For these reasons, the criminal justice system is not well suited to address the problem of neonaticide and abandonment.

"Safe Haven" Legislation

Recognizing the pitfalls of relying on detection and punishment to address the problem, and in an effort to reduce the number of newborns who are killed or die after being abandoned, nearly all states have enacted "safe haven," or infant abandonment, legislation that provides some immunity from prosecution to women who abandon their infant to a health care provider, emergency services personnel, or other authorized acceptors such as a fire station, police department, or place of worship. The first infant abandonment law was enacted in Texas in 1999 following a string of abandonment cases that made the news. This interest was fueled by high-profile cases such as teenager Amy Grossberg who in 1996 gave birth in a Delaware hotel room assisted by her boyfriend, Brian Petersen, and then discarded the infant in a dumpster; and Melissa Drexler, the New Jersey "prom mom" who in 1997 gave birth in a bathroom during her prom and left the infant in a trash can before returning to the dance.[75]

States rushed to enact their own laws, often spurred on by a local abandonment case. Today, all but two states (Alaska and Nebraska) have decriminalized infant abandonment to some degree.[76] Some states provide complete immunity from prosecution, while others permit the woman to raise an affirmative defense to prosecution, that is, one which, if found to be credible, would limit or excuse her criminal liability even if it is proven she abandoned her infant. Some laws also stipulate that no protection against prosecution is provided if the abandoned infant was found to have been abused. In 30 states, the anonymity of the person relinquishing an infant is preserved; 11 states require personnel to ask about the infant's medical history. The benefits of the safe haven program include the opportunity it affords for a woman to abandon her newborn without endangering the infant's life or risking prosecution. Potentially, it also provides women with an opportunity to receive medical treatment after the baby is delivered without fear of being reported to the police.

Despite popular support for these measures, criticism has arisen from a variety of quarters.[77] Conservative critics fear that safe haven programs promote teenage pregnancy by sending a message that it is okay to get pregnant and have a baby because someone else will assume responsibility for the child. Others argue that such laws could open the door to legalized abandonment on any grounds, such as an infant's gender or disability. Adoption advocates raise concern that anonymity prevents medical or genealogical information being made available to the child should she or he be adopted down the road.[78]

Perhaps the most basic question is whether safe haven programs even work. Caught up in the zeal to enact legislation, advocates and politicians simply issued empty and predictable proclamations, like, "Even if it was just one baby that was saved because of it, who could say that it was not worthwhile?" rather than evaluated the effectiveness of the legislation.[79] To date, there is scant evidence of any significant positive impact of infant abandonment legislation. Infants continue to be killed and abandoned despite the widespread passage of infant abandonment laws. Why is this?

In order for women and girls to take advantage of safe havens, they have to know they exist. Many of these laws were passed without providing funds to advertise the laws' existence to those who are at greatest risk of abandoning or killing their children. Furthermore, one cannot assume that women who *are* aware of the existence of a law are aware of the specifics. For that matter, it is unclear how strictly the infant abandonment laws will be construed. For instance, the laws vary on the age up to which an infant may be relinquished (72 hours to one year). Age limits are hard to enforce, given the difficulty of, say, distinguishing a 30-day-old infant from one who is 35 days old. Even law enforcement officials seem to acknowledge the arbitrariness of age limits in light of the overarching goals of the program. Consider the Massachusetts woman who left her three-month-old baby at a police station. Technically, the Massachusetts infant abandonment law did not protect the mother since it only provided for the abandonment of newborns up to seven days old.[80] Despite the age discrepancy, neither the police nor the Department of Social Services recommended prosecution.

There is also the question of how strictly the definition of "safe haven" is, or should be, enforced. Must a woman hand the baby to a hospital employee, or can she leave the baby in a hospital lobby or outside the entrance? In Columbus, Ohio, a security camera recorded a 16-year-old walking around the parking lot of a social service agency with a baby.[81] Eight hours later, the baby was found next to a trash can behind the agency. Ohio's law allows a parent to leave a newborn at a police station, fire station, or hospital without being criminally charged, but not a social services agency. A police spokesperson quoted in a news account describing the case said the police had not yet decided whether to file charges.

But perhaps the biggest reason that abandonments and neonaticide continue is that safe haven programs do nothing to either prevent unwanted pregnancies or to address why young women abandon their infants in the first place. Even if women are aware of the programs, they still may be reluctant to contact hospital, law enforcement, or other officials, either because of their prior negative experiences or because they fear that family, friends, and others will somehow find out about their pregnancies. The women who are most isolated and fearful are probably among those who are least likely to approach a hospital or law enforcement official or agency or other stranger to seek help. And infant abandonment legislation doesn't address the need to ensure that women receive prenatal care.

At the end of the day, safe havens may even spur a backlash. The overall result could be a more punitive response to women who do not deposit their newborns at a designated safe haven rather than a more compassionate and supportive reaction to those who do.[82]

Legal Defenses

Another reactive approach to the problem recognizes postpartum depression as a legal defense, something akin to the temporary insanity defense. Unlike the United States, more than two dozen countries recognize postpartum depression as a legal defense, including Britain, Canada, Australia, and Italy.[83] Postpartum depression was popularized in the United States by actress and celebrity Brooke Shields's 2006 account, *Down Came the Rain*, in which she detailed her own experience after the birth of her daughter. Medical research has shown that plummeting hormone levels (the "hypothalamic-pituitary-ovarian axis cascade") and altered neurotransmitter function in the central nervous system can cause mental status changes in the weeks and months after delivery.[84] The symptoms vary but can include feelings of worthlessness or excessive guilt, as well as recurrent thoughts of death and suicide.

Although infanticide laws vary among countries, generally speaking, they offer a woman legal protection by taking into account her mental condition within a year after giving birth (and in some cases, within a year after she has quit breastfeeding). The laws treat infanticide as an offense category distinct from homicide, provided the woman can prove that her mind is disturbed by the consequences of giving birth or lactating.[85] Advocates of these laws herald them as being more humane since infanticidal women are rarely incarcerated for their crimes. But the statutes are not without their problems.

For one, existing infanticide laws are based on a foundation that psychopathologizes motherhood and women's biology by associating the processes of giving birth and breastfeeding with mental illness. In addition, the law and the science do not appear to match up where neonaticide or abandonment are concerned. That is, the assumptions on which these laws are based about the connection between depression, child bearing, lactation, and diminished mental capacity (and thus, diminished culpability) are not supported by medical, clinical, and epidemiological facts.[86] As noted earlier, the vast majority of women who kill or abandon their newborns do not suffer from postpartum psychosis or postpartum depression that could account for their actions. It is not clear from existing evidence that new mothers experience more or different depression than women who don't bear children, or that this depression automatically justifies a finding of diminished capacity or of insanity.[87] In relation to neonaticide and abandonment, infanticide laws do not acknowledge directly the existence of pregnancy denial that took place early in the pregnancy before the presumed dramatic hormonal changes.

Yet, the practical result of infanticide laws, flawed as they may be, is that women are rarely incarcerated for their crimes. Instead, they often are put on probation and ordered to receive counseling that may help them address the circumstances that led to their actions. This itself seems more reasonable and humane than sentencing a woman to a prison term.

While addressing the root causes of unintended pregnancy will help reduce the incidence of neonaticide and abandonment, the problem also requires responses that reflect its unique character. We might consider recognizing a "neonaticide syndrome" that could be used as a legal defense, similar to the way in which battered woman's syndrome is recognized within the sphere of self-defense.[88] Instead of viewing women who kill their newborns as cold-hearted killers, a neonaticide syndrome defense would acknowledge that many are terrified, immature, or isolated women and girls whose denial of their pregnancy has contributed to a psychotic break at the time of giving birth. Such an approach would offer the benefit of shifting some of the responsibility for neonaticide and abandonment onto a society that continues to stigmatize female sexuality and offers no reliable safety net for women and girls facing an unwanted pregnancy. While recognizing neonaticide syndrome is far from a perfect solution, it would go a long way toward promoting a more understanding climate around unwanted or extramarital pregnancy, which, in turn, may prevent some cases of abandonment or neonaticide. At present, confusion remains regarding whether expert testimony on neonaticidal syndrome is admissible. In the absence of expert testimony that can help explain behavior patterns in neonaticide cases, consistent standards for determining guilt and punishment have yet to emerge.[89]

Conclusion

Many young women both know about contraception and are able to use it to avoid an unintended pregnancy.[90] But there remain those women and girls who remain ignorant of contraception, or, as in many cases of child sexual abuse or statutory rape, are far from empowered to prevent or terminate a pregnancy. They may have parents or men in their lives who have threatened to kill, evict, or disown them for having sex outside of marriage or getting pregnant. They may belong to religious communities where the leaders emphasize the immorality of extramarital sex. Shame, social isolation, and restricted access to information all contribute to the likelihood that some women and girls will, upon giving birth, be desperate to rid themselves of a newborn. In light of the fear and denial that mark some unintended pregnancies, killing or abandoning a newborn is a tragic, but not incomprehensible, reaction.

A climate of moral conservatism contributes to the problem. It increases the likelihood that if a young woman does become pregnant, she may be more likely to respond with denial and subterfuge than to seek help. Messages focused solely on condemning sex outside of marriage make some women so fearful of rejection and discovery that they resolve not to disclose a pregnancy to anyone, including people who might be in a position to help them.[91] It is easy to understand why some young women would deny that they are pregnant, not only out of the fear of the distant and abstract consequences of having a baby but also to avoid the immediate reality of being condemned as a whore and a sinner.

On a societal level, our responses to neonaticide and abandonment reflect mixed feelings about adolescent sexuality. On the one hand, the very existence of safe haven legislation suggests a degree of acceptance of the reality of unwanted and teenage pregnancy. Safe haven legislation reflects some level of concern for young, desperate mothers or at least a desire to save their babies. Similarly, a lack of consistent prosecution policies indicates that we do recognize the extreme isolation and fear that accompany many unwanted pregnancies. It is also possible that youth, vulnerability, and powerlessness are consistent with conventional notions of femininity and thus spare at least some women and girls the harshest official responses.

On the other hand, the failure to seriously advertise safe havens points to lingering reservations about any response short of outright condemnation of extramarital and adolescent pregnancy. Opposition to comprehensive sex education and ensuring access to contraceptive and other health services suggests that providing support to young and unmarried pregnant women is less important to some members of the public than upholding the hegemonic ideals of motherhood and womanly behavior—namely, that women should not have sex or get pregnant without the benefit of heterosexual marriage and, if they do, they should give birth and raise their child. For some members of the public, abandonment and neonaticide seem to animate fears about the erosion of the ideal of marriage being the sole site of procreation and motherhood. Our willingness to sentence women to lengthy prison terms indicates that neonaticidal women and girls are regarded by some as having committed a peculiarly horrific transgression against gender norms.

Neonaticide and abandonment pose the twin challenges of preventing these actions from occurring in the first place, and, failing that, addressing the physical and emotional needs of the women who experience an unwanted pregnancy. The criminal justice system seems especially ill equipped to deal with either concern. Relying on prosecution and punishment seems to be a script for what not to do. Killing and abandoning a newborn are not actions taken only by deranged women. Rather, they are symptoms, albeit rare and extreme ones, of a society that is neither comfortable talking about sexuality nor willing to guarantee support to women who face an unwanted pregnancy. While neonaticide and abandonment may not be excusable, they are also far from unthinkable in a society that is still not committed to frank discussions of adolescent sexuality and in which good-quality birth control, comprehensive sex education, and abortion services are not readily available to women of all ages.[92]

PART III

Bearing

5

"Innocent Preborn Victims"

Fetal Protectionism and Pregnant Women

In as many areas as we can, we want to put on the books that the embryo is a person. That sets the stage for a jurist to acknowledge that human beings at any stage of development deserve protection—even protection that would trump a woman's interest in terminating a pregnancy.

> —Samuel B. Casey, executive director, Christian Legal Society, quoted in *L.A. Times,* January 19, 2003

The problem isn't that we do not value unborn children. The problem is that we do not value the lives of the women who give them that life.

> —Lynn Paltrow, executive director and founder, National Advocates for Pregnant Women, 2007

In 2004, Oklahoma woman Theresa Lee Hernandez delivered a stillborn son at 32 weeks gestation who tested positive for methamphetamine. The Oklahoma prosecutor charged Theresa with first-degree murder, and she was incarcerated for three years before being convicted of second-degree murder in October 2007 and sentenced to 15 years incarceration.[1] In 2006, in the neighboring state of Kansas, Chelsea Brooks was 14 years old and nine months pregnant with a baby girl, Alexa, when she was murdered.[2] Police believe her abusive 20-year-old former boyfriend hired someone to kill her. Her family's outrage that the state could not file homicide charges in the death of the fetus reactivated interest in a state fetal homicide bill, House Bill 2300 (or "Alexa's Law"), which would treat the fetus as a second victim.

These two cases share more than a tragic, unexpected, and advanced pregnancy loss. Both the prosecutions of pregnant women who use illicit drugs and fetal homicide laws reflect attempts to legally recognize "fetal rights" or "fetal personhood." In recent years, we have witnessed an increase in laws that allow prosecutors to treat some crimes against pregnant women as having two victims, and the reanimation of long-standing and deeply rooted prejudice against women who use illegal drugs, targeting particularly those who are pregnant and continue to term. These trends reflect growing and highly contested claims that not only does a fetus have "rights" that must be protected but these rights are superior to those of pregnant women, indeed of all human beings.

As Brigham Young University law professor Marguerite Driessen explains, "There are many who feel that an unborn child is a living human being, regardless of the interests of its mother, who should be protected to the full extent of the law even against its parents if necessary." She continues this line of thought by pointing out, "If this is the case, there is no impediment to civil lawsuits or criminal prosecutions against mothers for actions during pregnancy that result in harm to their unborn children."[3] Pregnant women could be imprisoned for reckless endangerment if they did such things as drive too fast or ate unpasteurized cheese.

There are also those who feel, however, that while the law can and should recognize that others may have an interest in the unborn child, this is as far as the law should be permitted to go:

> Any attempt to go further, for instance by recognizing any rights of unborn children independent of their mothers, would be a step into the proverbial ether—wholly without legal support. If this is the case, civil or criminal enforcement actions against third parties are appropriate and welcome, but actions against the mothers on behalf of their unborn children are impossible given the fundamental inseparability of the pregnant woman and her unborn child.[4]

As I try to show here, claims of fetal rights and fetal protection have troubling implications for women's overall right to bodily sovereignty. Furthermore, the pursuit of such claims undermines any serious effort to address the problems of violence against women and women's drug dependency, and it actually endangers women's health.[5]

Violence against Pregnant Women

Violence against pregnant women warrants our strong concern, as does violence against any woman (see chapter 8). According to the Centers for Disease Control and Prevention (CDC), physical violence during pregnancy is associated with almost every reproductive health problem.[6] A pregnant woman who is beaten is less likely to gain the recommended maternity weight and is more likely to become anemic. She is more likely to smoke, drink alcohol, and use drugs. Being beaten may cause a pregnant woman's uterus to rupture or contribute to hemorrhage. Physical abuse can also harm the fetus and may lead to fetal death, distress, or bone fracture; an early onset of labor; or delivery of a pre-term, low birthweight infant.[7] Although domestic violence can adversely affect the health of a woman's pregnancy, much of this violence goes undetected by health care providers. Most women of reproductive age in the United States receive at least one reproductive health care service annually. Yet most health care providers do not routinely screen women for relationship violence.[8]

No reliable national estimate exists of the prevalence of violence against pregnant women by a male partner.[9] A multiyear 16-state study of the prevalence of physical abuse before and during pregnancy estimated that nearly 9 percent of women experienced abuse in the year before or during the pregnancy.[10] It is not possible to state definitively, though, that pregnant women are subject to higher rates of violence than other women because both violence and pregnancy are more common in younger women.[11] In general, both before and during pregnancy, abuse seems to be more prevalent among women who are young, unmarried, poor, uneducated, and nonwhite, and women who had not intended to become pregnant.[12]

In some cases, violence culminates in murder that stems from a man's desire to control the outcome of the pregnancy. Tjane Marshall, convicted of first-degree murder for killing his pregnant girlfriend, explained: "I got two kids. I didn't want the first one. I didn't want the second one."[13] Twenty-one-year-old Dan Leach II strangled his pregnant girlfriend and tried to make it look like a suicide after she told him she was pregnant with his child.[14] A 26-year-old college student was sentenced to 25 years to life for killing his pregnant girlfriend after she refused to get an abortion.[15] Other men are enraged because a woman wants to end the relationship or is considering an abortion. Robert Lopez, 35, killed his teenaged pregnant girlfriend, reportedly telling his mother, "I just flipped. She kept saying she was going to take the baby away from me."[16] Nineteen-year-old Anthony

O'Leary stabbed and strangled his pregnant ex-fiancee, Treasure Genaw, to death. Testimony revealed that O'Leary was upset that she was considering an abortion and ending their relationship.[17]

Again, however, data are not routinely collected, which makes it difficult to establish a reliable estimate of the incidence or the circumstances surrounding these murders.[18] The *Washington Post* spent a year compiling information on the traumatic deaths of pregnant women and new mothers in the United States, ultimately identifying 1,367 killings that took place nationally between 1990 and 2004.[19] The Centers for Disease Control and Prevention (CDC) documented 617 homicides of pregnant and postpartum women from 1991 to 1999, using data from more than 30 states.[20]

The data do suggest that homicide is a major cause of death for pregnant women and new mothers. The CDC study found that around one-third of maternal injury deaths were the result of homicide.[21] A Maryland study found that homicide was the fifth leading cause of death for women of childbearing years who had not been recently pregnant, and the leading cause among women who were or recently had been pregnant.[22] In Maryland, homicide was responsible for more than 20 percent of the maternal deaths over a six-year period, followed closely by cardiovascular disorders. Even after controlling for age and race, pregnant and new mothers were almost twice as likely as other women likely to die of homicide.[23] Pregnant women and new mothers who are younger (i.e., less than 20 years of age) are at much greater risk of homicide than those who are older, as are unmarried women and those who receive no prenatal care.[24] Race also seems to play a role: black women's maternal homicide risk was about seven times that of white women overall, and about 11 times higher for women between the ages of 25 and 29.[25]

Although black women face a greater likelihood of being murdered while pregnant, it was the murder of a pregnant white woman that was used to generate support for the passage of the federal Unborn Victims of Violence Act (UVVA) of 2004. Many states also have passed fetal homicide bills under the guise of being concerned about domestic violence. Evidence strongly indicates, however, that these laws are more about codifying into law the status of a fetus as a human being (thus justifying the need for greater policing of pregnant women) than about protecting women from violence.

The Unborn Victims of Violence Act of 2004 and Fetal Homicide Laws

On Christmas Eve of 2002, Laci Peterson disappeared from her home in Modesto, California.[26] She was almost eight months pregnant with a son that she and her husband had planned to name Conner. A jury later concluded that her husband, Scott Peterson, had killed her. California's definition of murder includes the unlawful killing of a fetus with malice aforethought, provided that the fetus has passed the embryonic stage (roughly between six and eight weeks). Scott Peterson was convicted of first-degree murder for killing Laci and second-degree murder for killing the fetus. He was sentenced to death.[27]

In 2004, President George W. Bush enacted "Laci and Conner's Law," as the federal Unborn Victims of Violence Act of 2004 (UVVA) eventually became known. Under the terms of the UVVA, if someone harms a pregnant woman and causes the death of her fetus while violating any one of 68 existing federal criminal laws, he or she can be charged for causing the mother's harm or death and face a second charge for killing the "unborn victim." Very few violent crimes are prosecuted in federal courts. The UVVA applies only to violent crimes committed in places like a military base, a post office, or a Native American reservation; its potential to have a broad impact on domestic violence, then, is similarly restricted.

In addition to the federal UVVA, at least 36 states permit homicide charges to be filed in the deaths of fetuses.[28] Fetal homicide laws were designed to be applied in cases where a pregnant woman is injured if her pregnancy is ended or harmed by an assault, a drunk driving accident, or other criminal act. Some laws require that the accused person act with "malicious foresight," while others allow charges of involuntary manslaughter when there is no intent to kill.[29]

State laws also differ in whether or not they, like the UVVA, extend the legal definition "person" and "human being" to mean a fetus. The UVVA and most state fetal homicide laws treat the fetus as an independent second victim that has legal rights distinct from the pregnant woman harmed by the criminal act: that is, when a pregnant woman is murdered or injured, two victims are claimed—the woman and her fetus—not one.[30] (Here I refer to this category of laws as "fetus-centered homicide laws.") Some of these laws consider the fetus a separate victim or a person only after certain stages of development or after a particular gestational age. Laws in at least 15 states apply to a fetus at any stage of development, starting at conception.[31] To date, fetal homicide laws have withstood challenges on the basis of their constitutionality.[32]

Opposing the legal recognition of a fetus as a second person may seem callous, especially when one considers the death of a wanted unborn baby due to violence late in the pregnancy. But while we can understand why people want prosecution to reflect the unique harm of an assault on a pregnant woman, this can be accomplished without recognizing the fetus as an entity separate from the mother who bears it.[33] In over a dozen states, lawmakers have adopted the enhanced penalty approach, applying stiffer penalties for murdering a pregnant women, instead of recognizing the death of the fetus as a separate crime.[34]

In other states, however, the need for political compromise prevented full consideration of this approach. In Alaska, for example, an early draft of a fetal homicide bill lacked a provision stipulating that the law should not be construed to permit the prosecution of a woman with respect to her fetus. Without this provision, for instance, a pregnant woman could be prosecuted for not leaving her abusive husband. After a battle to get the provision into the bill, a compromise was eventually reached. The provision was included, but it came at the expense of serious consideration of enhanced penalties, rather than recognizing a second victim.[35]

Fetus-Centered Laws as a Response to Domestic Violence

Lawmakers and politicians drafted and passed the Unborn Victims of Violence Act and fetus-centered homicide laws under the auspices of taking violence against women (and to a lesser extent, drunk driving) more seriously. But, there are reasons to question this claim. First, congressional and legislative testimony suggests that the attention lawmakers and advocates have heaped on murdered fetuses has not been accompanied by in-depth consideration of the causes, characteristics, and consequences of domestic violence against women more generally or by affirmative steps to deal with the problem. For instance, the Republican majority failed on multiple occasions to fully fund the Violence Against Women Act. As Rep. Jerrold Nadler (NY) pointed out in a hearing on the UVVA before the House of Representatives, "It appears that many of the Members who have signed on to this bill are the same ones who voted to divert funds from protecting women from violence to protecting stock dividends from taxation."[36]

Second, it is unclear how fetus-centered homicide laws can be expected to deter violence against pregnant women. What deters people from crime is not well understood. Even serious sanctions such as life imprisonment and capital punishment have not been found to be effective in deterring people from violent crime.[37] And in the present case, fetus-centered homicide laws offer no additional deterrent effect. One cannot hurt a fetus without in some way hurting a pregnant woman, and it is already against the law to hurt or kill a woman.

Rather, I would argue that one effect of these laws is to push the pregnant woman herself into the background. By separating the damage done to a woman's unborn child, these laws detract from the harm inflicted against the woman herself. For instance, when Kansas HB 2300 (mentioned at the beginning of this chapter) languished in the state senate judiciary committee, a state senator commented, "Now the bill is dead—and so is Chelsea's baby."[38] One feels the need to remind the senator that Chelsea is dead as well. Fetus-centered homicide laws contribute to the perception that the harm is defined by the harm to the fetus rather than to the woman. In doing so, they contribute to the devaluation of women that makes violence against women a problem in the first place. Fetal homicide laws imply that violence against a pregnant woman is, by definition, "worse" than violence against a woman who is not pregnant. Claims of fetal rights relegate "the women who are being hit, demeaned, and violated to the status of baby carriers" rather than human beings.[39]

If fetus-centered homicide laws which treat the fetus as a second victim do not ameliorate the problem of domestic violence (and may contribute to it), and if it is possible for legislators to acknowledge the distinct nature of an assault or murder of a pregnant woman without making killing a fetus a second, separate offense, why have such laws been passed with such zeal in the first place?

Anti-abortion activists deny that fetal protectionist homicide laws were created to erode abortion rights or to re-criminalize abortion.[40] But these denials should not be accepted at face value. The National Right to Life Committee maintains a website on unborn victims of violence that tracks changes in fetal homicide laws but dedicates no space on it to violence against women.[41] In the three-page UVVA, the terms "child," "unborn child," or "unborn children" are used no less than 28 times, consistent with the conservative, anti-abortion rights orientation of many of its drafters.

Elsewhere, champions of fetus-centered laws have co-opted the language of the women's movement to garner support for their position and arguably mask their intent. The executive director of the Christian Legal Society, Samuel B. Casey, was quoted in the *Washington Times* defending the UVVA claiming that "if there ever was a bill to protect a woman's right to choose, it is this bill that seeks to deter violence against or at least provide justice to the pregnant woman who is choosing life for her unborn child only to see her choice deprived by a crime of violence against her and/or her child."[42] As the reader may recall from the opening of this chapter, this is the same man who two years earlier had told the *Los Angeles Times* he intended to put as many laws as possible on the books recognizing that the embryo is a person in an effort to trump a woman's right to terminate her pregnancy.[43]

The Unborn Victims of Violence Act explicitly states that nothing in the act "shall be construed to permit the prosecution . . . of any woman with respect to her unborn child." But state statutes have used nearly identical language (often, as noted, only after hard-fought battles to get the language included in the first place) and then have gone on to prosecute pregnant women for their drug use in what has been called a "legislative bait and switch."[44] Fetal protection laws not only represent a backdoor to abolishing abortion but also they leave open the possibility that the laws used to prosecute those who assault pregnant women may be directed against pregnant women themselves. In Missouri, for example, the state argued that the exception articulated in their fetus-centered homicide statute applied only to a woman who indirectly harmed her unborn child, not to a woman whose drug use was claimed to have directly endangered the child.[45]

Claims of the need for fetal protection have been and will continue to be used to control and punish pregnant women, not protect them. Fetus-centered homicide laws are, at root, *fetal* protection laws. They simply are not designed to protect and support the woman who carries the fetus. I return to Marguerite Driessen for help in explaining the nature of what is at stake. She writes:

> That the mother and her unborn child are inseparably connected, that what affects the former affects the latter, and that access to the latter is accomplished only through the former, is obvious. These facts have led some to conclude that this creates an utter dependency of the unborn child upon its mother such that the mother has a duty to do all in her power to nourish and protect it. These same facts have led others to conclude that the unborn child is not a severable entity at all, but rather is a part of the mother, and thus she can have no externally imposed obligations to the unborn child.[46]

Arrests and prosecutions of women for continuing their pregnancy to term despite their use of illicit drugs, court orders, and civil commitments are examples of state-sanctioned efforts to externally impose such obligations. These efforts are rooted in our beliefs about who is fit to reproduce and what a "good mother" looks like (see chapters 7 and 8). These measures, purportedly undertaken in the interest of fetal and child health, result in "the normalization or standardization of motherhood. Only those who meet the state-enforced standard are permitted to reproduce without state interference."[47] These cases also serve a larger political purpose by distracting attention from significant social problems such as our lack of universal health care, the dearth of policies to support pregnant and parenting women, an absence of social supports for children, and the overall failure of the drug war. Instead, we focus our attention on "bad" pregnant women who are poor and who use drugs. We expect them to provide their fetuses with the health care and safety that they themselves have not been guaranteed.

The state cannot act this way without at least tacit public support. In general, the public seems increasingly, if grudgingly, willing to consider illicit drug use a public health or medical problem. Public animosity toward poor women who use illicit drugs and become pregnant and give birth, however, persists. The hostility has been fueled by the antiabortion movement's claims of fetal rights, combined with false and exaggerated claims about the effects of prenatal exposure to cocaine on pregnancy outcomes, fetal and infant health, and early childhood development.

The Panic over Maternal Drug Use

Fewer than 1 in 10 women, and around 4 in 100 pregnant women use illicit drugs; even fewer are dependent on them.[48] Pregnant women also smoke cigarettes and drink alcohol at much lower rates than other women.[49] Thus, the hysterical tone that often marks discussions of maternal drug use cannot be justified by pregnant women's rate of illicit drug use, drinking, and smoking.

In the 1980s and 1990s, a national panic ensued over "crack mothers" giving birth to "crack babies."[50] At a time when there was already evidence that there was no such thing as "crack babies" and that increasing poverty explained many of the health problems children were experiencing, *Time,* the *New York Times,* and other leading news outlets continued to report cocaine use during pregnancy as an epidemic destroying a generation of children. Women who used illicit drugs (especially cocaine) were portrayed as hypersexual, out-of-control women who would "do anything" for drugs and who were completely indifferent to any harm they might cause to themselves or others.[51]

The moral panic over women's use of cocaine abated in the mid-1990s, but the uncritical acceptance of misinformation about drugs and the stereotyping of the people who use them is being revisited today in the methamphetamine scare.[52] In the first years of the millenium, concern about methamphetamine jumped to the fore much like concern about crack cocaine did in the 1980s. Popular media accounts have decried an "epidemic" and a "scourge" of drug use, despite evidence that rates of methamphetamine use have stabilized since 1999 and have been declining since 2002.[53] Many reports play on exaggerated fears about the impact and addictiveness of methamphetamine, as well as the lack of an effective way to treat meth addiction.[54]

Media coverage of illicit drug use and drug dependency has improved somewhat since the 1980s and 1990s inasmuch as less of it is blatantly sensational and more of it makes some attempt to be factually correct. Researchers themselves have tried to insist that drug coverage be based on science, not emotions, asking that experts (rather than the local pediatrician or the local sheriff) be given the opportunity to address what, if any, risks have been linked to prenatal exposure to cocaine, methamphetamine, and other drugs. The public, however, is still fed a regular diet of accounts that distort and misrepresent the effects of illicit drug use, rely on nonexperts, and demonize the people who use illicit drugs.[55] This public, of course, includes not only lawmakers but also judges, police officers, and prosecutors, child protection workers, and health care providers. The latter, in particular, should play important roles in securing treatment and care for women who are addicted to drugs. Frequently, however, a hospital worker's report of a pregnant woman's drug use leads—directly or indirectly—to the involvement of the police and the criminal justice system.[56]

The front page story of the July 11, 2005, *New York Times,* "A Drug Scourge Creates Its Own Form of Orphan," typifies the problematic ways in which women who use illicit drugs are presented to the public, as well as the biases found among workers in the helping professions.[57] As with earlier media coverage of the crack epidemic, the story discussed the drug's "highly sexualized" users and depicted the "children of methamphetamine" as lost causes "with so many behavioral problems." The article mentioned not once, but twice, that some of the children had lice. The article's sources were harried social workers, a lawyer for a department of human services, a pediatrician involved in a state program that was run in conjunction with the Department of Justice, and other professionals with a stake in convincing the public of the gravity of the meth "scourge." Not one parent was quoted, or, for that matter, anyone qualified to express an opinion about the effects of prenatal exposure or who could speak directly to meth use trends, as distinct from trends in child welfare system intervention. Sources provided opinions that fell outside their areas of expertise, such as a pediatrician's opinion that "the parents are basically worthless." A state attorney general told an audience of hundreds: "People always ask, what can they do about meth? The most important thing you can do is become a foster parent, because we're just seeing so many kids being taken from these homes." The article never questioned whether removing so many children from their parents and their homes was justified.

The use of methamphetamine, cocaine, and other illicit drugs certainly present a valid public health concern. But medical and scientific evidence suggests that the harms associated with illicit drug use have been greatly overstated. By contrast, not only are alcohol and tobacco more widely used but also tobacco use and heavy alcohol use have known harmful consequences on fetal and child development.[58] Yet, our harshest responses have been reserved for those women who consume cocaine, heroin, and methamphetamine. Our responses to maternal drug use are simply not commensurate with the risks posed to the infant or child.

Pregnancy Loss

Estimates from the National Survey of Family Growth suggest there are about 1 million fetal losses each year in the United States, most of which occur before 20 weeks of gestation. When a pregnant woman uses illicit drugs and her pregnancy results in a miscarriage or a stillbirth, people often automatically and incorrectly conclude that her drug use was the cause. But there are many risk factors for fetal death. Even so, in many (and perhaps a majority) of cases of stillbirth and miscarriage, a cause cannot be determined. Though consuming some substances may increase the possibility of a pregnancy loss, the relationship is neither a causal one nor is it well understood. Our understanding is hindered by the challenge of conducting methodologically sound studies that take into account a wide range of risk factors and the relationships that may exist among them.

In the United States, a miscarriage commonly refers to the spontaneous abortion or loss of a pregnancy before the 20th week of pregnancy. When a fetal death occurs after 20 weeks gestation, it is often referred to as a stillbirth. Pregnancy loss after 20 weeks is extremely rare. The risk of miscarriage and stillbirth is higher for women who are over 35 years old.[59] The risk of stillbirth is also higher for black women and poor women, women who had previously delivered by cesarean section, and women who have conditions such as diabetes and high blood pressure.[60]

Miscarriages are common occurrences. Perhaps as many as one-half of all fertilized eggs are aborted spontaneously, before a woman even realizes she is pregnant.[61] About 15 percent of women who know they are pregnant will miscarry, usually between the 7th and 12th weeks of pregnancy.[62] Most miscarriages occur when the baby has deadly genetic problems, which are usually unrelated to the parents. In at least half of miscarriages that take place during the first trimester, there are chromosomal abnormalities. A smaller number of miscarriages are associated with maternal diseases and conditions, such as hyperthyroidism, poorly controlled diabetes, obesity, infections such as herpes simplex virus and chlamydia, and uterine defects and anomalies.

Environmental exposure may affect the likelihood of miscarriage, though difficulties in controlling for confounding factors and the absence of information on exposure or the dose of the toxin make it difficult to establish the nature of the relationship. The consumption of nicotine, alcohol, cocaine, caffeine, and other substances does seem to pose a dose-dependent heightened risk of miscarriage. That is, the more of a particular substance one consumes, the higher the risk of miscarriage.[63]

Stillbirths are far rarer than miscarriages but about 10 times more common than deaths due to Sudden Infant Death Syndrome (SIDS). According to the National Center on Birth Defects and Developmental Disabilities and the Centers for Disease Control and Prevention (CDC), each year in the United States, around 24,000–26,000 babies are stillborn.[64]

As with miscarriage, it is important to distinguish between risk factors and causes of stillbirth. Risk factors include characteristics like prior stillbirths, low socioeconomic status, race, maternal obesity, low education, advanced maternal age, diabetes mellitus, smoking, and an "overdue" pregnancy.[65] While these are associated with stillbirth, there is no known causal pathway that leads to the death. For instance, being poor or black is associated with increasing risk of stillbirth and adverse pregnancy outcomes, even after controlling for other factors. Researchers hypothesize that this may be due to subtle, yet-to-be-identified differences or inadequate medical care.[66]

Known causes of stillbirth include congenital anomalies, infection and asphyxia related to pre-eclampsia, placental abruption, umbilical cord accidents, Rh disease, and maternal and fetal trauma.[67] About one in four stillbirths are due to fetal disorders.[68] Another 25–30 percent are attributed to abnormalities of the placenta, umbilical cord, or fetal membranes.[69] Around 1 in 10 stillbirths is related to maternal diseases or conditions such as high blood pressure and diabetes.[70]

The important thing to note is that in a sizable proportion of miscarriages and stillbirths, *no* cause for the fetal death can be established. In about one-half of the cases of miscarriage in clinically recognized pregnancies, and possibly more, and in somewhere between 40 percent and two-thirds of all cases of stillbirth, no physical cause can be determined.[71] Concluding that an adverse pregnancy outcome has been caused by a woman's use of an illicit drug is simply not possible in light of existing medical evidence.

Early Childhood Outcomes

In the charged climate surrounding cocaine use, researchers who did *not* find adverse prenatal cocaine exposure effects had difficulty getting their research accepted at professional conferences.[72] Eventually, however, a body of research emerged demonstrating that poverty, environment, and their correlates such as poor nutrition and tobacco use influence children's development as much as or more than prenatal exposure to drugs.[73] A team of researchers concluded in 1998 that children exposed to cocaine in utero "are not hopelessly damaged and destined to become a burden to society."[74] In contrast to the devastating impact predicted by sensationalist media accounts, meta-analyses (i.e., studies of many other studies) found small or no effects on physical growth, cognition, language skills, motor skills, behavior, attention, affect, and neurophysiology.[75] In 2001, Deborah Frank and her colleagues published an article in the *Journal of the American Medical Association* in which they reviewed 74 studies of early childhood outcomes following prenatal cocaine exposure. After eliminating those which were methodologically unsound, Frank et al. concluded that although maternal cocaine use does add some risk, it does not automatically result in poor developmental outcomes. Many findings thought to be specifically the result of cocaine exposure are correlated with prenatal exposure to legal substances (e.g., tobacco and alcohol) and the quality of the child's environment.[76]

The best available medical evidence indicates that the use of illicit drugs and other substances is but one of many other factors that may affect pregnancy outcome and fetal and child outcomes. Recognizing this, scores of highly respected medical and public health organizations have voiced their opposition to the arrests and prosecutions of pregnant women who use illicit drugs, including the American Medical Association, the American Society of Addiction Medicine, the American Public Health Association, the American College of Physicians, the American College of Obstetricians and Gynecologists, the American Academy of Pediatrics, the March of Dimes, and the National Council on Alcoholism and Drug Dependence.

Neither being addicted nor being pregnant is a crime. Some law enforcement officials and prosecutors, operating under false assumptions that a woman's drug dependency is inevitably and irreversibly harming her unborn child, have persisted in pursuing charges against pregnant women. They define the problem as being one of a woman who uses drugs while she is pregnant. The problem is more accurately defined as being one of a woman becoming and remaining pregnant. If a woman who is already addicted to drugs becomes pregnant, the only way she can be assured of avoiding criminal charges is to get an abortion. In other words, it is a woman's decision to continue her pregnancy that is being criminalized, more so than the fact of her addiction and continued drug use.

Criminalizing the Pregnancies of Women Who Use Drugs

There are several hundred known cases from 1990 to 2006 in at least 40 states where pregnant women have been arrested for using drugs even when infants were born healthy or there was no evidence that women's drug use caused harm to the infant; there were over a dozen known arrests reported in 2006 and 2007 alone.[77] Typically, women have been charged with felonies, including murder or manslaughter, child abuse or neglect, and drug offenses. In 2003, Regina McKnight was found guilty in South Carolina of homicide by child abuse. Although she had no criminal record, she was sentenced to 20 years incarceration (with eight years suspended) because her addiction to cocaine was presumed to have caused her pregnancy to end in stillbirth.[78] If Regina had obtained an illegal third-trimester abortion rather than continued her pregnancy, she would have faced only about a two-year sentence.

In some cases, women have pleaded guilty or accepted plea bargains; many have been sentenced to incarceration or were detained while awaiting trial. When the arrests and prosecutions of women are challenged, the charges are virtually always found to be without legal basis or unconstitutional. With the exception of South Carolina (where an activist state supreme court with a bare majority twice rewrote state law to make the word "child" in the state child abuse and homicide statutes include viable fetuses), every state has dismissed prosecutions or overturned convictions. Many charges and convictions of child abuse and neglect, drug distribution, and manslaughter that are leveled against pregnant women have been dropped on the grounds that the legislation was never written with the intent that it be applied to the context of pregnancy.[79] Nonetheless, prosecutors continue to pursue charges against pregnant women. Defending women against these arrests and prosecutions continues to consume valuable resources of time, money, and expertise that could much better be spent providing direct support to women themselves.

Poor women of color have borne the brunt of criminal justice and other state intrusions into their reproductive lives, and it is their pregnancies that have been singled out for attention. Under the Fourteenth Amendment's equal protection clause, similarly situated persons will be treated similarly. White, black, and Hispanic women have comparable rates of drug use and substance dependence; the number in metropolitan areas who have used an illicit drug in the past month is 8.6, 8.4, and 5.6 percent, respectively.[80] Yet, despite the Fourteenth Amendment's equal protection clause, a 1992 survey of arrests and prosecutions of pregnant women found overwhelming evidence of race discrimination. An analysis of more recent cases is still under way; it suggests ongoing racial bias and an undeniable focus on low-income women.[81]

South Carolina remains a notoriously punitive state when it comes to its responses to pregnant women suspected of drug use. Until the Supreme Court ruled the practice unconstitutional in 2001 in *Ferguson,* pregnant women at the Charleston public hospital operated by the Medical University of South Carolina were secretly searched for evidence of drug use. About 30 women who tested positive were reported to the police by the nurse who oversaw the program and other health care workers. The hospital then helped to coordinate their arrests on charges of possession, drug delivery, or child abuse.[82] All but one of these women were black. The exception was a white woman who was identified by a nurse as someone who "lived with her boyfriend who is a Negro."[83]

Prosecutors also have singled out pregnant women, while ignoring men's exposures to substances that may affect fetal health. Men are nearly twice as likely as women to be classified with substance dependence or abuse.[84] Practically no studies have examined the possibility of paternal drug use affecting fetal health and pregnancy outcome, so it is not possible to say whether men's drug use has any effect.[85] Some studies, however, have found a correlation between men's exposure to certain kinds of chemicals (including pesticides, solvents used in paints, thinners, refineries, and the manufacturing of rubber products) and an increased risk of miscarriage and fetal defects.[86]

In addition to equal protection concerns, a wide range of other arguments can be leveled against efforts to criminalize women's pregnancies, but in this discussion I focus on three of the most basic: (1) the arrests and charges are based on flawed logic and faulty assumptions about maternal drug use and its effects; (2) criminalization is an ineffective and counterproductive means of promoting healthy pregnancies and birth outcomes; and (3) such measures open the door to a broad range of intrusions into pregnant women's rights to privacy and bodily integrity.

If a child is born prematurely or has a low birthweight or if a woman miscarries or delivers a stillborn baby, some hospital staff, medical examiners, and other state officials blame the women's actions for the outcome, especially if that woman has used any amount of an illicit drug, used too much alcohol, or in some way, through her race, class, or personality, offended the staff or officials. Some health care providers also see drug testing as part of defensive medicine. That is, if something has gone wrong with the birth and the staff fear that they may be sued, a positive drug test result provides them with a powerful defense, regardless of whether the harm was caused by the drug use.

The following conventional wisdom makes some sense: "Shooting a pregnant woman in the stomach is likely to harm the woman and her fetus. Therefore, a man who deliberately shoots his pregnant girlfriend has made a decision to harm the woman and her fetus, and he should be held accountable for his actions." Prosecutors and members of the public tend to adopt similar logic when faced with a pregnant woman who uses illicit and potentially harmful drugs, along the lines of: "Everybody knows that using drugs damages the fetus. Therefore, a woman who chooses to continue to use drugs (or chooses not to get off drugs) while she is pregnant has made a decision to harm her fetus, and she should be held accountable for her actions."

As noted, I am strongly opposed to treating a fetus as an independent entity, separate from a mother. Setting that aside for the moment, the logic that makes sense when applied to a man who deliberately shoots his girlfriend is problematic when extended to a pregnant woman who uses illicit drugs (or any other substance, for that matter).

First, one can infer a causal relationship between shooting someone in the stomach and the harm that results. As noted previously, however, the relationship between using a substance and fetal or infant health is much less straightforward. While a correlation may exist between the use of some substances (and, as discussed above, some medical conditions) and a higher risk of pregnancy loss, a causal relationship has not been unequivocally established in the medical literature. Most pregnant women who use substances such as cocaine, methamphetamine, nicotine, caffeine, or alcohol will give birth to healthy babies. And most pregnancy losses and other negative birth outcomes cannot be traced solely—or even mainly—to the use of an illicit substance, especially when that use is accompanied by other risk factors such as violence, heavy alcohol consumption, cigarette smoking, age, poverty, and so forth.

Second, the nature of addiction and dependency is such that not every person who uses a substance "chooses" or "intends" to continue to use it or can even be said to be indifferent to its consequences. Prolonged drug use can cause dramatic changes in brain function, making it very difficult for people to overcome drug dependence on their own without treatment.[87] The National Institute on Drug Abuse (which at the time of this writing is considering a name change to "The National Institute of Diseases of Addiction") defines addiction as "a chronic, relapsing brain disease that is characterized by compulsive drug seeking and use, despite harmful consequences." The American Psychiatric Association's *Diagnostic and Statistical Manual of Mental Disorders* (*DSM-IV*) recognizes that an "inability to control drug use" is often a key feature of chemical dependency.[88]

Women's attempts to cease using drugs completely during pregnancy are common.[89] Indeed, pregnancy and motherhood have been identified as catalysts for change among women who use drugs.[90] While many can and do stop or reduce their consumption and tolerance of potentially harmful substances while they are pregnant, permanent abstinence is no more attainable for many pregnant women than it is for other people. Wanting or intending to stop is an important part of recovery, but it is rarely sufficient. The physical, behavioral, and social aspects of dependence are such that many women will not succeed in their attempts to completely abstain from using a drug during pregnancy.

Moreover, in the absence of effective and comprehensive treatment on demand, it is unfair to punish women for not obtaining drug treatment. Many pregnant women do not enter drug treatment because they cannot afford to, there are no spaces available, or the program does not provide

childcare. A 1993 study of 294 drug treatment programs in five major cities showed that while most programs accepted pregnant women on some
basis, the method of payment accepted and the availability of child care
significantly limited access.[91] Only 55 percent of residential detoxification
programs accepted pregnant women on Medicaid or for free. Only one
in five programs accepted pregnant women *and* provided child care, even
though past research has found that lack of child care precludes addicted
women's participation in treatment.[92] Indeed, even those programs touted
as allowing women to bring their children typically limit the number and
ages of the children. This means that many women will have to split up
their family in order to get help. A survey conducted in 2008 found that
only 19 states have created drug treatment programs specifically for pregnant women, and only 7 states give pregnant women priority access to
state-funded drug treatment programs.[93] Even in these states, however, the
demand may exceed the number of available spaces in treatment programs.
And while there is strong evidence that treatment for addiction is at least as
effective as treatment for other chronic, relapsing conditions like asthma,
diabetes, and hypertension, treatment often fails patients.[94] As a result, it is
inappropriate to assume that simply entering treatment will be sufficient to
"cure" a woman of her dependency on drugs.

Abortion, like drug treatment, is frequently considered among pregnant
women who use illicit drugs, but less frequently obtained. Two-thirds of the
women in one study who reported using cocaine during their pregnancies
(and nearly as many of those who smoked cigarettes, but did not report using cocaine) considered having an abortion.[95] Some women either do not realize they are pregnant or delay making a decision until a stage in which a
legal abortion is no longer possible; others lack financial means or may have
religious reasons or a partner's desires that factor into their decision.[96]

The second argument I make against criminalizing the pregnancies of
women who use drugs is that it is a deeply misguided response to a public
health problem. Police officers, prosecutors, and judges (as well as the social
workers and hospital staff who often report women to law enforcement)
may claim that prosecution and other measures are necessary to safeguard
the health of the fetuses. They may use prosecution (or the threat of prosecution) to force women into drug treatment or to deter other women from
using drugs. In some cases, women have been incarcerated not because of
the offense they committed but because they were pregnant.

Simmone Ikerd, who was addicted to drugs, had been convicted in New
Jersey for welfare fraud. When she was eight weeks pregnant, she violated

the conditions of her probation. The judge sentenced her to a three-year prison term to be served at a facility that could treat her pregnancy and drug dependency, saying, "Not because we want to punish her, but because we want to save the baby. I don't want her using drugs. The only way I can do it is by putting her in jail."[97] After Simmone gave birth, she was released from prison. An appellate court later overturned her sentence for the probation violation on the grounds that it was imposed because she was a pregnant addict, it bore no relationship to her initial offense, and it was excessively punitive.[98]

Just as punishing a woman because she is pregnant is misguided and wrong, so is arresting a woman after she gives birth. If the intent is to protect fetuses, punitive surveillance and reporting strategies are more likely to have either no effect or an adverse effect on the problem of maternal drug use and dependence. On a strictly pragmatic level, arresting a woman after she gives birth will not have a retroactive impact on her pregnancy. By the time a pregnant woman has delivered a stillbirth or a baby is born testing positive for an illicit substance, valuable opportunities have been missed to provide a woman with support and access to good-quality health care, including drug treatment. As for any possible general deterrent effect caused by fear of prosecution and imprisonment, the nature of drug dependency (and the corresponding lack of effective drug treatment on demand) makes it more likely that a woman will avoid seeking medical care and drug treatment for fear of being reported, judged, prosecuted, and punished than that she will be deterred from using drugs.

Prosecutors, hospital and child protection workers, and concerned citizens alike frequently allude to a mythical figure: the hardened, uncaring pregnant addict with several children (who are all in state custody) who won't get treatment unless she is forced to do so. But it is not clear that such women exist, or if they do, that they comprise more than a tiny fraction of all the women who use or are addicted to illicit drugs.[99] Even so, energy spent condemning these women might be better invested in considering what role having one or more children taken away may play in women's drug dependency and view of future pregnancies and motherhood.

"Protecting the fetus" by incarcerating pregnant women wrongly assumes that jails and prisons consistently offer high-quality prenatal care programs, nutritional diets, and reproductive health care. As I document in chapter 6, this is very often not the case. Punitive approaches are simply no substitute for providing support, treatment, and services to women whose substance use, nutrition, and other aspects of their lives pose a threat to their health.

A third criticism leveled against mobilizing the criminal justice system to address a concern about drug use and pregnancy is that it creates a precedent for the supervision and punishment of pregnant women with regard to all aspects of their lives. Cases involving the arrest of pregnant women who use alcohol or who have refused a cesarean section demonstrate that this broader application of precedent is not only possible but already real. In Maryland, two women were convicted of reckless endangerment and sentenced to several years in prison for alleged cocaine use during pregnancy; three other women faced similar charges.[100] The Maryland Court of Appeals ruled that prosecution of such cases might open the way for pregnant women to be prosecuted for any number of injury-prone activities that might endanger the well-being of an unborn child, such as driving without a seatbelt, skiing, or horseback riding.

This ruling, like others before it, is a strong and important recognition of the larger issues of pregnant women's civil and human rights beyond the issue of drug use and addiction. Court decisions overwhelmingly reject the expansion of criminal law as a tool for policing pregnant women. While it is still true that, as of this writing, no state legislature has passed a law explicitly criminalizing pregnancy for drug users, many other kinds of laws and policies are being used to police and punish drug-using pregnant women. We have been sliding down the proverbial "slippery slope" for quite some time.

As mentioned earlier, hospital workers (including medical staff and social workers) and child welfare workers who are potentially best situated to provide important care and services to drug-dependent women are often the very ones who contact law enforcement authorities.[101] In 2003, the Child Abuse Prevention and Treatment Act (CAPTA) was amended to require health care providers involved in the delivery and care of infants to report to child protective agencies infants "affected" by illegal substance use. A state's receipt of federal child abuse funds depends on its compliance with the reporting provision. The law excluded from the reporting requirement those cases involving fetal alcohol effect or fetal alcohol syndrome which has well-documented indications and damaging effects. The act also failed to clearly define what is meant by "drug affected," leaving states to decide for themselves the criteria health care providers will use to identify infants to be reported to child protective services.

In some cases, a mother's positive drug test result may be treated as prima facie evidence of child abuse, without consideration of whether the child has been harmed or whether the woman is actually drug dependent.[102]

Neither CAPTA nor any of the civil state laws that predated it mandate universal drug testing. In other words, who gets tested and identified as a drug user, and thus who gets reported, is highly discretionary. Moreover, while neither CAPTA-inspired reporting laws nor the ones that predated CAPTA mandate that the information be turned over to the police, these laws typically do not prohibit it. The result has been that many women who used illicit drugs while they were pregnant are being reported to the police and are being arrested, detained, and prosecuted rather than receiving the services and care they need.

Pregnant women who do not use illicit drugs also find themselves being dragged down the slippery slope of state intervention. Women have become entangled in the court system not only for using drugs while pregnant but also for not obeying a doctor's or hospital administrator's orders.[103] In June 1987, Angela Carder's rare and fatal form of cancer came out of remission when she was 25 weeks pregnant. Angela's doctors told her that her condition was terminal. Angela, her husband and other family members, and her doctors decided to prolong her life as long as possible, at least until her 28th week of pregnancy, when it would be more likely that her fetus would survive if intervention was necessary. Despite Angela's wishes and the opinion of her doctors, the hospital's administrators (who were also its liability risk managers) obtained a court order for a cesarean. A few hours after the surgery, the fetus died. In 1990, a federal appeals court ruled that the judge was wrong to have given the hospital permission to perform the cesarean; Angela had the right to make health care decisions for herself and her fetus.[104] Unfortunately, it was too late for Angela. She died two days after the coerced surgery, with the cesarean listed as a contributing factor to her death.

More recently, in 1996, Laura Pemberton could not find a doctor in Florida who would permit her to attempt a vaginal birth after cesarean (VBAC) because of her vertical incision.[105] Doctors estimated she had a "substantial" and "unacceptably high" (i.e., 4 to 6 percent) risk of experiencing a uterine rupture, which might, in turn, cause the death of her baby.[106] Laura decided to give birth at home. During labor, she became dehydrated, so she went to the hospital to restore her fluids. The doctor, however, refused to give her an IV unless she agreed to have a cesarean. Laura and her husband surreptitiously left the hospital and went home, where Laura resumed labor. The sheriff and state attorney showed up at her home. They got a court order, and Laura was transported by ambulance to the hospital against her will, where she was forced to have a cesarean.

Laura subsequently brought a section 1983 civil rights action against state officials in federal court. The court, however, ruled that "whatever the scope of Ms. Pemberton's personal constitutional rights in this situation, they clearly did not outweigh the interests of the State of Florida in preserving the life of the unborn child." In his ruling, the judge dismissed as "bravado" Laura's confidence that she could have and would have delivered her son vaginally without harming him in any way."[107] Since 1996, Laura has had four successful vaginal births, unassisted.[108]

Singling out pregnant women and mothers for prosecution, court orders through family courts and drug treatment courts, and civil commitments contributes to a climate in which pregnant women are increasingly seen as adversaries of the fetuses they carry rather than people who have a stake in a healthy pregnancy and a positive outcome. There is no question that some women's drug use has become so chaotic and out of control that it may affect their parenting ability. No one is suggesting that such situations be ignored. Too often, however, unfitness to parent is based on a single, unconfirmed positive drug test rather than a thoughtful evaluation of whether drug use or any other factor has rendered someone incapable of parenting. As we should have learned from the crack panic, the distrust that stigma and prejudice engender among drug-using women may pose greater dangers to maternal and fetal health than the use of an illicit drug itself. Reporting pregnant women to child protection agencies and the police can be expected to have a chilling effect on physicians' relationships with their patients; no doubt, many pregnant women will be discouraged from seeking prenatal care or drug treatment, understandably afraid of being reported to authorities. Moreover, some health care providers will be discouraged from asking about drug use for fear they will have to turn patients over to punitive state authorities who have the resources to punish and separate families, but not to treat and support them.

Reporting requirements aside, women's fears of being judged by those who are assigned with helping them are not without foundation. Survey results suggest a sizable proportion of hospital medical staff and social workers already support defining illicit drug use as "child abuse" and coercive approaches to addressing a woman's drug use (e.g., incarceration, threatening women with loss of custody of their children to "encourage" them to complete drug treatment).[109]

Bystanders to Their Own Bodies

Portrayals of drug-dependent women often emphasize these women's (sometimes significant) personal failings while giving short shrift to other aspects of their lives, including past attempts to get help. Readers may recall the 2004 case of Melissa Rowland. Early media accounts cast Melissa Rowland as a vain, self-centered woman who had refused a cesarean section because she didn't want the scars.[110] She was charged with murder on the grounds that her refusal to have an immediate cesarean constituted "depraved indifference to human life."[111]

Melissa's reality was quite different. First, Melissa already had abdominal scars because she had delivered by cesarean in the past (which in itself increased her risk of a stillbirth). And media accounts were slow to point out that Melissa did agree later to having a cesarean in another hospital, where she gave birth to a stillborn boy and a liveborn girl who tested positive for cocaine. Much mainstream news coverage at the time ignored or downplayed the fact that Melissa was a deeply troubled woman with a history that included estrangement from her family, periodic homelessness, past suicide attempts, previous hospitalization in a mental hospital at the age of 12, and giving birth to twins at age 14.[112]

Much as we saw during the earlier negative eugenics campaigns, women like Melissa Rowland, Theresa Hernandez, Regina McKnight, and countless others are used to symbolize the women whose substance use, mental illness, poverty, troubled backgrounds, and race and ethnicity render them unsuitable for reproduction. With the possible exception of serial pedophiles, there are few groups more stigmatized and less likely to gain our support and protection (much less our compassion) than a poor pregnant woman of color who uses illegal drugs. By contrast, Laci Peterson symbolizes the ideal pregnant woman: one who is "white, suburban, middle class, married, not too young nor too old, pregnant at the right time and for the right reasons."[113]

The ways in which cases of fetal homicide and maternal drug use are presented to the public communicate volumes about whose pregnancies—and whose lives and whose deaths—deserve official compassion or condemnation.[114] Legislators and advocates tell us not only who "counts" as a victim but also what sort of protection is called for. In this way, they selectively use victims to legitimate their power to implement "protective" policies.[115]

That "fetal protection" measures and other attempts to recognize so-called fetal personhood continue to have traction with the public isn't surprising. People are genuinely and understandably pained by the tragedy of stillbirth and miscarriage, the violent end, or other negative result of a wanted pregnancy. They are sincerely and justifiably interested in ensuring that pregnancies yield healthy outcomes. Personally, I am comfortable recognizing that a fetus is a baby is a person in the eyes of some pregnant woman (e.g., those who want to be pregnant) without finding it necessary for a fetus to be recognized as a baby or a person in the eyes of the law.[116]

But, as we have seen with "safe haven" legislation that is purportedly designed to address neonaticide and infant abandonment, lawmakers and prosecutors manipulate public sentiment to their own ends. Concern for the living, already-born woman who uses drugs or who is being beaten by her husband or ex-boyfriend is too often overshadowed (and even discounted) by concern for the "preborn child." It wasn't Chelsea Brooks's life and death that inspired the fetal homicide bill but, rather, the fact of her pregnancy. Our concern for violence against pregnant women and maternal drug use emanates from women's position as the bearers of fetuses, not as people who are being beaten or struggling with addiction.

The message is clear. There are two types of pregnant women: the invisible, innocent, self-sacrificing vessel who carried the preborn victim of violence, and the indifferent, irresponsible, selfish drug-using woman who persisted in incubating a fetus. Both types of pregnant women are reduced to "fetal containers" whose lives and rights are rendered secondary to the interests of the "real" victim: the unborn child.[117] The distorted representations of who is sympathetic or blameworthy, who is the offender and who is the victim, make it hard for us to recognize how punishing these policies are for all women.

Whatever forms it takes, fetal protectionism ultimately results in women being treated as "bystanders to their own bodies."[118] The harms posed by institutionalizing coercive forms of state power simply do not outweigh any claimed benefits to holding women criminally culpable for a healthy pregnancy and birth outcome.[119] Arresting pregnant women for their drug or alcohol use reflects a belief "that being addicted to drugs or having another health problem is no different from a man shooting his pregnant girlfriend in the head."[120] Fetus-centered homicide laws and other attempts to recognize fetal rights and fetal protectionism create a legal foundation for policing pregnancy and punishing some women who carry their pregnancies to term. In the end, it seems far better, as one legal commentator observed, "that some tragic private wrongs transpire than that state-imposed coercion of pregnant women become part of our legal landscape."[121]

6

"Liars and Whiners"

Incarcerated Women's Right to Reproductive Health

During a natural gentle birth, a woman feels and senses the power of the birth and uses this energy to transform every part of her own being. A gentle birth is not rushed. The baby emerges at its own pace and in its own time, received into the hands of those who love and recognize it for the divine gift that it is.

—Barbara Harper, R.N., author of *Gentle Birth Choices,* 2005

My feet were still shackled together, and I couldn't get my legs apart.

—"Maria Jones," a pregnant Cook County (Ill.) jail inmate, describing her birthing experience, 1998[1]

Conditions in prisons, jails, and detention centers mirror the failure of social policies in the free world. Some of the most socially vulnerable and marginalized members of society are held behind bars, completely dependent on the institution to provide them with the basic necessities for life. If, to borrow from Dostoevsky, the degree of civilization in a society can be judged by the health care provided in its prisons, then the civilization of U.S. society has a long way to go, indeed.

Take, for instance, California, the second largest correctional system in the country. California's corrections system holds 1 in 10 of all the women incarcerated in the United States. In 2005, California spent $1.1 billion on health care for 164,000 male and female inmates, twice as much as it had seven years earlier.[2] Yet the quality of care remained so poor, with an inmate dying of medical incompetence or neglect, on average, once a week, that a receiver was appointed to improve the prison health care programs.[3]

California is hardly unique in the challenges it faces. Prison health care is located at the nexus of two enormous challenges facing U.S. society: the overall poor health of many low-income racial and ethnic minority women and men, and the massive scale of the correctional system. The U.S. Department of Health and Human Services' Agency for Healthcare Research and Quality tracks the nation's progress in improving quality and access to health care and in reducing health care disparities. As their 2005 report reveals, deficiencies in care are striking, particularly among racial and ethnic minority women.[4] Black women have higher death rates than other women due to heart disease, cancer, and stroke; their life expectancy is almost five years less than that of white women's.[5] Hispanic women receive poorer quality care than non-Hispanic white women for 60 percent of measures of health care, and they report poorer access to services on nearly 90 percent of all measures.[6] Chronic liver disease is one of the 10 leading causes of American Indian or Alaska Native females, though not for other racial groups; Hispanic women are more likely than other women to die from conditions that originated while they were pregnant.[7] Compared with high-income women, poor women are more likely to report fair or poor overall health and more likely to report being obese and having anxiety, depression, arthritis, asthma, diabetes, and high blood pressure. They also have lower rates of mammography and Pap tests.[8]

The unequal distribution of health in the United States is only part of the problem. There is also the matter of the immense scale and scope of the U.S. criminal justice system in general, and the correctional enterprise in particular, both of which ensnare disproportionate numbers of poor and racial and ethnic minority men and women. In 2006, the federal budget outlays for the administration of justice were $41 billion, including $6.1 billion for federal corrections.[9] By contrast, only $16.5 billion was allocated to social services and $39.7 billion to elementary, secondary, and vocational education.[10] Spending on corrections continues to outpace the growth in the correctional population. Between 1994 and 2004, local, state, and federal correctional expenditures increased by 78 percent.[11] During these same years, the number of people incarcerated in prisons or jails or on probation or parole increased 36 percent.[12]

Today, roughly 7 million men and women are detained, incarcerated, on probation or parole, or otherwise under the supervision of the criminal justice system.[13] Incarceration rates among women continue to rise, especially among women of color.[14] Women now comprise approximately seven percent of all inmates.[15] Black women are more than twice as likely as Hispanic women and over three times more likely than white women to be in prison.[16]

Overall, around 111,000 women were incarcerated in over 170 state correctional facilities and 15 women-only federal prisons in 2006, compared with 93,000 in 2000.[17] Another 98,500 women or so are held in jails.[18] Most women are incarcerated for nonviolent crimes.[19] The majority—around 85 percent—are of childbearing age: that is, between 18 and 44 years old.[20]

The history of the medical care and treatment of incarcerated women is long—and abysmal. It traces at least as far back as the early nineteenth century when women were housed in unsanitary, cramped quarters, and their keepers used women's presumed sexual immorality to justify neglect and sexual abuse.[21] Today, many correctional personnel competently provide services to incarcerated women and girls. But many prisons and jails still have systems of health care that assume the norm of a more violent male prison population, and which reflect and reinforce damaging sexist stereotypes about women who are behind bars.[22] And while correctional staff's sexual abuse and misconduct directed against incarcerated women may be less common than in the early penitentiaries, these crimes continue to be committed in facilities throughout the country.

Correctional Health Care

Florida's secure facilities provide many examples where women have suffered the consequences of substandard health care. In a Hillborough County facility, a pregnant inmate complained of back pain for 12 hours and asked to go to the hospital but was given Tylenol instead. Her premature baby died before medical personnel could get her to the hospital.[23] Correctional staff denied a Palm Beach County Jail pregnant inmate who was experiencing vaginal bleeding permission to go to the medical clinic because she had not previously put her name on a list. She deliberately slammed her thumb in a door so that she could see a doctor immediately.[24] A Broward County inmate nearly died from a tubal pregnancy misdiagnosed by medical personnel as constipation and pelvic inflammation.[25]

Women in other states do not necessarily fare any better. In 2002, some 33 plaintiffs filed a class action civil suit on behalf of the women prisoners at Tutwiler Prison in Alabama. The suit claimed that state officials and the for-profit medical care provider "delay or deny adequate treatment for serious medical, dental and mental health conditions, and willfully ignore warning signs of serious illness in anticipation that the women will be released from prison before they die."[26] For example, a 39-year-old woman began bleeding heavily and experienced severe cramping after her uterus prolapsed into her vagina. She started asking for help for the bleeding in June, but to no avail. She bled every day from August to September and eventually became anemic. Another prisoner had surgery for breast cancer. The sentencing judge assured her she would receive chemotherapy while incarcerated, but 18 months passed without her receiving treatment.

Inferior medical care contributed to the deaths of at least three women incarcerated at Tutwiler in 2004.[27] A few months before a lupus patient died of a brain hemorrhage, the primary doctor at Tutwiler had cancelled tests recommended by an outside cardiologist. Another patient's high cholesterol was never treated. A third inmate hanged herself after five days on suicide watch, without any record that she had been seen by a mental health professional during that time. The following year, three more Tutwiler inmates died in a two-month period.[28]

Indifference to prisoners' medical needs is not a new development. Up until the 1970s, it defined much correctional policy. The courts took a "hands off" approach to prisons and prisoners and refused to intervene. Eventually, the civil rights, prisoner rights, and women's movements of the 1960s and 1970s demanded recognition of basic human rights and led to a greater concern for the quality of medical care being provided to inmates. Today, courts recognize the Eighth Amendment rights of prisoners to obtain at least a modicum of medical care. But as the 1980 ruling in *Brown v. Beck* states, prisoners are not entitled to care that is "perfect, the best obtainable, or even very good."[29] In prisons across the United States, negligent medical care is common, but unless it can be demonstrated to be the result of "deliberate indifference to a serious medical need," it is not unconstitutional.[30]

The poor quality of incarcerated women's medical care to some extent reflects the lower quality of care provided to *all* prisoners, regardless of their gender. Poor and even unconstitutional medical care often continues undetected or unchecked. Many prisons are in rural areas and are isolated from population centers, prisoners' families and friends, and communities of activists and advocates who might be expected to take an interest in institutional conditions.[31] Prison officials may cover up abuses in their facilities by failing to document problems or by falsifying records.[32]

For example, the primary care doctor at Tutwiler, Dr. Samuel Engle-hardt, performed the death review of one of the women who died under his care. Not surprisingly, he concluded there were no problems with the health care the woman received.[33] Prison medical personnel are rarely held liable if they "fail to obtain and review a thorough medical history . . . misdiagnose and wrongfully prescribe treatment to a patient whom they have not examined personally, or if they disclose private or confidential details of a patient's medical condition to unauthorized persons."[34] Unless human rights investigators, advocates, or the media gain access to the prison, the conditions go undocumented and unaddressed.[35]

Even when poor conditions or appalling practices do become public, public outrage is rarely forthcoming. Many people subscribe to the "principle of less eligibility." Until every law-abiding citizen in the free world has health care, the reasoning goes, inmates should not expect it and, arguably, do not deserve it. The widespread public antipathy is part of what allows the maltreatment and abuse to continue.

Medical care also suffers when the providers are overextended and lack the resources to do their jobs. Many dedicated correctional health care providers become frustrated and outraged by the system within which they are expected to operate. Often, they play important roles in calling attention to the abuses taking place within a facility. But even committed personnel are frequently unable to secure what they need to provide adequate medical care. Dr. Valda Chijide, for example, resigned from her position as HIV doctor at Limestone Prison (AL) after repeatedly complaining to Prison Health Services about inadequate support and staffing. The month she resigned, the court monitor described a rat-infested HIV unit where broken windows were covered with tattered plastic sheeting.[36]

The growing trend toward privatizing prison health care by contracting out medical services to for-profit health care companies such as Prison Health Services has contributed to a lack of accountability.[37] By 2005, Prison Health, the largest for-profit provider of inmate medical care, had amassed 86 contracts in 28 states and cared for 237,000 inmates, or about 10 percent of the incarcerated population.[38] Prison Health's performance has generated much criticism and many lawsuits. The company has had to pay out millions of dollars in fines and settlements.[39] Oversight of the contracts appears to be spotty at best. In Alabama, the state official charged with making sure that Prison Health lives up to its contract, Associate Commissioner of the Alabama Corrections Department Ruth Naglich, was previously the vice president for sales and marketing at Prison Health.[40]

Reproductive Health Care

Every year, about 3,000 men and women prison inmates die, usually due to an illness.[41] Inside and outside of prisons and jails, heart disease and cancer are leading causes of death for both men and women, accounting for 27.3 and 23.3 percent of all deaths among prisoners.[42] Women prisoners are most likely to develop lung cancer, followed by breast cancer and ovarian cancer.[43] Breast, cervical, ovarian, and uterine cancer account for approximately one-quarter of all female cancer deaths among inmates.[44] Attention to the quality of reproductive health care in women's prisons, however, tends to focus narrowly on either HIV or pregnancy.[45]

Obstetric and gynecologic health is important for all female prisoners, not just those who are pregnant or infected with HIV. As discussed in chapter 3, it should include policies that provide access to abortion for incarcerated women who seek the procedures. Comprehensive reproductive health care includes breast exams, prenatal care, and measures designed to prevent, identify, and treat gynecologic cancers. Most U.S. correctional systems provided some level of female-specific health care.[46] For instance, of the 44 U.S. jurisdictions that responded to a 1999 national survey, 42 provided prenatal and postpartum services, and 44 provided mammography. The quality of the care provided is another matter. Prior research and complaints filed as part of lawsuits provide evidence that the quality of reproductive health care available to incarcerated women is lower than that available to the public and to incarcerated men, and falls well short of professional standards of care.

Pregnancy

Reproductive rights encompass the right to conditions that promote a safe and health pregnancy, as well as the right to give birth without fear of death, serious illness, or injury.[47] Between 5 and 10 percent of all incarcerated women are pregnant.[48] Most are pregnant at intake; others become pregnant during their incarceration, often by sexual contact with a correctional officer (a subject discussed below). About 2,000 women give birth while incarcerated every year.[49]

Fewer than one-fifth of federal and state departments of corrections place pregnant women in noninstitutional settings.[50] In some facilities, women are not permitted to breastfeed their newborns and may only have one to three days before their infant is turned over to a family member or the foster care system.[51] Other facilities offer programs where a woman and her infant remain together during her sentence (see chapter 7).

Findings regarding how incarceration affects pregnancy outcomes are mixed.[52] Some studies have found that incarceration is associated with lower birthweight and increased likelihood of maternal complications, perhaps due in part to the poor quality of the prenatal care received.[53] Other studies have found that being incarcerated may have a protective effect for some pregnant women and may result in higher birthweight babies and a lower likelihood of premature delivery.[54] It appears that some pregnant women have better access to shelter and prenatal care (and more support for abstaining from alcohol, cigarettes, and other drugs) when they are incarcerated. This seems to speak more to the low level of medical care available to many poor women in the free world, however, than to the overall high quality of care available in correctional facilities.

Prenatal care is supposed to promote the health of the pregnant woman and her fetus. Ideally, it will permit the prevention, early detection, and treatment of problems that may lead to a woman dying or miscarrying, or an infant being born with birth defects, low birthweight, or other preventable problems. The American College of Obstetricians and Gynecologists (ACOG) advises women to begin seeing their health care provider during their first trimester and to schedule more frequent visits as the pregnancy progresses.[55] Prenatal care is particularly important for incarcerated pregnant women because many of them have what would be considered "high-risk" pregnancies which are complicated by drug and alcohol abuse and sexually transmitted infections, including HIV and hepatitis B.[56] Many also have histories of abuse and poor social support networks which place them at greater risk for pregnancy-related complications.

Although the treatment of pregnant prisoners receives more attention than any other medical conditions incarcerated women face, the quality of care before, during, and after delivery still leaves much to be desired. Many women prisoners report that they receive little to no education about prenatal care and nutrition, do not receive regular pelvic exams or sonograms, and cannot alter their diets to suit their changing caloric needs. Many prisons do not routinely serve fruit because of concerns that inmates will make alcohol out of it. Vegetables may be habitually overcooked, thus reducing their nutritional value. A sample menu at the Central California Women's Facility included "pancakes with maple syrup for breakfast, bologna and American cheese sandwiches with chips and a sugar cookie for lunch, and corn dogs, potatoes, and Jell-o for dinner."[57] Pregnant women wanting to supplement their diets often must buy food from the commissary at prices completely disproportionate to the wages they earn.[58] Women may be expected to finish eating in less than 15 minutes and can be penalized for taking food out of the cafeteria to eat later.

To be sure, prenatal care in correctional facilities is not universally poor, and many pregnant women who are incarcerated receive compassionate treatment. In Washington state, the Birth Attendants Prison Doula project provides physical, emotional, and educational support to some incarcerated pregnant and postpartum women. In Arizona, "Boo," a pregnant jail inmate reports, "They're real good people to me . . . I get taken care of in here very well. They give us three pregnancy bags a day which contain two cartons of milk, two orange juices, and two fruits, and you get three pills three times a day during breakfast, lunch, and dinner."[59]

While humane and competent treatment is possible in prisons, in reality, the quality of medical care provided to pregnant women too often falls woefully short. Pregnant prisoners may endure degrading delivery experiences. A doctor ruptured pregnant inmate Samantha Luther's amniotic sac and then ordered her to shuffle the hallway of the local hospital for several hours wearing ankle shackles that provided only 18 inches of clearance. Her ankles were rubbed raw and she described the experience as "humiliating."[60] Sometimes the treatment reaches dangerous levels. Ajadyan Venny was nearly six months pregnant when she was booked into an Albany (NY) jail. Nine days later, she awoke with excruciating cramps. The nursing supervisor found Aja sitting on the toilet, crying, with blood everywhere. The nurse incorrectly assumed that Ajadyan had miscarried. Later, correctional officers looked in the toilet and found the infant, still in his placental sac. The nurse confirmed there was a faint heartbeat but did not try to restore the baby's breathing in the 15 minutes before ambulance workers arrived. The infant died after three days on a ventilator. Each of the three Prison Health nurses was placed on a year's probation and fined $500.[61]

In recent years, the practice of shackling pregnant women during transport and delivery has drawn the attention of organizations such as Amnesty International, with growing pressure to ban the practice. Leg irons or waist shackles that are fastened to the bed severely limit a woman's ability to move.[62] Moving during labor helps the labor progress and alleviates some of a woman's discomfort. A woman in labor also needs to shift positions for treatment. If complications like hemorrhage arise during delivery, a woman may need to be moved quickly to another setting; shackles can delay the move and create a hazardous situation for the mother and baby. A pregnant inmate, "Maria

Jones," was shackled to the bed even though she had no history of escaping or violence. The doctor determined that the baby's arrival was imminent and started to prepare the bed for delivery. "Because I was shackled to the bed, they couldn't remove the lower part of the bed for the delivery, and they couldn't put my feet in the stirrups. My feet were still shackled together, and I couldn't get my legs apart," Maria recalled. "The doctor called for the officer, but the officer had gone down the hall. No one else could unlock the shackles, and my baby was coming but I couldn't open my legs."[63]

In 2006, Amnesty International found that at least 38 states and the Federal Bureau of Prisons permit the use of restraints such as belly chains, shackles, handcuffs, or nylon "soft restraints" on women in their third trimester.[64] All but nine states and the District of Columbia permit the use of restraints during transport to the hospital. Once at the hospital, women may be shackled to their beds or restrained with flexible nylon soft restraints. Twenty-three states and the federal system permit restraints during labor. Only five states and the District of Columbia stipulate that no restraints are to be used on inmates during labor and birth.[65] Security concerns do not justify shackling, since correctional personnel accompany the women prisoners to the hospital. Further, most pregnant women are incarcerated for nonviolent offenses and pose no flight risk. As Dawn Davison, warden for the California Institution for Women in Chino, points out, "There is no woman in the throes of labor who is going to jump up and try to escape."[66]

Gynecologic Cancer and HPV

In general, ensuring women's babies are born healthy seems to be a greater priority for correctional staff and administrators than ensuring the health of the incarcerated women themselves. Gynecologic and reproductive health is a concern for all women, not just those who are pregnant, as all women are vulnerable to cervical cancer and other gynecologic cancers. Gynecologic cancers are those affecting the female reproductive organs, such as the ovaries, cervix, and uterus. Each year, about 72,000 women in the United States are diagnosed with a gynecologic cancer; about 27,000 women will die of such a cancer.[67] According to the American Cancer Society, uterine (endometrial) cancer is the most common gynecologic cancer but ovarian cancer is the most deadly; it is the fifth leading cause of death in American women.

Since the 1960s, the incidence and mortality of cervical cancer have declined significantly. Papanicolaou (Pap) smears and risk assessment tests can prevent gynecologic cancers or ensure they are detected in an early stage. Women diagnosed with cervical cancer in the United States tend to be those who have not had a Pap smear in the last three years.[68] With conscientious care, many gynecologic diseases do not have to be fatal. This care should include attention to human papillomavirus (HPV) and other genital infections.

HPV is the most common sexually transmitted infection and has been linked to cancers of the lower genital tract, including cervical cancer.[69] As of this writing, nearly all sexually active adult women have been exposed to HPV.[70] Most sexually active women at some point will become infected with HPV, but their immune system will fight off the infection.

Many incarcerated women's poverty, sexual histories, and lower access to health care place them at greater risk of having a persistent HPV infection or a suppressed immune system. Therefore, they are also at a higher risk for cervical cancer. For instance, a woman with a preexisting compromised immune system or a genital infection is 17 times more likely to develop HPV-related diseases.[71] Even women infected with HPV (including one of a handful of strains of high-risk HPV) probably will not develop cervical cancer.

With careful screening that includes a good physical examination and Pap smear testing, most lower genital tract disease can be prevented among incarcerated women.[72] A 1997 survey revealed that about 90 percent of all women state prison inmates and around 20 percent of jail inmates reported having received a gynecologic exam after admission.[73] Even when gynecological exams are performed on intake, however, there may be no follow-up, or the screening may not continue on the schedule recommended by national medical standards.[74]

Left undetected or untreated, sexually transmitted infections (STIs) can lead to serious complications that may jeopardize a woman or girl's reproductive health by, for example, increasing her risk of becoming infected if she is exposed to HIV, developing pelvic inflammatory disease (which is a major cause of infertility, ectopic or "tubal" pregnancy, and chronic pelvic pain), or passing the genital infection on to her child during pregnancy, labor, or delivery.[75] In a New York City juvenile detention facility, one full-time physician served the city's 19 juvenile centers and the 5,000 youth who passed through the system each year.[76] Fewer than one-third of the eligible girls received a Pap test, and only around one in five were tested for gonorrhea, chlamydia, and syphilis.[77]

Incarcerated women have higher rates of STIs and gynecologic infections.[78] A 2005 CDC study of persons entering correctional facilities examined the rates of chlamydia, gonorrhea, and syphilis among prisoners in a sample of states. About 7.4 percent of adult women tested positive for chlamydia at intake, 2.8 percent tested positive for gonorrhea, and 5.2 percent tested positive for syphilis. The same study found that young women entering juvenile corrections facilities were more likely than adult women to test positive for chlamydia and gonorrhea.[79]

HIV also jeopardizes many incarcerated women's health. Incarcerated women are 15 times more likely to be infected with HIV than are women who are free.[80] Nationally, about 2,000 women in state or federal prisons are known to be HIV-positive. At least 10 percent of women inmates in New York are infected with HIV, along with more than 1 in 20 in Florida, New Jersey, and Maryland.[81] Careful monitoring is necessary to maintain an HIV-positive women's reproductive health. A women infected with HIV should be offered multiple Pap smears throughout the year since, when a woman does have HPV, she is 30 times more likely than an uninfected women to develop cervical cancer.[82] Other disorders also may be more frequent, more severe, and less responsive to therapy in women infected with HIV, compared with other women. These include HPV-associated cervical disorders, recurrent yeast infections, and pelvic inflammatory disease.

Women in state and federal prisons are more likely than incarcerated men to be HIV positive.[83] Women are biologically more vulnerable to HIV infection; male-to-female transmission is thought to be more efficient than female-to-male transmission in the early stages of HIV disease.[84] Social factors that place many women at risk for incarceration also make them prone to HIV infection, including poverty, race, gender, and physical or sexual trauma.[85] Many women are injection drug users or sex partners of injection drug users. They are more likely than men to have supported themselves through sex work and to have exchanged unprotected sex for money, shelter, food, or drugs.[86] Fear of violence and a relative lack of power in sexual relations keep many women from insisting that their sex partner use a condom. Any serious efforts to prevent HIV infection or slow the spread or development of the disease among women involved with the criminal justice system must also address the factors that make these women socially vulnerable to infection.

Incarcerated women themselves play a significant role in primary prevention efforts. Arguably, investing in their health and education yields greater results than the same investment in men's health. Anne De Groot, M.D., co-chief editor of Brown Medical School's *Infectious Diseases in Corrections Report* and a prison physician, observes that, in her experience educating prisoners about HIV and other infectious diseases, male inmates tend to be narrowly focused on their individual situations. By contrast, educating women inmates has a "tremendous ripple effect" because they are more likely to share the information with the people in their lives.[87]

Correctional Staff Sexual Misconduct

Reproductive rights include the right to have sexual and reproductive security, including freedom from sexual violence and coercion. Conservative estimates suggest that between one-third and two-thirds of women incarcerated in the United States have experienced sexual abuse prior to being incarcerated; between 2 and 4 women in 10 experienced childhood sexual abuse.[88] Women's reproductive health may be indirectly affected by sexual abuse. Women who have been abused often have enhanced feelings of vulnerability and anxiety that discourage them from undergoing regular medical examinations. They may have a heightened need to control the time, place, and pace of a gynecological or obstetric exam or may fear having their body touched during the exam.[89]

Incarcerated women's sexual and reproductive security is also violated directly by correctional staff's misconduct.[90] Male correctional workers' sexual harassment and abuse has gone on for centuries. In early prisons and jails, it was not uncommon for women to be raped or forced into prostitution.[91] Recognition of the abuse brought about a period of penal reform in the late nineteenth century that led to sex-segregated facilities, including prisons and reformatories where women were supervised by female staff.[92]

In the wake of the passage of Title VII as part of the Civil Rights Act of 1964, male correctional officers were reintroduced into women's prisons. Though Title VII was intended to allow women to work in male prisons (which were greater in number and therefore presented greater opportunities for employment and advancement), men were able to use the provisions of Title VII to gain employment in female facilities.

Federal law stipulates that all sexual contact between prison staff and an inmate is abuse; "consent" is an irrelevant concept when one person holds tremendous power over the other's life, including the power to reward or retaliate.[93] Although all states have moved to make correctional officers' sexual misconduct toward individuals in custody a criminal offense (usually a felony), the practice continues.[94]

In January 2003, the Legal Aid Society of New York filed a class action lawsuit alleging that Department of Correctional Services (DOCS) officials at the highest levels failed to address the ongoing and obvious sexual abuse of female inmates.[95] The lawsuit describes many instances where male staff committed sexual abuse against women, ranging from verbal degradation and inappropriate visual surveillance to rape. Three of the plaintiffs in the case were impregnated by correctional officers. Male correctional officers were commonly stationed alone in women's dormitory-style housing block and could walk freely throughout these quarters and watch women while they changed their clothes or slept. According to the Correctional Association of New York's Women in Prison Project,

> Women prisoners [in New York] consistently report that male officers solicit sexual favors from and rape women inmates; watch women shower, dress, and use the bathroom; verbally harass them with epithets such as "bitch," "nigger-bitch," "whore," and "crack-whore"; and touch inmates inappropriately, particularly during routine "pat frisks." A number of women have become pregnant while incarcerated after being raped by corrections staff.[96]

Girls in two New York State secure facilities also report harassment, unwanted touching, and sexual contact. One girl recalled having sex in the office of a male staff member when another male employee walked in on them, saying, "Oh, oh, oh, oh I'm sorry" before leaving and closing the door.[97]

Housing of women in private facilities outside their home state makes some women more vulnerable to officers' sexual misconduct. Most of the women held at the 250-bed, privately run Brush Correctional Facility for Women in Colorado are from Hawaii, Colorado, and Wyoming. Some of the women reportedly had sex with members of the correctional staff because they believed this activity would lead to them being sent to a facility in their home state where they could be closer to relatives.[98] Reports of women and girls having sex in exchange for favors, food, money, and contact with their children are among the most common scenarios for misconduct. Sexual assaults and rapes occur less often, but these abuses do take place.[99] The harassment and other misconduct occur in an environment where the offending officer or staff's position grants him complete access to a woman wherever she goes, at all times of the day.

Women also face the challenge of proving the veracity of their claims, even when officers have a record of similar complaints being lodged against them. The Prison Rape Elimination Act of 2003 authorizing federal grants for programs to prevent and punish prison rape officially recognized the importance of stopping sexual misconduct within prisons. Without physical or medical evidence such as a semen sample, a pregnancy, a recently contracted sexually transmitted infection, or other incriminating evidence such as letters or photographs, however, a woman may face an uphill battle getting the prison staff and administration to take her complaint seriously. Even with such evidence, a woman's credibility is called into question because of her status as an inmate, a fact that offending correctional staff can exploit. Women who file grievances may face further harassment from the offending officer and potentially from others as well. Retaliation may affect her release date, reduce or deny her privileges, jeopardize her visiting rights, or have other adverse consequences.[100]

In some instances, it is striking the lengths that some prison officials and legislators have gone to in order to resist even acknowledging that a problem exists. The *Detroit News* conducted a five-month investigation that exposed how Michigan lawmakers and prison officials "stymied investigations of sexual abuse in women's prisons, stifled inmate complaints and stripped away the rights of assaulted prisoners to sue for damages."[101] Prosecuting correctional officers was a low priority, and one often left to the office of the attorney general—the same agency that defended the corrections department against lawsuits filed by the victimized women. All but 3 of the 31 prison employees convicted of sex-related crimes in the state were convicted of misdemeanors; nobody had been charged under a state law that made sex between guards and inmates a felony punishable by 15 years incarceration.

Legislators stripped away inmates' right to sue under Michigan's Elliott-Larsen Civil Rights Act in 1999. After restricting the office's power and cutting its staff, the Legislature finally closed down the office of the Legislative Corrections Ombudsman, which was responsible for investigating inmate complaints. They also changed the law so that unless a woman could prove she had sustained lasting physical injury, she could not obtain damages, even if she had been repeatedly groped, humiliated, or raped. The sexual abuse and rapes had been documented in investigations by the U.S. Justice Department's Civil Rights Division and Human Rights Watch, and even the United Nations. In response to increased public scrutiny, the state imposed restrictions designed to limit the media and the public's access to inmates and facilities.

In the wake of the publicity generated by the series in the *Detroit News* and as the result of growing concern, changes were eventually implemented. Most of the male correctional officers were replaced by female officers in the three women's prisons.[102] Male guards are no longer allowed to patrol areas where women inmates shower, sleep, or use the bathroom. In 2007, a federal judge struck down the state amendment to the civil rights law, restoring women's protection under the Eliott-Larson Act and their right to sue.

Why Does the Maltreatment and Abuse Occur?

Part of the problem of maltreatment stems from widespread prejudice against women who are incarcerated. This prejudice exists not only among correctional staff and administrators but also among the judges and law-makers who are responsible for redressing wrongs and among the public at large. The attitude prevails that because a woman has been arrested, charged, or convicted of a criminal offense, she is indifferent to intrusions on her privacy or has surrendered all rights to autonomy to her own body. In New York City, tens of thousands of women inmates were coerced into a pelvic exam, a Pap smear, and a breast exam. Until a class-action lawsuit was settled in 2005, every woman admitted to Riker's Island jail was told that if she did not consent to be examined she would be placed in medical isolation.[103] Adding insult to the injury, at least 40,000 men and women were forced to disrobe and sometimes squat for a strip search that took place in view of other inmates.[104]

Dehumanizing stereotypes contribute to a climate that encourages cal-loused care and disregard for women and their medical concerns. Many incarcerated women, but particularly those who are black or Hispanic, are stereotyped as shameless and sexually available. When asked during a tele-vision interview with journalist Ted Koppel whether prison medical staff were performing unnecessary pelvic exams, a California prison medical di-rector suggested that perhaps that some women liked having pelvic exams: "It's the only male contact [the women] get. . . . Maybe there's some gratifi-cation on their part."[105]

Correctional officers often claim women prisoners are chronic com-plainers and con artists who are only seeking attention or drugs.[106] There are thousands of examples where women's complaints were dismissed by correctional staff as unfounded whining or a ploy to secure narcotics when, in fact, their health was in jeopardy. For instance, Trina Brown, a Chowchilla (CA) inmate, was provided with pain medication stronger than Motrin only after her breast cancer had metastasized to her bones and eaten away both of her hips; prison doctors insisted that she was merely trying to feed her former addiction.[107]

Women who want to file an official complaint face obstacles that limit their access to the courts. The Prison Litigation Reform Act (PLRA) of 1996 has made it much harder for prisoners to file lawsuits in federal court. Also, PLRA's cap on attorney fees has made fewer attorneys willing to undertake litigation on behalf of incarcerated individuals. "Jailhouse lawyers"—or incarcerated persons who help others with litigation—are not as common in women's institutions. This makes it less likely that women will be able to call attention to the unconstitutional conditions inside their facilities.

Government funding tends to prioritize health and other initiatives in men's prisons while ignoring the potentially greater impact of educating and treating women.[108] The female population is small relative to the male population, and, overall, women have shorter sentences and are less violent than men. Courts often cite these differences in ruling that incarcerated women are not "similarly situated" to incarcerated men and therefore are not entitled to comparable services, funding for medical facilities, standards for care, and programs under the equal protection clause of the Fourteenth Amendment.[109] These obstacles, combined with common negative stereotypes of incarcerated women, make it less likely that outsiders will pay attention to conditions in women's prisons or that, if the conditions are noticed, the public will demand action.

Conclusion

Many people resist the notion of tax dollars being used to provide services to people who have broken the law. Such thinking is short-sighted. From a strictly economic standpoint, if we do not provide incarcerated women decent health care while they are incarcerated, their poor health will transfer to their communities upon release, and the public will still shoulder the expense of their care and the public health consequences.[110] Besides, even the most fiscally and politically conservative person would have trouble justifying using public funds to employ correctional staff to engage in sexual misconduct or medical malpractice. In relying on a form of punishment that deprives people of liberty, we are, in essence, taking custody and guardianship of them. We are assuming responsibility for inmates' physical health and well-being. This includes the responsibility for making sure that incarcerated women are safe from abuse and exploitation and have competent medical care.

The World Health Organization and most professional medical associations subscribe to the "principle of equivalence."[111] In contrast to the principle of less eligibility, the principle of equivalence holds that inmate-patients have the right to the same standards of medical care as non-inmates. That is, no distinction should be made with respect to medical care between inmates and citizens of the free world.[112] Clearly, we have fallen well short of that mark.

Uniquely female conditions such as menstruation, menopause, and obstetric and gynecological care for women in custody are too often regarded as an afterthought. Prisons have been designed along a "one-size-fits all" model based on a population of men. Women's prisons often operate under policies and procedures designed for prisons that house violent men, even though women are less likely to have a history of committing violence and are less likely to be involved in fatal violence.[113] "For years people apparently felt that an inmate was an inmate was an inmate," warden Dawn Davison points out. "What makes us think that when a woman comes to prison and becomes an inmate, she becomes the same as a man?"[114]

Davison's observation rings true. At the same time, the problem is not simply that women are subjected to a prison system designed with men in mind. Sexual misconduct against women and the neglect of women's gynecologic and reproductive health can only thrive in an environment that thoroughly devalues incarcerated women's worth. Mistreatment is an indication that we are intent on punishing not only a woman's violation of the criminal law but also her transgression against "womanly" behavior. Incarcerated women are categorized as having failed in this enterprise by virtue of their presence in the criminal justice system. In turn, their involvement in criminal activity is used to justify their continued abuse and neglect. Despite the improvement in prison conditions over the past 200 years, the contemporary plight of incarcerated women and girls highlights how far we still have to go to ensure that all women's rights to health and bodily integrity are protected and respected.

PART IV

Mothering

7

"Bad Mothers"
Incarcerated Women's Ties to Their Children

That's how much [my son] means to me, that words can't describe it. I mean, he get on my nerves, but it's okay to get on my nerves. . . . It's just, even when he goes away for the weekends, I'm just sick. I breathe for him. Without him, I don't know where I'd be.

When she said, "rights terminated," I just felt lost. I lost everything. I mean, I had already lost them when they snatched them from me, took them from me, you know what I'm saying? Those are my kids. I had those babies. And they was all I had because a lot of my peoples is dead. So, you snatch them, that was my world. You just took that! What I'm a fight for? What I'm a fight for? You took my babies. So I just continued using drugs. I didn't even think.

—Formerly incarcerated mothers, quoted in Venezia Michalsen, "Going Straight for Her Children? Mothers' Desistance after Incarceration," 2007

Most of the nation's 200,000 incarcerated women are mothers of children who are under the age of 18. Prior to being incarcerated, most women lived with their children.[1] During incarceration, most children of incarcerated women live with a female relative.[2] Over one-half of the mothers incarcerated in state prisons report never having a visit from their young children, and fewer than one in four report a monthly visit.[3] Nearly all of the women will be released eventually and intend to be reunited with their children.[4] Upon release, women will struggle to find good jobs and a reliable source of income.[5]

Despite the steady reminders of these well-worn facts, by and large, incarcerated women remain a nondescript feature of the prison landscape.

To the extent that incarcerated mothers are discussed at all, the discourse tends to be centered on the impact of their incarceration on children, while the women themselves are overlooked completely as both women and mothers.[6] When they are acknowledged outside of academic and activist circles, too often a criminal record or a history of drug abuse or mental disability is treated as de facto evidence of a woman's unsuitability to be a mother. To assume that incarcerated mothers exist only as a contradiction in terms, however, is neither fair nor accurate.

Prisons do house some women convicted of heinous acts of child abuse, but this is a very small proportion of the incarcerated population. In fact, fewer than 3 percent of all women are incarcerated for child abuse.[7] Prison and jails also house a sizable portion of women with mental disorders or drug problems.[8] While a woman's substance use, mental retardation, or mental illness may make it harder for her to be an effective parent, it does not automatically preclude her from being a parent, either legally or practically, or from benefitting from services to support her parenting.[9]

Research suggests that substance use is but one of many factors (such as maternal depression, domestic violence, incarceration, and homelessness) that may place some women at greater risk for parental stress and abusing or neglecting their children.[10] Much of the research that examines the direct effects of substance abuse on parenting has relied on small samples and yielded contradictory results.[11] It is still not clear that substance use, by itself, is associated with child abuse or neglect, and, if it is, how parenting behaviors are affected and what influence the type of substance and the drug using history has.

There also is a shortage of research on the ability of people with mental illnesses to be fit parents.[12] One study found family therapists' determinations of parental fitness were typically made solely on the basis of the parent's mental health status, without the therapist having seen the parent and child together before testifying in court.[13]

Part of the problem is that we lack standards for assessing parental mental health or fitness.[14] Mental health professionals and researchers tend to make their evaluations on the basis of optimal parenting responses.[15] Concluding that the parenting skills of an incarcerated mother with mental disabilities or a drug addiction fall short of *ideal* standards does not mean that a woman is incapable of parenting or that her parenting is so bad that her parental rights should be terminated.[16] Incarceration, drug abuse, mental illness, or mental retardation simply should not be treated as proxy indicators for the permanent inability to parent.

Furthermore, a mother has a well-established and fundamental right to raise her children without undue interference from the government.[17] Under the Constitution and the Fourteenth Amendment's due process clause, people have an essential right to create a home and to the custody, care, companionship, and nurturing of their children. The fundamental right to family relations encompasses the right to not have the state interfere in how a woman decides to raise and educate her children, as well as the right of relatives to live together. The right to parent does not automatically disappear when a woman is incarcerated or even when child abuse or neglect has occurred.

To be sure, a woman's right to parent is not absolute. The rights of an incarcerated woman to be a parent must be balanced against the right of a child to be safe from imminent harm and to receive adequate care. The thousands of cases each year of children being subjected to deplorable acts of cruelty make it clear that many people cannot and should not rear children. If the state has a compelling need to protect a child, and there is no less restrictive means to accomplish this, then a child may be removed from a parent. This does not mean, however, that states have the right to take a child away or terminate a woman's parental rights just because someone else would do a better job or because it would be less complicated from an administrative or family court standpoint.

Prison administrators' emphasis on security, order, and discipline, combined with a widely held tendency to view "incarcerated mothers" as an oxymoron, has led to the opportunity to mother one's children while incarcerated essentially being reduced to a privilege or a reward for good behavior, rather than a fundamental *right*. In this chapter, I adopt the position that the right to parent, by extension, guarantees that a woman has a right to maintain ties to her children while she is incarcerated. In the pages that follow, I highlight those aspects of prison administration, child welfare policy (including the Adoption and Safe Families Act), and post-conviction penalties that make it unnecessarily and unfairly difficult for women with criminal records to preserve and exercise their fundamental right to parent.

Motherhood, Race, Class, and Crime

Arguably no other concepts in this book are as fraught with multiple meanings as "mother" and "family." The yardstick by which all mothers are measured is that of a white, heterosexual, married, middle-class female.[18]

Single motherhood, extended families, female-headed households, family members residing in more than one residence, economic dependence, and mothers deciding not to marry are all arrangements that are less common among white families.[19]

In the wake of the maelstrom of criticism that followed the 1965 publication of what became known as the Moynihan Report (which blamed poverty on the pathology of black families),[20] we may hesitate to openly reproach poor single mothers of color and their families. Still, they are treated as being at odds with predominant ideas about what an American family is supposed to look like and how it is supposed to function.

In myriad ways, society communicates and reinforces the message that "good" mothers are married to male providers. Good mothers stay home to take care of young children. However, poor women who stay at home (as many do, especially when they realize most jobs do not pay enough to cover child care expenses) risk being branded undeserving "welfare queens." Poor minority mothers, whether incarcerated or not, rarely realize the status, social acceptance, protection, and other benefits that society promises to all mothers but, in reality, extends selectively and mainly to those who are white and middle-class.

Most mothers, including economically disadvantaged ones, do *not* turn to crime. Family often serves as a source of social control that protects women against a criminal lifestyle.[21] The responsibility of being a mother often curbs a woman's drug and alcohol use or otherwise protects against more entrenched involvement in crime and the criminal justice system.[22]

Kathryn Edin and Laura Lein interviewed almost 400 welfare and low-income single mothers. Fewer than 1 in 10 welfare-reliant mothers generated extra cash in the illegal underground economy; only 1 in 100 women who relied on wages felt that the risk of losing respectability outweighed the risk of being caught committing a crime.[23] Overwhelmingly, the women in Edin and Lein's study strove to be both good providers and good mothers who kept their children "off the streets, off drugs, out of gangs, not pregnant, and in school."[24] But the income the women earned from welfare and their jobs was insufficient to cover basic expenses. Most of them made up the difference by approaching their children's fathers, boyfriends, family members, and friends; seeking cash jobs in the informal economy; or appealing to charitable organizations.[25] Mothers who did commit crimes for economic reasons tended to do so as a last resort. Women see criminal activity as incompatible with good mothering, and the vast majority of them, Edin and Lein found, do not routinely commit crimes to make ends meet.

Mothers who do engage in crime are led to offend via a variety of pathways.[26] Women's routes to crime often feature childhoods of abuse, abandonment, and poverty and lives punctuated by serious violence.[27] Women report physically and emotionally brutalizing relationships and environments.[28] Many turn to illicit drugs to dull painful memories or violent or highly stressful realities. Getting pregnant at a relatively young age, leaving home, and dropping out of school, combined with the life circumstances that often precede teen pregnancy such as poverty, foster care placement, isolation, and low self-esteem, make it difficult to get a job, especially when one is unskilled or needs to arrange child care.[29] Some women engage in economic crimes (like commercial sex work, selling drugs, stealing, or fraud) to support themselves or their children or to support a drug addiction. In this regard, being a mother, for some women, may act as a "catalyst and a rationale for crime."[30]

Being separated from one's children as the result of illness, incarceration, or the child welfare system also may increase criminal activity or drug use. A team of researchers from the Vera Institute of Justice explored the relationship between drug offenses, maternal incarceration, and foster care in New York City. They drew on information about the mothers of children who entered foster care between July 1, 1996, and June 30, 1997, to examine the chronology of arrest, incarceration, and child placement.[31] The researchers had expected that the war on drugs would lead to more arrests and harsher punishments for minor drug offenses, which, in turn, would lead to more children entering foster care. While this may be taking place, the Vera researchers also found the opposite to be true. At least 90 percent of maternal incarcerations that overlapped with child placement in foster care (and 85 percent of the arrests that preceded the incarcerations) started *after* a child was placed in foster care.[32] Many women cite the pain of being separated from their children or the sense of having "nothing left to lose" as pushing them to resume or increase their use of drugs or alcohol.[33] The mental condition of parents with mental health issues also seems to worsen when children are removed from the home.[34]

Once arrested and convicted, whether or not a woman lives with her children also may influence the type or severity of her sentence.[35] A quantitative study of the sentencing of black men and women drug offenders in the mid-1990s found that when sentencing men, judges seemed mainly concerned with their prior record and the seriousness of the offense. When sentencing women, however, judges considered whether or not the woman lived with a child or with an adult family member.[36] Judges reserved their harshest treatment for women who had children but did not live with them.[37]

Mothering from the Inside

If a woman who has been living with her children is detained pretrial or is sentenced to serve time in a jail or prison, she is confronted with the question: "Who will take care of my children?"[38] Regardless of who is caring for their children or whether their children are in foster care, mothers who are incarcerated face the challenge of maintaining good ties to their children, worrying about their upbringing, and "mothering from the inside."[39] Sometimes, lip service is given to supporting incarcerated women in their efforts to maintain ties to their children, but this is not routinely upheld in practice.[40] Women have to arrange for and "manage" their children's caretakers, while at the same time negotiate their rights to their children.[41] Many also have to demonstrate that they are fit parents to official agencies and family courts.

Many incarcerated women acknowledge their parenting deficiencies and some have mixed feelings about raising their children.[42] But most incarcerated women who are also mothers subscribe to fairly traditional views, including a belief in the appeal of motherhood and a desire to be good mothers.[43] In the absence of benefits and protections extended to them, they still by and large value being mothers. For many, their ties to their children are inextricably entwined with their identity and their sense of self.[44] Separation can exact a huge psychological toll; feelings of grief, emptiness, anger, bitterness, guilt, and fear of loss or rejection are not uncommon among incarcerated mothers.[45]

The separation that accompanies incarceration also may lead to problems for women's children that are not easily overcome. These include emotional problems, aggressiveness, impaired concentration, anxiety, distrust, hostility, alienation, and delinquency, to name a few.[46]

But the impact of separation is neither automatic nor irreversible. Rather, it is shaped by a constellation of factors, such as the nature and strength of a child's attachment to her mother and other people, and the nature and severity of the separation itself. Visits between a mother and her child are a vital and effective means of reducing incarceration's potentially devastating impact on families.[47] "Without visitation," the authors of a report, *Hard Data on Hard Times*, observe, "the government imposes a double punishment on convicted parents: in addition to a loss of liberty, lack of contact may further strain parent-child relationships. In the worst case, lengthy separation without visits leads to the permanent dissolution of the family."[48]

Maintaining Ties and Visiting

Visits between parent and child have been associated with a greater likelihood of successful reunification after release from prison or jail, as well as several positive outcomes for children, including fewer behavior problems, heightened self-esteem, gains in nonverbal IQ scores, better emotional and school adjustment, and better adjustment to foster care.[49] Despite the well-established benefits of visiting, over one-half of women incarcerated in state prisons report never having a person visit with their children.[50] According to 1997 data, only around one in four women receive monthly visits with their children, and only around one-half reported monthly phone contact.[51] A more recent study of previously incarcerated women released in the New York City area found that nearly two-thirds had no visits from their children and almost one-half had no phone contact.[52]

Some caregivers, mothers, social service workers, and others prefer that the children do not visit. Especially when the visiting conditions are not suitable for family visits, they may have reservations about children visiting a prison. Caretakers and mothers may be embarrassed by the fact of the incarceration and do not want the children to experience similar shame. A mother may not want her children to see her locked up or to be subjected to intrusive searches and long waits. She may prefer to avoid the painful good-byes. The children themselves may not want to see their mother or may react badly to being separated from their mother by a pane of glass. These eventualities, however, do not negate the fact that mothers and children have a right to see one another.[53] And the experience of some children being hostile or indifferent to maintaining ties to their mothers is a much less common and pressing problem than that of families who wish to be or remain connected but are prevented from doing so.

An incarcerated mother's ability to maintain ties to her children depends on an array of factors, many of which are beyond her control.[54] It is nearly impossible for a woman to maintain a relationship with her child without the cooperation of the caregiver.[55] Her relationship with her children's caretaker; the emotional, physical, and financial well-being of the caretaker; the ages of the children; and the mother's relationship to her children before she was incarcerated all play a role.[56]

Other obstacles are structural or institutional, rather than interpersonal. The widespread use of incarceration, the lengthy sentences many women receive, and the imprisonment of women in prisons far from their homes all pose significant barriers. The impact of incarceration on families would be offset if the United States did not rely so heavily on incarceration to begin with. Incarceration rates in the United States are four times higher than the world average, and the United States incarcerates three times more women than any other nation.[57] Overall, women sentenced to state prison serve an average of about two years before they are released. Women convicted of violent offenses can expect to serve at least three to four years before they are released.[58] Even a short period of incarceration can make a lasting impression on a child.

Most women are imprisoned in geographically remote areas, which makes it difficult to transport children for visits. More than 60 percent of all parents in state prison are held more than 100 miles away from their last place of residence.[59] In New York, for instance, about 40 percent of women are held in Albion, a facility 370 miles away from New York City, the last residence of most of the women who are incarcerated.[60] In many states, women are sent outside of the state to serve their sentences.[61] In 2005, a survey of state departments of corrections recorded at least 499 women in 43 states (and 4,275 men) who had been transferred to out-of-state facilities; most of these were private facilities.[62] About one-half of state departments of corrections try to assign inmates to facilities near their families; the other half do not or cannot because there is only one prison.[63] In at least one state system, the department of corrections seems to treat living near one's family as a "reward" for good behavior rather than a desirable goal undertaken out of a commitment to preserving inmates' ties to family members.[64]

Other obstacles stem from the way the prisons themselves are run. There is much in the way of prison services, facilities, programming, and policies that should be reconsidered with an eye toward making it easier for incarcerated women (and men) to maintain ties with their families, including their children.[65]

PHONE CALLS

Without reliable access to information and telephones, incarcerated mothers probably will not be consulted in decisions about child-rearing, education, and medical care or even informed of the decisions that are made.[66]

Inmates' access to phones is extremely limited, and correctional facilities do not routinely offer reliable message-taking services for inmates. Typically, women can only make expensive collect calls to predesignated numbers; many caregivers cannot afford the additional expense of regular or frequent collect calls, especially when they must pay inflated rates. These rates can be as much as $17 for a 15-minute out-of-state call.

Across the country, telephone companies pay so-called commissions to state prison systems in return for a monopoly on the service. For instance, families of men and women in New York state correctional facilities paid phone rates 630 percent higher than normal consumer rates.[67] A kickback contract with a phone company gave New York State Department of Correctional Services 60 percent of the mark-up. In January 2007, Governor Eliot Spitzer agreed to forego the state's share of the markup, but the corporate mark-up remained. In June 2007, legislation was passed stating that future contracts for telephone services would be based on achieving the lowest possible cost to the telephone users, rather than making a profit. Nationwide, the Campaign to Promote Equitable Telephone Charges (eTc) continues to push for legislation that would put an end to prisoners' families being forced to foot the bill for exorbitantly priced phone calls.[68]

SPECIAL VISITING AREAS

Some facilities offer child-friendly visiting rooms, playgrounds, and separate visiting days in hopes of providing a less intimidating and more natural setting for the visits.[69] Some prisons arrange for volunteers (who may be other incarcerated women) to play with the children so that the adults can have at least a short conversation about "adult business" out of the child's earshot. But most prisons and jails fail to provide adequate or suitable space, staff, and resources to support family visiting. Visiting areas are often too crowded, too loud, or otherwise not conducive to good visiting. These poor conditions often discourage caregivers and social workers from arranging or encouraging visits between a mother and her child.

OVERNIGHT VISITS

Extended visits or contact with an infant or child without the presence of the substitute caregiver provide the opportunity to develop or solidify a mother-child relationship, as well as practical, hands-on parenting experience. Only a few facilities permit day-long or overnight visits between mothers and infants or small children without the presence of caregivers, or arrange for an infant to live with his incarcerated mother. Around one-fifth of state departments of corrections provide housing in at least one facility for mothers and their infants or small children.[70] Some of the housing options include in-facility nurseries (with or without special housing) and space for overnight visits. In 2001, only six agencies provided mother-child housing for children from infancy to the age of 18 months.

Bedford Hills Correctional Facility in Bedford, NY, is one of a growing number of women's prisons in the United States that allows a woman to keep her newborn with her in the nursery for the first year to 18 months of the baby's life.[71] A similar program at the neighboring Taconic facility requires that a mother remain with her child at all times, except when she attends a treatment program for an hour or two in the afternoon, during which time her infant is handed over to inmate caregivers, most of whom are also mothers. Preliminary data suggest that the babies in the prison nursery are developmentally the same as other babies, even a year after the mother is released.[72]

Another possibility is to permit women under criminal justice supervision to serve their sentences while living with their children in the community.[73] The Mother-Child Community Corrections Project undertook an inventory of such programs in 2001. Some programs are residential (e.g., a diversion program or halfway house), while others are nonresidential but involve day reporting, case management, work or education release, or home detention. Several of the residential programs restrict the number of children or specify that children must be younger than five or six years of age.[74]

Also, it seems that the number of spaces available in community programs is outstripped by the number of women who might benefit from participating in them. Of course, to avoid reinforcing stereotypes about what roles women "ought" to be occupying in society, opportunities for supervision in the community should be widely available to all women, not just those who are mothers.

Not all community supervision programs designed for mothers are inherently pro-woman in their approach. The Missouri Mothers Choosing Change drug court program targets women who have been charged with or who have pled guilty to endangering the welfare of a child because they gave birth to a child who tested positive for methamphetamine or cocaine at birth. Although the mothers are not incarcerated, they may be placed in short-term custody if they fail to comply with the program's rules. The program requires that women pay fees *in full* (ranging from $130 to $840, for a total of $1,970 for the 18-month program) before being permitted to move to the next level. These fees essentially put a price tag on women's rights to retain her parental rights to her children and raise serious equal protection issues.[75]

Foster Care and the Termination of Parental Rights

Whether or not an incarcerated woman has an open child protective services or family court case (i.e., a child in foster care), and if she does, whether or not the foster parent is a relative can have tremendous implications for a woman's ability to maintain a presence in her children's lives while she is imprisoned.[76] Each arrangement poses its own sense of challenges for an incarcerated woman who has children. Trying to "do mothering" from prison is hard on virtually every incarcerated woman who has children. Some mothers, particularly those whose children are in non-kin foster care, also face the heightened risk of having their parental rights terminated.

An estimated 70 to 80 percent of incarcerated mothers who lived with their children prior to being incarcerated have children living with their own parents or other family member, such as a sister or an aunt.[77] Good information does not exist with regard to the number or percentage of women whose children are not in the foster care system at all, are in kin foster care, or who are in non-kinship foster care. Information on the placement and whereabouts of prisoners' children is not routinely collected by state departments of correction. The most widely cited estimate is that about 10 percent of incarcerated women have children who reside in non-kin foster families.[78] Agency workers and others, however, suspect that this is probably an underestimate.[79]

The children of most incarcerated women live with a grandparent or other family member and are not under the supervision of family court or in the foster care system.[80] Having a child live with a relative who can provide not only a stable home but also cultural and community continuity is usually in the child's best interest. For instance, if a child is able to stay in her original home or neighborhood, or stay with a relative that she has grown up with, then the smells, sounds, tastes, and surroundings of the home will be familiar to her. She will be able to stay in the same school, play in the same playgrounds, see the same people, and shop in the same stores as before the incarceration.

A mother who is facing a short period of incarceration may grant temporary power of attorney to the relative who is providing full-time care for her child. In the case of longer sentences, a caregiver may be named the child's legal guardian or formally allocated the parental responsibilities (or "legal custody"). All of these arrangements permit the caregiver to make decisions about child-rearing, education, and medical treatment without the mother relinquishing all of her parental rights.

Each of these custody arrangement options has implications that must be weighed carefully. They vary in the decision-making rights that a parent retains and in whether and what sort of court involvement is required. For example, legal guardianship reduces a mother's decision-making authority. Unlike assigning power of attorney, guardianship can only be revoked or changed by a judge. But whereas the power of attorney must be renewed every year, guardianship allows for longer-term custody arrangements. If a woman cannot take care of her children because of mental disability, drug or alcohol dependency, or some other condition, child protective services could become involved and place the child with someone who is a stranger to the family. Assigning a legal guardian may prevent such intervention from taking place. Custody arrangements may determine whether the caregiver qualifies for benefits such as TANF (Temporary Assistance for Needy Families), Medicaid, and food stamps for the children.[81] The issue of caregivers' eligibility for public benefits is particularly important because many families of incarcerated women are already financially strapped; agreeing to care for another child adds to this burden.[82]

On the one hand, when there is no child protective services involvement, then there is no imminent risk of a woman having her parental rights terminated. On the other hand, the lack of child protective services involvement means that there is no system in place to compel the relative caring for the children to bring the children for visits, answer phone calls, or otherwise maintain contact. An incarcerated mother could petition the family court for help, but many women are reluctant to do so for fear that court involvement could make the situation worse.

Also, in some cases, the kin or legal guardian may, at some point, no longer be able to provide for the child or may themselves be accused of abuse or neglect, thus opening a family court case. In these instances, even though the mother is not the one who is accused of the neglect or abuse, she may be at risk of having her parental rights terminated under the provisions of the Adoption and Safe Families Act of 1997, discussed below.

Some women's children, then, live with a family member *and* are in the foster care system.[83] The Adoption and Safe Families Act has a kinship placement exception that allows the 15-month limit for a child leaving foster care to be extended if a child is living with a relative. However, at best, the timeline may be extended, not revoked, so some risk of terminating parental rights still exists.[84] Mothers potentially benefit from kin foster care (as opposed to legal guardianship) because the kin caregiver is technically subject to the same expectations as other foster families. These include not only keeping the child safe and providing an adequate level of care but also maintaining communication and regular visits with the mother while she is incarcerated. Often, however, caseworkers overseeing the case will let this latter expectation slide with kin foster parents because the foster parent is family and because underpaid and overworked caseworkers are preoccupied with the non-kin foster cases.[85] It is this latter group, women whose children are in long-term foster care with nonrelatives, who arguably have the most at stake. Although a minority of all incarcerated mothers, these women are at the greatest risk of having their parental rights involuntarily terminated.

The Adoption and Safe Families Act and the Termination of Parental Rights

The surrender or termination of parental rights is a required precursor to adoption, in cases where the parent does not surrender his or her rights voluntarily. A handbook produced by Legal Services of New Jersey explains the termination of parental rights in the following way:

> If your parental rights to your child are terminated, you will no longer have the right to visit with them, speak to them on the telephone, communicate with them by mail, or be told where they are or what is happening to them. Your relationship and your family's relationship with your children will be permanently and completely ended.[86]

Venezia Michalsen interviewed 100 formerly incarcerated women who had children for her doctoral dissertation. She found that around one-third of the women had their parental rights terminated for at least one of their children.[87] The circumstances under which an incarcerated mother's parental rights may be terminated can be roughly grouped into three categories.[88] One, a child may be living with a family member who is not a natural parent and the family member initiates the proceeding. While this might be less traumatic than having the state initiate the proceeding, it can still be a painful and demoralizing experience. One woman described how her own mother told her she needed to relinquish her parental rights so that her daughter would be eligible for some government assistance. "She wanted me to make that decision right then and there on the phone," she recalled. "I just dropped the phone. I was like wow! . . . I felt like just an incubator."[89]

Two, a parent can voluntarily surrender her rights. This may allow her to retain a sense of influence over her children's future. A woman described going to family court with her mother and asking the judge to let her mother take them, thus avoiding the involvement of the child protection system. "Now they grown," she noted. "They on they own now anyway, but they was never taken away from me."[90] In some instances, a woman will file a petition for voluntary termination because she recognizes that having her rights involuntarily terminated may adversely affect future proceedings in a case involving another child.[91] Mothers also may voluntarily (and in some cases, conditionally) surrender their rights because they believe that with an open adoption, they will be able to stay in touch or regain contact at some point down the road. However, open adoption agreements are not enforced in every state; adoptive parents in those states do not have to keep any promises they may have made about allowing the biological mother to have continued contact with or information about the child after the adoption.

Three, the child may be in the care and custody of the state already and the state initiates the termination proceeding. It is this situation that has been the cause of much concern, especially since the passage of the federal Adoption and Safe Families Act (ASFA) in 1997, which was intended to provide foster children with some stability so that they would not be shuttled from one temporary placement to another or languish in foster care.[92] The act assumes that every child needs permanency, even if this means moving to adoption (and severing ties with birth parents) much faster. Under this model, permanency is the goal of the process rather than keeping a family together or reunification.

ASFA's provisions stipulate that a plan for the child's permanent placement is prepared whenever a child enters foster care. A foster care agency's permanency plan typically involves making concurrent plans for permanency rather than sequential ones.[93] That is, child welfare staff must actively work toward one goal, which—at least initially—is usually keeping the family together or reunification, and at the same time prepare an alternative plan (such as adoption, placement with a relative, permanent or long-term foster care, or independent living) in case reunification is ruled out.[94]

Time Limits

When a child enters foster care, a clock starts to tick. ASFA requires states to seek to terminate parental rights after a child has been in foster care for 15 of the last 22 months. Some states specify shorter time limits, particularly for very young children, or may extend the time limit if it is deemed to be in the best interests of the child.[95] During this time period, the state must make "reasonable efforts" to prevent the removal of the child or to reunite the child with his or her family.

In some cases, the state does not need to wait 15 months to initiate the termination of parental rights (TPR) proceedings or demonstrate that it has made reasonable efforts. These include occasions where the parent has been convicted of certain crimes such as murdering another child, the parent has had their parental rights terminated with another child, or the child has been abandoned.

In some jurisdictions, courts consider incarceration an aspect of abandonment and use it to justify the termination of parental rights. Many women are sentenced to periods of incarceration that exceed the ASFA time limits. Women sentenced to state prison tend to serve 24–26 months before being released (or 36–45 months for women convicted of violent offenses), a period that exceeds the minimum number of months that a child can be in foster care before a termination proceeding must be filed under ASFA.[96]

In 2005, some 36 states had TPR statutes that explicitly mentioned incarceration.[97] Of these, 25 were time-driven: they permitted rights to be terminated on the basis of the sentence length. About one-half of these specified the time frame ("more than one year"), while the others did not (e.g., "for a period of years"). Only a handful of states stipulated that incarceration alone cannot be grounds for termination, and a few others provided for added flexibility in cases involving incarcerated parents.[98]

The Child Welfare League of America tried to measure ASFA's effect on incarcerated parents.[99] In many of the cases the researchers examined, serious child abuse or ongoing substance abuse problems would have been a concern even in the absence of ASFA. But in around one out of every five cases, ASFA time limits and other provisions—not child abuse or substance abuse—seemed to be the main reason for terminating incarcerated parents' rights.

Critics fear that without adequate information about the incarcerated woman's circumstances and her relationships with her children, foster care agencies and family courts may decide the children's future based on the number of months in foster care rather than what is best for the children. Virginia family judges' comments such as "[the parent] didn't remedy situation in a sufficient amount of time" or "although [the mother's] efforts are commendable, she did not make substantial improvements to her situation within the mandated period of time" corroborate these concerns.[100] The result is that permanency may be sacrificed in favor of expediency.[101]

Maintaining the Mother-Child Relationship

An agency caseworker is obliged to make efforts to support visiting between all children in foster care and their mothers, regardless of whether or not the mother is incarcerated. The failure to do so has more serious consequences for incarcerated parents, however, because of their dependence on others' cooperation to sustain contact with their children. For incarcerated mothers with children in foster care, the stakes are extremely high and the obstacles are many.[102]

ASFA permits extensions of the 15-month limit if a child is living with a relative (in states permitting such extensions), if the foster care agency has not made diligent or reasonable efforts to provide the services required by the reunification plan, or if the foster care agency documents other compelling reasons why termination would not be in the child's best interest (such as the emotional bond that exists between the mother and child).[103] Visiting and custody decisions rest mainly in the hands of family court judges who are expected to determine what is in the best interests of the child. The "best interests" standard is not articulated clearly. This leaves judges free to exert considerable discretion and allows considerable room for personal bias to shape the decisions.

Although incarcerated mothers can seek extensions of the time limits or other exemptions from termination, child protection agencies in many states do not routinely encourage such efforts, especially when the child is an infant. Caseworkers who don't realize that a child has a close and sustained relationship with the incarcerated parent are unlikely to request or invoke these exemptions in court. A mother's contact with her child may take place mainly through phone calls and the occasional visit. Many caseworkers will not witness that relationship firsthand and thus may not appreciate the reality, nature, and depth of the bond, much less be in a position to convince a judge of its existence. Martha L. Raimon, then of the Women's Prison Association, worried that "instead of looking closely at the circumstances, agencies push the button for termination. It's faster, it's cleaner, it doesn't take as much work. I'm afraid we're sucking large numbers of children and parents down a black hole who otherwise could have maintained their family ties."[104]

Although states vary in their requirements, in most states, foster families (both kin and non-kin) are required to support a mother's relationship with her children and her access to the services necessary to achieve reunification (if that is part of the permanency plan). Non-kin foster families are not required to deliver children to services or take the child to visit a parent in prison, however.[105] Even many kin foster families do not take children to visit their mothers. This situation often goes unnoticed and unaddressed by the foster care agency.

If foster parents cannot or will not arrange for a child to visit with the mother, some states require that the agency facilitate these visits as part of the "reasonable efforts to reunify" mandate. Courts may order (sometimes at the mother's request) collect phone calls, visits, plans for transporting the child to visits, and counseling. In some cases, the agency goes to court to suspend the visits.

Women have a right to a hearing in family court before they can be denied reasonable visitation rights, regardless of whether or not they are incarcerated.[106] However, many women are not aware that they have this right. Communication and transportation problems between courts and corrections may mean that mothers miss attending family court hearings even when the termination of parental rights is at stake. An incarcerated parent also must depend on the department of corrections to transport her so she can attend court dates. Some women must testify by telephone. Also, ASFA does not require continuity of legal representation. A woman may find that the attorney who defends her against abuse and neglect charges (who may be at least somewhat familiar with her case) is not the same attorney who deals with the termination of parental rights or other family court proceedings. And, while states provide attorneys for women facing the termination of parental rights, incarcerated women may have to represent themselves or retain a private attorney for visitation hearings.[107]

Even when termination is not imminent, agency workers and social workers must overcome significant hurdles in trying to arrange or facilitate visits, in part because they must navigate two large and confusing bureaucracies: the child protection system and the correctional system.[108] These bureaucracies are not in the habit of working together. This makes it difficult to arrange visits or establish whether a woman is able to care for her child upon her release. Agency workers have to coordinate schedules to make sure the mother and the child are both available for the visit. The longer a woman is incarcerated, the greater the likelihood that she or her child will experience a change in placement. Women may be relocated to another facility, and children may be moved to another foster home. In California, one-third of children who entered and remained in foster care for more than a year experienced three or more placements.[109]

Agency workers have to arrange transportation and either accompany the child or arrange for a staff member to do so, on day-long or overnight visits. In some cases, workers may not understand the nature of their obligation. For instance, in New York City, the Administration for Children's Services reimburses agencies for travel related to visits more than 50 miles away, while agencies are responsible for reimbursing for visits within a 50-mile radius.[110] Some workers, however, have misunderstood the policy to mean that they were not obligated to arrange visits for children whose parents were located more than 50 miles away.

Social workers' caseloads often do not permit them to meet with an incarcerated mother to arrange visits or to coordinate services. Courts do not routinely order mediation that could humanize and facilitate the relationship between the foster parent, the caseworker or social worker, and the mother. The power imbalance and the politically and emotionally charged context in which decisions are made means that a good working relationship among the key players is difficult to achieve without some form of mediation or routine contact to help them trust and respect one another.

A woman whose child was in foster care objected: "Don't go throwing words around like 'partnership.' Because no one who has the power to take away my child is my partner."[111] Another woman observed that "the foster families hold all the power . . . and the state already thinks that they do a better job than me. What chance do I have? They have a better house, more money, and there are two of them and one of me. I feel like they are judging me all of the time. Sometimes I think it would be easier if I just gave up . . . and then I say no, I love my kids and I can be a good mom to them."[112]

Demonstrating Rehabilitation

A mother with children in foster care must show meaningful participation with the state agency's case plan and complete the services outlined within a certain time frame if she is to avoid termination of her parental rights. The case plan may include instructions that she is to undergo counseling, attend classes on parenting and anger management, be subjected to random drug testing, complete a drug treatment program, and, if she is being released, obtain housing and a job. In many cases, it is virtually impossible for an incarcerated woman to demonstrate that she has been rehabilitated or is otherwise someone whose parental rights should not be terminated. Many of the services incarcerated women seek or need (e.g., drug treatment or parenting classes) are unavailable in the prison or have long waiting lists. Within the same state, there may be wide variation in the resources that women can access while incarcerated or under court supervision in the community. Almost all of the prisons in a 2002 national study provided parenting classes for their female inmates, but only 14 offered parenting classes with children present.[113] Most of the parent-child programs offered are run by outside providers, and the quality of the programs varies widely.[114] Some of the so-called programs may include only a few hours of general discussion on parenting.[115] Women may be deterred from participating if they must pay for the textbooks or materials used in the courses.

Mothers with mental illness face additional challenges to demonstrating they are rehabilitated.[116] Without high-quality mental health services, such women often accumulate disciplinary infractions on their record as they find themselves unable to adapt to and cope with the military-style routines and rules of prison life. Around one-half of women prisoners with mental health problems are charged with violating facility rules (compared with about one-third of women without mental problems).[117] Given correctional facilities' emphasis on security and order, such a history may make a woman ineligible to participate in the programs she needs to demonstrate that her parental rights should not be terminated. On other occasions, a woman may be labeled as mentally ill or addicted in order to help her gain access to reunification services, only to find later that these labels may be used against her in family court.[118]

On top of everything else, there is no guarantee that judges will recognize the efforts that women have made. A New Jersey woman, referred to in court records as "S.A.," was addicted to heroin.[119] Her rights to her young son were terminated in 2004. A few months later, while incarcerated on charges of possessing methadone without a prescription, S.A. gave birth to a girl, "Kate." S.A. was likely to be released before her daughter's first birthday. According to S.A., she and her mother called the Division of Youth and Family Services (DYFS) on several occasions but did not receive a return phone call. There was also unrefuted evidence that S.A. had been making substantial and largely successful efforts to address her addiction.

The family court terminated S.A.'s parental rights six months after Kate was born in proceedings that the appeals court described as "unjustifiably rushed." There was no inquiry about S.A.'s potential fitness as a parent or whether foster care was in Kate's best interest. As the appeals court later ruled, the speed with which the termination proceedings took place effectively barred S.A. from having contact with her daughter, frustrated any extended efforts at rehabilitation, and discouraged meaningful planning for her life after she was released. While DYFS was not required to offer services (since S.A.'s rights to another child had been terminated), the appeals court rejected the idea that this gave the state service agency the license to ignore S.A.'s efforts to have contact with her daughter, since her rights at that time remained intact. In February 2006 (a year after the termination proceeding), a New Jersey appeals court finally ruled that the family court had improperly terminated S.A.'s parental rights.

Post-Incarceration Issues

Women who are involved in the criminal justice system are held accountable to a mothering ideal that, by definition, their economic and social circumstances often preclude them from ever meeting. Upon release from prison, women who are mothers look forward to the prospect of reconnecting with their families and possibly reuniting with their children.[120] They are confronted with enormous challenges, though. Many mothers are unsure what they need to do to be reunited with their child or where they are in the reunification process. One study of 100 women released from prison found that nearly three-quarters had not yet reunified with their children, though most of these women were seeking reunification with at least one child.[121]

Some court orders are unrealistic, such as requiring a woman to complete drug treatment within 15 months, even though the available programs are 18 months long. Publicly funded community treatment slots often have wait lists of weeks or even months. Wait lists are longest for residential programs. Women transitioning from a jail or prison treatment program into the community need immediate admission into treatment. Even a delay of one day between release and treatment can result in a lost opportunity for a woman to begin or resume treatment.[122]

Mothers often only have a year to demonstrate that they have been rehabilitated as parents. They are not helped in their reunification efforts by family therapists who recommend that the "family needs at least 1 year of family therapy" or that the mother needs "at least 2 years of therapy."[123]

The post-release adjustment itself can be quite daunting.[124] One woman responded with anxiety to the news that she would be rejoined with her children a week after she was released:

> Now, I think that is pretty harsh. I've been on my own for a whole year, and then I come out and have the kids slammed on me, which anybody would think, "God, you'd think you'd want the kids back," but I don't know if I can cope. A week out, and that's all they're giving me to get my head back together again, and then I've got the routine of the children. I think that's a bit too much.[125]

Incarcerated women's lives are circumscribed by a web of regulation and surveillance. The same is also true for criminal justice-involved women who are not incarcerated but are expected to comply with probation, parole, or drug court requirements. The stress is keenly felt by single mothers, whose resources may already be strained.[126] In order to remain "free," women are expected to get a job and participate in some form of community supervision. Yet the more conditions to which they are subjected, the harder it is for them to meet all the demands, the greater the likelihood that they will violate, and the greater the likelihood that a violation will be noticed, risking a return to incarceration. As Alicia, a woman subject to intensive probation conditions, described:

> They expect us to have a full-time job, which is fine, counseling four times a week, on top of community service two hours a day; so that's ten hours a week, so where is the time for your kids? And they know some people have kids, but they don't care. You mess up any step of the law and they're violating you and putting you in prison. . . . And if you don't go to counseling when they say to go, you're violated even if you drop clean every day.[127]

Women also struggle to gain economic access to their right to bring up their children, as indicated by the challenges to securing housing and a stable source of income, such as a job.[128]

Housing

Parole conditions typically require a stable address so that parole officers can make home visits to check on the parolee's progress. In many areas, few housing alternatives exist for individuals who cannot live in public housing or with friends or relatives. Consequently, many previously in-carcerated women live in homeless shelters or other forms of temporary housing, which are correlated with higher rates of re-arrest.[129] In many cit-ies, gentrification also has reduced the amount of affordable housing. Al-though many women live with a family member once they're released from prison, this is not a viable option for all parolees. Families may already live in overcrowded conditions or are struggling to make ends meet. For some parolees, living with family members may be a source of stress and temp-tation rather than a safe haven; about 10 percent of the drug users in one study had at least one family member who had used cocaine in the past 30 days.[130]

Since 1996, public housing authorities and other providers of federally assisted housing have the option of denying housing to certain individuals, including those who use illegal drugs.[131] In 2002, the Supreme Court ruled that public housing officials could evict entire families if a guest or some-one in the household was convicted of a drug offense. As a result, many women cannot go home to public housing without putting their families and friends at risk of eviction.[132]

Although private landlords are not permitted to refuse to rent to some-one on the basis of a conviction for past drug use, a person convicted of the sale or manufacture of drugs, or someone who is currently a drug user, is not protected.[133] Furthermore, while the law ostensibly protects against discrimination on the basis of drug addiction, landlords do not necessarily refrain from acting on their biases, and the laws are not always enforced in a rigorous or timely fashion.

Income and Employment

Past or present drug use and criminal involvement makes it hard for many persons released from prison to obtain a stable source of income. The 1996 federal welfare law bans people convicted of drug felonies from receiving public assistance benefits and food stamps for the rest of their lives, even if they overcome a drug addiction or have otherwise demonstrated that they are rehabilitated. People convicted of other offenses (including violent of-fenses) are not subjected to such a ban. Some states have eliminated the ban entirely or limited the ban in some ways (for example, by requiring treatment), but 17 states have adopted the ban without modification.[134]

Poor women across the country are seriously disadvantaged when try-ing to enter the job market, and women recently released from prison face additional challenges. Some of the problems stem from the women's lack of marketable skills or human capital.[135] Nearly one-half of all persons incarcerated in state prison for drug convictions have not completed high school or earned their GED.[136] Many women have histories of extensive drug use or other medical problems that prevent them from qualifying for better-paying jobs that require heavy manual labor.[137]

Job discrimination and employment bans also get in the way of a woman with a criminal record securing employment or otherwise being able to support her children.[138] Job discrimination against persons with felony convictions is common. Most states permit public and private employers and occupational licensing agencies to disqualify applicants with any kind of criminal record, no matter how inconsequential the criminal history, how long ago the offense occurred, or how good the applicant's work history and qualifications.[139] Consequently, formerly incarcerated women are often banned from jobs for which they may be well suited or have practical experience. These include caring for children, disabled, or aged persons; working in assisted living facilities, nursing homes, camps, schools, or after-school programs; delivering meals-on-wheels; or working for transportation companies.

A report issued by the Boston Foundation and the Criminal Justice Institute highlighted some of the problems with criminal record reporting in Massachusetts.[140] Criminal record information is often inaccurate and may actually refer to another individual with the same date of birth and a similar name. Also, the system serves two very different end-users: law enforcement officials (who presumably have the skills necessary to read and interpret the report) and prospective employers outside the criminal justice system, who may not know how to accurately interpret the report. Employers may reject applicants with a long record, even if many of the charges listed in the report were dismissed or are years old. Many potential employers do not have guidelines to help them determine how particular criminal history information should be interpreted. This may result in their applying unnecessarily stringent standards. Also, in Massachusetts and elsewhere, felony and misdemeanor convictions are recorded for at least 15 and 10 years, respectively. Consequently, individuals may be held accountable for offenses that no longer have any bearing on their present ability to handle a job. David Nidus of the Fortune Society concludes that "law and reality often don't mix well, since an employer interested in keeping ex-offenders out of the workplace can almost always find some other element on which to base the rejection of a client."[141]

Conclusion

Despite mounting public concern about incarceration and conditions of confinement, in all likelihood, incarceration will figure prominently in our responses to crime for the foreseeable future. Without a fundamental shift in our approaches to punishment and parenthood, incarcerated women will continue to be scapegoated and widely assumed to be incompetent mothers, should their parenting be acknowledged at all. High-profile cases of often horrific neglect and abuse contribute to the perception that low-income women—not just those who are incarcerated—are unfit mothers. At the same time, we may idealize foster and adoptive parents who are perceived as having better incomes, better homes, and less chaotic lives.

The criminal justice system features the incarceration of thousands of women for a few years in geographically remote areas away from their families and other loved ones. The child protection system offers serious time constraints, an emphasis on the stability of the child's placement rather than reunification, and caseworkers and social workers burdened with heavy caseloads and scarce resources. Indeed, it is hard to imagine a situation that was better designed to fail incarcerated women and their children than the current one.

It is not clear that ASFA and the emphasis on terminating parental rights based on time frames provide any overall social benefit for children. ASFA and the policies described earlier also depend on and perpetuate a false dichotomy that pits parents' rights against children's rights. The tendency of some judges, agency workers, and foster parents to see the mother-child relationship as an adversarial one precludes serious consideration of how material and social assistance to mothers and other caregivers stands to benefit children as well.[142] In *Shattered Bonds: The Color of Child Welfare*, law professor Dorothy Roberts points out that the system in America emphasizes child protection, not child welfare. The system focuses not on assisting parents in providing for the welfare of their children but on protecting children by threatening to take women's children away. America has tolerated this *because* of the color of America's child welfare system, Roberts concludes. "This protective function falls heaviest on African American parents," Roberts asserts, "because they are most likely to suffer from poverty and institutional discrimination and to be blamed for the effects on their children."[143]

A more sympathetic view of incarcerated mothers as uneducated, victimized, downtrodden, world-weary women is, on the face, preferable to one that assumes their incompetence. This perspective, however, also masks the diversity of women's backgrounds and experiences. It ignores their strengths and mitigates against the possibility that many incarcerated women are or aspire to be capable, loving mothers.

Many of the known negative consequences of incarceration could be offset if we made it easier for incarcerated women and their families to become or stay connected, provided more support for the substitute caregivers, and addressed the problem of overburdened and underresourced foster care agencies. As sociologist Barbara Katz Rothman notes, motherhood is "a, and maybe *the,* prime relationship, primary in the lifespan of the person being mothered, primary in establishing our understandings of what it is to be connected with another human being."[144] By supporting an incarcerated mother's efforts to establish or maintain ties to her children, we are helping her in ways that play an important role in her own rehabilitation and well-being, as well as the households and communities of which she and her children are a part.[145] In doing so, we acknowledge society's stake in seeing a family succeed.

8

"Asking for It"

Battered Women and Child Custody

Every woman needs a good pounding every now and then.
— Donald R. Roberts, North Country (NY) village justice, who
refused a woman's request for an order of protection against her
husband (quoted in *New York Times*, September 25, 2006)

In 1999, Jessica Gonzales obtained a restraining order against
her estranged husband, Simon, who had a history of abusive and erratic
behavior. The order barred him from contact with her and their three
young daughters, ages 7, 9, and 10, and stipulated that the police were to
arrest Simon if he violated the order. A month later, Simon took the girls
without permission. Jessica called the police at 7:30 P.M. who told her to
call back at 10 P.M. if the girls had not returned. An hour later, Jessica called
the police again and told them that she had spoken to Simon on his cell
phone and he was at an amusement park. She requested that the police
arrest him there. They didn't. Jessica called two more times over the next
few hours, and each time was told to call back later. Jessica drove to her
husband's apartment and found it empty. She called the police, but after
40 minutes, no officer had arrived. Jessica drove to the police station and
filed an incident report. The officer who made the report left for a dinner
break without taking any action. At 3:20 A.M., Simon drove up to the police
station and started shooting a gun that he had purchased, as it turns out,
only an hour after he had taken the girls. During the gun battle, Simon was
killed. Afterward, police officers discovered Jessica's three daughters, dead,
in Simon's truck.

But the story doesn't end there. Jessica sued the town of Castle Rock,
Colorado, for refusing to enforce the restraining order against her husband.

In 2005, the Supreme Court ruled in *Castle Rock v. Gonzales* that police are exempt from legal action, even when their refusal to enforce a valid restraining order resulted in death.[1] As NOW president Kim Gandy observed, "The U.S. Supreme Court just hung a 'shoot here' sign around the necks of battered women and their children all across the country."[2]

Child abductions are not uncommon. Some 200,000 children are abducted by family members each year; in most of these cases, the abductor is a man in his 30s or 40s, typically the child's biological father.[3] In about 60 percent of all cases, the police are contacted, usually to recover the child from a known location or to help locate a missing child.[4] In the vast majority of cases, the child is returned; however, in more than one-half of all cases, the child is gone for a week or more. In around 44 percent of family abductions, the child is concealed, and in almost one in five cases, the children are moved out of state with the intent to make recovery difficult. Typically the abductor intends to prevent contact between the child and the mother and to change the custody arrangements permanently.

Intimate partner violence is an even bigger problem, accounting for one-fifth of all nonfatal violence and nearly one-third of fatal homicides among females 12 years of age and older.[5] According to estimates from the National Crime Victimization Survey, in 2001, an estimated 590,000 women experienced physical violence by their current or former intimate partners, who are usually—though not always—heterosexual men.[6] Most rapes and other physical assaults against women are committed by a current or former spouse, a live-in partner, or a date.[7] As many as one in five rapes are marital rapes (that is, nonconsensual sexual acts between a woman and her husband, ex-husband, or intimate long-term partner).[8] Around 1,200 women in the United States are killed each year by a husband, ex-husband, or boyfriend.[9]

Sociologist Michael Johnson distinguishes among four types of intimate partner violence, two of which are especially relevant to the present discussion.[10] "Intimate terrorism" (originally known as "patriarchal terrorism") escalates over time and is more likely to cause injury. Intimate terrorism is motivated by a man's need for power and control in the relationship; it helps us understand why an abuser's violence against a woman may actually escalate when the woman leaves or attempts to leave the relationship. Also, men who engage in intimate terrorism are most likely to institute custodial challenges as a means of scaring a woman into returning to or staying with him, or to punish her for leaving.[11] Women are more likely than men to engage in "violent resistance." Violent resistance includes fighting

166 "Asking for It"

back against a violent and controlling partner. Police officers may interpret a woman's violent resistance in a way that justifies her arrest.

Prior to the 1980s, police were reluctant to make arrests in domestic violence cases, and prosecutors were reluctant to pursue charges because of widely shared perceptions that the victim wouldn't cooperate, that court action was a waste of time, or that the courts should stay out of "private" matters between a man and his family. In 1983, Tracey Thurman nearly died from injuries she sustained when her estranged husband attacked her in broad daylight for 27 minutes, stabbing her repeatedly in the chest, neck, and throat; kicking her in the head; breaking her neck; and leaving her partially paralyzed. Police officers had repeatedly ignored Tracey's requests for a warrant for her husband's arrest. When she called the police on the day of the attack, it took nearly a half hour for a single Torrington (Connecticut) police officer to respond. Tracey successfully sued the police force, claiming that the Torrington police were negligent in failing to protect her as they would any other crime victim simply because she was married to her attacker.[12]

Thurman v. City of Torrington and other cases have dramatically altered how the criminal justice system responds to domestic violence; arrests and prosecutions for domestic violence have increased.[13] Most states have adopted laws specifically aimed at domestic violence and battery.[14] These laws stiffen the penalties for domestic violence (especially repeat offenses) in an attempt to ensure that the assaults and other offenses committed in a domestic violence context are taken as seriously as other crimes. All states have introduced laws that authorize police to arrest domestic violence offenders without a warrant in misdemeanor cases based solely on a probable cause determination that an individual had engaged in domestic violence.[15]

Although we have come to regard domestic violence as a crime, we have yet to recognize it as a violation of women's reproductive rights. Some of the criminal justice and family court responses are anchored in the same patriarchal assumptions that make domestic violence such a pervasive problem in the first place. Our responses too often fail to support battered women's rights to bodily integrity and actively undermine a woman's right to care for her children. In this way, our responses embolden abusers while reinforcing women's second-class position in society.

A Violation of Bodily Integrity

Except for victims of child abuse, victims of intimate partner violence are more likely than other victims to sustain injuries.[16] Over 40 percent of spousal victims and over 50 percent of other intimate partner victims received at least "minor" injuries (such as black eyes, swelling, cuts, and chipped teeth); nearly 20 percent sustained serious injuries (including gunshot wounds and rape). Violence between intimates accounts for nearly one in six murders; women are far more likely than men to be killed by their intimate partner.[17] Although it is not common for women to become pregnant as the result of rape, pregnancy is more likely to occur when the sexual assault is not an isolated incident, as is the case with marital rape and incest.[18] Like other rape victims, women who are raped by a current or former intimate partner may suffer from depression, memory loss, and other serious emotional problems.[19] A woman may avoid going to see a doctor even for routine appointments or annual pelvic exams (or be prevented from doing so by her partner), because of fear that her abuse will be detected.[20]

All women have the right to be free from exploitation, sexual assault, and other forms of violence. Women also have the right to enjoy freedom of movement and security of one's person. Engaging in violence against a woman clearly violates her bodily integrity. Few people in the United States would dispute this. But some aspects of our official responses to violence against women suggest that we are not fully committed to protecting this right or to ensuring that all women have access to it.

Take, first, the example of marital rape. Being in an intimate relationship does not erase a woman's right to say "no" to sex. Since 1993, marital rape has been defined as a crime in all 50 states in at least one section of the sexual offense codes. This is not the watershed achievement one might imagine, however. Most states treat being raped by one's past or present husband or boyfriend less seriously than being raped by a stranger. As of May 2005, around one-half of all states still had exemptions that provided men some immunity from being prosecuted for marital rape under certain circumstances.[21] For example, some states require that the spouses must have been living apart or that the abusive spouse must have inflicted physical injury on the victim by the use of force or violence (rather than "only" the threat of it by say, holding a gun to her head). Some 20 states exempt men from sexual offense charges when their wives are mentally incapacitated (e.g., very drugged or intoxicated) or physically helpless (i.e., unconscious or in a coma); in some states, husbands are immune from rape charges even when they *themselves* administered the intoxicants that rendered the wives mentally incapacitated or otherwise incapable of consenting.[22]

As the case of marital rape shows, not all of our laws articulate a respect for women's bodily integrity. In other instances, laws offer some recourse or protection against violence, but they are not implemented or enforced. Such is the case with restraining orders. Both criminal and civil courts can issue restraining orders or orders of protection, though they are usually sought in the civil system through family court.[23] Court orders of protection either require the abuser to have peaceful contact with the victim (if they still live together or share child custody) or prohibit the offender from having contact with the victim. They also typically prohibit firearms possession and order the abuser to surrender any weapons. Most states and the District of Columbia treat violating a civil court order of protection as a separate criminal offense, usually a misdemeanor.[24]

But the statutes present only one part of the picture. There is also the matter of practice. Many restraining orders are never issued or served, and when that happens, batterers cannot be prosecuted for violating those orders. In 2005, a California task force found that 17 courts weren't issuing restraining orders, even when required by law, or lacked a procedure for entering them into their database. And many abusers were allowed to own firearms in violation of the orders.[25] In 2006, the *Orange County Register* surveyed all 58 California counties and interviewed judges, law enforcement officials, advocates, and victims of domestic violence.[26] About 260,000 active restraining orders were on record in California, about 147,000 of which were criminal protective orders issued when domestic violence cases were prosecuted or as a condition of probation. At least one in every seven restraining orders had not been served, including one in three civil orders.

In Maryland, shoddy record keeping has had fatal consequences. In 2003, Lisa Spicknall filed a $20 million lawsuit claiming that the failure of the state to maintain correct information on a court protective order in a state computer database and a lack of training of county clerks allowed the father of her children to buy a handgun.[27] Richard Spicknall II used the handgun in the slaying of her two children. A county sheriff's clerk had conducted an audit of a database eight months earlier, saw the word "consent" in the restraining order, and thought it meant Richard was permitted to buy a gun. In reality, it meant that both parties had agreed to the restraining order.[28] Lisa Spicknall's lawyer said an internal audit of the system that was completed before the shootings indicated an error rate of 85.7 percent.[29]

Furthermore, in 11 California counties, people filing for a temporary restraining order issued in family court must first provide advance notice to the person they are accusing of abuse. In some cases, this requires women to call their abuser and then read a script, "I am getting a domestic violence restraining order against you because [reason] at 1:30 today [date] at the Lamoreaux Justice Center at 341 The City Drive in Orange, California." The advance notification requirement endangers many victims since many abusive partners react to the notice with threats, intimidation, and violence.[30]

The National Center for Victims of Crime points out that protective orders "are effective only when the restrained party is convinced the order will be enforced."[31] They also noted that batterers subject to family court orders tend to be more dangerous than those subject to orders issued in the criminal court.

For restraining orders to have teeth, they must be consistently enforced not only within a jurisdiction but also across state and tribal boundaries. The "full faith and credit provision" of the federal Violence Against Women Act (VAWA) stipulates that a valid protection order issued in another state must be enforced everywhere throughout the country. Prior to the passage of VAWA in 1994, only a handful of state statutes provided any type of full faith and credit to protection orders from other jurisdictions.[32] Implementation has been checkered. Some jurisdictions have failed to act or have been slow to submit orders to the national registry. In May 1997, the FBI began accepting protective orders for a national registry. A year later, however, the national registry contained fewer than 5 percent of the 2 million orders believed to qualify for entry.[33] In February 2003, the National Protection Order File held only around 750,000 protection orders from 43 states.[34]

Some states passed legislation that imposes additional requirements in order to recognize an out-of-state order. Some states enforce only out-of-state orders that could be issued under the laws of the enforcing states. Unstandardized practices, the lack of trust and connections across jurisdiction, fees being charged for out-of-state or out-of-jurisdiction queries, and the lack of standardized and recognizable language in the orders themselves all have interfered with implementing full faith and credit.[35] Judicial officers, court administrators, advocates and service providers, law enforcement personnel, and attorneys who are involved in the enforcement of the orders often find the process confusing, as do the victim-petitioners who are trying to have the order enforced.

In sum, legislation is an important part of addressing the problem of domestic violence. The existence of laws sends a message about the value placed on women's physical safety and well-being, a message that needs to be heard by both men and women. At the same time, the failure to enforce the existing laws also sends a message and undermines the intent of the laws themselves.

The Right to Be a Mother

Intimate partner violence is thought to have damaging externalized effects (e.g., antisocial behavior, including delinquency and aggression) and internalized effects (e.g., anxiety, depression, and low self-esteem) on the children who witness it. Much attention is also given to the intergenerational transmission of violence. The metaphors of "transmission" and a "cycle of violence" suggest that violence is inevitable among men who witnessed family violence as children; in point of fact, the vast majority of these men do not commit serious acts of violence.[36] Two noted experts on intimate partner violence, Michael Johnson and Kathleen Ferraro, point out that most studies have found only small (even tiny) intergenerational effects. Quite possibly, the effect of witnessing violence varies depending on the severity of violence in the family, the extent to which a child was exposed to or experienced the violence personally, and other stressors present in the home, as well as the presence of protective factors and the child's own psychological make-up.[37]

Battering can impede a woman's ability to be an effective parent. The injuries and psychological duress associated with severe abuse can make it tough to hold down a job that supports one's family. A partner's violence can inflict physical, emotional, and cognitive damage that makes it harder for a woman to care and provide for her children. It does *not* automatically render a woman an unfit or neglectful parent, however. Even in the face of serious violence and stress, women systematically take steps to reduce the effects of the violence on their children such as offering a strong, reassuring presence and arranging for the child to stay with a friend or relative. A child's safety and behavior often weigh heavily in a woman's decision whether or not to leave, as does the need to ensure continued economic support.

Again, however, our official responses to violence against women do not adequately support women's efforts to parent. They often overlook how domestic violence is rooted in patriarchy and a desire for male control. In some cases, they miss the mark entirely. For instance, children are far more likely to be abducted by a male family member than a stranger. Partners' and ex-partners' credible threats of child abduction and homicide instill incredible fear and distrust in mothers and are often quite effective in controlling women's actions. Stereotypical child kidnappings committed by strangers (like the high-profile case of Polly Klass) are rare; there are fewer than 200 such cases a year.[38] Rather than allocate resources to address the problem of family abductions and custody disputes, however, the Department of Justice spent $12 million to create the national AMBER Alert system.[39] The lobbying for the AMBER Alert legislation preyed on the public's fear that strangers—not fathers and ex-husbands—would kidnap their children. The discourse was dominated by stranger kidnapping and overwhelmed any discussion of dangers associated with more likely (and proximate) sources of harm to children and families: that is, a male relative.

Interestingly, anecdotal accounts suggest that law enforcement officials are reluctant to issue AMBER alerts every time a family member kidnaps a child or a child runs away, for fear that the public will eventually ignore the alerts. A spokesperson for the Texas Department of Public Safety told a reporter, "You don't want to be in a position where you get Amber fatigue where people say, 'It never ends, another Amber Alert,' and they tune out."[40] An Ohio police chief pointed out that law enforcement officers usually err on the side of caution to protect people, but with the AMBER Alert, "If you erred on the side of caution, this thing would be going off all the time."[41] Perhaps it is not entirely surprising that from 1996 to January 2007, the AMBER Alert System led to the safe return of only around 300 children.[42]

Just as AMBER Alert downplays the role of family violence in child abduction, the same is true of many decisions about custody and visitation. When the victim is the mother of a minor, her domestic abuse case is often heard in family court rather than criminal court.[43] Court officials and case workers frequently fail to understand the complex context in which domestic violence occurs, and they may blame the victim for her abuse. In the remainder of this chapter, I examine how this bias affects women's rights to mother. An abused mother may face an uphill battle to obtain sole custody of her child or to avoid visiting arrangements that subject her to continued violence and control. Also, abused women may have to defend themselves against charges of neglect if they are unable to protect a child from directly or indirectly experiencing violence.

Custody, Visiting, and the Impact of "Fathers' Rights"

Historically, common law considered children as property and awarded custody to fathers. In the twentieth century, the approach shifted to the "tender years doctrine," which held that women should have custody of very young children. But since the 1980s, the custodial presumption favoring mothers has eroded. In particular, the so-called fathers' rights movement has led to judges prioritizing joint custody over a woman's safety when making custody and visitation rulings. Fathers' rights advocates have been effective in convincing judges and others that men are being unfairly denied involvement in their children's lives after separation, even if the reason for the separation is domestic violence.

Child psychiatrist Richard Gardner invented the term "parental alienation syndrome," or PAS, to describe cases that he believed involved false allegations of sexual abuse.[44] In serious cases of alleged PAS, Gardner recommends that custody of the child be transferred from the beloved parent to the rejected parent for deprogramming. Gardner originally asserted that PAS was present in approximately 90 percent of the children whose families were involved in custody litigation, though he did not provide any empirical evidence to support his claims about PAS, its frequency, or its context.[45] The notion of PAS has been thoroughly discredited on empirical and legal grounds by mental health and legal communities, including the National Council of Juvenile and Family Court Judges, the National District Attorney's Association National Center for the Prosecution of Child Abuse, and the American Psychological Association's Presidential Task Force on Violence and the Family.[46] Despite its scientific invalidity, the term "PAS" has been applied to a wide range of cases in which a child refuses to visit the noncustodial parent, regardless of whether or not the child objects on the basis of alleged abuse.

The result of Gardner and the fathers' rights lobbying has been that judges, assessors, arbitrators, and other state agents are afraid of appearing biased if they don't support joint custody and liberal visitation for male parents, even if these arrangements compromise the safety of women and children.[47] In one case of fathers' rights run amok, an Indiana woman, Kim Linetty, was ordered by a judge to take her three children to visit their father in prison, even though the father, Henry J. Weldy, is serving time for raping Kim in 2002.[48]

The fear of not being believed or taken seriously keeps many women trapped in abusive relationships. When there are no previous police reports on file, a woman's claims may be doubted. But many women take out orders of protection or call the police only as a last resort. Also, violence or the risk of a father kidnapping a child escalates while or after a woman separates from her abusive partner.[49] Thus, it may not be until after the separation that a woman is impelled by circumstance to seek an order of protection or report the abuse to the police.[50] Cases like that of Lori Jean Smith are not unusual. Lori Jean filed for a divorce in December 2004 and planned to move out after the holidays. Her husband refused to accept her decision and began drinking heavily and making threats. On December 27, Lori Jean tried to get a temporary restraining order, but the clerks failed to process it. That night, according to the police, Gary Smith shot Lori Jean in the head with a 12-gauge shotgun. He later told the police, "I'm 61 years old. I have no future, so I might as well just make sure that she has no future, too."[51]

The myth persists, fueled in large part by father's rights activists, that women routinely and intentionally lie about being abused (or about their children being physically or sexually abused) in order to gain an advantage in a custody or divorce case. Women are accused of misusing orders of protection to kick men out of their homes or to deny them contact with their children. In reality, abusers' false denials or false accusations (e.g., that their partners are lying unfit, aggressive, vindictive brainwashers) are more common than victims' false claims of abuse.[52] A Canadian study found that in cases involving a custody dispute, the rate of intentionally false allegations of child abuse is about 12 percent, with noncustodial parents (usually fathers) most frequently making intentionally false reports.[53] Another study of 215 cases of sexual abuse allegations in divorce cases found that adults knowingly made false allegations in fewer than 5 percent of all cases.[54]

Lawyers and judges tend to be cynical and too willing to assume a woman is fabricating an allegation of abuse.[55] Judges and other family court personnel may wrongly believe that considering domestic violence "is tantamount to being partisan to mothers."[56] Essentially, the situation constitutes a form of "equality with a vengeance." Equal treatment is not inherently fair treatment, and "special" treatment that takes into account a parent's abuse is not inherently unfair. "Although some abusive men genuinely want a relationship with their children and desire an improved post-separation relationship, many batterers pursue visitation as a way of gaining access to their ex-partner," Peter Jaffe and his co-authors of *Child Custody and Domestic Violence* note. "For many women, the burden of battling their former partner, traversing a court system that is highly suspicious of allegations of violence, and coping with a visitation schedule that delivers their children into the arms of their abuser can be crushing."[57]

Most states have adopted one of two approaches for addressing domestic violence in their custody statutes: (1) rebuttable presumption statutes, which presume that the abuser will not have custody of the children; or (2) factor tests, which encourage judges to weigh the effects of domestic violence in determining a child's best interests.[58] Organizations such as the National Council of Juvenile and Family Court Judges, the American Psychological Association, the American Bar Association, and even the U.S. Congress recommend that a finding of domestic violence should create a presumption that the abuser will not have sole or joint custody of children.[59] Abusive parents can rebut the presumption by, for example, completing a treatment program for batterers. The problem with this is that completing a batterer's program does not guarantee that the batterer even attended all of the required sessions, much less that he was rehabilitated. In fact, there is much reason to question whether court-ordered treatment of spouse abuse is effective; programs often fail to challenge the batterers' sense of entitlement to a patriarchal dividend that underlies women's subordination.[60]

Another problem is that mandatory arrest policies may result in a woman being arrested for domestic violence, even if she is acting in self-defense or is not the primary aggressor. This arrest may label her a domestic violence perpetrator and thwart her efforts to obtain custody if the family court judge must apply the rebuttable presumption standard.[61]

Thirty-four states and the District of Columbia have factor tests that make domestic violence one factor that judges must consider in determining custody.[62] Most states mandate that all factors must be weighed equally, though some states give greater weight to domestic violence. Predictably, fathers' rights advocates prefer factor tests because it makes it easier for men to get custody of their children in cases involving domestic violence.

Another problematic practice is using parenting coordination and mediation as a means of resolving disputes for "high-conflict" families, including those that involve past or present domestic violence. As the American Bar Association has pointed out, such measures are inappropriate in domestic violence cases.[63] Batterers may use the parenting coordination or mediation process to threaten victims or to manipulate the coordinator or mediator in order to gain concessions. Mediators often encourage the victim to be cooperative, flexible, and willing to negotiate, while discounting the fear that prevents her from asserting her needs. Mediation, for instance, presumes that participants can maintain a balance of power and reach a mutually satisfactory resolution. In cases of domestic violence, the abuser's desire to maintain power and control over the victim undermines the entire method and purpose of mediation. The process and the outcome can be unfair—and even dangerous—if the imbalance of power is great or goes unrecognized. Furthermore, the mediator's neutrality and the process's focus on the future may discourage discussions of past abuse. This, in turn, may strengthen the abuser's belief that his behavior is acceptable.[64]

In some jurisdictions, domestic violence may be so prevalent that it is "tuned out" except in the most egregious cases. The high prevalence of domestic violence in caseloads may cause law enforcement, mental health, and legal professionals to view common acts of domestic violence like pushing, slapping, and threatening as insignificant. A study of supervised and unsupervised visitation in New York City found that more than three-quarters of the study's 242 participants had experienced severe forms of physical and psychological abuse, and nearly one-half had reported severe injuries.[65] A history of abuse or injuries did not influence whether a father was ordered to a supervised visitation center, family-supervised visits, or unsupervised visitation.[66]

Many judges do not adequately take into account domestic violence when determining custody or visitation schedules. In Massachusetts, the Battered Mothers' Testimony Project (BMTP) conducted extensive interviews with 39 women who had experienced violence from an intimate partner and were engaged in custody litigation with the abusive ex-partner.[67] BMTP found that physical custody and/or unsupervised visitation was granted or recommended to men who had used violence against the mothers, the children, or both. When child custody was disputed, judicial actors either did not accept or did not consider documentation of violence against women or children.

Child Protective Services

Women who leave their abusers face battles over custody and visitation. Women who do not leave, however, risk being charged with neglect or abuse for exposing the children to violence and having their children removed from their custody.[68] A tendency exists to focus narrowly on a woman's failure to leave. Family court and child protective service workers often assume that women who leave their abusers are better parents than those who stay.[69] Women are expected to report abuse to the police, get a restraining order, and file for divorce, even though these measures provide no guarantee that the abuse will end and may actually fuel violent retaliation. At the same time, women take many protective measures to shield their children from serious harm. These steps, however, are often ignored or unacknowledged. For example, one woman described some of the routine ways in which she protected her very young children from being harmed by her husband's violence, including

> putting the kids to bed very early (waking very early with them and getting them down for naps before he'd even awakened for his day), feeding them in a different room and not at the same time as his meals were being served, and not nursing them in front of him ever (he didn't like me nursing). I also did a lot of emotional labor (telling him how good he was with them or how cute they were and how much they looked or acted like him to help him feel too connected to them to want to hurt them or to hurt me in front of them, and such). I also used sexual advances and promises of sex to distract him. And, of course, I was agreeable to his every demand if he was using threats against them or if he was escalating to the point of violence in front of them. And, I left them in their cribs for longer than is healthy to prevent their seeing the violence.[70]

Family court and child protective service workers may discount these efforts, as well as the many reasons why a battered woman doesn't report the abuse or leave her abuser. She may be economically or emotionally dependent on the abuser's support or that of his family. Immigrant women may fear deportation; lesbian and bisexual women may fear being outed to employers or family members.[71] A woman may have her own legal problems that make her leery of court involvement. She also likely fears the retaliatory violence that makes her point of exit so dangerous and may jeopardize the safety and well-being of their children.[72] As child and family advocate Mary Raines puts it, "When a court assumes that a mother who stays compromises the safety of her children, it ignores the lethality of the decision to leave."[73]

When the system focuses more on blaming mothers for failing to protect children rather than holding the batterer accountable, it echoes and reinforces the dynamic between a woman and her abuser. On some occasions, it is not only the abuser but also court actors and social workers who mock a woman's decisions or her authority or even question her sanity.[74] They, and the state they represent, can become an extension of the maltreatment. They may treat common signs of trauma (such as crying, emotional flatness, high levels of anxiety, nervousness, or anger) as evidence that a woman is crazy, unstable, or otherwise an unfit parent. As one woman described, "I can't stress enough how awful it is, how awful it is to be battered . . . and not to be able to get away from that, to go to a court and have them give you more of the same—not only not protect you from it, but give you more of the same."[75]

Sharwline Nicholson's boyfriend (and the father of one of her children), Barnett, hit Sharwline's son. Following that incident, Sharwline told Barnett she wanted to end their relationship. Barnett became enraged and viciously beat her. Sharwline was hospitalized with a broken arm and a rib. While she was in the hospital, Child Protective Manager Nat Williams placed her two small children in foster care, even though Sharwline had requested the children be placed with family members in the Bronx and New Jersey. Williams ignored the fact that the abuser lived in South Carolina, visited only once a month, and did not have a key to Sharwline's home. Moreover, Sharwline had clearly indicated that she wanted to end the relationship with Barnett; it was that disclosure that precipitated the beating.[76] Five days passed before Williams sought family court approval for the placement. Sharwline could not see her children for over a week and saw them only once during the 14 days it took for her children to be returned to her.

Before *Nicholson v. Scoppetta* was decided in 2004, New York City Administration for Children's Services (ACS) workers used charges and the threat of taking away children to pressure women to leave their abusers. In Sharwline Nicholson's case, as well as in approximately 234 others that same year, ACS charged victims of domestic violence with neglect for failing to protect children from witnessing such violence. The threat or actual removal of children to foster care was used to coerce women who were victims of violence into getting help. Once a victim of domestic violence agreed to services such as emergency housing and safety planning, her children would usually be returned to her. But in at least some instances, the threat of or actual separation of women from their children was used to punish women, "initially for the mothers' alleged neglect, and then continually for any failure to comply with the demands of ACS."[77] Ultimately, the court ruled that ACS unnecessarily separated mothers from their children and circumvented women's rights to due process.

A battered woman who is also a mother faces a situation not unlike being between a rock and a hard place under a load of bricks. If her victimization comes to the attention of the family court, she may be charged with neglect or abuse. Yet, if she seeks services from child welfare in an attempt to mitigate the impact of her victimization on the child, she stands a good chance of not receiving services (because of the limited resources available) or being treated the same as a woman who was mandated by the court to receive such services.[78] Harvard School of Public Health assistant professor

Jay Silverman describes the "perilous irony" of battered women's situations. Judges, law enforcement officials, and other authorities pressure women to leave abusive men in order to protect their children. But, he observes, "women who can make this break then face family courts, another authority that often ignores this history of abuse as a threat to children's safety and, perversely, concludes that women's attempts to protect their children from these men actually demonstrate their own lack of fitness as mothers."[79]

A Safety Net or a Web of Surveillance and Regulation?

Responses to domestic violence feature a lack of coordination among battered women advocates, child protective services, the criminal justice system, and community-based or nongovernmental organizations. Instead of cooperating to support a woman's efforts to ensure that she and her children can be safe and together, too often the involvement of multiple agencies becomes a web of surveillance and regulation that gets in the way of her attempts to escape violence and raise her children. The situation is further complicated by a climate of mutual distrust and conflict that can develop between battered women's advocates on the one side and child protection workers on the other.

Social service workers may be able to provide battered women with the housing and employment assistance they need to escape the violence. Again, though, a battered woman may be reluctant to seek help from social services, knowing that social service workers are mandated reporters of child abuse and neglect who might blame her for not protecting her children. Unless the social workers have been trained to understand domestic violence, they also may assume that a battered woman who has not left her abuser is exposing her child to danger and report her to child protective services.

A tendency exists—as exemplified by news headlines like "Horrific Rash of Mother Murders" and "Mom's Killer on Loose"—to treat violence against a woman as if it is more wrong or more tragic because the victim is a mother. The flip side of this, however, is that some women's status as mothers subjects them to harsher scrutiny of their actions. The focus of family court and foster care agency personnel, instead of being on the violence committed against a woman and her need for support, may shift toward her children and concern about their safety. When that shift takes place, it is often the woman who is held accountable for the children's safety, even though her own is not assured by the state. The predominant attitude seems to be, "We will help you, but our first priority is the safety of your children. If you can help us ensure their safety, then we will help you." Once again, we find that concern for women who are mothers takes second place to concern for her children.

When systems come into conflict, we are likely to see a pitting of the battered mother's rights and needs against the perceived rights and needs of the children, as though they were separate, independent entities. We talk about a *family* court, but it is not clear to what extent the court sees the family, as opposed to lots of broken pieces. Our systems focus on "units" or individuals (that is, criminal courts focus on the adult batterer, child protective services focuses on the child); a woman and her children may get ground up in separate mills.[80]

Passed in 1994, the Violence Against Women Act (VAWA) was the first piece of U.S. federal legislation designed to address domestic violence. It was hoped that the act might encourage interagency collaboration. In reality, however, few states have managed to achieve this goal. Coordination is still wanting in many, if not most, jurisdictions. For example, an abuser is presumed innocent of domestic violence in a criminal court, but a family court judge will be expected to make a finding of domestic violence in order to make custody and visiting arrangements. This situation requires coordinating different services at different stages of the process in both criminal and family proceedings. Consider as well some victims' immigration concerns or language barriers. Little wonder, then, why many abused women return to their abusers, discouraged by the delays and complexities of the proceedings and the difficulty in piecing together resources they need to escape the violence.

Obstacles loom particularly large for poor women whose lives already are subject to considerable governmental social control. Poor women, for example, may seek relief from a variety of different programs, including housing assistance (rent vouchers, public housing), employment assistance (job training), food assistance (food stamps, school lunches), medical care (Medicaid, state-subsidized health insurance), childcare subsidies, and cash assistance (TANF [Temporary Assistance for Needy Families], SSI [Supplemental Security Income]). Women who are mothers may deal with family court, foster care agencies, and the board of education on behalf of their children. Women victims of domestic violence may face court appearances; meetings with attorneys, counselors, and social workers; required education or psychological evaluations; and so forth. Such contacts may be required (with serious sanctions for noncompliance) or "optional" (but in women's best interests) and involve face-to-face appointments, phone calls, or written documentation. Regardless of their form, these contacts obligate women to invest time, money, and effort arranging and attending appointments, establishing eligibility, providing documentation, completing and submitting paperwork, and so on.[81]

A culture of fear and concern about liability also pressures many people in social services and the family court to err on the side of recommending removal and supervision. Many child protective services administrators and supervisors work in fear of another high-profile child abuse case like Elisa Izquierdo, Nixzmary Brown, or Lisa Steinberg. Such cases focus intense attention on the system and force the reallocation of resources and the adjustment strategies to allay heightened public concern in the short term rather than to implement needed changes over the long term.[82] In the wake of such cases, surveillance and documentation often assume priority over the actual provision of services.[83]

Conclusion

That violence is a form of patriarchal oppression is not news. But our official responses to violence against women in general, and women who are mothers in particular, suggest that at least some responses also are grounded in patriarchal assumptions about a man's "right" to abuse and control.

Too often, our policies and state agents perform in ways that replicate disempowering patriarchal structures. Men's battering is not only about hurting a woman but also about using fear and intimidation to gain power and control over every aspect of the victim's life. For instance, while mandatory arrest and prosecution policies may restrict the abuser's power to control outcome, in effect, the decision-making power is shifted to the state, not the individual victim. Similarly, forcing a woman to engage in mediation with her batterer may have the unintended effect of undermining the victim's efforts to assert control over her own life and reinforce her belief that she is incompetent to survive on her own. Approaches that dictate solutions ("You will leave your abuser or else we will take your kids away") undermine a woman's sense of autonomy and agency rather than empower her to make decisions on her own timetable.

While individual policies may have been designed to help women, many of them, at least in their implementation, fail to respect that women are decision makers and experts of their own life, even when they are victims.[84]

Women may remain in abusive relationships for a variety of reasons, including fear, love, and shame, as well as financial dependence and a lack of confidence that leaving or mobilizing the criminal justice system will end the violence. Women typically have good reasons for not trusting the system to make the violence stop or to provide them with the support they need if they decide to leave.

Also, some policies and procedures seem oriented more toward protecting children rather than supporting a woman's efforts to protect herself and her children. The system's treatment of domestic violence seems to be another vehicle for linking a woman's value to our assessment of whether she is a good wife or mother. It also reflects a gendered double standard. If a woman's partner beats her, then she risks being deemed a bad mother for failing to protect her child from violence. By contrast, it is possible for a man to be deemed a suitable father even when it has been established that he has beaten or killed the children's mother.

The state plays at least two key roles in ensuring that violence against a woman does not jeopardize her reproductive rights. The state is in a position to protect and defend a woman's right to be free from violence. It also can practically support her in her attempts to raise her children in a safe environment. A commitment to reproductive justice requires us to examine how women can accomplish this in ways they would like with help from the state. How to undertake real advocacy on behalf of battered women without simply increasing the surveillance and further disempowering them is but one of the critical questions that remain to be answered.

Conclusion
Being

There is something drastically wrong with a conception of reproductive freedom that allows [the] wholesale exclusion of the most
disadvantaged from its reach.

—Dorothy Roberts, *Killing the Black Body,* 1998

The impact of the state's policing of reproduction affects every woman, including women who will never see the inside of a patrol
car, courtroom, or cell. But the failure to ensure reproductive justice lands
hardest on the most vulnerable members of society.

This book is not only about misguided policies like, as I have argued,
fetal homicide laws, parental notification statutes, no-procreation orders,
and the time-driven and involuntary termination of parental rights. This
book is also about regulating women's social citizenship and understanding how citizens are formed, valued, and, ultimately, judged. I have tried
to show how respect for a woman's reproductive rights is doled out on the
basis of how well she conforms to societal norms about "womanly" or feminine behavior. I have also shown the place of girls and women in society
and the need to make sure they are situated such that they can access and
exercise their rights. Identifying how our system of criminal justice curtails
women's reproductive justice is but one step toward addressing this much
bigger challenge.

Roe v. Wade was decided in 1973, legalizing abortion and freeing women
from governmental intrusion during the first trimester of pregnancy. The
decision was meant to expand women's citizenship and autonomy. Access
to safe abortions would make it easier for women to participate in social and economic life because it would permit women to defer marriage

and motherhood, perhaps indefinitely. In the years since *Roe* articulated the state's compelling interest in a viable fetus, however, the state has approached women not as human beings and citizens but as past, present, or potential baby carriers and mothers. Today, the state weighs in not only on whether a woman can terminate her pregnancy but also on whether a woman can continue a pregnancy and give birth (and under what conditions), raise her children, and enjoy reproductive health free from violence or fear.

As they did over 100 years ago, our criminal justice system and our laws reflect and reinforce longstanding and deeply held ideas about who deserves the protections and entitlements that social citizenship has to offer. Citizenship, unfortunately, continues to be attached to classist and racist notions about which women are morally, socially, and economically fit to reproduce.[1] (Men, however, are not held to the same standards.) Women whom we perceive to have failed to establish themselves as responsible citizens by controlling their reproduction in socially acceptable ways do not have their contributions to society recognized. Instead, their status as citizens is discounted, and their access to society's benefits is extremely restricted.[2]

In this regard, regulating women's reproduction plays an important role in maintaining citizenship as an exclusionary process. Citizenship builds identities on the basis of a common or created solidarity. For women, some behaviors and statuses—specifically, being black or Hispanic or poor or addicted to drugs or battered or young or procreating outside of marriage—have come to be seen as at sharp odds with being a good (reproductive) citizen.

The nature of the criminal justice system is such that it is empowered to impose its will on an individual for the good of society. In intruding on women's reproductive lives, though, it oversteps its charge. While we may trust that the criminal justice system rehabilitates people or protects society, features of the system (i.e., its immense scale and expense, its harsh punishments, its devastating impact on families and communities) strongly suggest such trust is misplaced. Having reviewed how the criminal justice system responds to women's reproductive capacities in various contexts, I conclude that, where women are concerned, enforcing existing social arrangements and standards of femininity is as much of a priority for the criminal justice system as is enforcing the law and seeking justice. Claims that the actions of police, prosecutors, judges, and correctional administrators are undertaken for the "woman's own good" or to "protect children" simply do not ring true.

That the system fails to ensure people have what they need in order to meaningfully participate in society (and actually interferes with their ability to do so) is a charge that can be leveled against other institutions as well. School officials claim to be concerned about teen pregnancy, but then forego comprehensive sex education in favor of ineffective and misleading abstinence-only-until-marriage programs. Although programs such as Temporary Assistance to Needy Families are supposed to provide material public assistance to women and children, in reality they do not help raise people out of poverty but maintain the status quo. Similarly, child and public welfare agencies do not provide a safety net for mothers or girls seeking to leave an abusive household or women at risk of neglecting or abusing their children.

Our formal systems of criminal justice and public welfare maintain invidious distinctions between bad women and girls and good ones, welfare recipients and workers, offenders and mothers. Not coincidentally, the welfare and the criminal justice systems reinforce these distinctions by effectively barring women who use drugs, commit crimes, or are battered from ever being considered "good" or deserving of societal benefits and protections. As women of color have become overrepresented among the populations of offenders and welfare recipients, "minority" has become a code word for "welfare recipient" and "offender," with the understanding that these, in turn, imply "bad" and "undeserving." Reproductive justice, as Dorothy Roberts observes of racial justice, "demands aggressive government programs to relieve poverty and redress longstanding barriers to housing, jobs, and political participation." Yet "white Americans have resisted the expansion of welfare precisely because of its benefits to Blacks."[3]

At the same time, calls to expand the reach of the criminal justice system continue, perhaps because such expansion reinforces the marginalization of poor and racial and ethnic minority groups while protecting the interests of a largely white male elite.[4] The stigmatizing, isolating, and punitive nature of the criminal justice system has spread to the family courts and the public welfare and child welfare systems.[5] Even agencies purportedly guided by a social work orientation that should emphasize social change, problem-solving, and the empowerment of human beings have instead shifted toward an approach that emphasizes adherence to rules and time frames. Agencies that are charged with providing practical support and assistance instead respond with the surveillance, enforcement, and punitive mindsets that are the hallmarks of the criminal justice system.

Underlying these societal mores is a view that poor women are society's bane. As feminists have long been aware, a defining characteristic of our responses to pressing social problems such as violence against women, teen or unintended pregnancy, and substance abuse has been to blame women for their situation.[6] In setting after setting, judges, lawyers, medical staff, social workers, and caseworkers scrutinize, judge, and insert themselves into poor women's and girls' lives. Officials and workers in a variety of roles and settings often evaluate a woman's position based on how "compliant" or willing she is to defer to their authority and accept their judgment of herself.

Women become entrapped in multiple systems with no coordination of services or requirements. A charitable explanation for this is that the criminal justice system, the family courts, the public welfare system, education, public housing, and the like tend to operate as independent entities with their own set of goals. Each bureaucracy sees a problem through that system's lens exclusively. When systems are underresourced and overburdened, it is far too easy, as one observer notes, "to look at the hammer in your hand and see nothing but a succession of nails in front of you."[7] Yet emerging out of these seemingly chaotic and uncoordinated institutions is a web of state regulation that acts in patterned, systematic ways that reinforce patriarchy and racial inequality and, ultimately, as I have shown, can serve to deny women reproductive rights.

Our public policies with regard to crime and reproduction reveal a conservative bent that stresses free will, places great stock in deterrence, and is concerned with controlling female sexuality and reproduction. District attorneys who pursue criminal charges against drug-using women who continue their pregnancies to term communicate to all women that their behavior while they are pregnant may be grounds for prosecution. Further, such prosecutions put all women on notice that they can be prosecuted *because* they are pregnant. Similarly, lawmakers who oppose comprehensive sex education do so because they fear such measures do not send a harsh message about the dangers and immorality of extramarital sex. Wanting to control who reproduces while at the same time opposing access to abortion, the strategy of people on the far right (and not so far right) seems to be to make some women's future appear so bleak that they will be deterred from getting pregnant or having additional children. Such actions also warn other women about what may happen to them if they violate dominant norms regarding who can reproduce and under what conditions.

The contradictions are obvious. Restrictions on abortion and the lack of quality drug treatment coexist with the arrests and prosecutions of women for continuing their pregnancies to term. While socially and economically privileged women are able to access expensive technologies to become pregnant by means of artificial insemination and other technologies, incarcerated women's reproductive health is ignored. The state can compel a woman to remain pregnant and give birth to a child that she cannot afford, but, at the same time, it neglects to secure child support from fathers who are able to pay.

Our failure to develop a better understanding of women and families has led to policies that undermine the status of women rather than elevate it. Safe haven statutes, AMBER Alerts, and fetal homicide laws are examples of measures motivated by the desire to make a symbolic statement rather than a sincere commitment to addressing the root causes of unwanted pregnancy, violence against women, and other social problems. Increasingly, the state acts as if it has the obligation to intervene in women's reproductive lives, while absolving itself of any responsibility for ensuring that the basic needs for health care (including drug treatment), education, housing, and financial support are met. Ironically, at some of the very points at which women may benefit the most from support (e.g., when a teenager becomes pregnant, when a mother is beaten by her partner, when a woman who uses drugs becomes pregnant or gives birth, when a woman is locked up), our official (and unofficial) responses are the harshest.[8]

This is typical of classical perspectives that ignore the context in which women's "choices" about crime and reproduction occur. Does a pregnant girl, panic-stricken and terrified of being thrown out of her home, freely "choose" to kill or abandon her newborn? Can a woman who is struggling to feed, clothe, and shelter herself "choose" to decline $250 from a nonprofit organization in exchange for being sterilized? Does a mother on probation for a drug offense freely ignore her probation officer's or attorney's urging that she have her tubes tied? Does an incarcerated woman voluntarily opt out of having access to decent gynecologic care? Does any girl "choose" to be sexually harassed by correctional staff? Does a woman prefer not to leave a batterer or report him to the police when doing so will not guarantee her safety? Time and again, we fail to acknowledge, much less address, the limited economic resources, racism, violence, geography, and social isolation that restricts women's options to the point of obliterating them. We ignore the connections between individual tragedies like abandoned babies and assaults on pregnant women and the larger structures and institutions that permit these tragedies to take place in the first place. What does it even mean for a poor woman to claim her body as her "own" when her body is so thoroughly regulated and devalued by the state?[9]

In 1967, activists and theorists of the Black Power movement, Stokely Carmichael and Charles Hamilton, wrote:

> When white terrorists bomb a black church and kill five black children, that is an act of individual racism, widely deplored by most segments of the society. But when in that same city—Birmingham, Alabama—five hundred black babies die each year because of the lack of proper food, shelter and medical facilities, and thousands more are destroyed and maimed physically emotionally, and intellectually because of conditions of poverty and discrimination, that is a function of institutional racism.[10]

Decades after these words were written, we still have not redressed the structural barriers posed by our drug laws and child welfare policies that disproportionately and adversely affect poor and minority women. Ordinary Americans have yet to react to evidence of institutionalized forms of gender and racial discrimination and inequality with the same sense of moral outrage and urgency that we heretofore have reserved for the acts of individuals.

Admittedly, there are some women whose actions or inactions pose a direct and serious threat to their children's well-being. But visceral reactions to a particular woman's failures take on a different cast when they are used by lawmakers and judges who can mobilize the force of the law and the courts. It is not clear how condemnation, either personal or official, leads to a better outcome for a woman or society—or any child, for that matter. Perhaps most important, the fact that some women's actions may cause serious and irrevocable harm to children and other people does not absolve society from its responsibility. The state must respect and uphold the dignity of each person because of the kind of society we are or aspire to be: one that values and supports its citizens because they are human beings, not because an individual's actions lend themselves to respect.

Lynn Paltrow, founder of National Advocates for Pregnant Women, has been at the forefront of defending the rights of pregnant women. She points out that vicious labeling of women who have abortions (not to mention abortion providers or abortion advocates) "murderers" is part of a larger trend. As my choice of chapter titles highlights, the vicious rhetoric isn't confined to abortion but also surrounds women who use drugs, incarcerated women, girls who abandon their newborns, and women who have not yet left their abusers. "You can't have that level of hateful rhetoric and just limit it to abortion," Paltrow concludes. "Once pregnant women are seen as capable of heinous crimes like murder, they are dehumanized."[11] When we deny a poor woman her say over whether or not she will become pregnant or give birth, when we fail to support her efforts to raise her own children in a safe and healthy environment, and by stripping away control over her reproductive health and other central aspects of her reproductive life, we place a woman in the same category as an animal that we neuter or breed. We are not simply saying, "You are a second-class citizen," but also, "You are not worthy of being considered a human being at all."

If we aspire to promote the health and well-being of women and children, our purposes would be better served by recognizing all women as allies—not adversaries, or incompetents, or hapless victims—who share a goal of freely chosen reproductive decisions that result in healthy outcomes for women and, ultimately, their children and communities. True empowerment seems an essential ingredient to ensure this. But while empowerment is a noble goal, it is not easily achieved. The trust needed for effective cooperation and alliances may not be readily forthcoming after centuries of women-blaming. Too, it is not in the best interest of our patriarchal systems to promote women's empowerment. As Jennifer Reich, sociologist and author of *Fixing Families* points out in her powerful study of mothers accused of abuse or neglect:

> [Women] who were truly empowered could address the social inequalities that they endure. However, they may also question the role of the state in their private family life. They may advocate for themselves in interactions with welfare officials. They may question their lack of resources and opportunity. They may notice that they have been forced to transfer their subordination from men to the state, but have not become independent or self-sufficient.[12]

Empowered women might be more inclined to opt out of reproduction and traditional caregiving and nurturing gender roles. Women might elect to not have children or to leave the care of their children and other dependents to others.[13] And this is what I think people find so deeply troubling. When women are truly empowered, then we will be at the mercy of neither men nor the state. We will make our decisions and live our lives as human beings, not fettered by social convention or social pressure. Our social arrangements will look very different. And they will not serve the interests of patriarchy.

Is there reason to think that the foreseeable future includes pro-woman laws, policies, and practices? Writing in *At Women's Expense,* Cynthia R.

Daniels was cautious: "Although women's rights may ultimately be upheld in the courts, a broader public culture may continue to endorse resentment toward women and more subtle forms of social coercion against those who transgress the boundaries of traditional motherhood."[14] Considerable energy is currently consumed by women's anxiety not so much about pregnancies and childrearing per se, but about how others will view their reproductive lives. It is not just poor and minority women who are mindful of others' harsh judgments. Even white upper-class and middle-class women face social disapproval if they enjoy a glass of wine, a cup of coffee or a soda, or eat a tuna sandwich or soft cheese while they are pregnant or nursing. Federal guidelines stipulate that all women capable of conceiving should be considered as "pre-pregnant," regardless of whether they plan to get pregnant.[15] Under such scrutiny, it is not surprising that many women lack the confidence and resolve required to resist unnecessary and unwanted medical intervention in their pregnancies, labor, and deliveries, hang onto their children through a custody battle or incarceration, or insist that their bodily integrity be respected.

Until we dismantle patriarchy, our systems and our laws will continue to fail women. Until there are fundamental shifts in the way society is structured, introducing marginally more supportive measures or passing less punitive laws is only making a substantively sexist and racist system slightly less sexist and racist. At root, the answers to complex social problems will not be found in laws and court rulings alone but, rather, in broad-based measures that strengthen women's economic status, education, choice-making, autonomy, sexual power, and health care.

Perhaps naively, I do have hope. Domestic violence and rape are now widely recognized as crimes in the United States. Prison conditions, while still appalling, have generally improved compared with 100 years ago. Some criminal and appellate court judges have been champions of women's rights to privacy and bodily sovereignty. Many legal and medical professionals have proven to be outspoken allies in the fight to recognize women's fundamental right to reproductive decision making.

I take solace in the fact that many people on all sides of the abortion debate are troubled by our collective failure to remedy the social conditions that keep millions of women and children living in poverty. I'm mindful that my own conservative, Midwestern, religious upbringing did not lend itself to recognizing reproductive rights, much less trying to write a book about them or participating in a larger social movement devoted to their advancement. And yet I did. I continue to believe in the capacity of people to think for themselves, despite the power of institutions and our compromised democracy. I also am convinced that women's strength and resilience, our ability to survive and to persevere in the face of tough social circumstances, are forces to be reckoned with.[16]

The consequences of maintaining the status quo (or worse) are simply too troubling to entertain the possibility that the pursuit of reproductive justice is a futile endeavor. Far more is at stake than the right to an abortion. As long as women's worth is measured in terms of our reproduction—whether we successfully reproduce or reproduce "correctly"—we will fail to meet the standards for good citizens. In varying degrees, we will all be vulnerable to state intrusion into the most basic and intimate facets of our lives. And as long as reproduction is the standard for all women's social citizenship, no woman will be respected as a true citizen or recognized fully as a human being.[17]

Notes

This book owes a considerable intellectual debt to Lynn Paltrow's and Dorothy Roberts's scholarship and advocacy, as well as that of Rickie Solinger and Rachel Roth. These women, among others, have been at the forefront of advancing our understanding of reproductive rights in the twentieth and twenty-first centuries. Some material presented in this book previously appeared in Jeanne Flavin (2007), "Slavery's Legacy in Contemporary Attempts to Regulate Black Women's Reproduction," in Mary Bosworth and Jeanne Flavin, eds., *Race, Gender, and Punishment: From Colonialism to the War on Terror* (New Brunswick, NJ: Rutgers University Press).

1. No doubt realizing his gaffe, he added, "That would be an impossible, ridiculous, and morally reprehensible thing to do, but your crime rate would go down."

2. In this book, names appearing in quotation marks are pseudonyms that are used either when no public record (e.g., a news account or a court case) exists that links an event or situation to a specific person, when the identity of the person is not known, or when the person wishes to remain anonymous. Also, convention dictates that I routinely refer to scholars and public officials by their last name, as, for example, "Solinger" rather than "Rickie." In referring to individuals whose stories illustrate some of the problems with the policies I describe, however, I use the person's first name: for example, "Sharwline." This is not to suggest disrespect to the latter group but out of a hope that using first names will remind the reader of these women's humanity in a way that using their last name only does not.

3. This woman also channeled much of her energy into developing programs at a women's correctional facility to help women maintain ties to their children, as well as address the needs of incarcerated women who were infected with HIV.

4. Dorothy E. Roberts (1998), *Killing the Black Body: Race, Reproduction, and the Meaning of Liberty* (New York: Vintage).

5. There are limits to thinking only in terms of rights, however, as sociologist Barbara Katz Rothman points out in both *Recreating Motherhood* and, more recently, *Weaving a Family*. This is particularly true in a consumer society that has reduced many discussions of rights to the idea that if you can pay for it, you have a right to have it. Rothman reminds her readers of the civil rights movement and the black students seated at a Woolworth's counter with "a dollar in hand and a right to buy." But, she goes on to say, "In truth, at that moment in American history, a bigger problem for the blacks of the American South was their poverty: how many of them didn't have the

dollar? Economic inequality is, for most Americans, just the way things are, not really fixable. . . . We have a focus on individual rights rather than social justice in America." Rothman (2005), *Weaving a Family: Untangling Race and Adoption* (New York: Beacon), 35. See also Rothman (1989), *Recreating Motherhood: Ideology and Technology in a Patriarchal Society* (New York: Norton). Bearing this in mind, I prefer the term "reproductive rights" or "reproductive justice." The terms "reproductive choice" and "reproductive freedom" fail to adequately acknowledge that, for many women, their choices are so restricted or limited as to be nonexistent and fall far short of anything approximating freedom.

6. Gregg Barak, Jeanne Flavin, and Paul Leighton (2001), *Class, Race, Gender, and Crime: Social Realities of Justice in America* (Los Angeles: Roxbury).

7. Kenneth Neubeck and Noel Cazenave (2001), *Welfare Racism: Playing the Race Card against America's Poor* (New York: Routledge).

8. Adrienne Rich (1984 [1977]), *Of Woman Born: Motherhood as Experience and Institution* (London: Virago), 13.

9. Later in this volume I use the terms "state actors" and "state agents" to encompass a broad range of people who work in official agencies and institutions. These include but are not limited to lawmakers, law enforcement officials, child protective service caseworkers and social workers, prosecutors and defense attorneys, criminal and family court judges, and correctional and community supervision administrators and staff. Their actions and decisions are not merely perceived as those of an individual but carry the weight of the institutions they represent.

10. Mary Bosworth (1999), *Engendering Resistance: Agency and Power in Women's Prisons* (London: Ashgate).

11. In general, however, judges are more likely to restrict women's reproduction than men's and more likely to do so in cases where the crime was not directly related to children. Rachel Roth (2004c), "Searching for the State: Who Governs Prisoners' Reproductive Rights?" *Social Politics: International Studies in Gender, State and Society* 11(3): 411–438, at 418–419.

12. Todd R. Clear and Dina R. Rose (1999), *When Neighbors Go to Jail: Impact on Attitudes about Formal and Informal Social Control* (Washington, D.C.: National Institute of Justice, U.S. Department of Justice); Todd R. Clear, Dina R. Rose, and Judith A. Ryder (2001), "Incarceration and the Community: The Problem of Removing and Returning Offenders," *Crime and Delinquency* 47(3): 335–351.

13. Rickie Solinger (2005), *Pregnancy and Power: A Short History of Reproductive Politics in America* (New York: New York University Press).

14. These divisions, of course, are artificial, given that the processes of sex, conception, pregnancy, birth, and parenting are "potentially contiguous" rather than "intrinsically separate." Lealle Ruhl (2002), "Dilemmas of the Will: Uncertainty, Reproduction, and the Rhetoric of Control," *Signs* 27(3): 641–663, at 643.

15. Vickie Welborn (2004), "Mother Pleads Guilty: Woman Negligent in Baby's Death Agrees to Sterilization," *Shreveport Times*, November 5, A1.

16. Victoria Frye (2001), "Examining Homicide's Contribution to Pregnancy-Associated Deaths," *Journal of the American Medical Association (JAMA)* 285(11): 1510–1511.

17. Adam Liptak (2006), "Prisons Often Shackle Pregnant Inmates in Labor," *New York Times,* March 2, A16. See also Anne De Groot and Susan Cu Uvin (2005), "HIV Infection among Women in Prison: Considerations for Care," *Infectious Diseases in Corrections Report* 8(5–6): 1–4.

18. Shalini Bhargava (2004), "Challenging Punishment and Privatization: A Response to the Conviction of Regina McKnight," *Harvard Civil Rights–Civil Liberties Law Review* 32: 513–542.

19. Ibid., 514; emphasis in the original.

20. Roberts (1998).

CHAPTER 1

1. Kristin Luker (1984), *Abortion and the Politics of Motherhood* (Berkeley: University of California Press), 14–15.

2. Roger Rosenblatt (1992), *Life Itself: Abortion in the American Mind* (New York: Random House), 83; Leslie Reagan (1997), *When Abortion Was a Crime: Women, Medicine, and Law in the United States, 1867–1973* (Berkeley: University of California Press), 8.

3. Rosalind Pollack Petchesky (1990), *Abortion and Woman's Choice: The State, Sexuality, and Reproductive Freedom,* 2nd ed. (Boston: Northeastern University Press), 78.

4. Luker (1984), 17–20. Many estimates are based on the reports of physicians who wanted to convince the public that abortion was a big problem; therefore, they may be inflated.

5. For example, in the cellar of an 83-year-old Philadelphia abortionist, police found the remains of 21 infants who, according to the news account, had been born alive. "Dr. Hathaway's Crimes" (1883), *New York Times,* June 24, 1.

6. James Mohr (1978), *Abortion in America* (Oxford: Oxford University Press), 147–170; Luker (1984), 14–15; Petchesky (1990), 78.

7. Mohr (1978).

8. The same article cited a test case in which John Lang, "an aged German," was prosecuted and convicted for practicing medicine without a license, a misdemeanor offense for which he was fined $50. "Crusade against Quack Doctors" (1876), *New York Times,* October 5, 5.

9. Abortion, unlike alcoholism, sexually transmitted diseases, prostitution, and other medical/bioethical concerns of the time, permitted physicians the opportunity to claim to save lives. Luker (1984), 31.

10. Women were generally aware of the continuous nature of conception and pregnancy. Where the general public and the antiabortion physicians disagreed was on the moral implications of the biological facts. The public tended to be of the mind that embryos were not, *morally* speaking, as alive as the mother, at least not until quickening. Luker (1984), 25–26.

11. Any abortions not deemed by physicians to be medically necessary were defined as criminal and, as such, came under the purview of the legal profession, a division of labor that served the purposes of both the legal and the medical professions.

Ministers' concerns could be dismissed as theoretical in the face of the hard medical science and expertise that were being claimed. Women not only lacked the credentials to challenge doctors but also were excluded from the discussion because their vested interest in the outcome rendered them incapable of being "objective." To the extent that Protestant clergy objected to abortion, their opposition seems to be based more on racist fears of the declining birthrates among Protestants than on their deeply held religious principles. Mohr (1978), 188–190; Luker (1984), 12, 43.

12. Linda Gordon (2002), *The Moral Property of Women: A History of Birth Control Politics in America* (Chicago: University of Illinois Press); Rosenblatt (1992), 87.

13. Medicalization and medical control are not confined to abortion, either, but extend to pregnancy and childbirth. Pregnancy and childbirth have come to be treated as potentially dangerous processes requiring medical intervention rather than natural and potentially empowering women-centered experiences. See Ann Oakley (1984), *The Captured Womb: A History of the Medical Care of Pregnant Women* (Oxford: Basil Blackwell); Barbara Katz Rothman (1989), *Recreating Motherhood: Ideology and Technology in a Patriarchal Society* (New York: Norton); see also the review in Bonnie Fox and Diana Worts (1999), "Revisiting the Critique of Medicalized Childbirth: A Contribution to the Sociology of Birth," *Gender & Society* 13(3): 326–346.

14. Rosenblatt (1992), 88.

15. Petchesky (1990), 73.

16. For example, between 1894 and 1932, there were 40 indictments and 5 convictions in Alabama; from 1911 to 1930, there were 100 indictments and 31 convictions; and between 1849 and 1858, there were 32 indictments and 1 conviction in Massachusetts. Taussig and Harris cited in Luker (1984), 53.

17. Thomas Harris (1936), "Statutes Relating to Abortion, Appendix A," in Frederick J. Taussig, *Abortion, Spontaneous and Induced: Medical and Social Aspects* (St. Louis: Mosby), 453–475.

18. Scholars are largely silent with regard to abortion among black women during this time. Enslaved women knew how to abort or arrange the death of a newborn if they did not want children, and high infant mortality and miscarriage rates meant that these deeds would not easily be detected. Eugene Genovese, (1974), *Roll, Jordan, Roll: The World the Slaves Made* (New York: Vintage), 496–497.

19. Reagan (1997), 133.

20. A note on terminology is warranted here. Miscarriages are considered a form of "spontaneous" abortions, as opposed to "induced" or intentional abortions. The definition of "therapeutic abortion" has changed over time. Generally speaking, therapeutic abortions are those where a pregnancy is terminated to save the woman's life or preserve her health (possibly to include her emotional or mental health), to terminate a pregnancy that would result in a child being born with defects incompatible with life or associated with significant morbidity, to terminate a pregnancy that is not viable, or to selectively reduce a pregnancy involving multiple fetuses. Denise James and Natalie E. Roche (2006) "Therapeutic Abortion," *eMedicine,* at http://www.emedicine.com/med/topic3311.htm (retrieved September 1, 2007).

21. Luker (1984), 58–59.

22. Ibid.

23. Ibid.

24. Gordon (2002), 299; Luker (1984), 56.

25. Reagan (1997), 205–207.

26. Ibid.

27. Jennifer Nelson (2003), *Women of Color and the Reproductive Rights Movement* (New York: New York University Press), 8–10.

28. Gordon (2002), 299.

29. Nelson (2003), 8–9.

30. Psychiatrists were among the first to criticize the hospital abortion system, having been called on to diagnose severe depression to justify therapeutic abortions. Attorneys argued that criminalization could no longer be justified on the grounds that it was needed to protect women from dangerous surgery. Civil liberties lawyers also raised concerns that anti-abortion statutes undermined women's right to privacy and equal protection under the law. Protestant clergy constructed abortion as a social problem rather than a medical issue, having been drawn into the campaign for legal abortion by helping women acquire safe (though illegal) abortions. Some physicians recognized not only the powerful demand for abortion but also the need to keep the procedure safe and legal. In contrast to attorneys and clergy being neutralized during the physicians' original movement to criminalize abortion, here these very groups took an active role in liberalizing the laws. In the 1950s and 1960s, this awareness led doctors (joined by lawyers and members of the clergy) to begin campaigning for reform. Nelson (2003), 10–11; Reagan (1997), 145–147.

31. Carole Joffe (1995), *Doctors of Conscience: The Struggle to Provide Abortion before and after* Roe v. Wade (Boston: Beacon).

32. Wendy Kline (2001), *Building a Better Race: Gender, Sexuality, and Eugenics from the Turn of the Century to the Baby Boom* (Berkeley: University of California Press), 2.

33. Ibid., 11.

34. Petchesky (1990), 78.

35. Kline (2001), 33.

36. While horrific, some small solace can be taken in the fact that this figure falls far short of the goal among many eugenicists to sterilize 14 million people—"the lower one-tenth"—in the United States. For example, Edwin Black (2003), *War against the Weak: Eugenics and America's Campaign to Create a Master Race* (New York: Four Walls Eight Windows), xvi; Johanna Schoen (2005), *Choice and Coercion: Birth Control, Sterilization, and Abortion in Public Health and Welfare* (Chapel Hill: University of North Carolina Press); Nelson (2003).

37. Physicians benefitted personally from their widespread use of sterilization. Performing hysterectomies and tubal ligations was more financially lucrative for physicians than other methods of birth control. Also, some doctors used minority women as a means of gaining experience in obstetrics and gynecology. This practice traces back as far as the origins of modern gynecology. The so-called Father of Modern Gynecology, J. Marion Sims, conducted surgical experiments in his Alabama backyard hospital for slaves. Area slave owners sent slaves to Sims so he could attempt to restore their health; in return, Sims was able to experiment on the women, inventing instruments and medical procedures.

38. *Roe v. Wade,* 410 U.S. 113; 93 S. Ct. 705 (1973); *Doe v. Bolton,* 410 U.S. 179; 93 S. Ct. 739 (1973).

39. There is no national definition of fetal viability in the United States. Medically, it is defined as the point at which a fetus can sustain independent life. This "anatomical threshold" typically is not reached before at least the 23rd or 24th week of gestation. Even so, the incidence of fetal mortality at 24–25 weeks of estimated gestational age is quite high, around 66 percent. Edward C. Grendys Jr. (2004), "Pregnancy: Neoplastic Diseases," in Lee Goldman and Dennis Ausiello, eds., *Cecil Textbook of Medicine* (Philadelphia: Saunders).

40. Rosenblatt (1992), 92–93.

41. Nelson (2003).

42. Before the 1960s and 1970s, many academics blamed the problems of the black family on black women's matriarchy and the cultural and economic emasculation of black men. The dominant rhetoric advocated federal birth control and sterilization programs as a means of alleviating poverty. Black Nationalist men, including members of the Nation of Islam and the Black Panther Party, embraced a hypermasculinized identity in part to counter this view. They pressured black women to have many children as a means of contributing male warriors for the revolution. As black women became integrated into the party leadership, they denounced this strategy and advocated for voluntary fertility control, a position the Black Panthers eventually accepted. The Young Lords Party was formed after the Black Panthers in 1968. According to Jennifer Nelson, author of *Women of Color and the Reproductive Rights Movement,* the Young Lords "were among the first to demand both an end to sterilization abuse and a right to abortion and contraception on demand within an organization whose politics grew from both nationalist and feminist roots" (69–70). This was possible in part because being Puerto Rican did not carry the same emasculated or emasculating stigmas as being black did. The Young Lords were able to deconstruct machismo within their own ranks much more swiftly and readily than the Black Panthers had. Unlike the Black Panthers, the Young Lords Party was founded when the women's liberation movement was picking up steam. Women succeeded in advancing their demands for an organization that was both nationalist and feminist. Ultimately, the Lords revised their platform to include a call for equality for women and to redefine machismo to connote recognizing women as comrades and equals. Leith Mullings (1997), *On Our Own Terms: Race, Class, and Gender in the Lives of African American Women* (New York: Routledge).

43. Rickie Solinger (2001), *Beggars and Choosers: How the Politics of Choice Shapes Adoption, Abortion, and Welfare in the United States* (New York: Hill and Wang).

44. Ibid., 170–171.

45. Nanette Davis (1985), *From Crime to Choice: The Transformation of Abortion in America* (Westport, CT: Greenwood), 31–32; Solinger (2001), 11–12.

46. Nelson (2003), 138–139.

47. Solinger (2001), 12.

48. Lawrence H. Tribe (1990), *Abortion: The Clash of Absolutes* (New York: Norton), 156. The indifference to indigent women's suffering was quite pointed. Senator

Jesse Helms of North Carolina went so far as to make the ridiculous argument that an exception for pregnancies that endangered a woman's life was not necessary since the woman and her doctor could always claim "self-defense" were they to be arrested and tried for deliberately killing the fetus. Solinger (2001), 11–13.

49. Some liberals may have been reluctant to advocate vigorously for federal funding of abortion because, in the context of the Vietnam War, they had previously argued from the position that taxpayers should *not* have to fund government activities they find immoral. Tribe (1990), 158.

50. Solinger (2001).

51. Ibid., 19.

52. Center for Reproductive Rights (2003), Roe v. Wade *and the Right to Privacy,* 3rd ed. (New York: Center for Reproductive Rights), 44, at http://www.reproductiverights. org/pdf/roeprivacy.pdf (retrieved September 1, 2007).

53. Tribe (1990), 23.

54. *Planned Parenthood of Southeastern Pennsylvania v. Casey,* 505 U.S. 833; 112 S. Ct. 2791 (1992).

55. Petchesky (1990), 289.

56. *Webster* (Blackmun, J., concurring in part and dissenting in part), at 560.

57. Solinger (2001), 21–22.

58. As of October 2007, only 26 states required insurers with prescription drug benefit plans to cover the full range of FDA-approved contraceptive drugs and devices. In 16 states, certain employers and insurers can refuse to cover contraceptives on religious or moral grounds. Guttmacher Institute (2007c), "Insurance Coverage of Contraceptives," *State Policies in Brief,* at http://www.guttmacher.org/statecenter/spibs/ spib_ICC.pdf (retrieved November 1, 2007).

59. It wasn't until male impotence drugs (like Viagra and Cialis) started being widely covered that many states passed legislation mandating that insurance plans which cover prescription drugs must also cover the range of FDA-approved prescription contraceptive drugs and devices. Laura Fasbach (2005), "Assembly OKs Birth Control Benefit Bill," *Bergen County (NJ) Record,* December 13, A1. See also Meika Loe (2005), *The Rise of Viagra: How the Little Blue Pill Changed Sex in America* (New York: New York University Press).

60. Guttmacher Institute (2007c); Guttmacher Institute (2007g), "Refusing to Provide Health Services," *State Policies in Brief,* at http://www.guttmacher.org/statecenter/spibs/spib_RPHS.pdf (retrieved September 1, 2007).

61. Radical feminist organizations like the Redstockings did openly acknowledge that legal abortion freed women from the psychological and physical dangers of pregnancy, and thus affirmed women's sexual pleasure. Nelson (2003), 51; Reagan (1997), 36.

62. Reagan (1997), 36.

63. Ibid., 32–33.

64. William Saletan (2003), *Bearing Right: How Conservatives Won the Abortion War* (Los Angeles: University of California Press), 102–104.

65. Ibid.

66. Ibid.

67. Solinger (2001), 64.

68. Hillary Rodham Clinton (2005), "Remarks by Senator Hillary Rodham Clinton to the NYS Family Planning Providers," January 24, at http://clinton.senate.gov/~clinton/speeches/2005125A05.html (retrieved September 1, 2007).

69. Lealle Ruhl (2002), "Dilemmas of the Will: Uncertainty, Reproduction, and the Rhetoric of Control," *Signs* 27(3): 641–663, at 644.

70. Linda L. Layne (2003), *Motherhood Lost: A Feminist Account of Pregnancy Loss in America* (New York: Routledge), 241.

71. Ruhl (2002), 644.

72. Davis (1985), 121.

CHAPTER 2

1. Matter of Bobbijean P., *In re Bobbijean P.,* N.Y. Slip Op. 7173 (2007); N.Y. App. Div. (2004); No. NN 03626-03, N.Y. Slip Op. 50286(U) (2004) (Fam. Ct., Monroe County, March Mar. 31, 2004); Michael Ziegler (2005), "No-More-Kids" Judge Orders Another Mom: Stop Procreating," Rochester (NY) Democrat and Chronicle, January 5.

2. *Matter of Bobbijean P. v. Stephanie P.,* N.Y. Slip Op. 7173 (N.Y. App. Div., 2007).

3. Mark Fass (2007), "Panel Rejects Court's Ban on Pregnancy," *New York Law Journal* 8(67): 1.

4. U.S. Census Bureau (2006), *Table 2: Annual Estimates of the Population by Selected Age Groups and Sex for the United States: April 1, 2000 to July 1, 2005,* NC-EST2005-02 (Washington, DC: U.S. Census Bureau, Population Division).

5. Neglect-only cases account for about one-third of these fatalities; another approximately one-third are due to physical abuse only, and the remaining one-third are due to some combination of maltreatment. U.S. Department of Health and Human Services, Administration on Children, Youth and Families (2006), *Child Maltreatment 2004* (Washington, DC: U.S. Government Printing Office), table 2.

6. Rachel Roth (2004b), "'No New Babies?' Gender Inequality and Reproductive Control in the Criminal Justice and Prison Systems," *Journal of Gender, Social Policy and the Law* 12(3): 391–425, at 413.

7. Accompanying the negative eugenics methods of promoting sterilization of the "unfit" was a positive eugenics approach that emphasized marriage and reproduction of the fit. In the early 1900s, marriage was encouraged as a means of permitting female sexual pleasure (i.e., by channeling it into marriage) while at the same time reducing promiscuity and promoting marriage. Even certain "high-grade" feebleminded women who had been sterilized could be released from institutions and counted on to marry and create homes for themselves and their husbands. And this is what many women did. Many of them, in fact, first learned that they had been sterilized only after they had gotten married and sought professional advice to determine why they could not conceive. Elaine Tyler May (1995), *Barren in the Promised Land: Childless Americans and the Pursuit of Happiness* (Cambridge: Harvard University Press).

8. Wendy Kline (2001), *Building a Better Race: Gender, Sexuality, and Eugenics from the Turn of the Century to the Baby Boom* (Berkeley: University of California

Press), 36–37; Nicole Hahn Rafter (1997), *Creating Born Criminals* (Urbana: University of Illinois Press), 10.

9. Rafter (1997), 10.

10. Ibid.

11. Rosalind Pollack Petchesky (1990), *Abortion and Woman's Choice: The State, Sexuality, and Reproductive Freedom*, 2nd ed. (Boston: Northeastern University Press), 84.

12. Although Brockway focused on reforming prisoners, his experiments with Elmira's "incorrigibles" set the stage for Lombroso and criminal anthropology. Lombroso considered heredity as the main organic cause of criminal behavior. He stopped short, though, of asserting that "born criminals" would produce criminalistic children. While he did recommend that born criminals be imprisoned for life or executed, this stemmed from his concern with preventing crime in the current generation, not in successive ones. American criminal anthropologists reformulated Lombroso's ideas, however, and merged them with the doctrine of eugenics. If the cause of criminality was an inherited "taint," then the solution was to prevent born criminals from reproducing more of their kind. Anthropologists also recognized a significant implication of Lombroso's work: namely, that if the criminal was morally and biologically primitive, then he or she must also be intellectually backward. So it came to pass that by the end of the nineteenth century, the idea of the criminalistic imbecile had merged with the idea of the "imbecilized" criminal. Rafter (1997), 11–12; Edwin Black (2003), *War against the Weak: Eugenics and America's Campaign to Create a Master Race* (New York: Four Walls Eight Windows), 76–83.

13. Kline (2001), 25.

14. Mary Odem (1995), *Delinquent Daughters: Protecting and Policing Adolescent Female Sexuality in the United States, 1885–1920* (Chapel Hill: University of North Carolina Press), 3.

15. Ibid., 4.

16. Ibid.

17. Kline (2001), 29. Around 1915, psychiatrists "broke with the view that intellectual and moral weakness must go hand in hand in born criminals" and thus diluted the idea of innate criminality (12). Instead, they returned to a view that psychopaths were "constitutionally inferior" but not necessarily feebleminded. Also, most did not claim that psychopathy was heritable. While psychiatrists "slowed the hunt for defective delinquents . . . the eugenics movement retained sufficient vigor to make a final push for defective delinquent legislation." Rafter (1997), 12–13.

18. Rafter (1997), 48–49.

19. Ibid., 35; Kline (2001), 37.

20. Rafter (1997), 41.

21. Although institutions for feebleminded and sexually wayward young women had been established as early as 1848, separate institutions for defective delinquents were not established until 1921. New York and Pennsylvania established independent institutions exclusively for "defective delinquents." Pennsylvania had separate facilities for delinquent males and females, with young women sent to an institution modeled after one in New York. Virginia established a state farm in 1926 that received a range

of offenders, both felons and misdemeanants, and a diverse population of drug addicts, feebleminded, mentally retarded, psychopaths, and tubercular, as well as those with venereal diseases. The widespread adoption of intelligence testing helped pressure criminal justice agencies to isolate the defective delinquents they identified. Also, in New York and possibly elsewhere, World War I had depopulated the prisons, thus making it easier for the legislature to rationalize designating an institution for defective delinquents. World War I also heightened anxieties about extramarital sex and the spread of venereal disease among the troops. Young women were considered to transmit feeblemindedness and immorality, as well as syphilis. Rafter (1997); Kline (2001).

22. Kline (2001), 3.

23. Ibid., 78.

24. Black (2003), 58–59. The balance was to be comprised of 3 million people who were "equally defective, but not under the state's care" and 7 million "borderline" cases. Their cause was aided by some of the wealthiest people in the country, including John D. Rockefeller Jr., who supported eugenic plans to incarcerate feebleminded criminal women for lengthy periods to keep them "from perpetuating [their] kind . . . until after the period for child bearing had been passed." Quoted in Black (2003), 93. Rockefeller also formed the Bureau of Social Hygiene to investigate prostitution. Rafter (1997), 154.

25. Rafter (1997), 33.

26. Ibid., 153.

27. Quoted in Black (2003), 57. The committee's main legal advisor suggested that it would probably be constitutional if the original sentencing judge were to order the sterilization of a convicted offender, but to venture farther and sterilize other offenders might be problematic. The legal advisor also warned against the dangers of sterilizing someone who could be reformed (and mentioned specifically juvenile offenders who were rendered habitual criminals but went on to become exemplary citizens as adults). To deprive such a person "all hope of progeny" through sterilization would "approach closely to the line of cruel and unusual punishment." Quoted in Black (2003), 59–60.

28. Mike Anton (2003), "Forced Sterilization Once Seen as Path to a Better World," *Los Angeles Times,* July 16, A1.

29. Rafter (1997), 227.

30. Kline (2001), 59.

31. Asexualization encompassed a broader category of procedures than "sterilization," which typically involved vasectomies in men and tubal ligations in women. California's laws permitted castrating a man or removing a woman's ovaries. "An act to permit asexualization of inmates of the state hospitals and the California Home for the Care and Training of Feeble-Minded Children and of convicts in the state prisons," approved April 26, 1909, date of approval: June 13, 1913, 1913 Cal Stat Chapter 363.

32. The Lynchburg Training School and Hospital, the country's largest institution for the retarded, sterilized thousands of men, women, and children without notification. Many of the women were led to believe they were going to have an appendectomy. Most of the sterilizations were performed on whites, though it is not clear the extent to which this was the result of the hospital's restrictive whites-only admissions

policy or an attempt to focus specifically on poor whites. Robert Reinhold (1980), "Virginia Hospital's Chief Traces 50 Years of Sterilizing the 'Retarded,'" *New York Times*, February 23, 6; Johanna Schoen (2005), *Choice and Coercion: Birth Control, Sterilization, and Abortion in Public Health and Welfare* (Chapel Hill: University of North Carolina Press), 82.

33. Rafter (1997), 227.

34. Quoted in James W. Weir (1929), "West Virginia Aims at Crime Reduction," *New York Times*, May 12, E2.

35. Kline (2001), 81.

36. For example, women represented only a slight majority of those sterilized at Sonoma. However, while men were typically sterilized for their own benefit, women were sterilized to protect society from their perceived "sexual delinquency." Of the patients sterilized between 1922 and 1925, some 25 percent of the women were sent to Sonoma for the sole or primary purpose of being sterilized, compared with only 2 percent of the men. Having sex outside of marriage became a code for class and a marker for hereditary inferiority. Rafter (1997), 160; Kline (2001), 53, 59; May (1995), 203.

37. Nancy Ordover (2003), *American Eugenics: Race, Queer Anatomy, and the Science of Nationalism* (Minneapolis: University of Minnesota Press), 31.

38. Rafter (1997), 153.

39. Ordover (2003), 134–135.

40. Ibid., 134.

41. Ibid., 78–79.

42. Just as negative eugenic campaigns began to peak in the 1930s, "positive eugenics"—designed to strengthen the white race through pronatalist campaigns to promote marriage and family among white, college-educated couples (as opposed to working-class, sexually suspect, institutionalized "moron girls")—became more popular. Kline (2001), 126.

43. *Skinner v. Oklahoma*, 316 U.S. 535 (1942).

44. Ibid., at 541.

45. Black (2003), xvi.

46. Schoen (2005).

47. Michael Katz (2001), *The Price of Citizenship* (New York: Owl), 4.

48. Schoen (2005).

49. Jennifer Nelson (2003), *Women of Color and the Reproductive Rights Movement* (New York: New York University Press).

50. Ibid., 66.

51. In some parts of the South, sterilization abuse was so common that tying a woman's fallopian tubes or removing her uterus without her knowledge or consent was known as a "Mississippi appendectomy."

52. Many white women, who had been denied sterilization because they were unmarried or because they were deemed as not having had enough children, objected to the introduction of a waiting period and other measures designed to eliminate sterilization abuse. As physician and medical activist Helen Rodriguez-Trias explains, "While young white middle-class women were denied their requests for sterilization, low income women of certain ethnicity were misled or coerced into them." Quoted in

Joyce Wilcox (2002), "The Face of Women's Health: Helen Rodriguez-Trias," *American Journal of Public Health* 92: 566–569, at 568. See also Jane Lawrence (2000), "The Indian Health Service and the Sterilization of Native American Women," *American Indian Quarterly* 24: 400–419.

53. This figure includes 20,000 in California (between 1909 and 1953), and 8,000 in North Carolina and about 7,000 in Virginia (between the late 1920s and the mid-1970s). Schoen (2005), 82.

54. Ordover (2003), 161.

55. Beth Warren (2005), "Calls, Emails Hammer DA on Sterilization Case," *Atlanta Journal-Constitution,* February 18, 20E.

56. Vickie Welborn (2004), "Mother Pleads Guilty: Woman Negligent in Baby's Death Agrees to Sterilization," *Shreveport Times,* November 5, A1.

57. Jeff Newell (2000), "Court: No More Children for Mom," *Northwest Daily News,* February 25, B1.

58. Alex Wayne (2002), "Child's Parents Avoid Prison Term: A Superior Court Judge Says Christian Eddins' Parents Aren't Wholly to Blame for His Death," *Greensboro (NC) News and Record,* August 2, B1.

59. Guillermo Contreras (2000), "Defendant Told She Should Be Sterilized," *Albuquerque Journal,* October 12, A1.

60. Jennifer McMenamin (2006), "The Roots of Child Abuse," *Baltimore Sun,* May 4.

61. The discussion of "fundamental rights" draws significantly from the explanation provided in Evelyn Holmer (2004/2005), "How *Ohio v. Talty* Provided for Future Bans on Procreation and the Consequences That Action Brings," *Journal of Law and Health* 19: 141–176.

62. Cynthia R. Daniels (1993), *At Women's Expense: State Power and the Politics of Fetal Rights* (Cambridge: Harvard University Press), 33.

63. Ibid.

64. *Olmstead v. United States,* 277 U.S. 438 (1928), at 478 (Brandeis, J., dissenting). See also *Planned Parenthood v. Casey,* 505 U.S. 833; 112 S. Ct. 2791 (1992).

65. *Skinner v. Oklahoma,* 316 U.S. 535 (1942), at 541; *Roe v. Wade,* 410 U.S. 113; 93 S. Ct. 705 (1973), at 163; *Planned Parenthood of Southeastern Pennsylvania v. Casey,* 505 U.S. 833 (1992).

66. Shalini Bhargava (2004), "Challenging Punishment and Privatization: A Response to the Conviction of Regina McKnight," *Harvard Civil Rights–Civil Liberties Law Review* 32: 513–542, at 526.

67. *Eisenstadt* extended the right to obtain contraceptives to unmarried couples. *Eisenstadt v. Baird,* 405 U.S. 438; 92 S. Ct. 1029 (1972), at 453.

68. New York Civil Liberties Union (2004), "Legal Issues in Rochester Ruling" at http://www.nyclu.org/rrp_rochester_ruling_issues_062904.html (retrieved September 1, 2007).

69. Roth (2004b).

70. Ibid., 418–419. Some men charged with abuse or neglect have been ordered not to procreate. On other occasions, men who owe back child support have been ordered not to procreate, a situation that has been referred to as "pay up or zip up." For example, a judge issued a "no-procreation order" to Sean Talty in 2002 as part of

his sentence for failing to pay $38,000 child support to three of the seven children he fathered by five women. The Ohio Supreme Court tossed out that order because there was no method for lifting the procreation ban if Talty fulfilled his parenting obligations. In a similar case in 1999, however, the Wisconsin Supreme Court upheld the order that David Oakley (a father of nine children who was sentenced to three years in prison and five years of probation for owing $25,000 in child support) to father any children during probation unless he could prove he could support them all. Robert Pierre (2004), "In Ohio, Supreme Court Considers Right to Procreate," *Washington Post,* May 11, A2; Christina Leonard (2004), "Inmates' Advocates Challenge Arpaio's Abortion Roadblocks," *Arizona Republic,* October 15, n.p. Appellate courts generally have not upheld sexual and reproductive restrictions on women. Their reasons for overturning the restrictions include (a) the restrictions bear no direct relationship to the crime, (b) they restrict noncriminal conduct or coerce conduct (by pressuring men and women to get married in order to procreate), (c) they are overbroad, and (d) they cannot be enforced. But, it should be noted, defense attorneys often do not challenge a charge or conviction, either out of respect for the defendant's wishes or even, possibly, the defense attorney's disquietude about some women continuing to procreate.

71. Rachel Roth (2000), *Making Women Pay: The Hidden Costs of Fetal Rights* (Ithaca, NY: Cornell University Press).

72. Personal Responsibility and Work Opportunity Reconciliation Act of 1996 (PRWORA), Pub. L. 104-193, 110 Stat. 2105. This legislation reduced benefits and abolished Aid to Families with Dependent Children. See also Alejandra Marchevsky and Jeanne Theoharis (2006), *Not Working: Latina Immigrants, Low-Wage Jobs, and the Failure of Welfare Reform* (New York: New York University Press).

73. Congressional Budget Office (2003), *Baby Boomers' Retirement Prospects: An Overview* (Washington, DC: Congressional Budget Office), 2.

74. Ibid.

75. Roth (2000), 4.

76. Germaine Greer (1985), *Sex and Destiny* (New York: Harper and Row), 331.

77. *Matter of Bobbijean P., In re Bobbijean P.,* 5.

78. Margaret Sanger (1920), *Women and the New Race* (New York: Brentano's), n.p., at http://infomotions.com/etexts/gutenberg/dirs/etext05/7wmnr10.htm (retrieved January 20, 2008). The pseudonymous Jukes family was described in Richard L. Dugdale (1910), *The Jukes: A Study in Crime, Pauperism, Disease and Heredity* (New York: Putnam).

79. U.S. Government Printing Office (2006), *Budget of the United States Government: Public Budget Database, Fiscal Year 2006,* at http://www.gpoaccess.gov/usbudget/fy06/browse.html (retrieved September 1, 2007); Genaro Armas (2003), "Poverty Climbs, Incomes Slide" (Washington, DC: Associated Press); Children's Defense Fund (2004), *Basic Facts on Welfare* (Washington, DC: Children's Defense Fund), at http://www.childrensdefense.org/site/PageServer?pagename=familyincome_welfare_basic-facts (retrieved September 1, 2007).

80. Congressional Budget Office (2005), *Changes in Participation in Means-Tested Programs* (Washington, DC: Congressional Budget Office), at http://www.cbo.gov/showdoc.cfm?index=6302&sequence=0 (retrieved September 1, 2007).

81. Ibid.

82. Congressional Budget Office (2007), *Estimated Funding for Operations in Iraq and the War on Terrorism* (Washington, DC: Congressional Budget Office), at http://www.cbo.gov/publications/collections/iraq.cfm and http://www.cbo.gov/ftpdocs/77xx/doc7793/02-07-CostOfWar.pdf (retrieved September 1, 2007).

83. Citizens for Tax Justice and the Institute on Taxation and Economic Policy (2004), *Corporate Income Taxes in the Bush Years,* at http://www.ctj.org/corpfed04an.pdf (retrieved September 1, 2007).

84. Robert G. Lynch (2005), "Early Childhood Investment Yields Big Payoff," *Policy Perspectives* at http://www.wested.org/online_pubs/pp-05-02.pdf (retrieved September 1, 2007).

85. Leslie Calman and Linda Tarr-Whelan (2005), *Early Childhood Education for All: A Wise Investment* (New York: Family Initiative), at http://web.mit.edu/workplace-center/docs/Full%20Report.pdf (retrieved September 1, 2007).

86. Dennis Chaptman (2001), "High Court Limits Dad's Procreation," *Milwaukee Journal Sentinel,* July 11, A1.

87. The NYCLU warned that the judge's financial logic could be extended to the exercise of other fundamental rights: "For example, can New York City ban all protests (protected by the First Amendment) during the Republican convention [in the summer of 2004] because of the extra security costs the protests will entail?" New York Civil Liberties Union (2004).

88. ACLU Fund of Michigan (2003), amicus brief filed in *Family Independence Agency v. Renee Gamez* (1999).

89. Newell (2000), B1.

90. Deborah Frank, Marilyn Augustyn, Wanda Knight, et al. (2001), "Growth, Development, and Behavior in Early Childhood Following Prenatal Cocaine Exposure," *Journal of the American Medical Association (JAMA)* 285: 1613–1625; Barry Lester, Linda LaGasse, and Ronald Seifer (1998), "Cocaine Exposure and Children: The Meaning of Subtle Effects," *Science* 282: 633–634.

91. Quoted in Lynn Paltrow (2001), "The War on Drugs and the War on Abortion," *Southern Law Review* 28(3): 201–253, at 247.

92. U.S. Department of Health and Human Services (2006), *The AFCARS Report* (Washington, DC: Administration for Children and Families, Administration on Children, Youth and Families, Children's Bureau), at www.acf.hhs.gov/programs/cb and http://www.acf.hhs.gov/programs/cb/stats_research/afcars/tar/report13.htm (retrieved September 1, 2007).

93. Rickie Solinger (2005), *Pregnancy and Power: A Short History of Reproductive Politics in America* (New York: New York University Press), 252.

94. Jennifer Reich (2005), *Fixing Families: Parents, Power, and the Child Welfare System* (New York: Routledge).

95. Project Prevention, "Statistics," at http://www.projectprevention.org/ (retrieved January 10, 2008). The program used to give clients more money if they were permanently sterilized than if they undertook a form of temporary sterilization.

96. On the website, Project Prevention responds to the frequently asked question, "Are you targeting blacks?" with the answer, "The reality is, not all drug addicts

are black." See also Amy Allina (2002), "Cash for Birth Control: Discriminatory, Unethical, Ineffective and Bad Public Policy," *Network News* 27(1): 5–6; Christopher Zehnder (2003), "Not Medicine, but Social Control," *Los Angeles Mission,* at http://www.losangelesmission.com/ed/articles/2003/1103cz.htm (retrieved September 1, 2007).

97. Project Prevention, "Statistics" (retrieved May 18, 2007).

98. Quoted in Zehnder (2003).

99. Project Prevention, at http://www.projectprevention.org/help/donations.html#otherways (retrieved September 1, 2007).

100. Quoted in Zehnder (2003).

101. *Family Independence Agency v. Renee Gamez,* Mich. App. LEXIS 2529 (2003) (unpublished opinion).

102. See also Laurence H. Tribe (1990), *Abortion: The Clash of Absolutes* (New York: Norton), 97.

103. Rafter (1997), 212.

104. Suzanne C. Tough, Christine Newburn-Cook, David W. Johnston, et al. (2002), "Delayed Childbearing and Its Impact on Population Rate Changes in Lower Birth Weight, Multiple Birth, and Preterm Delivery," *Pediatrics* 109(3): 399–403.

105. J. A. Martin, B. E. Hamilton, P. D. Sutton, et al. (2006), *Births: Final Data for 2004* (Hyattsville, MD: National Center for Health Statistics).

106. L. Keith and J. J. Oleszczuk (1999), "Iatrogenic Multiple Birth, Multiple Pregnancy and Assisted Reproductive Technologies," *International Journal of Gynecology and Obstetrics* 64: 11–25; J. A. Martin, M. F. MacDorman, and T. J. Mathews (1997), "Triplet Births: Trends and Outcomes, 1971–94," *Vital and Health Statistics* 55: 1–20.

107. William M. Gilbert, Thomas S. Nesbitt, and Beate Xen (2003), "The Cost of Prematurity: Quantification by Gestational Age and Birth Weight," *Obstetrics and Gynecology* 102: 488–492.

108. Tribe (1990), 92.

CHAPTER 3

1. *Thornburgh v. American College of Obstetricians,* 476 U.S. 747; 106 S. Ct. 2169 (1986).

2. Judy Mann (2000), "N.Y. Suit Shows Fragility of Abortion Rights," *Washington Post,* March 29, C15.

3. New York Civil Liberties Union (2000), "On Monday to Argue Court Order Prohibiting Former Inmate from Having Abortion Is Unconstitutional," *NYCLU News,* March 5, 2000, n.p., at http://www.nyclu.org/news2000.html (retrieved October 12, 2006).

4. John R. Sullivan (2000), "Judge Temporarily Bars County Inmate from Having Abortion," *New York Times,* March 4, B2.

5. Soon after the order was entered, Barbara was released from jail and was no longer dependent on the county sheriff for her medical care. Bizarrely, she was still forbidden to undergo the medical procedure under the original restraining order.

6. *Planned Parenthood of Southeastern Pennsylvania v. Casey,* 505 U.S. 833; 112
S. Ct. 2791 (1992); *Roe v. Wade,* 410 U.S. 113; 93 S. Ct. 705 (1973); *Doe v. Bolton,* 410 U.S.
179; 93 S. Ct. 739 (1973).

7. Upon being admitted to a Louisiana correctional facility in 1999, Victoria
W. found out that she was around 14 weeks pregnant. Victoria wanted an abortion.
Because an abortion was considered elective surgery, the unwritten prison policy
required Victoria to get a court order allowing her to leave the prison. Her attorney,
Howard Marcello, did not contact prison officials to arrange the court order; the sheriff's attorney suspected this was because Marcello was morally opposed to abortion.
Unbeknownst to Victoria, when Marcello did file a motion, he did not ask for a court
order but for early release from the remainder of her sentence. The judge temporarily
set the motion aside pending a medical evaluation, which Victoria was told by her attorney would cost $1,500. Victoria eventually filed her own motion for early release,
citing problems with one of her children. By the time she was released, however, it was
too late for her to get an abortion. The U.S. Court of Appeals ruled that it was her attorney's action, not the policy, that denied Victoria her right to an abortion. *Victoria
W. v. Larpenter,* 369 F.3d 475; 205 F. Supp. 2d 580 (Eastern District of Louisiana, 2004).

8. Around 4 million women in the United States will give birth each year.
Stephanie Ventura, Joyce C. Abma, William D. Mosher, and Stanley Henshaw (2003),
"Trends in Pregnancy Rates, 1976–1997, and New Rates for 1998–1999: United States,"
National Vital Statistics Reports 52(7): 1–15.

9. Lawrence B. Finer and Stanley K. Henshaw (2006a), "Disparities in Rates of
Unintended Pregnancy in the United States," *Perspectives on Sexual and Reproductive
Health* 38(2): 90–96.

10. Rachel K. Jones, Mia R. S. Zolna, Stanley K. Henshaw, and Lawrence B.
Finer (2008), "Abortion in the United States: Incidence and Access to Services, 2005,"
Perspectives on Sexual and Reproductive Health 40: 6–16; National Center for Health
Statistics (2005), *Health, United States, 2005* (Washington, DC: U.S. Government Print-
ing Office), table 16, at http://www.cdc.gov/nchs/data/hus/hus05.pdf; Lilo Strauss, Joy
Herndon, Jeani Chang, et al. (2005), *Abortion Surveillance: United States, 2002* (Atlanta:
Centers for Disease Control and Prevention, National Center for Chronic Disease Pre-
vention and Health Promotion, Division of Reproductive Health).

11. Lilo T. Strauss, Sonya B. Gamble, Wilda Y. Parker, et al. (2006), "Abortion
Surveillance: United States, 2003," *Morbidity and Mortality Weekly Report* 55(S S11):
1–32.

12. Ibid.

13. F. C. Notzon, Y. M. Korotkova, S. P. Ermakov, et al. (1999), "Maternal and
Child Health Statistics: Russian Federation and United States, Selected Years, 1985–95,"
Vital and Health Statistics (Washington, DC: National Center for Health Statistics),
table 17.

14. Jack M. Balkin (2005), "*Roe v. Wade:* An Engine of Controversy," in Jack
M. Balkin, ed., *What* Roe v. Wade *Should Have Said* (New York: New York University
Press), 3–27.

15. Rosemary Nossiff (2007), "Gendered Citizenship: Women, Equality, and
Abortion Policy," *New Political Science* 29(1): 61–76.

16. Ibid., 62.

17. *Gonzales v. Carhart,* 127 S. Ct. 1610; 167 L. Ed. 2d 480 (2007), at 1649; *Bradwell v. State,* 83 U.S. 130 (1873).

18. *Gonzales v. Carhart,* at 1649.

19. Ibid.

20. Nossiff (2007).

21. Center for American Women in Politics, at www.cawp.rutgers.edu (retrieved September 1, 2007).

22. Nossiff (2007).

23. Balkin (2005).

24. Julia S. O'Connor, Ann Shola Orloff, and Sheila Shaver (1999), States, Markets, Families: Gender, Liberalism and Social Policy in Australia, Canada, Great Britain and the United States (Cambridge: Cambridge University Press).

25. Jones et al. (2008).

26. Evelyn Nieves (2005), "S.D. Makes Abortion Rare through Laws and Stigma: Out-of-State Doctors Come Weekly to 1 Clinic," *Washington Post,* December 27, A1.

27. Ibid.

28. Stanley K. Henshaw and Lawrence B. Finer (2003), "The Accessibility of Abortion Services in the United States, 2001," *Perspectives on Sexual and Reproductive Health* 35(1): 16–24.

29. Lawrence B. Finer and Stanley K. Henshaw (2006b), *Estimates of U.S. Abortion Incidence: 2001–2003* (New York: Alan Guttmacher Institute), at http://www.guttmacher.org/pubs/2006/08/03/ab_incidence.pdf (retrieved September 1, 2007); Jones et al. (2008).

30. Carole Joffe (1995), *Doctors of Conscience: The Struggle to Provide Abortion before and after* Roe v. Wade (Boston: Beacon).

31. Ibid., 142.

32. Guttmacher Institute (2007g), "Refusing to Provide Health Services," *State Policies in Brief,* at http://www.guttmacher.org/statecenter/spibs/spib_RPHS.pdf (retrieved September 1, 2007).

33. Ibid.

34. Hillary Frey and Miranda Kennedy (2001), "Abortion on Trial: The Prosecution of Dr. Pendergraft," *Nation,* June 18, 12–14.

35. "Man Pleads Guilty to Breaking into Iowa City Abortion Clinic" (2006), *Associated Press,* July 20; "Davenport Man Gets Probation for Breaking into Abortion Clinic" (2006), *Associated Press,* September 2.

36. Eric Rich (2006), "Bomb Suspect's Father Tipped Off Authorities," *Washington Post,* June 10, B1; "Robert Weiler Indicted on Charges of Possessing, Making Unregistered Destructive Device" (2006), *U.S. Federal News,* June 19, n.p.

37. "Accessory to Firebomb Gets One Year" (2006), *Associated Press,* August 4.

38. Each year, the FMF conducts a national survey of anti-abortion violence, harassment, and intimidation directed at clinics' patients and health care workers. The survey is among the most comprehensive study of its kind. In 2005, some 739 abortion providers were identified, and 337 responded to the survey. Nearly one-half were nonprofit clinics, around one-third were for-profit facilities, and one-fifth were private

doctor's offices. Michelle Wood, Susie Gilligan, Patty Campos, and Daisy Kim (2006), *2005 National Clinic Violence Survey* (Arlington, VA: Feminist Majority Foundation).

39. FMF noted that effective law enforcement corresponds with lower levels of violence. According to FMF, of those clinics that had contact with local, state, or federal law enforcement, 75 percent or more rated law enforcement response as "good" or "excellent." News accounts suggest that serious crimes are prosecuted vigorously and sentenced severely. For instance, the five persons convicted in the United States for anti-abortion-related murders were given sentences ranging from 25 years to life all the way up to the death penalty. Michael F. Griffin is serving a life sentence for the 1993 murder of a doctor in Pensacola. Paul Hill received the death penalty for two murders outside a Pensacola clinic in 1994; he was executed in 2003. John Salvi was sentenced to life without parole for killing two receptionists at a Boston-area clinic in 1994 in Massachusetts; he committed suicide in prison. Eric Rudolph was sentenced to life imprisonment in 2005 for a 1998 bombing that killed a police officer at an Alabama abortion clinic. James Kopp murdered an Amherst (NY) physician in 1998; in 2003, he was sentenced to 25 years to life. National Abortion Federation (NAF) statistics echo these findings. In 2005, NAF recorded nearly 15,000 incidents against abortion providers in the United States and Canada. The most common incidents were picketing (13,415), followed by trespassing (633), hate mail and harassing calls (515), and vandalism (83). There were also two incidents of arson and six bombing or arson attempts. Other incidents included assault and battery, death threats, burglary, and stalking. From 1991 to 2005, there were 7 murders and 17 attempted murders. Wood et al. (2006); National Abortion Federation (2006), *NAF Violence and Disruption Statistics,* at http://www.prochoice.org/pubs_research/publications/downloads/about_abortion/violence_statistics.pdf (retrieved October 12, 2006).

40. According to the New York State Department of Health, Office of Professional Misconduct and Physician Discipline, medical misconduct includes "practicing fraudulently, practicing with gross incompetence or gross negligence; practicing while impaired by alcohol, drugs, physical disability or mental disability; being convicted of a crime; filing a false report; guaranteeing that treatment will result in a cure; refusing to provide services because of race, creed, color or ethnicity; performing services not authorized by the patient; harassing, abusing or intimidating a patient; ordering excessive tests; and abandoning or neglecting a patient in need of immediate care." New York State Department of Health, Office of Professional Misconduct and Physician Discipline, at http://www.health.state.ny.us/nysdoh/opmc/main.htm (retrieved September 1, 2007).

41. Sharon Lerner (2002), "When Medicine Is Murder," *Village Voice,* April 2.

42. Women went as far as developing their own nonmedical and illegal abortion networks, such as California's Society for Humane Abortion and the Chicago Women's Liberation Union's "Jane." The Jane collective hired someone they thought was a doctor to perform abortions, but upon finding out he was not, they began to train themselves to perform abortions. From 1969 to 1973, "Jane" performed 11,000 illegal abortions for an average fee of $50. Nanette Davis (1985), *From Crime to Choice: The Transformation of Abortion in America* (Westport, CT: Greenwood), 181, 216; Jennifer Nelson (2003), *Women of Color and the Reproductive Rights Movement* (New York: New York University Press), 47.

43. Leslie J. Reagan (1997), *When Abortion Was a Crime: Women, Medicine, and Law in the United States, 1867–1973* (Berkeley: University of California Press); Rickie Solinger (2001), *Beggars and Choosers: How the Politics of Choice Shapes Adoption, Abortion, and Welfare in the United States* (New York: Hill and Wang).

44. Reagan (1997).

45. Solinger (2001).

46. Reagan (1997), 200.

47. Finer and Henshaw (2006); Jones et al. (2008).

48. "Florida: Illegal Abortion Clinic Busted" (2005), *Tampa Tribune*, January 6.

49. Paul Rubin (2004), "No Choice Scenes from a 'Clown Show,'" *Phoenix New Times*, January 8.

50. "Late Term Abortion Cases" (2001), *Associated Press State and Local Wire*, April 7.

51. Elizabeth Fernandez (2000), "Jailed for Mistake in Abortion: Doctor Says He Was Singled Out," *Cleveland Plain Dealer*, September 24, 22A.

52. Phyllida Burlingame (2000), *Preventing Unfair Prosecution of Abortion Providers: An Investigation into Political Bias by the Medical Board of California* (San Francisco: ACLU of Northern California), at http://www.aclunc.org/news/press_releases/aclu_investigates_political_bias_by_the_medical_board_of_california.shtml?ht=burlingame%20burlingame (retrieved September 1, 2007).

53. Nationally, one study found, nearly 100,000 people die each year in the United States as a result of medical error, but only 10 doctors had been charged with murder in the last dozen years. Burlingame (2000).

54. Jodi Wilgoren (2005), "Kansas Prosecutor Demands Files on Late-Term Abortion Patients," *New York Times*, February 25; "Former AG's Case against Abortion Doctor Now Dead" (2007), *Kansas City Star*, February 14.

55. Tiller's clinic is one of only a few in the country to perform late-term abortions and has long been a target of anti-abortion protesters. Kansas state health records indicate that 491 abortions were performed after the 22nd week of pregnancy in 2003.

56. Stephanie Simon (2006), "Kansas Judge Dismisses Abortion Charges," *Los Angeles Times*, December 23, A22.

57. Kansas was not the only state to seek to prosecute abortion providers under the pretense of being concerned for statutory rape victims. In Florida, a bill was introduced in the House and the Senate requiring health care professionals to call the police if they "reasonably should know" that a girl 15 years old or younger might be pregnant. The bill also requires doctors who provide abortions to these girls to collect a DNA sample to the Florida Department of Law Enforcement. As in Kansas, the sponsors of the bill claimed that the bill was intended to target sexual abuse of minors, not to make it more difficult for girls to obtain abortions. However, Representative Dennis Baxley was quoted as saying, "It doesn't make me unhappy that a few more children may live." Jennifer Liberto and Rebecca Catalenello (2007), "Legislators Want Pregnant Girls Reported," *St. Petersburg Times*, March 7.

58. A few months later, Kansas Attorney General Paul Morrison filed 19 new misdemeanor charges that Tiller failed to secure an independent second opinion before performing a late-term abortion. Dion Lefler (2007), "New Judge Assigned to

Hear Case against George Tiller," *Wichita Eagle,* August 22, n.p. Furthermore, Kansas is among a handful of states that permit citizens to petition for a grand jury to convene. Anti-abortion groups organized a citizen petition drive that led to a grand jury being convened in January 2008 to investigate Tiller. Ron Sylvester (2008), "Grand Jury Sworn in to Investigate Wichita Abortions," *Wichita Eagle,* January 8, n.p.

59. Susan Saulny (2007), "Abortion Charges Filed against Kansas Clinic," *New York Times,* October 18, A26.

60. Ann Friedman (2006), "Mail-Order Abortions," *Mother Jones,* November/December, at http://www.motherjones.com/news/outfront/2006/11/mail_order_abortions.html (retrieved September 1, 2007).

61. Mark A. Rosing and Cheryl D. Archbald (2000), "The Knowledge, Acceptability, and Use of Misoprostol for Self-Induced Medical Abortion in an Urban US Population," *Journal of the American Medical Women's Association* 55(3): 183–185.

62. Cytotec is less effective than the RU-486 "cocktail," but it is also far less expensive.

63. Rosing and Archbald (2000).

64. "Woman Faces Charges for Performing Abortion on Self" (2005), *Columbia State,* May 1, B3.

65. Ibid. See also Brian R. Ballou and Raja Mishra (2007), "Alleged Bid to Abort Leads to Baby's Death," *Boston Globe,* January 25.

66. "Pregnant Woman Charged with Attempting to Abort Fetus" (2007), *Associated Press Wire Service,* April 11.

67. Linda A. Bartlett, Cynthia J. Berg, Holly B. Shulman, et al. (2004), "Risk Factors for Legal Induced Abortion-Related Mortality in the United States," *Obstetrics and Gynecology* 103(4): 729–737.

68. Jones et al. (2008).

69. Ibid.

70. Lawrence B. Finer, Lori F. Frohwirth, Lindsay A. Dauphinee, et al. (2006), "Timing of Steps and Reasons for Delays in Obtaining Abortions in the United States," *Contraception* 74(4): 334–344. A study found that over 1 in 4 pregnant women who used cocaine (and around 1 in 16 other women) who gave birth in Washington, D.C., hospitals considered abortion when they discovered they were pregnant but could not afford it. Jeanne Flavin (2002), "A Glass Half Full? Harm Reduction among Pregnant Women Who Use Cocaine," *Journal of Drug Issues* 32: 973–998.

71. Guttmacher Institute (2007h), "State Funding of Abortion under Medicaid," *State Policies in Brief,* at http://www.guttmacher.org/pubs/spib_SFAM.pdf (retrieved September 1, 2007).

72. Ibid.

73. Finer et al. (2006).

74. *Maher v. Roe,* 432 U.S. 464; 97 S. Ct. 2376 (1977) (Brennan, J., dissenting).

75. Guttmacher Institute (2007d), "Mandatory Counseling and Waiting Periods for Abortion," *State Policies in Brief,* at http://www.guttmacher.org/statecenter/spibs/spib_MWPA.pdf (retrieved September 1, 2007).

76. Ibid.

77. *Planned Parenthood of Southeastern Pennsylvania v. Casey,* 505 U.S. 833; 112 S. Ct. 2791 (1992).

78. Guttmacher Institute (2007d).

79. Chinué Turner Richardson and Elizabeth Nash (2006), "Misinformed Consent: The Medical Accuracy of State-Developed Abortion Counseling Materials," *Guttmacher Policy Review* 9(4): 6–11.

80. American Cancer Society (2006), *Can Having an Abortion Cause or Contribute to Breast Cancer?* at http://www.cancer.org/docroot/CRI/content/CRI_2_6x_Can_Having_an_Abortion_Cause_or_Contribute_to_Breast_Cancer.asp (retrieved September 1, 2007); National Cancer Institute (2003), *Summary Report: Early Reproductive Events and Breast Cancer Workshop,* at www.cancer.gov/cancerinfo/ere-workshop-report (retrieved September 1, 2007).

81. Susan J. Lee, Henry J. Pater Ralston, Eleanor A. Drey, et al. (2005), "Fetal Pain: A Systematic Multidisciplinary Review of the Evidence," *Journal of the American Medical Association (JAMA)* 294: 947–954.

82. U.S. House of Representatives (2006), *False and Misleading Health Information Provided by Federally Funded Pregnancy Resource Centers* (Washington, DC: Committee on Government Reform–Minority Staff), at http://www.democrats.reform.house.gov/Documents/20060717101140-30092.pdf (retrieved September 1, 2007).

83. Patrik Jonsson (2007), "Ultrasound: Latest Tool in Battle over Abortion," *Christian Science Monitor,* May 15.

84. The (admittedly anecdotal) experience of a friend of mine suggests that the counseling process may, in some instances, contribute to a woman's anxiety rather than alleviate it. "Erin" was the mother of two young children. She discovered she was pregnant at the same time that her marriage was falling apart. She felt strongly that an abortion was in her best interest and promptly arranged for an abortion. She scheduled an appointment at the abortion clinic in the predominately Catholic, middle-sized town where she lived. She sat in the waiting room, which featured a bulletin board where women could leave notes for their fetus. As she read the notes on the bulletin board, Erin became increasingly anxious—not about the abortion procedure itself, but about how she should act. She feared that the counselor might view her certainty that she wanted an abortion as abnormal and insist that Erin undergo additional counseling.

85. Strauss et al. (2005), table 16.

86. Ibid.

87. Finer et al. (2006).

88. Helena Silverstein (2007), *Girls on the Stand: How Courts Fail Pregnant Minors* (New York: New York University Press).

89. All of these states allow a minor to obtain an abortion without parental involvement if she receives approval from a court or in a medical emergency. Guttmacher Institute (2007f), "Parental Involvement in Minors' Abortions," at http://www.guttmacher.org/statecenter/spibs/spib_PIMA.pdf (retrieved November 1, 2007).

90. Center for Reproductive Rights (2001), *Mandatory Parental Consent and Notification Laws* (New York: Center for Reproductive Rights), at http://www.reproductiverights.org/pub_fac_mandconsent.html (retrieved September 1, 2007).

91. Silverstein (2007), 3–18.

92. Stanley K. Henshaw and Kathryn Kost (1992), "Parental Involvement in Minors' Abortion Decisions," *Family Planning Perspectives* 24: 196–209.

93. Silverstein (2007), 52.

94. Ibid., 69.

95. Ibid., 59.

96. Ibid.

97. *Ex parte Anonymous,* 905 So. 2d 845 (2005). See also http://www.birminghambar.org/data/SlipOpinions/CivApp/2040267.htm (retrieved January 21, 2008).

98. Ex parte Anonymous.

99. Ibid., 850–851.

100. Child Custody Protection Act (CCPA) and Child Interstate Abortion Notification Act (CIANA), H. R. 748; S. 8, 396, 403.

101. As summarized by the Center for Reproductive Rights on its website:

This section will make it a federal crime for a physician to perform an abortion on a minor who resides in another state unless the minor has a court order from her home state authorizing an abortion or her parent is notified and the abortion provider provides federal notice (explained below) before performing the abortion. The bill does not provide any way for a minor to obtain a judicial waiver of the federal notice and delay requirement if her home state does not have a judicial bypass procedure. The requirements of this Section apply if the non resident minor obtains an abortion in any of 24 states or the District of Columbia. In order to provide the federal notice required by the second section of the bill, the physician must try to provide "actual notice"—which is defined as written, in person notice to a parent—and then wait 24 hours before performing the abortion. Therefore, even if the minor comes to the clinic with a parent, the physician will have to wait 24 hours before performing the abortion. If, after making a "reasonable effort," the physician is unable to provide actual notice, the physician must provide "constructive notice," which means that a period of over 72 hours will have to elapse before the abortion may be performed.

Center for Reproductive Rights (2006b), *The Teen Endangerment Act: Harming Women Who Seek Abortions* (New York: Center for Reproductive Rights), at http://www.crlp.org/pub_fac_ccpa.html (retrieved September 1, 2007).

102. For instance, a pregnant 14-year-old from Lancaster, Pennsylvania, wanted to keep and raise her baby. Her boyfriend's parents drove her to New Jersey to circumvent Pennsylvania parental notification law. They then refused to take her home until she ended her pregnancy. Laurie Kellman (2006), "Senate Set to Pass Parental Notification Requirement for Minors Seeking Abortions," *Associated Press,* July 25.

103. David Sharp (2007), "Plea Deal Approved in Parental Abduction Case in Maine," *Associated Press,* October 12.

104. Carla Crowder (2005a), "DYS Chalkville Abuse Charges Go Back to '94," *Birmingham News,* August 9; Amy Singer (2002), "Investigation: Girls Sentenced to Abuse," *Marie Claire,* June.

105. Ultimately, the original lawsuit merged with two others and had as many as 40 plaintiffs (including five of the girls' mothers). Eventually, seven employees retired or resigned, four were fired, three appealed to the State Personnel Board, and one died. Of those who appealed, at least one has returned to work at a different facility. Val Walton (2002), "Most Sex Abuse Claims Dropped in DYS Lawsuit," *Birmingham News,*

April 12; Carla Crowder (2003), "DYS Campus Superintendent, Psychologist on Leave in Probe," *Birmingham News,* March 14.

106. *Monmouth County Correctional Institutional Inmates v. Lanzaro,* 834 F. 2d 326 (1987) at 349. See also Corinne Carey (2008), "Access to Reproductive Health Care in New York State Jail Facilities" (New York: New York Civil Liberties Union).

107. *Doe v. Arpaio, et al.,* 214 Ariz. 237 (2007).

108. Ibid.

109. Christina Leonard (2004), "Inmates' Advocates Challenge Arpaio's Abortion Roadblocks," *Arizona Republic,* October 15, n.p.

110. Quoted in ibid.; *Doe v. Arpaio, et al.* In 2007, the Court of Appeals of Arizona upheld the lower court's ruling in favor of the inmate. See also *Roe v. Crawford,* 396 F. Supp. 2d 1041 (Western District of Missouri, 2005).

111. *Monmouth County Correctional Institutional Inmates v. Lanzaro.*

112. *Estelle v. Gamble,* 429 U.S. 97; 97 S. Ct. 285 (1976).

113. The discussion that follows draws significantly, but not exclusively, from the results of Roth's meticulous research, which encompassed 44 states and the District of Columbia. Rachel Roth (2004a), "Do Prisoners Have Abortion Rights?" *Feminist Studies* 30(2): 353–381.

114. Ibid., 363–364. This dismal state of affairs is mitigated somewhat by advocacy organizations who have intervened with prison officials and provide support on an unofficial or ad hoc basis.

115. Ibid.

116. Ruth Marcus (2003), "'Partial Birth': Partial Truths," *Washington Post,* June 4, A27.

117. Center for Reproductive Rights (2006a), *The Federal Abortion Ban* (New York: Center for Reproductive Rights), at http://www.federalabortionban.org/press_statements/060221-court-review.asp (retrieved September 1, 2007).

118. Carole Joffe (2007), "The Abortion Procedure Ban: Bush's Gift to His Base," *Dissent* (Fall): 57–61.

119. These 27 states have passed laws prohibiting partial-birth abortions that permit such procedures only to save a woman's life (not her health). As of October 1, 2007, at least 17 of these bans were specifically blocked by a court and 8 bans remained unchallenged. Guttmacher Institute (2007a), "Bans on 'Partial-Birth' Abortion," *State Policies in Brief,* at http://www.guttmacher.org/statecenter/spibs/spib_BPBA.pdf (retrieved November 1, 2007).

120. The media's use of terms like "partial-birth abortion" lends it credibility that is not justified. For example, Miranda Kennedy (2000), "Partial Truth Abortion Coverage," *Fair and Accuracy in Reporting,* at www.fair.org (retrieved September 1, 2007).

121. Ivan Oransky (2003), "U.S. Congress Passes 'Partial-Birth Abortion' Ban," *Lancet* 363: 1464.

122. The intact dilation and evacuation procedure was developed as a means of reducing complications associated with late-second-trimester abortions. An intact dilation and evacuation usually takes place over the course of two to three days and often requires collapsing the fetal calvaria so the fetal skull can pass through the patient's cervix and the intact fetus can be removed from the womb. The cervix is dilated,

usually about a day before the surgical procedure. The fetus is then separated into pieces and removed using forceps and a vacuum. Alexi A. Wright and Ingrid T. Katz (2006), "*Roe* versus Reality: Abortion and Women's Health," *New England Journal of Medicine* 355: 1–9; Oransky (2003).

123. *Carhart v. Gonzales,* 413 F. 3d 791 (8th Cir. Neb., 2005); *National Abortion Federation v. Ashcroft,* 330 F. Supp. 2d 436, LEXIS 17084 (S.D.N.Y., 2004); *Planned Parenthood Federation of America v. Ashcroft,* 320 F. Supp. 2d 957 (N.D. Cal., 2004).

124. See the Supreme Court ruling in *Stenberg v. Carhart,* 530 U.S. 914; 120 S. Ct. 2597 (2000).

125. For an abortion provider's account of some of the stress and confusion around what constitutes the banned procedure and its implications for his patients and his practice, see Warren M. Hern (2003), "Did I Violate the Partial-Birth Abortion Ban? A Doctor Ponders a New Era of Prosecution," *Slate,* October 22, at http://www.slate.com/id/2090215/ (retrieved September 1, 2007).

126. *Gonzales v. Carhart, et al.,* 550 U.S. ___ (2007).

127. Quoted in Joffe (2007), 59.

128. *Planned Parenthood Federation of America v. Ashcroft,* at 92–93.

129. Ibid., at 1019.

130. American College of Obstetricians and Gynecologists (2006), amicus brief filed in *Gonzales v. Carhart, et al.,* 550 U.S. ___ (2007); see also Joffe (2007).

131. American College of Obstetricians and Gynecologists (2006); Physicians for Reproductive Health and Choice (2006), amicus brief filed in *Gonzales v. Carhart, et al.,* 550 U.S. ___ (2007).

132. Christine Vestal (2007), *States Probe Limits of Abortion Policy,* June 11, at http://www.stateline.org/live/ViewPage.action?siteNodeId=136&languageId=1&contentId=121780 (retrieved September 13, 2007).

133. Laurence H. Tribe (1990), *Abortion: The Clash of Absolutes* (New York: Norton), 241.

134. American Civil Liberties Union (ACLU) (2004), *Public Funding for Abortion: Promoting Reproductive Freedom for Low-Income Women,* at http://www.aclu.org/ReproductiveRights/ReproductiveRights.cfm?ID=9039&c=146 (retrieved September 1, 2007).

CHAPTER 4

1. This subject is included in the "conceiving" section of the book rather than, say, the section on "bearing" or "mothering" because women who kill or abandon a newborn tend not to be invested in their pregnancies, much less the birth and rearing of the child. Typically, they were in a state of denial that they were even pregnant. Unlike many of the women described in the "bearing" section of this book, their pregnancies have not been noticed, much less subject to official forms of social control. And, in contrast to the women described in chapters 7 and 8, these women appear never to have had any intention of being a mother and raising the infant they had delivered. For this reason, I refrain from calling the women and girls who kill their newborns "mothers." By all accounts, they never saw themselves in that light

and had no plans to assume the responsibilities and roles that are commonly associated with the term.

2. In this chapter, I focus mainly on abandonment and neonaticide, but other categories of infanticide do exist. Infanticide refers to the act of a parent killing his or her infant or child. The term encompasses both neonaticide (killing of an infant within 24 hours after birth) and filicide (killing an infant child who is more than one day old). When a woman fatally injures an older infant (as opposed to a newborn), it seems to be at least partly a reaction to the stress of normative expectations of mothering. In contrast, women and girls who kill or abandon their newborns seem to be reacting against the idea of having conceived to begin with. Martha Smithey found that women who fatally injure their older infants (non-newborns up to the age of 36 months) do so, in part, because of a self-perception that they are bad mothers who can neither make their infants comply nor escape the stress of an intense, escalating situation. Martha Smithey (2001), "Maternal Infanticide and Modern Motherhood," *Women and Criminal Justice* 13(1): 65–83. Meyer and Oberman et al. (2001) developed a typology of women who kill their children. They identified and reviewed 219 cases of infanticide reported in the news between 1990 and 1999 and found that the majority were "purposeful" cases, both with and without mental illness ($n = 79$), and neglect cases ($n = 76$), followed by neonaticide cases ($n = 37$). The smallest number were abuse cases in which the mother acted alone ($n = 15$) or with a partner ($n = 12$). Cheryl Meyer and Michelle Oberman et al. (2001), *Mothers Who Kill Their Children: Understanding the Acts of Moms from Susan Smith to the "Prom Mom"* (New York: New York University Press).
"Abandonment" is a term that has been used in a variety of ways and in a variety of legal contexts, but here it refers to occasions in which a woman or girl gives birth outside of a hospital and leaves her infant in a public or private setting with the intent of disposing of the child.

3. Estimates based on media accounts are problematic since some cases never attract media attention or are not covered because of injunctions against revealing the name of a minor. Consequently, an increase in media coverage may reflect an increase in attention rather than a real increase in the incidence of neonaticide or abandonment. K. Drescher-Burke, J. Krall, and A. Penick (2004), *Discarded Infants and Neonaticide: A Review of the Literature* (Berkeley, CA: National Abandoned Infants Assistance Resource Center); Meyer and Oberman et al. (2001).

4. The U.S. Department of Health and Human Services reports that around 450 children under one year of age died as the result of abuse or neglect in 2005. Fatality rates are highest among the youngest children; as the age of the children increases, fatality rates drop. Among all child fatalities, around 40 percent are due to neglect only, and around one in four are due to physical abuse only. The FBI reports that, each year, between 200 and 300 children under the age of one are murdered, usually by a parent. This estimate, however, is based on crimes that come to the attention of the police. It is easier to kill a newborn without anyone discovering the crime than an older child or an adult who is more likely to be missed and whose body is harder to conceal. Many cases of neonaticide (possibly even a majority) never come to the attention of law enforcement. U.S. Department of Health and Human Services, Administration on

Children, Youth and Families (2007), *Child Maltreatment 2005* (Washington, DC: U.S. Government Printing Office); H. Snyder, T. Finnegan, and W. Kang (2006), "Easy Access to the FBI's Supplementary Homicide Reports: 1980–2003," Federal Bureau of Investigation, *Supplementary Homicide Reports 1980–2003*, machine-readable data files, at http://ojjdp.ncjrs.org/ojstatbb/ezashr/ (retrieved September 1, 2007); Katie Pollock with Lupe Hittle (2003), *Baby Abandonment: The Role of Child Welfare Systems* (Washington, DC: Child Welfare League of America Press), 2.

5. Meyer and Oberman et al. (2001), 47–48.

6. Susan Hatters Friedman, Sarah McCue Horwitz, and Phillip J. Resnick (2005), "Child Murder by Mothers: A Critical Analysis of the Current State of Knowledge and a Research Agenda," *American Journal of Psychiatry* 162(9): 1578–1587; Meyer and Oberman et al. (2001).

7. Kathryn Edin and Maria Kefalas (2005), *Promises I Can Keep: Why Poor Women Put Motherhood before Marriage* (Los Angeles: University of California Press), 64–65.

8. Meyer and Oberman et al. (2001).

9. Edin and Kefalas (2005).

10. Holly Auer and Charity Vogel (2003), "Trapped by Pregnancy, Young Woman Turns Desperate: Unwanted Baby Placed in Dumpster," *Buffalo News*, October 27.

11. Quoted in ibid.

12. Ibid.

13. She was later charged with second-degree murder. Chrisena Coleman (2005), "Girl Faces Slay Rap in Newborn's Fall," *New York Daily News*, March 23, 7.

14. Jennifer Lee (2005), "After Her Baby Dies, Girl Only Wants School," *New York Times*, January 26, B8.

15. U.S. Department of Health and Human Services (2005), *Depression during and after Pregnancy*, at http://www.4woman.gov/faq/postpartum.htm (retrieved January 21, 2008); Velma Dobson and Bruce Sales (2000), "The Science of Infanticide and Mental Illness," *Psychology, Public Policy and Law* 6: 1098–1112; Drescher-Burke et al. (2004).

16. Meyer and Oberman et al. (2001).

17. Ibid., 46.

18. Both physical abuse during the pregnancy and unplanned pregnancies may contribute to a woman's decision to abandon or kill her newborn. Both of these factors have been associated with poor weight gain (i.e., less than 20 pounds) during pregnancy for adolescents. Abbey B. Berenson and Constance M. Wiemann (1997), "Inadequate Weight Gain among Pregnant Adolescents: Risk Factors and Relationship to Infant Birth Weight," *American Journal of Obstetrics and Gynecology* 176(6): 1220–1224. Personally, on at least two occasions I was completely oblivious to the dramatic physical changes of people whom I saw regularly. In one case, I did not notice that one of my best students had lost 40 pounds during the course of the semester before she was involuntarily hospitalized for anorexia. In another instance, a colleague was seven months pregnant before the thought even crossed my mind that perhaps her weight gain was due to pregnancy. Social norms prevent one from comfortably commenting on a woman's weight gain or pressing the issue of pregnancy, making it likely that a pregnancy can pass, if not unnoticed, at least unremarked upon.

19. Meyer and Oberman et al. (2001), 171.

20. John Futty (2004), "Baby's Death Shocks Somalis," *Columbus Dispatch,* September 9, B2.

21. Quoted in ibid.

22. Central Ohio Crime Stoppers, at http://www.stopcrime.org/wanted.asp (retrieved January 18, 2008).

23. Melisa Holmes, Heidi Resnick, Dean Kilpatrick, and Connie Best (1996), "Rape-Related Pregnancy: Estimates and Descriptive Characteristics from a National Sample of Women," *American Journal of Obstetrics and Gynecology* 175(2): 320–325; Judith McFarlane and Ann Malecha (2005), *Sexual Assault among Intimates: Frequency, Consequences and Treatments* (Washington, DC: National Institute of Justice).

24. Sex with a minor under a certain age is against the law in every state, although the age of consent may differ. "Child sexual abuse" refers to the sexual assault of a minor. In 2005, about 84,000 children were sexually abused. Most of the sexual assaults reported to law enforcement are against girls under the age of 18; one-third of the offenders in these cases are family members, and 60 percent are acquaintances. "Statutory rape" commonly refers to nonforcible sexual intercourse between an adult and a person who is younger than the statutory age of consent. The "typical" victim of statutory rape is a 14- or 15-year-old girl; in around 60 percent of the statutory rape cases, the offender is an acquaintance who is 20 or 21 years old. Some state laws also take into account sexual contact with a minor by someone who is a defined number of years older than the minor or by an authority figure such as a coach or a teacher. In around 29 and 7 percent of the cases, respectively, the offender is a boyfriend or a family member. U.S. Department of Health and Human Services, Administration on Children, Youth and Families (2007); Howard N. Snyder (2000), *Sexual Assault of Young Children Reported to Law Enforcement* (Washington, DC: U.S. Department of Justice, Bureau of Justice Statistics); Karyl Troup-Leasure and Howard Snyder (2005), *Statutory Rape Known to Law Enforcement* (Washington, DC: U.S. Department of Justice, Office of Justice Programs); Holmes et al. (1996).

25. Judith McFarlane and Ann Malecha (2005) conducted a study of sexual assault among intimates using a sample of 148 adult women who obtained court orders of protection. Some 100 of the women had been sexually assaulted by the person named in the court order, 20 percent reported at least one rape-related pregnancy, and 20 percent terminated their pregnancy with an elective abortion.

26. At the time of this writing, the attorney generals of Kansas and Indiana were aggressive in their attempts to obtain the medical records of minor patients of family planning and abortion clinics under the guise of determining whether the clinics were complying with the states' requirements to report statutory rape. Florida was considering legislation that would require health care professionals to call the police if they know or suspect a patient 15 years or younger is pregnant. Supporters claim these actions stem from a larger state and federal effort to reduce the incidence of teen pregnancy (and thus the number of children who become wards of the state) by deterring men from having sex with teenage girls. To date, however, no empirically supported link between statutory rape enforcement and teen pregnancies has been established. Clinic administrators and medical professionals are concerned about safeguarding

minors' privacy rights, in part out of concern that overly broad reporting requirements may deter adolescents from seeking health care or reducing the quality of care
received. As the authors of a Guttmacher report observed:

> Statutory rape reporting requirements can present a challenge for those who
> recognize the value in both assuring that minors have access to confidential
> health care and protecting adolescents from sexual exploitation. This is par-
> ticularly true for reproductive health care providers, who usually are obliged to
> report suspected cases of sexual abuse—and often are uniquely positioned to
> detect it. At the same time, they are ethically, and sometimes legally, required to
> honor a patient's privacy rights.

Chinué Turner Richardson and Cynthia Dailard (2005), "Politicizing Statutory Rape
Reporting Requirements: A Mounting Campaign?" *Guttmacher Report on Public Policy,* at www.guttmacher.org/pubs/tgr/08/3/gr080301.pdf (retrieved January 21, 2008).
According to the DHHS Office of the Inspector General, federally funded family planning clinics *are* complying with state law and are upholding their legal obligation to
report suspected cases of child abuse and sexual abuse. Assistant Inspector General
for Evaluation and Inspections (2005), Memorandum (OEI-02-03-00530), April 25, at
http://opa.osophs.dhhs.gov/titlex/OEI-02-03-00530.pdf (retrieved January 21, 2008);
George Grob (2005), *Federal Efforts to Address Applicable Child Abuse and Sexual
Abuse Reporting Requirements for Title X Grantees,* OEI-02-03-00530, April 25 memorandum (Washington, DC: Department of Health and Human Services), at http://opa.
osophs.dhhs.gov/titlex/OEI-02–03–00530.pdf (retrieved September 1, 2007). Thus, the
actions of the Kansas and Indiana attorney generals and the Florida legislature not only
are unwarranted but also contradict the position articulated by all major medical professional organizations. Jennifer Liberto and Rebecca Catalanello (2007), "Legislators
Want Pregnant Girls Reported," *St. Petersburg Times,* March 7. For a comprehensive
discussion of the issues involved with statutory rape enforcement and child abuse reporting, see Abigail English and Catherine Teare (2001), "Statutory Rape Enforcement
and Child Abuse Reporting: Effects on Health Care Access for Adolescents," *DePaul
Law Review* 827(50): 838–863; Society of Adolescent Medicine (2004), "Confidential
Health Care for Adolescents: A Position Paper of the Society for Adolescent Medicine,"
Journal of Adolescent Health 35(5): 420–423.

27. Ramesh Raghavan, Laura Bogart, Marc Elliott, et al. (2004), "Sexual Victimization among a National Probability Sample of Adolescent Women," *Perspectives on
Sexual and Reproductive Health* 36(6): 225–232.

28. Jonathan Miller (2006b), "Woman Admits She Threw Baby Down Air Shaft,"
New York Times, March 29, B6; "Two Infants Found in Trash, and a Darker Tale Unfolds" (2005), *New York Times,* September 17.

29. The father pleaded guilty to aggravated manslaughter, aggravated assault,
and aggravated sexual assault and was sentenced to 35 years in prison. Miller (2006b);
Jonathan Miller (2006a), "Man Is Sentenced in Baby's Death," *New York Times,* December 14, B9; "Jersey City: Sentence in Baby's Death" (2007), *New York Times,* April 26.

30. Dennis Gilbert (2006), *Hamilton College Hot Button Issues Poll: Guns, Gays,
and Abortion,* at http://www.hamilton.edu/news/polls/HotButtonFinalReport.pdf (retrieved September 1, 2007).

31. See literature cited in Drescher-Burke et al. (2004); Friedman et al. (2005).

32. At 40.4 births for every 1,000 women, the birthrate for this age group was lower in 2005 than it had ever been, having declined by nearly one-third since its peak in 1991. Most teenage pregnancy occurs among 18- and 19-year-olds. Guttmacher Institute (2006b), *U.S. Teenage Pregnancy Statistics: National and State Trends and Trends by Race and Ethnicity*, at http://www.guttmacher.org/pubs/2006/09/12/USTPstats.pdf (retrieved May 27, 2007); B. E. Hamilton, J. A. Martin, and S. J. Ventura (2006), *Births: Preliminary Data for 2005* (Hyattsville, MD: National Center for Health Statistics), tables 2, 5, at http://www.cdc.gov/nchs/products/pubs/pubd/hestats/prelimbirths05/prelimbirths05.htm (retrieved January 21, 2008).

33. See review in Todd Melby (2007), "A Flurry of Good News," *Contemporary Sexuality* 41(2): 1–3.

34. Kristin Luker (2006), *When Sex Goes to School* (New York: Norton).

35. Ibid.; Kristin Luker (1996), *Dubious Conceptions: The Politics of Teenage Pregnancy* (Cambridge: Harvard University Press).

36. Luker (2006).

37. Guttmacher Institute (2007e), "Overview of Minors' Consent Laws," *State Policies in Brief*, at http://www.guttmacher.org/statecenter/spibs/spib_OMCL.pdf (retrieved October 15, 2007).

38. Laura M. Carpenter (2005), *Virginity Lost: An Intimate Portrait of First Sexual Experiences* (New York: New York University Press).

39. Ibid.

40. Christopher Trenholm, Barbara Devaney, Ken Forson, et al. (2007), *Impacts of Four Title V, Section 510 Abstinence Education Programs* (Princeton, NJ: Mathematica Police Research); Rebecca Maynard (2005), *First-Year Impacts of Four Title V, Section 510 Abstinence Education Programs* (Princeton, NJ: Mathematica Policy Research,); Debra Hauser (2004), *Five Years of Abstinence-Only-Until-Marriage Education: Assessing the Impact* (Washington, DC: Advocates for Youth), at http://www.advocatesforyouth.org/publications/stateevaluations.pdf (retrieved January 21, 2008).

41. Trenholm et al. (2007), xvii.

42. When used consistently and correctly, condoms are about 98 percent effective in preventing pregnancy and do reduce the risk of STIs, including chlamydia. The virus that causes AIDS can be transmitted only through the direct exchange of certain body fluids such as blood, semen, vaginal secretions, or breast milk. Saliva, tears, and sweat have never been found to lead to HIV transmission. SEICUS (2005), *In Their Own Words: What Abstinence-Only-Until-Marriage Programs Say*, http://www.siecus.org/policy/in_their_own_words.pdf (retrieved September 1, 2007); Kimberly A. Workowski and Stuart M. Berman (2006), "Sexually Transmitted Diseases Treatment Guidelines 2006," *Morbidity and Mortality Weekly Report* 51(RR-6): 1–94.

43. SEICUS (2005).

44. See literature cited in Carpenter (2005).

45. As of July 2008, at least 22 states had decided to forego the federal grants for abstinence-only sex education. Feminist Majority Foundation (2007), *Washington State Refuses Abstinence-Only Programs*, at http://www.feminist.org/news/newsbyte/uswirestory.asp?id=11118 (retrieved July 18, 2008).

46. For instance, women who do not get prenatal care are three to four times more likely to die of pregnancy-related causes than women who receive any prenatal care. Centers for Disease Control and Prevention (2003c), "Pregnancy-Related Mortality Surveillance: United States, 1991–1999," *Morbidity and Mortality Weekly Report,* February 21.

47. Young women, especially those who are younger than 17 years of age, are more likely than women in their 20s to experience pregnancy-related complications and to die in childbirth. A. P. McCauley and C. Salter (1995), "Health Risks of Early Pregnancy," *Population Reports* (Baltimore: Johns Hopkins School of Public Health, Population Information Program), at http://www.infoforhealth.org/pr/j41/j41chap2_3.shtml#top (retrieved September 1, 2007).

48. Lourdes Medrano Lesli (2003), "14-Year-Old Mom Charged in Her Newborn's Death," *Minneapolis Star Tribune,* October 7, B3.

49. Christine Clarridge (2004), "Manslaughter Charges Filed in Infant's Death," *Seattle Times,* August 31, B4; Sam Skolnik (2004), "Woman Pleads Guilty in Death of Newborn," *Seattle Intelligencer,* September 14, B4.

50. Jessica Heslam (2002), "N.H. Police Save Newborn Dumped by Teen Mom," *Boston Herald,* August 23, 6.

51. Meyer and Oberman et al. (2001).

52. Ibid., 58.

53. Sarah Miltimore (2000), "Neonaticide: A Comparison Study of Cases Found in the United States with Cases Found in Britain and Canada," M.S. thesis, University of California at Irvine.

54. Christina Nuckols (2005), "Del. Cosgrove Pulls Bill after Internet Fuels Fiery Protest," *Norfolk Virginian-Pilot,* January 11, B1. Cosgrove's misguided bill did not encourage the reporting of fetal deaths because all states already have fetal death reporting requirements. For example, 38 states require reporting fetal deaths that occur at 20 weeks or more. Centers for Disease Control (1997), *State Definitions and Reporting Requirements for Live Births, Fetal Deaths, and Induced Terminations of Pregnancy* (Hyattsville, MD: National Center for Health Statistics, Division of Vital Statistics), 3.

55. Quoted in "Del. Cosgrove: Don't Relax Just Yet" (2005), *Well-Timed Period,* January 8, at http://thewelltimedperiod.blogspot.com/2005/01/del-cosgrove-dont-relax-just-yet.html (retrieved September 1, 2007).

56. Nuckols (2005).

57. Gabrielle Maple (2004), "Miscarriage Proof Frees Woman," *New Orleans Times-Picayune,* August 18, 1.

58. Michelle went to the hospital complaining of stomach pain and excessive bleeding. The doctor determined that she had recently given birth and called the police. During an interview with the police, Michelle told them she had delivered a stillborn baby in the bathroom and then disposed of the body about four days later when the trash was scheduled to be collected. (The body was never recovered.) Maple (2004).

59. Meyer and Oberman et al. (2001), 58–59.

60. Tom Kertscher (2004), "Punishment Varies in Newborn Deaths," *Milwaukee Journal Sentinel,* September 20, 1.

61. Ibid.

62. Miltimore (2000), 36.

63. Texas Department of Criminal Justice (2006), *Women on Death Row,* at http://www.tdcj.state.tx.us/stat/womenondrow.htm (retrieved October 12, 2006).

64. Kenisha Berry (killed her newborn), Linda Carty (kidnapped a newborn), Darlie Routier (killed her two sons, aged 5 and 6), Cathy Henderson (abducted and killed a 3-month-old infant). Texas Department of Criminal Justice (2006).

65. Kertscher (2004).

66. Beth Bookwalter (1998), "Note: Throwing the Bath Water Out with the Baby: Wrongful Exclusion of Expert Testimony on Neonaticide Syndrome," *Boston University Law Review* 78: 1185–1210.

67. Ibid.

68. Norman Finkel, John Burke, and Leticia Chavez (2000), "Commonsense Judgments of Infanticide: Murder, Manslaughter, Madness, or Miscellaneous," *Psychology, Public Policy and Law* 6: 1113–1137.

69. Ibid., 1113.

70. Ibid., 1130.

71. Michele Connell (2002), "The Postpartum Psychosis Defense and Feminism: More or Less Justice for Women?" *Case Western Reserve Law Review* 53: 143–153, at 144.

72. Quoted in Kertscher (2004).

73. Ibid.

74. Ibid.

75. Melissa Drexler pleaded guilty to aggravated manslaughter a month and a half after Brian Petersen and Amy Grossberg were sentenced in Delaware, having pled guilty to manslaughter. Robert D. McFadden (1996), "Teen-Age Sweethearts Charged with Murdering Their Baby," *New York Times,* November 18, B1; Ruth Padawer (2006), "Lives after Death: Baby-Killing Drama Still Haunts Some of Those It Touched," *Bergen County (NJ) Record,* November 12, A1; Abby Goodnough and Bruce Weber (1997). "The Picture of Ordinary: Before Prom Night, a Suspect Was the Girl Next Door," *New York Times,* July 2, B1; Robert Hanley (1997), "Woman Indicted in Killing of Newborn Son at Prom," *New York Times,* September 18, B6.

76. Guttmacher Institute (2007b), "Infant Abandonment," *State Policies in Brief,* at http://www.guttmacher.org/statecenter/spibs/spib_IA.pdf (retrieved September 1, 2007).

77. Debbe Magnusen (2000/2001), "From Dumpster to Delivery Room: Does Legalizing Baby Abandonment Really Solve the Problem?" *La Verne Law Review Journal of Juvenile Law* 22: 1–28.

78. A 2003 review of infant abandonment legislation found that most states' statutes do not make diligent efforts to locate the father before terminating his parental rights. Some states explicitly state that a search for parents and notice are unnecessary if the identities of the relinquishing parties are unknown. Ian Bolling (2003), "Infant Abandonment and Safe Haven Legislation," in *Report on Trends in the State Courts* (Williamsburg, VA: National Center for State Courts), 25–26.

79. Paul DeCarlo (2005), "Experts Explain Roots of Infanticide," *Riverside Press Enterprise,* May 14, B1.

80. "Mom Finds Safe Haven for Infant" (2005), *Boston Herald,* March 19, 6.

81. Alayna DeMartini and Penny Moore (2004), "Police Not Naming Girl Who Left Her Baby in Alley," *Columbus Dispatch*, September 23, C1.

82. When prevention efforts fail, a more promising variation on the idea of a "safe haven" is offered by a nonprofit organization based in Los Angeles. Project Cuddle operates a hotline for pregnant women who want help turning their newborns over to authorities or telling their parents about their pregnancies. The founder, Debbe Magnusen, favors helping young mothers-to-be in finding resources before their babies are born and supporting them in their decision whether to keep the child or give it up for adoption. The goal is not to retrieve abandoned newborns but to prevent the abandonment in the first place. Between the time of its founding in 1996 and 2005, Project Cuddle offered confidential assistance to over 600 women and girls. Project Cuddle (2007), *No Baby Deserves to Die before Having a Chance to Live* (Los Angeles: Project Cuddle), at www.projectcuddle.org (retrieved September 1, 2007).

83. Michelle Oberman (2003), "Lady Madonna, Children at Your Feet: Tragedies at the Intersection of Motherhood, Mental Illness and the Law," *William and Mary Journal of Women and Law* 33: 35–67; Michelle Oberman (2004), "Mothers Who Kill: Coming to Terms with Modern American Infanticide," *DePaul Journal of Health Care Law* 8: 3–107.

84. Margaret G. Spinelli (2001), "A Systematic Investigation of 16 Cases of Neonaticide," *American Journal of Psychiatry* 158: 811–813; B. Harris (1994), "Biological and Hormonal Aspects of Postpartum Depressed Mood," *British Journal of Psychiatry* 164: 288–292.

85. For example, the Criminal Code of Canada Section 233 states: "A female person commits infanticide when by a wilful act of omission she causes the death of her newly born child, if at the time of the act or omission she is not fully recovered from the effects of giving birth to the child and by reason thereof or of the effect of lactation consequent on the birth of the child her mind is then disturbed." The punishment for infanticide is a maximum term of five years of imprisonment. This is the only form of homicide in Canada for which a life sentence is not possible.

86. Dobson and Sales (2000); Finkel et al. (2000).

87. While it may not be a factor in neonaticide and abandonment cases, acknowledging the reality of postpartum depression and psychosis reminds us that sometimes some women are ensnared by biology and hormonal fluctuations, and with serious consequences. This recognition opens the door to erroneous assumptions that all women are (or potentially are) "hormonal," too emotional, too unstable, and so on and therefore unsuited for certain duties, such as military service or public office. At the same time, ignoring or downplaying the reality of postpartum depression denies help and information to women who are suffering the very real consequences of it and need assistance and support.

In contrast to postpartum depression, which affects between 5 and 20 percent of new mothers, postpartum psychosis is rare, affecting only one to two mothers out of every 1,000 births. Most psychosis is the result of affective disorders that are triggered by the stress of the pregnancy. Postpartum psychosis, such as that experienced by Andrea Yates (who was charged in the 2001 drowning deaths of her five children, including an infant) often involves hallucinations or delusions, severe depression, and thought disorder. The onset is usually within the first few weeks after (not immediately after) childbirth; the first year after delivery is a time of high risk for mental disturbance. Andrea had an extensive history of mental illness that included medications, multiple psychiatric hospitalizations, and suicide attempts. She unsuccessfully asserted a defense of postpartum psychosis in her first trial but was convicted and sentenced to life imprisonment. Her original conviction was overturned and a retrial ordered when it became known that a prosecution witness falsely testified that an episode of *Law and Order* featured a similar case when, in fact, no such episode had aired on the show. On July 26, 2006, she was found not guilty by reason of insanity and was committed to a state mental hospital. U.S. Department of Health and Human Services (2005); Dobson and Sales (2000); Deborah Denno (2003), "Who Is Andrea Yates? A Short Story about Insanity," *Duke Journal of Gender Law and Policy* 1: 1–139; Drescher-Burke et al. (2004).

88. Bookwalter (1998).
89. Ibid.
90. Edin and Kefalas (2005).
91. Doris Vallone and Lori Hoffman (2003), "Preventing the Tragedy of Neonaticide," *Holistic Nursing Practice* 17: 223–228.
92. Meyer and Oberman et al. (2001), 171.

CHAPTER 5

I am grateful to Tiloma Jayasinghe and Lynn Paltrow of the National Advocates for Pregnant Women for their comments on an earlier draft of this chapter.

1. Murray Evans (2007), "Woman Enters Plea in Death of Baby," *Associated Press Wire Service,* September 21.
2. Rick Montgomery (2006), "Regulating the Rights of the Unborn," *Kansas City Star,* July 9, A1.
3. Citations in the original passage have been deleted. Marguerite A. Driessen (2006), "Avoiding the Melissa Rowland Dilemma: Why Disobeying a Doctor Should Not Be a Crime," *Michigan State Journal of Medicine and Law* 10: 1–56, at 15.
4. Ibid.
5. The issues surrounding fetal protectionism are so numerous and so complex that it is impossible to do them justice in one chapter. Fortunately, these issues have been the subject of scores of books and articles and have enjoyed the benefit of attention from reproductive rights scholars and advocates, most notably, Lynn Paltrow, Dorothy Roberts, Rachel Roth, and Cynthia Daniels.
6. Laurie F. Beck, Christopher H. Johnson, Abrian Morrow, et al. (2003), *PRAMS 1999 Surveillance Report* (Atlanta: Division of Reproductive Health, Centers for Disease Control); see literature cited on 38, 70.
7. Ibid.
8. Ibid.
9. U.S. General Accounting Office (2002), *Violence against Women: Data on Pregnant Victims and Effectiveness of Prevention Strategies Are Limited* (Washington, DC: U.S. General Accounting Office).
10. Some women are abused before they become pregnant but not while they are pregnant. Women also may be at greater risk of abuse in the year after they give

birth. Linda E. Saltzman, Christopher H. Johnson, Brenda Colley Gilbert, and Mary M. Goodwin (2003), "Physical Abuse around the Time of Pregnancy: An Examination of Prevalence and Risk Factors in 16 States," *Maternal and Child Health Journal* 7(1): 31–43; Beck et al. (2003).

11. Harold B. Weiss and his colleagues concluded that pregnant women do suffer high rates of assault, but it may be because they are part of a demographic group of young women that is more vulnerable to violence in general. For this reason, they propose that pregnant women be considered a "sensitive" population that requires extra care rather than an "at-risk" population, per se. Harold B. Weiss, Bruce A. Lawrence, and Ted R. Miller (2004), "Pregnancy-Associated Assault Hospitalizations: Prevalence and Risk of Hospitalized Assaults against Women during Pregnancy," *Obstetrics and Gynecology* 100(4): 773–780. See also Beck et al. (2003); Saltzman et al. (2003); U.S. General Accounting Office (2002).

12. Saltzman et al. (2003); Beck, et al. (2003).

13. Quoted in Donna St. George (2004b), "Violence Intersects Lives of Promise," *Washington Post,* December 20, A1.

14. Eric Hanson (2004), "A Matter of Conscience," *Houston Chronicle,* March 26, A1.

15. Barbara Ross (2005), "Beau's Guilty of Killing His Girlfriend Refused Abortion," *New York Daily News,* April 8, A1.

16. Lopez had previously attacked another girlfriend so severely that a piece of the knife snapped off in her skull and had to be removed surgically, and she lost one of her eyes. Michael Duck and the Associated Press (2005), "Murder Suspect Was Guilty in Valley Stabbing," *Allentown (PA) Morning Call,* July 25, A1.

17. Brian Dekoning (2005), "Jury Deciding Fate of Man Who Killed His Pregnant Girlfriend," *Manchester (NH) Union Leader,* June 22, A6.

18. In 2003, the U.S. Standard Certificate of Death was revised to include five categories related to the woman's pregnancy status: not pregnant within past year; pregnant at time of death; not pregnant, but pregnant within 42 days of death; not pregnant, but pregnant 43 days to one year before death; and unknown if pregnant within the past years. As states revise their certificates, they are expected to introduce the standard item. This should permit better information to be collected regarding violence and pregnancy in years to come. U.S. Standard Certificate of Death, rev. November 2003, at http://www.cdc.gov/nchs/data/dvs/DEATH11-03final-ACC.pdf (retrieved October 22, 2007).

19. Donna St. George (2004a), "Many New or Expectant Mothers Die Violent Deaths," *Washington Post,* December 19, A1.

20. Automobile accidents accounted for 44 percent. Jeani Chang, Cynthia J. Berg, Linda E. Saltzman, and Joy Herndon (2005), "Homicide: A Leading Cause of Injury Deaths among Pregnant and Postpartum Women in the United States, 1991–1999," *Journal of Public Health* 95(3): 471–477. Both the *Washington Post* and the CDC figures probably reflect a serious undercount. For instance, 13 states have no way of telling how many pregnant and postpartum women have been killed. In part, this reflects a larger problem of the underreporting of maternal deaths (due to any cause) on death certificates. Researchers have found that in half or more of cases involving a maternal death, physicians completing death certificates fail to report that a woman was pregnant or

had a recent pregnancy. See studies cited in Isabelle L. Horon (2005), "Underreporting of Maternal Deaths on Death Certificates and the Magnitude of the Problem of Maternal Mortality," *American Journal of Public Health* 95(3): 478–482.

21. Chang et al. (2005); St. George (2004a).

22. Isabelle L. Horon and Diana Cheng (2001), "Enhanced Surveillance for Pregnancy-Associated Mortality: Maryland, 1993–1998," *Journal of the American Medical Association (JAMA)* 285: 1455–1459.

23. Ibid.

24. Chang et al. (2005); Patricia M. Dietz, Roger W. Rochat, Betsy L. Thompson, et al. (1998), "Differences in the Risk of Homicide and Other Fatal Injuries between Postpartum Women and Other Women of Childbearing Age: Implications for Prevention," *American Journal of Public Health* 88: 641–643.

25. Chang et al. (2005).

26. Henry K. Lee (2003), "Vigil for Missing Modesto Mother-to-Be," *San Francisco Chronicle,* January 1, A17; Andrew Murr and Nadine Joseph (2003), "A Husband in Trouble," *Newsweek,* April 28, 38; Kimberly Edds (2005), "Peterson Sentenced to Death by Injection," *Washington Post,* March 17, A10.

27. Scott Peterson was sentenced to death in 2005.

28. National Conference of State Legislatures (2007), *Fetal Homicide,* at http://www.ncsl.org/programs/health/fethom.htm (retrieved August 16, 2007); Christine Vestal and Elizabeth Wilkerson (2006), *States Expand Fetal Homicide Laws,* at http://www.stateline.org/live/details/story?contentId=135873 (retrieved October 12, 2006).

29. National Conference on State Legislatures (2006), *Fetal Homicide,* at http://www.ncsl.org/public/help.htm (retrieved October 12, 2006).

30. *Roe v. Wade* established that the state has an enforceable interest in protecting viable fetuses. The courts and the legislatures have not explicitly established, however, that an unborn child is a being with rights that the state can enforce. And indeed, in *Roe,* the Supreme Court held that "the word 'person,' as used in the Fourteenth Amendment, does not include the unborn." The courts *have* recognized that unborn children will have legal rights if they are subsequently born alive. For instance, if a man dies while his wife is pregnant with their child, the law recognizes that he most likely would have wished to provide for the child of his pregnant wife. Therefore, once the child is born, the child is entitled to a share of the dead man's estate. But this is not the same as recognizing a fetus as a person with rights on par with people who are born alive. Driessen (2006), 16–17.

31. National Conference of State Legislatures (2007); Vestal and Wilkerson (2006).

32. For example, a defense attorney argued that the Pennsylvania fetal homicide law was unconstitutional because the state abortion law permitted a woman to end her pregnancy until the 24th week of pregnancy, but a person could be charged with fetal homicide at any stage of fetal development. A Michigan case raised the issue of equal protection. A 16-year-old couple conspired to end an unwanted pregnancy by inducing a miscarriage. The boyfriend was charged for repeatedly striking his girlfriend (who was six months pregnant) with a souvenir baseball bat. Under Michigan statutes, however, the girlfriend could not be charged with causing her own miscarriage even though she was a willing participant. (The girl could have sought a legal abortion, but

she would have needed a judge's or parental permission to obtain it.) Federal Legislative Office of the National Right to Life Committee (2006), *Constitutional Challenges to State Unborn Victims (Fetal Homicide) Laws,* at http://www.nrlc.org/Unborn_Victims/ statechallenges.html (retrieved September 1, 2007); Shannon M. McQueeney (2005), "Recognizing Unborn Victims over Heightening Punishment for Crimes against Pregnant Women," *New England Journal on Criminal and Civil Confinement* 31: 461–483; Matthew T. Mangino (2005), "When a Murder Victim Is Pregnant," *Pennsylvania Law Weekly* 28(10): 8.

33. When people mourn the unexpected loss of a pregnancy, the loss could also be characterized as that of the loss of an anticipated child—the child that they looked forward to being born—as opposed to that of the fetus or unborn child, per se. Driessen (2006).

34. An alternate proposal to the federal UVVA, the Motherhood Protection Act, sponsored by Senator Dianne Feinstein (D-CA), would have enhanced the punishment for offenses that injured or caused the death of a pregnant woman but would not have recognized the fetus or embryo as a separate victim. It was voted down in both the Senate (49–50) and the House (229–186). Elizabeth Hurley (2005), *More States Are Passing Fetal Homicide Laws* (Washington, DC: Concerned Women for America), at http://www.cwalac.org/article_202.shtml (retrieved October 12, 2006); 108th U.S. Congress (2003–2004), S. 2219[108]: Motherhood Protection Act; 108th U.S. Congress (2003–2004), H. R. 2247[108]: Motherhood Protection Act of 2003; Vestal and Wilkerson (2006).

35. An early draft of the bill made it a crime of murder if the person "knowingly engages in conduct that results in the death of an unborn child under circumstances manifesting an extreme indifference to the value of human life." Senate Judiciary Committee (2005), *CS for Senate Bill No. 20 (JUD,* April 21, 2005); Tiloma Jayasinghe (2007), staff attorney, National Advocates for Pregnant Women, personal communication, September 4.

36. Committee on the Judiciary (2003), *Unborn Victims of Violence Act of 2003 or Laci and Conner's Law,* hearing before the Subcommittee on the Constitution of the Committee on the Judiciary, House of Representatives, 108th Congress.

37. For instance, the vast majority of the top criminologists and most police chiefs in the United States believe that capital punishment has no significant deterrent effects. Michael L. Radelet and Ronald L. Akers (1996), "Deterrence and the Death Penalty: The Views of the Experts," *Journal of Criminal Law and Criminology* 87(1): 1–16.

38. Quoted in Montgomery (2006).

39. Jacquelyn Campbell (1998), "Abuse during Pregnancy: Progress, Policy, and Potential," *American Journal of Public Health* 88(2): 185–187.

40. In 2005, state lawmakers proposed more fetal homicide bills rather than bills directly restricting abortion. Vestal and Wilkerson (2006).

41. National Right to Life Committee, *Unborn Victims of Violence,* at http:// www.nrlc.org/Unborn_Victims/index.html (retrieved September 1, 2007).

42. Quoted in Joseph Curl (2004), "Bush Signs Fetus-Protection Bill: Affirms 'Two Victims' in Crime on Pregnant Woman," *Washington Times,* April 2, A3.

43. Aaron Zitner (2003), "Abortion Foes Attack *Roe* on New Research: As Science Advances, Some Find Arenas in Which to Seek a Special Status Denied the Embryo and Fetus in the High Court's 1973 Ruling," *Los Angeles Times,* January 19, A1.

44. Howard Minkoff and Lynn M. Paltrow (2006), "The Rights of 'Unborn Children' and the Value of Pregnant Women," *Hastings Center Report* 36(2): 26–28, at 27.

45. Ibid.

46. Citations in the original passage have been deleted. Driessen (2006), 27.

47. April L. Cherry (2007), "The Detention, Confinement, and Incarceration of Pregnant Women for the Benefit of Fetal Health," *Columbia Journal of Gender and Law* 16: 147–197, at 148.

48. In 2005, the Substance Abuse and Mental Health Administration reported that about 15 million women had used illicit drugs in the past year. Among all women in the United States, marijuana and hashish are the most commonly used illicit drug, followed by the nonmedical use of psychotherapeutics, including pain relievers. Substance Abuse and Mental Health Services Administration (2006b), *Results from the 2005 National Survey on Drug Use and Health: National Findings* (Rockville, MD: U.S. Department of Health and Human Services, Office of Applied Studies); U.S. Department of Health and Human Services (2003), *Drug Use among Racial/Ethnic Minorities* (Bethesda, MD: National Institute on Drug Abuse), table 10.

49. Fewer than one in five pregnant women smoked cigarettes in the past month (compared with around almost one in three who were not pregnant). Around one in eight pregnant women report drinking alcohol, and fewer than 4 percent report binge drinking. By contrast, over one-half of nonpregnant women report currently drinking alcohol, and nearly one in four report binge drinking. Substance Abuse and Mental Health Services Administration (2006b). The multisite Infant Development, Environment, and Lifestyle (IDEAL) study of 1,632 mothers, which focused on prenatal methamphetamine exposure, revealed similar findings. At some point during the pregnancy, about one-quarter of the women smoked tobacco, 23 percent drank alcohol, 6 percent used marijuana, and 5 percent used methamphetamine. The study selected geographic regions with notable methamphetamine use. Amelia M. Arria, Chris Derauf, Linda L. LaGasse, et al. (2006), "Methamphetamine and Other Substance Use during Pregnancy: Preliminary Estimates from the Infant Development, Environment, and Lifestyle (IDEAL) Study," *Maternal and Child Health Journal* 10(3): 293–302.

50. Drew Humphries (1999), *Crack Mothers: Pregnancy, Drugs, and the Media* (Columbus: Ohio State University Press).

51. Ibid.; Jimmie L. Reeves and Richard Campbell (1994), *Cracked Coverage: Television News, the Anti-Cocaine Crusade, and the Reagan Legacy* (Durham, NC: Duke University Press).

52. Methamphetamine, also known as speed, crystal, or crank, is a synthetic stimulant that can be dissolved in liquid, ingested orally, snorted, or injected. Some people have used the drug recreationally ever since the 1960s. A researcher at the Sentencing Project reports that meth is among the least commonly used drugs; the rate of meth use has remained stable since 1999, and the rate of use by high school students actually declined between 1999 and 2005. The rate of use is higher in areas such as Los Angeles, San Diego, San Jose, Omaha, and Portland, Oregon. Ryan S. King (2006), *The

Next Big Thing? Methamphetamine in the United States (Washington, DC: Sentencing Project).

53. Ibid.; Jack Shafer (2007), "About That Methedemic," *Slate,* January 31, at http://www.slate.com/id/21487391 (retrieved January 21, 2008).

54. King (2006).

55. Jack Shafer has published several articles in *Slate* documenting the shortcomings of the press corps' drug coverage, including "Why Does Drug Reporting Suck?" (August 10, 2005), "Methamphetamine Propaganda" (March 3, 2006), and "Pfft Goes the Methedemic" (July 1, 2006). Shafer offers the following advice:

> Start your article with an anecdote, preferably one about a user who testifies about how methamphetamine destroyed his life. Toss out some statistics to indicate that meth use is growing, even if the squishy numbers don't prove anything. Avoid statistics that cut against your case. Use and reuse the words "problem" and "epidemic" without defining them. Quote law enforcement officers extensively, whether they know what they're talking about or not. Avoid drug history except to make inflammatory comparisons between meth and other drugs.
>
> Gather grave comments from public-health authorities but never talk to critics of the drug war who might add an unwanted layer of complexity to your story.

Jack Shafer (2006), "How Not to Report about Meth," *Slate,* March 21, at http://www.slate.com/id/21338398/ (retrieved January 28, 2008).

56. Ellen M. Weber (2007), "Child Welfare Interventions for Drug-Dependent Pregnant Women: Limitations of a Non-Public Health Response," *University of Missouri UMKC Law Review* 75: 789–845.

57. Kate Zernike (2005), "A Drug Scourge Creates Its Own Form of Orphan," *New York Times,* July 11.

58. See review of medical and scientific literature in Weber (2007).

59. Gordon C. S. Smith, Jill P. Pell, and Richard Dobbie (2003), "Cesarean Section and Risk of Unexplained Stillbirth in Subsequent Pregnancy," *Lancet* 362: 1779–1784. Stillbirths occur once in approximately every 115–150 births in the United States. The most common causes of stillbirth are placental problems, birth defects, growth restrictions, and infections. Sven Cnattingius and Olof Stephansson (2002), "The Epidemiology of Stillbirth," *Seminars in Perinatology* 26: 25–30.

60. Smith et al. (2003); Cnattingius and Stephansson (2002).

61. Raj Rai and Lesley Regan (2006), "Recurrent Miscarriage," *Lancet* 368: 601–611.

62. Ibid.

63. Ibid.

64. Marian F. MacDorman, Donna L. Hoyert, Joyce A. Martin, et al. (2007), "Fetal and Perinatal Mortality, United States, 2003," *National Vital Statistics Reports* 55(6): 1–20.

65. See literature cited in R. L. Goldenberg, R. Kirby, and J. F. Culhane (2004), "Stillbirth: A Review," *Journal of Maternal-Fetal and Neonatal Medicine* 16: 79–94.

66. Ibid.; Anthony M. Vintzileos, Cande V. Ananth, John C. Smulian, et al. (2002), "Prenatal Care and Black–White Fetal Death Disparity in the United States: Heterogeneity by High-Risk Conditions," *Obstetrics and Gynecology* 99: 483–489.

67. Goldenberg et al. (2004).

68. Alexandra Grosvenor Eller and Janice L. B. Byrne (2006), "Stillbirth at Term," *Obstetrics and Gynecology* 108(2): 442–447.

69. Ibid.

70. Ibid.

71. Cnattingius and Stephansson (2002); R. C. Fretts (2005), "Etiology and Prevention of Stillbirth," *American Journal of Obstetrics and Gynecology* 193: 1923–1935; Goldenberg et al. (2004).

72. G. Koren, K. Graham, H. Shear, and T. Einarson (1989), "Bias against the Null Hypothesis: The Reproductive Hazards of Cocaine," *Lancet* 2: 1440–1442.

73. Deborah Frank, Marilyn Augustyn, Wanda Knight, et al. (2001), "Growth, Development, and Behavior in Early Childhood Following Prenatal Cocaine Exposure," *Journal of the American Medical Association (JAMA)* 285: 1613–1625. See also Howard W. Kilbride, Cheri A Castor, and Kathryn L. Fuger (2006), "School-Age Outcome of Children with Prenatal Cocaine Exposure Following Early Case Management," *Journal of Developmental and Behavioral Pediatrics* 27(3): 181–187; Cassandra Schiller and Pat Jackson Allen (2005), "Follow-Up of Infants Prenatally Exposed to Cocaine," *Pediatric Nursing* 31(5): 427–436.

74. Barry Lester, Linda LaGasse, and Ronald Seifer (1998), "Cocaine Exposure and Children: The Meaning of Subtle Effects," *Science* 282: 633–634, at 634.

75. Frank et al. (2001); Lester et al. (1998).

76. Many of the early studies were methodologically flawed in ways that biased the results. For example, some studies did not use a control or comparison group, the examiners knew whether the children had been exposed to cocaine, or there were inadequate controls for alcohol and tobacco use and other factors. Fifteen of the studies did not adequately control for alcohol and tobacco use, poverty and environmental factors, and HIV infection. This makes it impossible to establish that it is cocaine that is actually the source of any impairments as opposed to, say, the mother's poor diet, stress, or tobacco use. For instance, in my 2002 study, I found that almost 90 percent of the women who used cocaine also smoked. Tobacco use has been associated with many pregnancy and delivery complications, increased infant mortality and morbidity, and lower birthweights. Frank et al. (2001); Jeanne Flavin (2002), "A Glass Half Full? Harm Reduction among Pregnant Women Who Use Cocaine," *Journal of Drug Issues* 32(3): 973–998; U.S. Department of Health and Human Services (2001), *Women and Smoking: A Report of the Surgeon General* (Atlanta: U.S. Department of Health and Human Services, Public Health Service, CDC, National Center for Chronic Disease Prevention and Health Promotion, Office on Smoking and Health).

77. National Advocates for Pregnant Women (2007), data file shared with the author.

78. *State v. McKnight*, 352 S.C. 635 (2003).

79. *Whitner v. South Carolina*, 492 S.E. 2d 777 (S.C., 1997). For example, the court held that it is impossible for a fetus to "possess" the drugs since a fetus would not be capable of handling, manipulating, or using drugs. *Ward v. State*, 184 S.W. 3d 874 (Tex. App., 2006). See also *Reinesto* 894 P. 2d 733 (1995), at 736–737, and other cases

cited in *State v. Martinez,* brief of Amici Curiae Sutin, Thayer & Browne, P.C. et al., in support of respondent.

80. Substance dependence is highest among American Indians and Alaska Natives and lowest among Asians. Native Hawaiians or other Pacific Islanders, whites, and Hispanics all report slightly higher rates of substance dependence than blacks. U.S. Department of Health and Human Services (2003), table 10; Substance Abuse and Mental Health Services Administration (2006).

81. Lynn M. Paltrow (1992), *Criminal Prosecutions against Pregnant Women: National Update and Overview* (New York: American Civil Liberties Union, Reproductive Freedom Project); National Advocates for Pregnant Women (2007).

82. *Ferguson v. City of Charleston* 532 U.S. 67; 121 S. Ct. 1281 (2001). The *Ferguson* ruling did not examine the question of whether the viable fetus was a person or whether mandatory child abuse reporting laws could be used to prosecute maternal drug use. Rather, the Court ruled narrowly on the issue of whether a hospital could test pregnant women for drugs without their knowledge or specific consent, given Fourth Amendment protections against unlawful searches and seizure. Consequently, the *Ferguson* ruling "left South Carolina free to explore just how far it could go toward criminalizing women's behavior during pregnancy by scrutinizing pregnancy outcome." Brigitte M. Nahas (2001), "Drug Tests, Arrests, and Fetuses: A Comment on the U.S. Supreme Court's Narrow Opinion in *Ferguson v. City of Charleston,*" *Cardozo Women's Law Journal* 8: 105–142; Nancy D. Campbell (2006), "The Construction of Pregnant Drug-Using Women as Criminal Perpetrators," *Fordham Urban Law Journal* 33: 463–485, at 468.

83. This sentence was included in the notes in the medical records of the white nurse who reported the women to the police. Lynn Paltrow (2006), *Background Concerning* Ferguson et al. v. City of Charleston et al., at http://advocatesforpregnantwomen.org/issues/criminal_cases_and_issues/background_concerning_ferguson_et_al_v_city_of_charleston_et_al.php (retrieved September 1, 2007).

84. Substance Abuse and Mental Health Services Administration (2006a), *National Survey on Drug Use and Health, 2004 and 2005* (Rockville, MD: Office of Applied Studies, U.S. Department of Health and Human Services).

85. Hillary Klonoff-Cohen and Phung Lam-Kruglick (2001), "Maternal and Paternal Recreational Drug Use and Sudden Infant Death Syndrome," *Archives of Pediatric and Adolescent Medicine* 155: 765–770.

86. For example: M. L. Lindbohm, K. Hemminki, M.G. Bonhomme, et al. (1991), "Effects of Paternal Occupational Exposure on Spontaneous Abortions," *American Journal of Public Health* 81(8): 1029–1033; G. Stemp-Morlock (2007), "Reproductive Health: Pesticides and Anencephaly," *Environmental Health Perspectives* 115(2): A78; M. Hooiveld (2006), "Adverse Reproductive Outcomes among Male Painters with Occupational Exposure to Organic Solvents," *Occupational and Environmental Medicine* 63(8): 538–544. Of course, however, the answer is not to prosecute men with the same fervency as we ordinarily reserve for prosecuting some pregnant women.

87. Some people experience remission or recover from substance dependence without formal treatment (a phenomenon referred to in the literature as "maturing out," "spontaneous remission," or "spontaneous recovery"). F. Termorshuizen, A. Krol,

M. Prins, and E. J. C. van Ameijden (2005), "Long-Term Outcome of Chronic Drug Use: The Amsterdam Cohort Study among Drug Users," *American Journal of Epidemiology* 161(3): 271–279; G. Bischof, H. J. Rumpf, C. Meyer, et al. (2005), "Influence of Psychiatric Comorbidity in Alcohol-Dependent Subjects in a Representative Population Survey on Treatment Utilization and Natural Recovery," *Addiction* 100(3): 405–413; C. Steensma, J. F. Boivin, L. Blais, and E. Roy (2005), "Cessation of Injecting Drug Use among Street-Based Youth," *Journal of Urban Health* 82(4): 622–637.

88. American Psychiatric Association's *DSM-IV* distinguishes between chemical (or drug) abuse and drug dependence. Both conditions involve "a maladaptive pattern of drug use, leading to impairment or distress." A person who abuses drugs meets one or more criteria in a 12-month period—"1) recurrent use leading to failure to fulfill major obligations; 2) recurrent use which is physically hazardous; 3) recurrent drug-related legal problems; and 4) continued use despite social or interpersonal problems"— but does not meet the criterion for dependency. A person is drug dependent (what some may think of as addicted) when he or she presents three or more of the following in a yearlong period: "1) tolerance to the drug's actions, 2) withdrawal; 3) drug is used more than intended; 4) there is an inability to control drug use; 5) effort is expended to obtain the drug; 6) important activities are replaced by drug use; 7) drug use continues despite knowledge of a persistent physical or psychological problem." Dependence may or may not be physiological. American Psychiatric Association (2000), *Diagnostic and Statistical Manual of Mental Disorders,* 4th ed., text revision (Washington, DC: American Psychiatric Association).

89. Sheigla Murphy and Marsha Rosenbaum (1999), *Pregnant Women on Drugs* (New Brunswick, NJ: Rutgers University Press); Claire E. Sterk (1999), *Fast Lives: Women Who Use Crack Cocaine* (Philadelphia: Temple University Press).

90. Caroline Mallory and Phyllis Noerager Stern (2000), "Awakening as a Change Process among Women at Risk for HIV Who Engage in Survival Sex," *Qualitative Health Research* 10(5): 581–594; Murphy and Rosenbaum (1999); Suzanne Pursley-Crotteau and Phyllis Noerager Stern (1996), "Creating a New Life: Dimensions of Temperance in Prenatal Cocaine Crack Users," *Qualitative Health Research* 6(3): 350–367.

91. Vicki Breitbart, Wendy Chavkin, and Paul Wise (1994), "The Accessibility of Drug Treatment for Pregnant Women: A Survey of Programs in Five Cities," *American Journal of Public Health* 84: 1658–1661.

92. Pursley-Crotteau and Stern (1996).

93. Guttmacher Institute (2007i), "Substance Abuse during Pregnancy," *State Policies in Brief,* at http://www.guttmacher.org/statecenter/spibs/spib_SADP.pdf (retrieved January 21, 2008).

94. Charles Marwick (1998), "Physician Leadership on National Drug Policy Finds Addiction Treatment Works," *Journal of the American Medical Association (JAMA)* 279: 1149–1150; Charles P. O'Brien and Thomas A. McLellan (1996), "Myths about Addiction," *Lancet* 347(8996): 237–240.

95. Flavin (2002).

96. Murphy and Rosenbaum (1999); Sterk (1999).

97. Quoted in "Appellate Court Rules Judge Overstepped Authority by Jailing Pregnant Woman" (2004), *Associated Press State and Local Wire,* June 15.

98. *State of New Jersey v. Ikerd,* 69 N.J. Super. 610; 850 A.2d 516 (2004).

99. Some women may present a public face of being indifferent to the toll their drug use is taking on their lives perhaps to cover their fear, confusion, and rage at a system that holds them accountable for a healthy pregnancy without providing them the support and services to do so. Jennifer Reich's study of the child protective system provides a thoughtful and rich analysis of the ways in which men and women who have their children removed from their custody respond to being similarly mired in the family court system. Jennifer Reich (2005), *Fixing Families: Parents, Power, and the Child Welfare System* (New York: Routledge).

100. *Kilmon v. State of Maryland,* 905 A. 2d 306 (Md. App. 2006). See also Susan Kinzie (2006), "Charges Rejected for Moms Who Bear Babies Exposed to Illegal Drugs," *Washington Post,* August 4, B6; Lynn Harris (2006), "Drugs While Pregnant: Dangerous vs. 'Endangerment'?" *Salon,* at www.salon.com/mwt/broadsheet/2006/09/06/drugs_as_endangerment/index.html (retrieved October 12, 2006).

101. The conditions that trigger mandatory reporting laws vary widely across and even within states. Some states require only a positive toxicology screen at birth or physical signs of addiction or dependence, while other states require an assessment of the newborn's imminent risk of harm or need for protection. Weber (2007); National Clearinghouse on Child Abuse and Neglect Information (NCCANI) (2002), *Current Trends in Child Maltreatment Reporting Laws* (Washington, DC: NCCANI); National Clearinghouse on Child Abuse and Neglect Information (NCCANI) (2003), Reporting Child Maltreatment in Cases Involving Parental Substance Abuse, at http://www.calib.com/nccanch/pubs/usermanuals/subabuse/report.cfm (retrieved October 12, 2006).

102. While drug tests can tell whether a woman ingested a drug within the previous two to three days, there is much information these tests cannot report. They cannot tell how much of the drug was taken or how often a woman uses the drug. It is not possible to determine from a drug test result whether drug use has caused a miscarriage, stillbirth, or fetal injury or illness. A drug test cannot measure whether the drug use has impaired a woman's ability to care for herself or others and, if it has, to what extent. Only a narrow range of information can be gleaned from a drug test result. Drew Humphries, John Dawson, Valerie Cronin, et al. (1995), "Mothers and Children, Drugs and Crack: Reactions to Maternal Drug Dependency," in Barbara Raffel Price and Natalie J. Sokoloff, eds., *The Criminal Justice System and Women* (New York: McGraw-Hill), 167–179. See also Guttmacher Institute (2007i); Cherry (2007).

103. See cases cited in Cherry (2007).

104. Many of the court orders have been obtained against white, middle-class women. This suggests a move toward greater regulation of all women's pregnancies rather than a move away from the oppressive policies that have mainly focused on the pregnancies of poor women of color. Terry E. Thornton and Lynn Paltrow (1991), "The Rights of Pregnant Patients: Carder Case Brings Bold Policy Initiatives," *HealthSpan* 8(5), n.p., at http://advocatesforpregnantwomen.org/articles/angela.htm (retrieved October 12, 2006).

105. *Pemberton v. Tallahassee Memorial Regional Medical Center, Inc.,* 66 F. Supp. 2d 1247 (N.D. Fla. 1999); Barbara Behrmann (2007), *Pregnant? In Labor? Your Rights Are under Attack,* at http://www.breastfeedingcafe.com/ReflectionsOnNAPWSummit.htm

(retrieved January 28, 2008); Linda C. Fentiman (2006), "The New 'Fetal Protection': The Wrong Answer to the Crisis of Inadequate Health Care for Women and Children," *Denver University Law Review* 84: 537–599.

106. The physicians at the hospital hearing ruled that vaginal birth posed a "substantial" and "unacceptably high" risk of uterine rupture (or "four to six percent") and resulting death of the baby. *Pemberton,* at 1250, 1253.

107. Ibid., at 1252.

108. In 2004, Amber Marlowe sought to deliver her seventh child. She had previously given birth to six children, each weighing over 11 pounds. She was told, however, that it was not safe to deliver her seventh vaginally because the fetus was so large. The hospital obtained a court order compelling her to undergo the cesarean surgery. By the time she learned of the order, Amber had already delivered her baby at another hospital, a natural delivery she described as a "piece of cake." David L. Caruso (2004), "Court Cases Revive Debates about Rights of Mothers during Childbirth," *Boston Globe,* May 19.

109. Weber (2007); Ernest L. Abel and Michael Kruger (2001), "Physician Attitudes Concerning Legal Coercion of Pregnant Alcohol and Drug Users," *American Journal of Obstetrics and Gynecology* 186: 768–772; National Center on Addiction and Substance Abuse at Columbia University (CASA) (1999), *No Safe Haven: Children of Substance-Abusing Parents* (New York: CASA).

110. The district attorney, Kent Morgan, stated that "we are unable to find any reason other than the cosmetic motivations by the mother" for her decision not to have the cesarean, a report widely circulated in early media accounts. Melissa denied that those were her reasons and pointed out that her two older children had been delivered by cesarean. Alexandria Sage (2004), "Woman Charged with Murder after Allegedly Refusing C-Section: She Denies She Feared Scars," *Associated Press,* March 12.

111. Later, the murder charges were dropped in exchange for Rowland pleading guilty to two felony counts of child endangerment based on her cocaine use during her pregnancy; she was sentenced to 18 months probation and drug treatment.

112. Katha Pollitt (2004), "Pregnant and Dangerous," *Nation,* April 26.

113. Jennifer K. Wood (2005), "In Whose Name? Crime Victim Policy and the Punishing Power of Protection," *NWSA (National Women's Study Association) Journal* 17(3): 1–17, at 4.

114. Ibid.

115. Ibid., 5.

116. It is useful to distinguish between the cultural and the legal or inherent construction of personhood. Anti-abortion activists and supporters of fetal rights subscribe to the logic of the latter. By contrast, anthropologist and noted pregnancy loss expert Linda Layne and others accept a view of personhood that assumes it is a culturally constructed and gradual process. Linda L. Layne (2003), *Motherhood Lost: A Feminist Account of Pregnancy Loss in America* (New York: Routledge), 240–241.

117. Lynn M. Paltrow (1999), "Pregnant Drug Users, Fetal Persons, and the Threat to *Roe v. Wade,*" *Albany Law Review* 62: 999–1054.

118. Lucinda Finlay, quoted in Marc Santora (2004), "Albany Court Reverses Rule on Stillbirths," *New York Times,* April 2.

119.Cynthia R. Daniels (1993), *At Women's Expense: State Power and the Politics of Fetal Rights* (Cambridge: Harvard University Press), 28.

120.Lynn Paltrow (2004), "The Pregnancy Police," *Alternet.org,* April 4, quoted in Wood (2005), 7.

121.Nancy K. Rhoden (1986), "The Judge in the Delivery Room: The Emergence of Court-Ordered Cesareans," *California Law Review* 74: 1951–2030, at 1953.

CHAPTER 6

1.The paired quotations in the epigraph to this chapter were used in a column by Robert C. Koehler of Tribune Media Services, n.d., "Secure Birth," *Common Wonders,* at http://commonwonders.com/archives/c01239.htm (retrieved September 1, 2007).

2.James Sterngold and Mark Martin (2005), "Hard Time: California's Prisons in Crisis," *San Francisco Chronicle,* July 3, A1.

3.Prisoners "are denied access to medical specialists, timely delivery of medical services, technologically advanced diagnostic techniques, the latest medication and drug therapies, and up-to-date surgical procedures." Michael Vaughn and Leo Carroll (1998), "Separate and Unequal: Prison versus Free-World Medical Care," *Justice Quarterly* 15(1): 3–41, at 32; "Receiver Ordered for Prison Health System" (2005), *New York Times,* July 1. In 2001, the California Policy Research Center (CPRC) issued a 142-page report that stemmed from a systematic review of more than 1,000 files containing women prisoners' complaints. The final report thoroughly documented the need for better access to health care for California's women prisoners. The CPRC study found that missed medications was the most common complaint, particularly among women with HIV whose quality (and length) of life is affected when medication schedules are disrupted or not adhered to. One-third of the women reported gynecological and reproductive health problems. Of the 1,072 prisoner files examined containing usable data, slightly more than one-third reported treatment errors that led to adverse health consequences, and slightly less than one-third reported gynecological or reproductive health care problems. Including some of the CPRC's findings here should not be interpreted as singling California out for criticism. The problems that exist in the California correctional system exist in other states as well. It is entirely possible that, due to the efforts of the incarcerated women, their attorneys, and other advocates, the problems are better documented in California than elsewhere. Nancy Stoller (2001), *Improving Access to Health Care for California's Women Prisoners* (Santa Cruz: California Policy Research Center), at http://prisonerswithchildren.org/pubs/stoller.pdf (retrieved September 1, 2007).

4.Agency for Healthcare Research and Quality (AHRQ) (2005), *Women's Health Care in the United States: Selected Findings from the 2004 National Healthcare Quality and Disparities Reports,* Publication No. 05-P021 (Rockville, MD: AHRQ), at http://www.ahrq.gov/qual/nhqrwomen/nhqrwomen.htm (retrieved September 1, 2007).

5.Elizabeth Arias (2006), "United States Life Tables, 2003," *National Vital Statistics Reports* 15(14): 1–40; S. Harper, J. Lynch, S. Burris, and G. Davey Smith (2007),

"Trends in the Black-White Life Expectancy Gap in the United States, 1983–2003," *Journal of the American Medical Association (JAMA)* 21(11): 1224–1232.

6. Agency for Healthcare Research and Quality (2005).

7. National Center for Health Statistics (2006), *Health, United States, 2006* (Hyattsville, MD: U.S. Government Printing Office).

8. Agency for Healthcare Research and Quality (2005).

9. Office of Management and Budget (2006), *Budget of the United States Government* (Washington, DC: U.S. Government Printing Office), at http://frwebgate5. access.gpo.gov/cgi-bin/waisgate.cgi?WAISdocID=008454473655+6+0+0&WAIS action=retrieve pp. 66, 72 (retrieved June 15, 2007). To put the idea of $1 billion into perspective, consider that a person making $1,000 a day would take 2,740 years to earn $1 billion. It would take over 1,900 years to spend $1 billion at the rate of $1 per minute.

10. Ibid.

11. In fiscal year 2004, federal, state, and local governments spent an estimated $194 trillion in direct expenditures on the criminal justice system, one-third of which was for correctional activities. Kristen Hughes (2006), *Direct Expenditures by Criminal Justice Function, 1982–2004* (Washington, DC: U.S. Department of Justice, Bureau of Justice Statistics).

12. Lauren Glaze and Seri Pella (2005), *Correctional Populations in the United States* (Washington, DC: U.S. Department of Justice, Bureau of Justice Statistics).

13. Ibid.

14. While women's incarceration rates (number of prisoners sentenced to more than one year per 100,000 population) are growing, they remain much lower than those for men. The incarceration rate for women was 47 in 1995 and 65 in 2005. The comparable figures for men are 781 and 929, respectively. Paige Harrison and Allen Beck (2006b), *Prisoners in 2005* (Washington, DC: U.S. Department of Justice).

15. Ibid.

16. In 2006, the incarceration rate for black women was 358 per 100,000 compared with 152 and 94 per 100,000 for Hispanic and white women, respectively. Ibid. See also William J. Sabol, Todd D. Minton, and Paige M. Harrison (2007), *Prison and Jail Inmates at Midyear 2006* (Washington, DC: U.S. Department of Justice); U.S. General Accounting Office (1999), *Women in Prison: Issues and Challenges Confronting U.S. Correctional Systems* (Washington, DC: General Accounting Office).

17. Harrison and Beck (2006b); Sabol et al. (2007); U.S. General Accounting Office (1999).

18. Paige M. Harrison and Allen J. Beck (2006a), *Prison and Jail Inmates at Midyear 2005* (Washington, DC: U.S. Department of Justice).

19. About one-half of men in state prisons are serving sentences for violent offenses compared with only one-third of women. Paige Harrison and Allen Beck (2005), *Prisoners in 2004* (Washington, DC: U.S. Department of Justice, Bureau of Justice Statistics).

20. Harrison and Beck (2006a, 2006b).

21. Nicole Hahn Rafter (1992), *Partial Justice: Women, Prisons, and Social Control* (New Brunswick, NJ: Transaction).

22. Assaults on inmates and staff are perceived as being less common in women's prisons, though this may be based more on myth than fact. Dana Britton (2003), *At Work in the Iron Cage: The Prison as Gendered Organization* (New York: New York University Press). See also Miles D. Harer and Neil P. Langan (2001), "Gender Differences in Predictors of Prison Violence: Assessing the Predictive Validity of a Risk Classification System," *Crime and Delinquency* 47(4): 513–536.

23. John Pacenti (2004), "Prenatal Care at Jail Criticized," *Palm Beach Post,* May 9, 1C.

24. Ibid.

25. Ibid.

26. *Laube v. Haley,* 242 F. Supp. 2d 1150 (M.D. Ala., 2003), at 3.

27. Carla Crowder (2005b), "Prison Medical Care Tied to Deaths," *Birmingham News,* April 21, 1A.

28. Poor care seemed to be the rule rather than the exception. The court monitor (and an expert in correctional health care), Dr. Michael Puisis, concluded that the Tutwiler medical contractor had administered substandard care to 19 of 22 prisoners whose charts he reviewed. Ibid.

29. *Brown v. Beck,* 481 F. Supp. 723 (S.D. Ga., 1980).

30. According to the standards established in *Estelle v. Gamble,* 429 U.S. 97; 97 S. Ct. 285 (1976), for correctional health care to be considered a violation of the Eighth Amendment, a person who is incarcerated must pass a two-part test and show that (1) there was a serious medical need and (2) prison officials showed "deliberate indifference: that is, they both knew of a medical condition and did not respond to it in a reasonable manner. This standard is difficult to meet and far higher than the free-world requirement to prove that care has been negligent. Maissa Boulos, Alicia D'Addario, and Rachel Meeropol (2005), *The Jailhouse Lawyer's Handbook* (New York: Center for Constitutional Rights and the National Lawyers Guild).

31. Cynthia Chandler (2003), "Death and Dying in America: The Prison Industrial Complex's Impact on Women's Health," *Berkeley Women's Law Journal* 18: 40–60, at 44.

32. Ibid.

33. Crowder (2005b).

34. Vaughn and Carroll (1998).

35. Chandler (2003).

36. The spotty record keeping suggested that thousands of doses of prescribed medication had never been administered. Paul Von Zielbauer (2005b), "Company's Troubled Answer for Prisoners with H.I.V.," *New York Times,* August 1, A1.

37. Jenifer Warren (2005b), "U.S. to Seize State Prison Health System," *Los Angeles Times,* July 1, A1.

38. Paul Von Zielbauer (2005a), "As Health Care in Jails Goes Private, 10 Days Can Be a Death Sentence," *New York Times,* February 27.

39. For example, *New York Times* reporter Paul Von Zeilbauer wrote a series of articles documenting the appallingly poor medical care Prison Health Services provided to New York City inmates. He found that 10 psychiatrists should have been fired for failing to pass the necessary test for state certification but instead were permitted to practice for more than a year. When they were finally fired on the city's orders, Prison

Health left one-third of the full-time psychiatrist positions vacant. Prison Health "employed five doctors with criminal convictions, including one who had been jailed for selling human blood for phony tests to be billed to Medicaid. In all, at least 14 doctors who have worked for Prison Health have state or federal disciplinary records, among them a psychiatrist forbidden to practice in New Jersey after state officials blamed him for a patient's fatal drug overdose." In November 2005, city health officials found that the Prison Health contract appeared to be illegal because jail doctors are answerable to Prison Health executives rather than physicians. Paul Von Zielbauer (2005c), "In City's Jails, Missed Signals Open Way to Season Suicides," *New York Times,* February 28, A1; Paul Von Zielbauer (2005d), "Investigators Called Rikers Medical Contract Illegal, State Panel Says," *New York Times,* November 22, B1.

40. Von Zielbauer (2005b).

41. Nearly 80 percent of prison inmates' deaths are due to an illness other than HIV/AIDS; another 9 and 6 percent of deaths are caused by AIDS and suicide, respectively. Mortality rates are highest among men and white inmates. Christopher Mumola (2005), *Suicide and Homicide in State Prisons and Local Jails,* NCJ 210036 (Washington, DC: U.S. Department of Justice, Bureau of Justice Statistics); Christopher J. Mumola (2007), *Medical Causes of Death in State Prisons, 2001–2004,* NCJ 216340 (Washington, DC: U.S. Department of Justice, Bureau of Justice Statistics).

42. Mumola (2007).

43. Carol Caldwell, Mack Jarvis, and Herbert Rosefield (2001), "Issues Impacting Today's Geriatric Female Offenders," *Corrections Today* 63(5): 110–113; Mumola (2007).

44. Mumola (2007).

45. For instance, in 2006, the CDC Correctional Health Care website devoted to women's health focused almost exclusively on HIV, pregnancy, substance abuse, and mental health, while ignoring gynecologic cancer and HPV screening and treatment. Centers for Disease Control and Prevention (2006), *About Correctional Health,* at http://www.cdc.gov/nchstp/od/cccwg/WH_General.htm (retrieved October 12, 2006).

46. U.S. General Accounting Office (1999).

47. Center for Reproductive Rights (n.d.), *Safe Pregnancy* (New York: Center for Reproductive Rights), at http://www.reproductiverights.org/ww_iss_mother.html (retrieved September 1, 2007).

48. American Correctional Association (1990), *The Female Offender* (Lanham, MD: American Correctional Association). Another study reported that one out of every four adult women in prison is pregnant at the time of incarceration or has given birth at some point during the previous year.

49. Adam Liptak (2006), "Prisons Often Shackle Pregnant Inmates in Labor," *New York Times,* March 2, A16.

50. Eight state departments of correction (DOCs) and the Federal Bureau of Prisons have the authority to place a pregnant inmate in noninstitutional settings such as home detention, day reporting, or community facilities. LIS, Inc. (2002), *Services for Families of Prison Inmates* (Longmont, CO: National Institute of Corrections).

51. Ibid.

52. See literature cited in Diana Mertens (2001), "Pregnancy Outcomes of Inmates in a Large County Jail Setting," *Public Health Nursing* 18(1): 45–53.

53. Ibid.

54. Katherine Baldwin and Jacquelyn Jones (2000), *Health Issues Specific to Incarcerated Women: Information for State Maternal and Child Health Programs* (Washington, DC: Health Resources and Services Administration).

55. Pregnant women are advised to take prenatal vitamins and mineral supplements, stop smoking, and gain an appropriate amount of weight. They should exercise; eat a variety of foods (including fruits, vegetables, and grains) that provide enough basic nutrients; and avoid alcohol, tobacco, and excessive salt or caffeine.

56. Prison doctors seem to have been successful at preventing pregnant women infected with HIV from transmitting HIV to the fetus or child during pregnancy, labor and delivery, or breastfeeding. In the absence of any intervention, the risk of a pregnant, HIV-positive woman transmitting the virus to her infant is 15 to 45 percent. Taking antiretroviral drugs during pregnancy and labor, undergoing an elective cesarean delivery, and other interventions lowers the risk of mother-to-child transmission to below 2 percent. Department of HIV/AIDS and Department of Reproductive Health and Research (2004), *Antiretroviral Drugs for Treating Pregnant Women and Preventing HIV Infection in Infants* (Geneva: World Health Organization), 4.

57. Chandler (2003), 50.

58. Ibid.

59. Quoted in Kathleen J. Ferraro and Angela M. Moe (2003), "Mothering, Crime, and Incarceration," *Journal of Contemporary Ethnography* 32(1): 9–40, at 25.

60. Quoted in Amnesty International (2006), *Abuse of Women in Custody: Sexual Misconduct and Shackling of Pregnant Women* (New York: Amnesty International), at http://www.amnestyusa.org/women/custody/abuseincustody.html (retrieved September 1, 2007).

61. The State Commission of Correction found that prenatal training for nurses consisted of email messages with instructions copied from a university web site. Von Zielbauer (2005a).

62. Amnesty International (2006).

63. Testimony reported in Amnesty International (1999), *Not Part of My Sentence: Violations of the Human Rights of Women in Custody* (New York: Amnesty International).

64. Amnesty International (2006).

65. Ibid.

66. Quoted in Jenifer Warren (2005a), "The State: Rethinking Treatment of Female Prisoners," *Los Angeles Times,* June 19, A1.

67. U.S. Cancer Statistics Working Group (2006), United States Cancer Statistics: 2003 Incidence and *Mortality Web-Based Report* (Atlanta: U.S. Department of Health and Human Services, Centers for Disease Control and Prevention and National Cancer Institute), at www.cdc.gov/cancer/npcr/uscs (retrieved June 12, 2007).

68. Cynthia Dailard (2003), "HPV in the United States and Developing Nations," *Guttmacher Report* 6(3): 4–6.

69. Annekathryn Goodman (2002), "Human Papillomavirus Infections in Incarcerated Women," *Infectious Diseases in Corrections Report* 5(1): 1–5.

70. "Human Papillomavirus (HPV) 101" (2006), *Infectious Diseases in Corrections Report* 9(6–7): 8.

71. Ibid.

72. Goodman (2002).

73. Lawrence A. Greenfeld and Tracy L. Snell (1999), *Women Offenders* (Washington, DC: U.S. Department of Justice, Bureau of Justice Statistics).

74. K. Weatherhead (2003), "Cruel but Not Unusual Punishment: The Failure to Provide Adequate Medical Treatment to Women in the United States," *Health Matrix: Journal of Law and Medicine* 13(2): 429–472; U.S. General Accounting Office (1999). National guidelines recommend a Pap test every 2–3 years after a woman has had three Pap tests in a row and the results show there are no problems. Other women should be screened annually. Centers for Disease Control and Prevention (2003a), *Cervical Cancer: Basic Facts on Screening and the Pap Test*, at http://www.cdc.gov/cancer/nbccedp/bccpdfs/cc_basic.pdf (retrieved September 1, 2007).

75. Centers for Disease Control and Prevention (2005), *STD Surveillance 2005* (Atlanta: U.S. Department of Health and Human Services, Centers for Disease Control and Prevention). A woman infected with chlamydia has a greater chance of becoming infected with HIV if she is exposed to the virus. She may develop complications such as inflammation of the cervix, urethra, uterine lining, uterus, fallopian tubes, or ovaries; develop a pelvic infection; or become infertile. Between 50 and 75 percent of babies born to mothers with chlamydia will get the infection (including in their eyes, the back of their throat, or their rectum or vagina); between 30 and 40 percent of babies infected with chlamydia at birth will develop complications such as conjunctivitis ("pink-eye") or pneumonia.

If not detected and treated, around one-third of people infected with syphilis will progress to the tertiary (late) stage, the most destructive stage of syphilis. During this stage, syphilis may cause serious blood vessel and heart problems, mental disorders, blindness, central nervous system problems, and even death. Without treatment, tertiary or "late" syphilis may then involve any of the organ systems, including the central nervous system. A woman may pass syphilis on to the baby during pregnancy, labor, and delivery. Women with untreated gonorrhea increase their risk of developing pelvic inflammatory disease, an abscess in or near the ovaries, an ectopic (tubal) pregnancy, or chronic pelvic pain or of becoming infertile.

76. Despite these problems, New York's Department of Juvenile Justice gave Prison Health Services, the contractor providing the care, mostly satisfactory evaluations during its four-year contract. Paul Von Zielbauer (2005e), "A Spotty Record of Health Care at Juvenile Sites in New York," *New York Times,* March 1, A1.

77. Ibid. Also, HPV vaccines exist which help prevent genital HPV infection. Detained and incarcerated girls might benefit from being offered vaccination for HPV prior to the onset of sexual activity.

78. Anne De Groot and Susan Cu Uvin (2005), "HIV Infection among Women in Prison: Considerations for Care," *Infectious Diseases in Corrections Report* 8(5–6): 1–4.

79. Centers for Disease Control and Prevention (2005).

80. De Groot and Cu Uvin (2005).

81. Laura M. Maruschak (2007), *HIV in Prisons, 2005* (Washington, DC: U.S. Department of Justice, Office of Justice Programs).

82. In fact, the only AIDS-defining illness exclusive to women is invasive cervical cancer. M. Sara Rosenthal (2003), *The Gynecological Sourcebook* (New York: McGraw-Hill), 53–70.

83. Maruschak (2007).

84. De Groot and Cu Uvin (2005); C. D. Pilcher, H. Tien, J. J. Eron Jr., et al. (2004), "Brief but Efficient: Acute HIV Transmission and the Sexual Transmission of HIV," *Journal of Infectious Diseases* 189(10): 1785–1792.

85. De Groot and Cu Uvin (2005); Kimberly Arriola, R. Jacob, Ronald L. Braithwaite, and Cassandra F. Newkirk (2006), "At the Intersection between Poverty, Race, and HIV Infection: HIV-Related Services for Incarcerated Women," *Infectious Diseases in Corrections Report* 9(6–7): 1–7.

86. De Groot and Cu Uvin (2005).

87. Anne De Groot (2005), personal email communication with the author, July 27.

88. De Groot and Cu Uvin (2005).

89. Ibid.

90. This section draws on information presented in a 2004 unpublished paper, "Sexual Abuse in Prison," written by Leslie Smith, then-M.A. student in sociology at Fordham University. See also "Sex, Contraband to Private Prison for Women" (2005), *Casper Star Tribune,* February 25; Women in Prison Project (2004), *Coalition for Women Prisoners: Proposals for Reform* (New York: Correctional Association of New York), 20; *Amador v. Superintendents of the Department of Correctional Services* (S.D.N.Y., Sept. 13, 2005); Human Rights Watch and ACLU (2006), *Custody and Control: Conditions of Confinement in New York's Juvenile Prisons for Girls,* at http://hrw.org/reports/2006/us0906/ (retrieved September 1, 2007); *Laube v. Haley*; Amnesty International (1999); Avery Calhoun and Heather Coleman (2002), "Female Inmates' Perspectives on Sexual Abuse by Correctional Personnel," *Women and Criminal Justice* 13(2/3): 101–124.

91. Rafter (1992).

92. Ibid.; Britton (2003).

93. Sexual Abuse of a Minor or a Ward, 18 U.S.C. § 2243 (2006).

94. NIC/WCL (National Institute of Corrections/American University, Washington College of Law) Project on Addressing Prison Rape (2006), *State Criminal Laws Prohibiting Sexual Abuse of Individuals in Custody* (Washington, DC: NIC/WCL Project on Addressing Prison Rape).

95. *Amador v. Superintendents of the Department of Correctional Services* (2005). See also *Kidd v. Andrews*, 340 F. Supp. 2d 333, U.S. Dist. (W.D.N.Y., 2004); Gary Craig (2006), "Inmate Despair Hints at Abuse: Was She Raped? Lawyer Calls for New Inquiry into 3-Year-Old Suicide," *Rochester (NY) Democrat and Chronicle,* July 13; Jeffrey Blackwell (2005), "Father, Son Prison Guards Charged in Alleged Sex Abuse," *Rochester (NY) Democrat and Chronicle,* March 31.

96. In 2006, the Correctional Association noted that reports of physical and sexual abuse of prisoners were not common in Bedford Hills and Albion facilities, but neither were they unheard of. Women in Prison Project (2004); Women in Prison Project (2006a), *Bedford Hills Correctional Facility* (New York: Correctional Association of New York).

97. Human Rights Watch and the American Civil Liberties Union (2006), 65.
98. "Sex, Contraband to Private Prison for Women" (2005).
99. Cindy Struckman-Johnson and David Struckman-Johnson (2006), "A Comparison of Sexual Coercion Experiences Reported by Men and Women in Prison," *Journal of Interpersonal Violence* 21: 1591–1615; Melvin Claxton, Ronald J. Hansen, and Norman Sinclair (2005), "Guards Assault Female Inmates," *Detroit News*, May 22.
100. Struckman-Johnson and Struckman-Johnson (2006).
101. Norman Sinclair, Melvin Claxton, and Ronald J. Hansen (2005b), "Prisoner Complaints Unheeded," *Detroit News*, May 24; see also Norman Sinclair, Melvin Claxton, and Ronald J. Hansen (2005a) "Michigan Faces Conflict of Interest," *Detroit News*, May 24; Claxton et al. (2005).
102. "Guarding against Sexual Abuse" (2006), *Grand Rapids Press*, January 7, A10.
103. Michael Weissenstein (2005), "NY Jails Ban Forced Exams for Women," *Associated Press*, July 14, n.p.
104. Tracy Connor (2005), "City's 30M Mea Culpa: Paying for Illegal Strip Searches," *New York Daily News*, July 13, 5.
105. Quoted in Walter Goodman (1999), "Of Camera and Consequences at a Women's Prison," *New York Times*, November 2.
106. Britton (2003).
107. Chandler (2003), 55.
108. De Groot (2005), personal email communication.
109. Michelle Maloney, Rachel Wilgoren, Milissa Rothstein, and Shelly Inglis (2005), "Special Issues of Women Prisoners," in *A Jailhouse Lawyer's Manual*, 6th ed. (New York: Columbia Human Rights Law Review), 246–248; *Women Prisoners v. District of Columbia*, 93 F.3rd 910 (1996); *Klinger v. Department of Corrections*, 107 F.3d. 609 (8th Cir., 1997); *Keevan v. Smith*, 100 F.3d 644 (8th Cir., 1996).
110. The United States is the only major industrialized nation in the world without a universal health insurance system. It is hard to argue that prisoners "take away" medical care from nonincarcerated citizens in a country where 41.6 million people, or 16 percent of the entire population under the age of 65, has no health insurance coverage. National Center for Health Statistics (2006).
111. According to the National Commission on Correctional Health Care, all correctional institutions should subscribe to guidelines established by professional groups such as the American Cancer Society and the American College of Obstetricians and Gynecologists.
112. Vaughn and Carroll (1998).
113. Warren (2005); Britton (2003).
114. Quoted in Warren (2005).

CHAPTER 7

1. Christopher J. Mumola (2000), *Incarcerated Parents and Their Children*, NCJ 216340 (Washington, DC: U.S. Department of Justice, Bureau of Justice Statistics).
2. Tracy L. Snell (1994), *Women in Prison* (Washington, DC: U.S. Department of Justice, Bureau of Justice Statistics), table 9; Mumola (2000).

3. Mumola (2000).

4. Venezia Michalsen (2007), "Going Straight for Her Children? Mothers' Desistance after Incarceration," Ph.D. diss., City University of New York; Barry Krisberg and Carolyn Engel Temin (2001), *The Plight of Children Whose Parents Are in Prison* (Oakland, CA: National Council on Crime and Delinquency).

5. Patricia O'Brien (2002), *Reducing Barriers to Employment for Women Ex-Offenders: Mapping the Road to Reintegration* (Chicago: SAFER Foundation Council of Advisors to Reduce Recidivism through Employment); Patricia O'Brien (2001), *Making It in the "Free World": Women in Transition from Prison* (Albany: SUNY Press).

6. I use the term "mother" to refer to a woman whose rights to parent have neither been voluntarily surrendered nor involuntarily terminated. Terms like "biological mother" or "birth mother" are more appropriately used in cases where a woman's parental rights have been permanently relinquished or transferred to someone else.

7. About two-thirds of all women are incarcerated for drug offenses (32 percent) or property offenses, including writing bad checks and other forms of fraud (29 percent). Child abuse is one of the offenses included in the category "other violent crimes." Bureau of Justice Statistics (2005), *Profile of Jail Inmates, 2002* (Washington, DC: U.S. Department of Justice); Paige Harrison and Allen Beck (2006b), *Prisoners in 2005* (Washington, DC: U.S. Department of Justice).

8. About one-fourth of women in state prisons and local jails report that they had been diagnosed with a mental disorder in the past year, with young white women being more likely to report symptoms. About three-quarters of women prisoners who had a mental health problem also met the criteria for substance dependence or abuse. Doris J. James and Lauren E. Glaze (2006), *Mental Health Problems of Prison and Jail Inmates* (Washington, DC: U.S. Department of Justice).

9. Corina Benjet, Sandra T. Azar, and Regina Kuersten-Hogan (2003), "Evaluating the Parental Fitness of Psychiatrically Diagnosed Individuals: Advocating a Functional-Contextual Analysis of Parenting," *Journal of Family Psychology* 17(2): 238–251.

10. Prasanna Nair, Maureen E. Schuler, Maureen M. Black, et al. (2003), "Cumulative Environmental Risk in Substance Abusing Women: Early Intervention, Parenting Stress, Child Abuse Potential and Child Development," *Child Abuse and Neglect* 27(9): 997–1017.

11. Benjet et al. (2003).

12. Nina Wasow (2006), "Planned Failure: California's Denial of Reunification Services to Parents with Mental Disabilities," *New York University Review of Law and Social Change* 31: 183–224.

13. Lenore McWey, Tammy L. Henderson, and Susan N. Tice (2006), "Mental Health Issues and the Foster Care System: An Examination of the Impact of the Adoption and Safe Families Act," *Journal of Marital and Family Therapy* 32(2): 195–214.

14. R. K. Otto and J. F. Edens (2003), "Parenting Capacity," in T. Grisso, R. Borum, J. F. Edens, et al., eds., *Evaluating Competencies: Forensic Assessments and Instruments* (New York: Kluwer Academic/Plenum). Furthermore, many people with mental health problems fear losing custody or visiting rights. This fear may actually deter them from seeking treatment. Alisa Busch and Allison D. Redlich (2007), "Patients'

Perception of Possible Child Custody or Visitation Loss for Nonadherence to Psychiatric Treatment," *Psychiatric Services* 58(7): 999–1002.

15. Benjet et al. (2003).

16. See research cited in Wasow (2006); Benjet et al. (2003).

17. See cases cited in Pamela Lewis (2004), "Behind the Glass Wall: Barriers That Incarcerated Parents Face Regarding the Care, Custody, and Control of Their Children," *Journal of the American Academy of Matrimonial Lawyers* 19: 97–115, at 104 n.61.

18. Patricia Hill Collins (1999), "Shifting the Center," in Stephanie Coontz, ed., *American Families: A Multicultural Reader* (New York: Routledge), 197–217.

19. Barrie Thorne (1992), "Feminism and the Family: Two Decades of Thought," in Barrie Thorne and Marilyn Yalom, eds., *Rethinking the Family: Two Decades of Thought,* 2nd ed. (Boston: Northeastern University Press), 1–30.

20. Daniel P. Moynihan (1965), *The Negro Family: The Case for National Action* (Washington, DC: U.S. Department of Labor, Office of Planning and Research).

21. Many delinquent girls have experienced structural dislocation: that is, the "removal, by choice, force, or some combination of circumstances, from a social institution—with little chance of reassociation due to the nature of the rift between the individual and the institution." Criminologist Regina Arnold found that many poor black girls experience abuse in the home (including sexual abuse committed by a male relative or stepfather). Their age, gender, and size often make fighting back an unrealistic option, which is why many young girls remain in the abusive situations. Others resist the violence or marginalization by running away, stealing, or being truant. Their inexperience and lack of job skills limit the options they have to legitimately earn a living to meet their needs; economic marginality can lead to stealing, prostitution, and drug dealing as a means of survival. Regina A. Arnold (1995), "Processes of Victimization and Criminalization of Black Women," in Barbara Raffel Price and Natalie J. Sokoloff, eds., *The Criminal Justice System and Women,* 2nd ed. (New York: McGraw-Hill), 136–146. See also Eleanor M. Miller (1986), *Street Woman* (Philadelphia: Temple University Press).

22. One woman reported that now that she has a son, "I have him to go home for. I don't have to go buy weed or drugs with my money, I could buy my *son* stuff with my money." Quoted in Kathryn Edin and Maria Kefalas (2005), *Promises I Can Keep: Why Poor Women Put Motherhood before Marriage* (Los Angeles: University of California Press), 172–173. See also Dana D. Dehart (2004), *Pathways to Prison: Impact of Victimization on the Lives of Incarcerated Women* (Columbia, SC: Center for Child and Family Studies); Kathleen J. Ferraro and Angela M. Moe (2003), "Mothering, Crime, and Incarceration," *Journal of Contemporary Ethnography* 32(1): 9–40.

23. Kathryn Edin and Laura Lein (1997), Making Ends Meet: How Single Mothers Survive Welfare and Low-Wage Work (New York: Russell Sage).

24. Ibid., 7.

25. The majority of 379 single mothers in their study saw full financial independence through legal paid employment as their overarching goal, since it was the only strategy that didn't require a loss of self-respect. But since they couldn't make ends meet on their wages or welfare alone to support their families at subsistence levels, they had to consider other alternatives. The second-best alternative was to seek help

from one's social network, preferably the father of a child or a live-in boyfriend rather than a relative or friend. If the social network support didn't pan out, then the third-best alternative to generate extra income was to take cash work or a side job in the informal economy (e.g., cleaning houses, babysitting, collecting aluminum cans). When these strategies didn't work, many women appealed to churches or private charities to pay the rent or cover a utility bill. Engaging in criminal activity was undertaken only as a last resort, when other strategies had failed. Edin and Lein (1997), 176.

26. See literature cited in Sandra Enos (2001), *Mothering from the Inside: Parenting in a Women's Prison* (Albany: SUNY Press). See also Dehart (2004); Beth E. Richie (1996), *Compelled to Crime: The Gender Entrapment of Battered Black Women* (New York: Routledge).

27. Enos (2001); Richie (1996).

28. Dehart (2004).

29. Arnold (1995); Barbara Owen (1998), *"In the Mix": Struggle for Survival in a Women's Prison* (Albany: SUNY Press), 12.

30. Ferraro and Moe (2003), 19.

31. Timothy Ross, Ajay Khashu, and Mark Wamsley (2004), *Hard Data on Hard Times: An Empirical Analysis of Maternal Incarceration, Foster Care, and Visitation* (New York: Vera Institute of Justice).

32. Ibid.

33. Ferraro and Moe (2003), 30.

34. McWey et al. (2006).

35. Jeanne Flavin (2001), "Of Punishment and Parenthood: Family-Based Social Control and the Sentencing of Black Drug Offenders," *Gender & Society* 15(4): 609–631.

36. Judges were less likely to incarcerate those single women who lived with their children and women who didn't have children but did live with an adult family member.

37. Information on the judges' reasoning was not available, though one cannot rule out the possibility that women who had children but did not live with them were being punished twice: once for their offense, and once for being perceived as bad mothers. It is also possible that sentencing a woman who does not have custody of her children alleviates judges' practical concern for who would care for the children if she were incarcerated.

38. When a woman is taken into custody, there is often no time to make arrangements for what to do with the child. In some jurisdictions, the police may routinely notify child protective services when they arrest a woman whose children are present. Elsewhere, the police may only call child protective services in cases where there is evidence of severe abuse or neglect. In some cases, a woman may not tell the arresting officers she even has children for fear of the children entering the system. From the child's perspective, an arrest followed by detention may lead to the conclusion that her mother has disappeared or abandoned her, especially if the child is not told about the arrest.

39. Kerry Kazura (2001), "Family Programming for Incarcerated Parents: A Needs Assessment among Inmates," *Journal of Offender Rehabilitation* 32: 67–83.

40. Owen (1998), 13.

41. Enos (2001).

42. Incarcerated women are not always sympathetic to those others' ambivalence about aspects of parenting. Sociologist and author of *Mothering from the Inside,* Sandra Enos, reported that a woman who expressed relief that someone else would be dealing with her child during the "terrible twos" was scolded by her fellow participants in a group session. Enos observes that "there was very little tolerance for women who expressed anything but an eagerness to return to care for children, at least in some capacity." Enos (2001), 81.

43. Ferraro and Moe (2003); Owen (1998), 12.

44. Ferraro and Moe (2003), 24; Phyllis E. Berry and Helen M. Eigenberg (2003), "Role Strain and Incarcerated Mothers: Understanding the Process of Mothering," *Women and Criminal Justice* 15(1): 101–119.

45. Other pains related to mothering include the lack of privacy and frequent strip searches (including before and after every visit), the limited access to health care, the poor quality or inadequate provision of basic toiletries, and the limited telephone access and isolation. Human Rights Watch (2002), *Ill-Equipped: U.S. Prisons and Offenders with Mental Illness* (New York: Human Rights Watch). At the same time, for some women, incarceration provides some respite from the stress and demands of their lives on the outside. For example, a woman with several young children described her time in jail as a "vacation": "When I was at home with the kids, I never got a chance to sit down and read books. It's impossible to find the time to write when you have to work and you have to get the kids off to school or you have to do all of the things." Quoted in Ferraro and Moe (2003), 13.

46. See review in Joycelyn M. Pollock (2002), "Parenting Programs in Women's Prisons," *Women and Criminal Justice* 14(1): 131–154.

47. In general, courts have held that denying the right to visiting between incarcerated parents and their minor children is unconstitutional. But this is a relatively low burden. A prison regulation restricting visits is not considered unconstitutional if it is reasonably related to legitimate penological goals (such as security, order, and discipline). Lewis (2004), 103.

48. Ross et al. (2004), 1.

49. Lisa Barnard and Jeanne M. Flavin (2007), *The Impact of Visiting: Fact Sheet and Bibliography* (New York: Fordham University Interdisciplinary Center for Child and Family Advocacy); Arthur L. Cantos, Leonard T. Gries, and Vikki Slis (1997), "Behavioral Correlates of Parental Visiting during Family Foster Care," *Child Welfare* 76(2): 309–329; Susan C. Mapp (2002), "A Framework for Family Visiting for Children in Long-Term Foster Care," *Families in Society* 83(2): 175–182; Lenore M. McWey and Ann K. Mullis (2004), "Improving the Lives of Children in Foster Care: The Impact of Supervised Visitation," *Family Relations* 53(3): 293–300; Diane S. Young and Carrie Jefferson Smith (2000), "When Moms Are Incarcerated: The Needs of Children, Mothers, and Caregivers," *Families in Society* 81(2): 130–141.

50. Mumola (2000); Elizabeth I. Johnson and Jane Waldfogel (2002), "Parental Incarceration: Recent Trends and Implications for Child Welfare," *Social Service Review* 76(3): 460–479.

51. Mumola (2000).

52. Michalsen (2007), 74.

53. Lewis (2004), 104, nn.61, 64.

54. Incarcerated mothers often want to be consulted in decisions about medical treatment, religious upbringing, how the child is to be disciplined, or where he will attend school. Matters such as what food the child will be permitted to eat, how her hair will be styled, or the kind of clothing she wears, which may seem ordinary, often are extremely important to maintaining a cultural or familial identity.

55. Martha L. Raimon (2001), "Barriers to Achieving Justice for Incarcerated Parents," *Fordham University Law Review* 70: 421–426, at 425.

56. Staying in touch with children is particularly hard when the child is too young to read or write or doesn't have a clear or favorable sense of his mother. Ann Adalist-Estrin (2003), *The Caregivers' Situation* (Palmyra, VA: Family and Corrections Network), 2; Enos (2001).

57. The United States accounts for fewer than 5 percent of the world's people but nearly 25 percent of those who are incarcerated. The magnitude of the difference between U.S. incarceration rates and other countries' cannot be explained solely by our higher crime rates. Christopher Hartney (2006), *U.S. Rates of Incarceration: A Global Perspective* (Washington, DC: National Council on Crime and Delinquency), at http://www.nccd-crc.org/nccd/pubs/2006nov_factsheet_incarceration.pdf (retrieved September 1, 2007).

58. Timothy A. Hughes, Doris James Wilson, and Allen J. Beck (2001), *Trends in State Parole, 1990–2000* (Washington, DC: U.S. Department of Justice), table 8.

59. Christopher J. Mumola (2007), *Medical Causes of Death in State Prisons, 2001–2004* (Washington, DC: U.S. Department of Justice, Bureau of Justice Statistics).

60. Women in Prison Project (2007), *Imprisonment and Families Fact Sheet* (New York: Correctional Association of New York).

61. Amnesty International (1999), *Not Part of My Sentence: Violation of the Human Rights of Women in Custody* (New York: Amnesty International).

62. LIS, Inc. (2006), *Interstate Transfer of Prison Inmates in the United States* (Longmont, CO: National Institute of Corrections). This figure is an undercount since some states did not respond to the survey. For instance, Hawaii, which did not respond to the survey, housed 175 women in a private Kentucky facility in 2006.

63. In 2002, the National Institute of Corrections reported the responses from 48 state departments of corrections, the Federal Bureau of Prisons, the District of Columbia, New York City, Guam, Saipon, and the Correctional Service of Canada. LIS, Inc. (2002), *Services for Families of Prison Inmates* (Longmont, CO: National Institute of Corrections).

64. Pennsylvania DOC inmates can move closer to their home region as a reward for good work, program participation, conduct, and reduced security level. LIS, Inc. (2002).

65. In 1998, Joycelyn Pollock, a professor of criminal justice at Southwest Texas State University, conducted a national survey of parenting programs in women's prisons, receiving responses from 40 states. The following section relies heavily, though not exclusively, on the findings of her survey. Pollock (2002).

66. Women's Advocacy Project (2005), *Policy Recommendations: Making Family Reunification a Reality for Criminal Justice-Involved Women* (New York: Women's

Prison Association), at http://66.29.139.159/pdf/Recommendations_2005.pdf (retrieved September 1, 2007); Denise Johnston and Katherine Gabel (1995), "Incarcerated Parents," in Katherine Gabel and Denise Johnston, eds., *Children of Incarcerated Parents* (New York: Lexington), 3–20.

67. New York Campaign for Telephone Justice (2007), *Family Connections Bill Passes in New York State Legislature,* press release, June 21, at http://www.telephonejustice.org/about/whats_new_content.asp?ID=41 (retrieved September 1, 2007).

68. In 2007, rates for interstate collect calls made from correctional facilities ranged from as little as $3.75 for a 15-minute call in Nebraska to more than $17.00 in Arizona and several other states. Within-state area (IntraLATA) collect calls range from less than $2.00 to more than $13.00 for a 15-minute call. Campaign to Promote Equitable Telephone Charges (2007), *Current Status by State,* at http://www.etccampaign.com/etc/current_status.php (retrieved September 1, 2007).

69. Pollock (2002).

70. LIS, Inc. (2002).

71. Susan Conova (2006), "Do Babies Belong in Prison?" *In Vivo* 5(1): 1, at http://www.cpmc.columbia.edu/news/in-vivo/v014_6_feb-mar_06/imprisoned_mother.html (retrieved September 1, 2007).

72. Ibid.

73. Mary K. Shilton (2000), *Resources for Mother-Child Community Corrections* (LaCrosse, WI: International Community Corrections Association).

74. Mother Child Community Corrections Project (MCCP) (2001), *Preliminary Mother Child Program Inventory* (Silver Spring, MD: MCCP), at http://www.nicic.org/pubs/2001/016737.pdf (retrieved October 17, 2007).

75. MCC Drug Court (Missouri) (n.d.), *Mothers Choosing Change Drug Court Handbook for Participants,* on file with the author.

76. I am grateful to Tanya Krupat of the Osborne Association and Fran Raguso of Montclair State University for their help with this chapter, and this section in particular.

77. Mumola (2007); Johnson and Waldfogel (2002).

78. Snell (1994), table 9.

79. Tanya Krupat (2007), personal email communication, June 26; Pollock 2002.

80. Slightly different patterns emerge across racial and ethnic lines in the longer-term arrangements to take care of the child. Black and Hispanic women are more likely to place children with a grandmother, while white women are more likely to rely on husbands and non-relative foster care. Snell (1994).

81. Barbara S. Bosley, Christie Donner, Carolyn McLean, and Ellen Toomey-Hale, eds. (2002), *Parenting from Prison: A Resource Guide for Parents Incarcerated in Colorado* (Denver: Parenting from Prison Guide Committee).

82. Pollock (2002).

83. Children also may move between placements with family members and non-kin foster homes, or some combination thereof. Lorrie L. Lutz of the National Resource Center for Foster Care and Permanency Planning (now the National Resource Center for Family-Centered Practice and Permanency Planning) oversaw dialogues with mothers, foster or "resource" families, public child protection agency administrators, and line social workers in 11 states. Although her research did not focus

on the situation of incarcerated mothers, the participants' comments shed light on the precarious nature of the relationship between child protection agencies, foster families, and mothers. Her findings suggest that many placements occur in an environment that is ripe for misunderstanding, distrust, and sincere differences of opinion. An Arizona caseworker described a foster family that "sabotaged the reunification efforts to the point that I had to remove the child. In this resource family's mind there was nothing that the birth family could do right. I got so tired of hearing every single thing that the birth Mom had did wrong. I knew that the birth Mom was doing her best and I could see she was making progress. The resource parents just could not see it." Lorrie L. Lutz (2005), *Relationship between Public Child Welfare Workers, Resource Families and Birth Families* (New York: National Resource Center for Family-Centered Practice and Permanency Planning), 9.

84. Much depends on the caseworker, the foster care agency, the judge, and the particular relationships that have developed among them, the mother, and the substitute caregiver. If these relationships are good, long-term kinship foster care may be an option for the child. If not, termination of parental rights is still a possibility.

85. A shortage of experienced and qualified child protection workers plagues the foster care system. The average tenure of social workers working in child protective services is less than two years; supervisors often have only three years of experience. Fewer than one-third of caseworkers have degrees in social work. They also are underpaid and overworked. In 2001, their average salary was around $33,000. And, although the Council on Accreditation recommends caseloads of no more than 18 children per worker, the average caseload is between 24 and 31; caseloads sometimes reach 100 children per worker. National Association of Social Workers (2003), *Child Welfare Workforce*, at http://www.socialworkers.org/advocacy/updates/2003/082003_a.asp (retrieved September 1, 2007). See also U.S. General Accounting Office (2003), *HHS Could Play a Greater Role in Helping Child Welfare Agencies Recruit and Retain Staff* (Washington, DC: U.S. General Accounting Office).

86. Beatrix Shear (1999), *Termination of Parental Rights* (Edison,: Legal Services of New Jersey), 7, at http://www.acwc.org/intranet/DV%20Toolkit/termparentrights.pdf (retrieved September 1, 2007).

87. The average number of children affected by the termination was three. Michalsen's study was among the first (and possibly *the* first) to look at the role children and motherhood play in women's lives after they are released from prison. Michalsen (2007).

88. Lewis (2004).

89. Quoted in Michalsen (2007), 106.

90. Ibid.

91. Involuntary termination can constitute an "aggravated circumstance" that negates the need for child protective services to make reasonable efforts toward promoting reunification. *In the Matter of the Adoption of A.M.B.*, 812 A.2d 659 (Pennsylvania Superior Court, Oct. 17, 2002).

92. Every state had 18 months to adapt the federal legislation. Some states made largely semantic changes, while others undertook more extensive revisions.

93. The concern with sequential planning was that children remained in "temporary care" for much of their childhood, often with multiple foster care placements.

94. Parental rights are not terminated unless a permanency plan exists, in a process sometimes known as "home finding." Independent living is typically an option for older teens who are unlikely to be and may not want to be adopted. Permanent foster care may be recommended when a foster parent is willing to keep a child until emancipation but does not want to adopt the child. Long-term foster care involves placing a young person in a residential or group home setting or foster home, when there is some chance that the goal could be changed to reunification, relative placement, or adoption at a future date.

95. Child Welfare Information Gateway (2004), *Grounds for Involuntary Termination of Parental Rights: Summary of State Laws* (Washington, DC: U.S. Department of Health and Human Services), at www.childwelfare.gov/systemwide/laws_policies/statutes/groundterminall.pdf (retrieved September 1, 2007).

96. Hughes et al. (2001).

97. Arlene F. Lee, Philip M. Genty, and Mim Laver (2005), *The Impact of the Adoption and Safe Families Act on Children of Incarcerated Parents* (Washington, DC: Child Welfare League of America).

98. California and New York are the only two states to specifically require that certain provisions be made to incarcerated parents and their families (e.g., transportation and visiting services). Ibid.

99. Child Welfare League of America researchers conducted a Lexis search to identify TPR proceedings involving incarcerated parents. Most state court cases are not reported and will not show up in Lexis. They did locate information on 394 proceedings that took place in 2002 that served as the basis for a significant part of their analysis. Lee et al. (2005).

100. It is not known whether the parents in these cases were incarcerated. Reported in McWey et al. (2006).

101. Raimon (2001), 425; McWey et al. (2006).

102. Ross et al. (2004).

103. Around 10 percent of incarcerated mothers' children are in non-kin foster homes and do not qualify for such an exemption. Mumola (2007). See also David Crary (2003), "Love Locked Away: A Civil Rights Group Is Helping Imprisoned Mothers Keep Custody of Their Children," *Washington Post*, March 23, F1.

104. Quoted in Crary (2003).

105. In some instances, the foster family may have been told that the child was most likely not going to go home; they may even expect to adopt the child. The foster family may be confused and frustrated by efforts to involve the mother and move toward reunification. If the foster family expects to adopt the child, the dynamics of visiting become quite complicated and reduce the likelihood of successful reunification. Lutz (2005), 43.

106. In part, this hearing is to determine whether visits are in the best interest of the child. Lewis (2004).

107. Ibid., 105.

108. Women in Prison Project (2006b), When "Free" Means Losing Your Mother: The Collision of Child Welfare and the Incarceration of Women in New York State (New York: Correctional Association of New York); Lee et al. (2005).

109. B. Needell, D. Webster, S. Cuccaro-Alamin, et al. (2005), *Child Welfare Services Reports for California*, University of California at Berkeley, Center for Social Services Research, at http://cssr.berkeley.edu/ucb%5Fchildwelfare/ (retrieved September 1, 2007).

110. Children's Services Visiting Improvement Task Force (2005), *Family Visiting Improvement Action Plan* (New York: Children's Services Task Force).

111. Lutz (2005), 14.

112. Ibid., 13.

113. LIS, Inc. (2002).

114. Ibid.; Pollock (2002).

115. Pollock (2002).

116. Human Rights Watch (2002).

117. James and Glaze (2006).

118. Women's Advocacy Project (2005).

119. Jennifer R. Sentivan (2006), "Parent and Child: The Mother's Parental Rights Were Improperly Terminated under the Facts of This Case," *New Jersey Lawyer* 15(7): 22.

120. Christine E. Grella and Lisa Greenwell (2006), "Correlates of Parental Status and Attitudes toward Parenting among Substance-Abusing Women Offenders," *Prison Journal* 86(1): 89–113.

121. Michalsen (2007).

122. Patricia Kassebaum (1999), *Substance Abuse Treatment for Women Offenders: Guide to Promising Practices* (Rockland, MD: U.S. Department of Health and Human Services).

123. McWey (2006).

124. Much is made of the fact that many women with criminal justice records have been sexually and violently victimized, a background that not only places them at greater risk of drug or alcohol abuse and mental disorders but also has implications for programming and reentry. At the same time, I'm reminded of something Jody M., a former resident of Bedford Hills Correctional Facility (NY), once told me. While specific programs exist for women who have children, battered women, women with a history of mental illness or addiction, victims of violence, or woman infected with HIV, the woman who does not fit into any of these categories may find herself without support. And heaven help her, or any other inmate, for that matter, who is convicted of a violent offense and is thus ineligible for many programs and services.

125. Quoted in Mary Bosworth (1999), *Engendering Resistance: Agency and Power in Women's Prisons* (London: Ashgate), 107.

126. Ferraro and Moe (2003).

127. Quoted in ibid., 21.

128. For the economic aspect of reproductive justice, see the discussion of CARASA's efforts in Jennifer Nelson (2003), *Women of Color and the Reproductive Rights Movement* (New York: New York University Press).

129. Venezia Michalsen's dissertation relied on a nonprobability sample of previously incarcerated women in New York City. She found that over one-half of the women were residing in a homeless shelter, while almost one-quarter were in rental

housing. Michalsen (2007). See also Stephen Metraux and Dennis P. Culhane (2004), "Homeless Shelter Use and Reincarceration Following Prison Release," *Criminology and Public Policy* 3(2): 139–160; Council of State Governments (2006), *Homelessness and Prisoner Re-Entry* (New York: Council of State Governments Eastern Regional Conference), at http://www.csgeast.org/pdfs/Re-Entry/RPC_Homelessness%20one-pager_v8.pdf (retrieved September 1, 2007).

130. Eileen Sullivan, Milton Mino, and Katherine Nelson (2002), *Families as a Resource in Recovery from Drug Abuse: An Evaluation of La Bodega de la Familia* (New York: Vera Institute of Justice).

131. In only three states, however, do local housing authorities flatly ban applicants with a range of criminal histories. Legal Action Center (2004), *After Prison: Roadblocks to Reentry* (New York: Legal Action Center), 16, at http://www.lac.org/lac/upload/lacreport/LAC_PrintReport.pdfhttp://www.lac.org/lac/upload/lacreport/LAC_PrintReport.pdf (retrieved September 1, 2007). In New York, people with criminal records must finish parole and then wait up to six years before renting in public-housing projects, even though they may otherwise be eligible for low-income housing.

132. *Department of Housing and Urban Development v. Rucker, consolidated with Oakland Hous. Auth. v. Rucker et al.*, 535 U.S. 125 (2002).

133. Mary Ann Hallenborg (2004), *The New York Landlord's Law Book*, 2nd ed. (New York: Nolo).

134. Legal Action Center (2004).

135. Nearly one of every three state prisoners has a reported learning disability, a hearing or vision problem, or a mental or physical condition; the prevalence of speech disabilities among prisoners is three times higher than among the general public. Laura Maruschak and Allen J. Beck (2001), *Medical Problems of Inmates, 1997* (Washington, DC: U.S. Department of Justice, Bureau of Justice Statistics), 1.

136. Caroline Wolf Harlow (2003), *Education and Correctional Populations* (Washington, DC: U.S. Department of Justice, Bureau of Justice Statistics).

137. Richard B. Freeman (1996), *Why Do So Many Young American Men Commit Crimes and What Might We Do about It?* Working Paper No. W5451 (Cambridge, Mass.: National Bureau of Economic Research), at http://papers.ssrn.com/s013/papers.cfm?abstract_id=10140 (retrieved September 1, 2007).

138. A shortage of jobs also impedes women's efforts to earn a living. Since the 1960s, the number of industrial-sector jobs (which historically have employed unskilled or uneducated workers), has been halved. This has significantly affected local employment opportunities. The manufacturing industry lost the highest proportion of jobs, while construction and service jobs showed a slight gain. Jobs in the service sector, however, tend to be fewer and lower-paying than those in the industrial sector. Available low-skill jobs, such as dishwasher or delivery worker, are generally extremely low paying while requiring long hours. Women may be offered better work "off the books," but such work is forbidden by the conditions of parole.

139. Only 14 states require that public employers consider an individual applicant's qualifications and ability to do the job. In terms of granting occupational licenses (such as barber, beautician, nail technician, butcher, nurse, therapist, or plumber), only 21 states require a direct, rational, or reasonable relationship between

the license sought and the applicant's criminal history in order to deny the license. In New York, the law permits employers to ask applicants if they have ever been convicted of a crime but only permits an employer to use an applicant's prior felony convictions as a basis for denying employment if there is a legitimate business interest related to the job or if the applicant poses a risk to people or property. Legal Action Center (2004).

140. CEK Strategies (2005), *CORI: Balancing Individual Rights and Public Access* (Boston: Boston Foundation and the Criminal Justice Institute), at http://www.tbf.org/uploadedFIles/CORI%20Report.pdf (retrieved September 1, 2007).

141. David Nidus (2002), personal communication (email) with the author, October 21.

142. Theodore Stein (2000), "The Adoption and Safe Families Act: Creating a False Dichotomy between Parents' and Children's Rights," *Families in Society* 81: 586–592.

143. Dorothy Roberts (2002), *Shattered Bonds: The Color of Child Welfare* (New York: Basic Civitas), 274.

144. Barbara Katz Rothman (2005), *Weaving a Family: Untangling Race and Adoption* (Boston: Beacon), 53.

145. Barbara J. Myers, Tina M. Smarsh, Kristine Amlund-Hagen, and Suzanne Kennon (1999), "Children of Incarcerated Mothers," *Journal of Child and Family Studies* 8(1): 11–25.

CHAPTER 8

1. Jessica had obtained the restraining order in an attempt to make him stop making harassing calls to her. He had stalked her, broken into her house, and attempted to kill himself in front of his daughters. *Gonzales v. City of Castle Rock* 545 U.S. 748; 125 S. Ct. 2796; 366 F.3d 1093 (10th Cir. Colo., 2005).

2. National Organization for Women (2005), *Supreme Court Ruling Leaves More Women Vulnerable to Domestic Violence,* press release, June 28, at http://www.now.org/press/06-05/06-28.html (retrieved September 1, 2007).

3. Heather Hammer, David Finkelhor, and Andrea Sedlak (2002), *Children Abducted by Family Members: National Estimates and Characteristics* (Washington, DC: Office of Juvenile Justice and Delinquency Prevention).

4. A desire to resolve the problem alone or with family and a belief that the police wouldn't help (sometimes based on past experience) were common reasons cited for not reporting the case to the police.

5. Shannon Catalano (2006), *Intimate Partner Violence in the United States* (Washington, DC: U.S. Department of Justice, Bureau of Justice Statistics).

6. Callie Marie Rennison (2003), *Intimate Partner Violence, 1993–2001* (Washington, DC: U.S. Department of Justice, Bureau of Justice Statistics).

7. See literature review presented in Sherry Lipsky, Victoria Holt, Thomas Easterling, and Cathy Critchlow (2005), "Police-Reported Intimate Partner Violence during Pregnancy: Who Is at Risk?" *Violence and Victims* 20(1): 69–78. Abuse is so pervasive and varies so widely in terms of degree and frequency that it makes it problematic

to use generic terms like "victims of domestic violence" and "survivors of intimate partner violence." Poverty, low educational levels, unemployment, and other indicators of low socioeconomic status all have been associated with a higher risk of intimate partner violence, perhaps because poverty produces a more stressful household and neighborhood environment. Findings with regard to the influence of race and ethnicity are mixed. Most often, intimate partner violence involves a white man abusing a white woman, though blacks appear to be overrepresented in cases involving intimate partners who are not married. Matthew Durose, Caroline Wolf Harlow, Patrick Langan, et al. (2005), *Family Violence Statistics,* NCJ 207846 (Washington, DC: U.S. Department of Justice, Bureau of Justice Statistics). Since intimate partner violence, race, poverty, and a lack of social and health support systems are intricately linked within the U.S. social structure, race and ethnicity may serve as a proxy for socioeconomic status. At least one study has found that the effects of race dropped out after income level was taken into account. Lipsky et al. (2005), 71; Callie Rennison and Mike Planty (2003), "Nonlethal Intimate Partner Violence: Examining Race, Gender, and Income Patterns," *Violence and Victims* 18(4): 433–443; Durose et al. (2005). Another study suggests that black and white women report similar patterns of victimization, while Hispanic and American Indian women are at significantly higher risk of intimate partner violence. Ross Macmillan and Candace Kruttschnitt (2005), *Patterns of Violence against Women: Risk Factors and Consequences—Final Report,* IJ CX-0011 (Washington, DC: National Institute of Justice). While the physical experience of being battered is the same for all women, women who are racial and ethnic minorities may face barriers to seeking help in the form of shelter or other economic support. Racial and ethnic minority women must decide whether to seek assistance from an outsider who "may not look like her, sound like her, speak her language, or share any of her cultural values." Jenny Rivera (1997), "Domestic Violence against Latinas by Latino Males: An Analysis of Race, National Origin, and Gender Differentials," in Adrien Katherine Wing, ed., *Critical Race Feminism: A Reader* (New York: New York University Press), 259–266.

8. Raquel Bergen (2006), *Marital Rape: New Research and Directions* (Harrisburg, PA: VAWNet), at http://www.wcsap.org/advocacy/PDF/MaritalRapevawnet.pdf (retrieved September 1, 2007).

9. Rennison (2003); James Alan Fox and Marianne Zawitz (2004), *Homicide Trends in the United States* (Washington, DC: U.S. Department of Justice, Bureau of Justice Statistics), at http://www.ojp.usdoj.gov/bjs/pub/pdf/htius.pdf (retrieved September 1, 2007). Nearly one-third of all women murder victims are killed by a spouse, ex-spouse, or boyfriend (compared with fewer than 6 percent of men murder victims).

10. The other two types are "mutual violent control" and "common couple violence." Mutual violent control is rare and involves two partners who are *both* violent and controlling. By contrast, most couples engage in common couple violence at some point. It includes arguing, shouting, pushing, shoving, and other acts that cause little or no physical injury and is not part of any pattern of control. Michael Johnson (1995), "Patriarchal Terrorism and Common Couple Violence: Two Forms of Violence against Women," *Journal of Marriage and the Family* 57: 283–294; Michael Johnson and Kathleen Ferraro (2000), "Research on Domestic Violence in the 1990s: Making Distinctions," *Journal of Marriage and the Family* 62: 948–963.

11. Geraldine Butts Stahly (1999), "Women with Children in Violent Relationships: The Choice of Leaving May Bring the Consequence of Custodial Challenge," *Journal of Aggression, Maltreatment and Trauma* 2(4): 239–251.

12. *Thurman v. City of Torrington*, 595 F. Supp. 1521 (1984).

13. There is also growing recognition that domestic violence deprives society of women's contributions to human and social capital. Violence against women costs companies nearly $73 million each year due to lost productivity. Centers for Disease Control and Prevention (2003b), *Costs of Intimate Partner Violence against Women in the United States* (Atlanta: U.S. Department of Health and Human Services, Centers for Disease Control and Prevention, National Center for Injury Prevention and Control); Ileana Arias and Phaedra Corso (2005), "Average Cost per Person Victimized by an Intimate Partner of the Opposite Gender: A Comparison of Men and Women," *Violence and Victims* 20(4): 379–391.

14. Neil Miller (2004), *Domestic Violence: A Review of State Legislation Defining Police and Prosecution Duties and Powers* (Alexandria, VA: Institute of Law and Justice), at http://www.ilj.org/publications/DV_Legislation-3.pdf (retrieved September 1, 2007).

15. Even today, however, criminal justice system responses to domestic violence are hardly uniform or adequate from state to state. States vary in the breadth of police authority to arrest domestic violence offenders without a warrant. They also differ in how well they integrate domestic violence with states' victims rights acts and the degree to which officers provide victim assistance—for example, by informing victims of their rights, transporting them to a medical facility or shelter, or helping them remove personal belongings. Some states train police and prosecutors on domestic violence-related issues, while others do not. Ibid.

16. Durose et al. (2005). The report is not without its flaws, however. In addition to the usual problem that much violence goes unreported to the police or in victimization surveys, the authors of *Family Violence Statistics* defined "family violence" in such a way that excluded violence between current or former unmarried partners. Wherever possible, however, I recalculated the statistics to include violence against boyfriends and girlfriends. Here, I use the term "intimate partner violence" to refer to violence against a spouse, as well as a current or former partner.

17. Durose et al. (2005).

18. Strangely, even though marital rape is a form of *both* intimate partner violence and sexual assault, it often is not addressed by scholarship or advocacy in either area. Sexual assault programs often treat marital rape as a family violence problem, while scholars and advocates for battered women may leave sexual assault programs to deal with the issue of marital rape. Raquel Bergen (2003), "Studying Wife Rape: Reflections on the Past, Present, and Future," *Violence against Women* 10(12): 1407–1416.

19. Barbara Ehrenreich (2000), "How 'Natural' Is Rape?" *Time Magazine,* January 31. Feminists in the nineteenth century recognized that women should control marital intercourse as a means of allowing them to determine the conditions under which they bore and raised children and undertook the work of motherhood. The women's rights movement of the time demanded "both a legal right to refuse and real socioeconomic alternatives to submission." Jill Hasday (2000), "Contest and Consent: A Legal History of Marital Rape," *California Law Review* 88: 1373–1505.

20. Stephanie Riger and Susan Staggs (2004), *The Impact of Intimate Partner Violence on Women's Labor Force Participation,* NIJ 207143 (Washington, DC: National Institute of Justice), at http://www.ncjrs.gov/pdffiles1/nij/grants/207143.pdf (retrieved September 1, 2007).

21. Bergen (2006); Michelle Anderson (2003), "Marital Immunity, Intimate Relationships, and Improper Inferences: A New Law on Sexual Offenses by Intimates," *Hastings Law Journal* 54: 1463–1572.

22. Anderson (2003), 1487 nn. 73, 74.

23. A California task force found that law enforcement and prosecutors in the counties they studied "rarely and inconsistently enforce violations of such orders when issued by family court." Task Force on Local Criminal Justice Response to Domestic Violence (2005), *Keeping the Promise: Victim Safety and Batterer Accountability* (Sacramento, CA: Office of the Attorney General), 4.

24. Miller (2004).

25. Task Force on Criminal Justice Response to Domestic Violence (2005).

26. Monica Rhor (2006), "Orders Often Fail to Restrain Violence," *Orange County Register,* March 18.

27. "State Fights Gun Lawsuit by Child-Killer's Ex-Wife" (2003), *Annapolis (MD) Capital,* July 16; Craig Whitlock (1999), "Lapses in Gun Check Decried: Legislators Scold Md. Police Agencies," *Washington Post,* November 23.

28. Brian Shane (1999), "Restraining Order Loophole Enrages Committee Members," *Capital News Service,* November 30, at http://www.newsline.umd.edu/crimeold/spickna1112.htm (retrieved September 1, 2007).

29. "State Fights Gun Lawsuit by Child-Killer's Ex-Wife" (2003); Whitlock (1999).

30. Rhor (2006).

31. National Center for Victims of Crime (2002), *Enforcement of Protective Orders,* NCJ 189190 (Washington, DC: Office for Victims of Crime).

32. Emily J. Sack (2004), "Domestic Violence across State Lines: The Full Faith and Credit Clause, Congressional Power, and Interstate Enforcement of Protection Orders," *Northwestern University Law Review* 98(3): 827–906.

33. National Center for Victims of Crime (2002).

34. Peter M. Brien (2005), *Improving Access to and Integrity of Criminal History Records,* NCJ 200581 (Washington, DC: U.S. Department of Justice, Office of Justice Programs).

35. National Center for State Courts and the National Criminal Justice Association (2004), *Crossing Borders: Regional Meetings on Implementing Full Faith and Credit* (Washington, DC: Office on Violence against Women).

36. Johnson and Ferraro (2000).

37. Ibid. See also Jeffrey Edleson, Lyungai F. Mbilinyi, and Sudha Shetty (2003), *Parenting in the Context of Domestic Violence* (San Francisco: Judicial Council of California), at http://www.courtinfo.ca.gov/programs/cfcc/pdffiles/fullReport.pdf (retrieved January 21, 2008).

38. "Stereotypical kidnappings" are defined as "abductions perpetrated by a stranger or slight acquaintance and involving a child who was transported 50 or

more miles, detained overnight, held for ransom or with the intent to keep the child permanently, or killed." In 40 percent of these cases, the child was killed. Each year, an estimated 58,200 children are victims of nonfamily abduction, which includes "all nonfamily perpetrators (friends and acquaintances as well as strangers) and crimes involving lesser amounts of forced movement or detention in addition to the more serious crimes entailed in stereotypical kidnappings." David Finkelhor, Heather Hammer, and Andrea J. Sedlak (2003), *Nonfamily Abducted Children: National Estimates and Characteristics* (Washington, DC: Office of Juvenile Justice and Delinquency Prevention).

39. The America's Missing: Broadcast Emergency Response (AMBER) Alert System began in 1996 in Texas; other states and communities soon followed suit. Once law enforcement officials determine that a child abduction has taken place that meets AMBER Alert criteria (e.g., the child is at risk of serious injury or death and sufficient descriptive information of the child, captor, or captor's vehicle exists), broadcasters and state transportation officials are notified. AMBER Alerts interrupt regular programming, are broadcast on radio and television, and appear on highway signs. Office of Justice Programs (2006), "Frequently Asked Questions on AMBER Alert," at http://www.amberalert.gov/faqs.html (retrieved September 1, 2007).

40. "Some Fear Popularity Is Weakening Amber Alerts" (2006), *New York Times*, March 19, A21.

41. Ibid.

42. Office of Justice Programs (2006); "AMBER Alert Awareness Day 2007," at http://www.amberalert.gov/newsroom/AMBERCoorMessage2007.htm (retrieved September 1, 2007).

43. Adrienne Lockie, director of the Domestic Violence Advocacy Project at Rutgers-Newark School of Law, explains why a victim may prefer to obtain a recourse in the civil or family court rather than try to mobilize the criminal justice system on her behalf. First, unlike in a criminal case, the victim-petitioner has more control over the process; she can decide to withdraw her case and what evidence to put forth. She also has some input into scheduling court dates. The victim-petitioner only has to provide evidence that a family offense was committed on a "preponderance of evidence" rather than that a crime was committed by "beyond a reasonable doubt." She has a right to legal representation; in a criminal case, she is not represented or even considered a party. Also, as noted earlier, many victims do not want to call the police for fear of the consequences of doing so. Even a woman who does call the police may find that an arrest or prosecution will not protect her from future violence. Adrienne Lockie (2005), "New York's Failure to Protect All Victims of Domestic Violence," *American Journal of Family Law* 18(4): 234–241.

44. Richard A. Gardner (1998), *The Parental Alienation Syndrome*, 2nd ed. (Creskill, NJ: Creative Therapeutics).

45. Gardner has since lowered his original estimate substantially, but he still does not provide empirical support for his assertion that abuse allegations in a divorce context are usually false. Carol S. Bruch (2002), "Parental Alienation Syndrome and Alienated Children: Getting It Wrong in Child Custody Cases," *Child and Family Law Quarterly* 14(2): 381–400.

46. Jennifer Hoult (2006), "The Evidentiary Admissibility of Parental Alienation Syndrome: Science, Law, and Policy," *Children's Legal Rights Journal* 26: 1–61; Stephanie J. Dallam (1999), "The Parental Alienation Syndrome: Is It Scientific?" in E. St. Charles and L. Crook, eds., *Expose: The Failure of Family Courts to Protect Children from Abuse in Custody Disputes* (Los Gatos, CA: Our Children Our Children Charitable Foundation). See also information presented on www.stopfamilyviolence.org.

47. Peter Jaffe, Nancy Lemon, and Samantha Poisson (2003), *Child Custody and Domestic Violence* (Thousand Oaks, CA: Sage).

48. Patrick M. O'Connell (2006), "Delicate Balancing Act: Local Case Highlights Problems in Court Rulings," *South Bend Tribune,* April 30.

49. Angela Browne (1995), "Fear and the Perception of Alternatives: Asking 'Why Battered Women Don't Leave' Is the Wrong Question," in Barbara Raffel Price and Natalie J. Sokoloff, eds., *The Criminal Justice System and Women* (New York: McGraw-Hill), 228–245; Cathy Humphreys and Ravi K. Thiara (2003), "Neither Justice nor Protection: Women's Experiences of Post-Separation Violence," *Journal of Social Welfare and Family Law* 25(3): 195–214.

50. Browne (1995).

51. Quoted in Rhor (2006), n.p.

52. Jaffe et al. (2003), 11, 17.

53. Nico Trocme and Nicholas Bala (2005), "False Allegations of Abuse and Neglect When Parents Separate," *Child Abuse and Neglect* 29(12): 1333–1345. An Australian study similarly found that fewer than 1 in 10 allegations of child abuse were false. T. Brown, M. Frederico, L. Hewitt, and R. Sheehan (2000), "Revealing the Existence of Child Abuse in the Context of Marital Breakdown and Custody and Access Disputes," *Child Abuse and Neglect* 24(6): 849–859.

54. Kathleen Coulbourn Faller and Ellen DeVoe (1995), "Allegations of Sexual Abuse in Divorce," *Journal of Child Sexual Abuse.* 4(4): 1–25.

55. Jaffe et al. (2003), 11, 17.

56. Ibid., 13.

57. Ibid., 18.

58. According to a 2003 survey, 17 states and the District of Columbia have adopted rebuttable presumption statutes. Amy Levin and Linda Mills (2003), "Fighting for Child Custody When Domestic Violence Is at Issue: Survey of State Laws," *Social Work* 48(4): 463–470.

59. Jaffe et al. (2003), 18–19.

60. Kristina C. Evans (2004), "Can a Leopard Change His Spots? Child Custody and Batterer's Intervention," *Duke Journal of Gender Law and Policy* 11: 121–139; Barry D. Rosenfeld (1992), "Court-Ordered Treatment of Spouse Abuse," *Clinical Psychology Review* 12: 205–226; Douglas P. Schrock and Irene Padavic (2007), "Negotiating Hegemonic Masculinity in a Batterer Intervention Program," *Gender & Society* 21(5): 625–649.

61. Levin and Mills (2003).

62. Ibid.

63. Nina Zollo and Robin Thompson (2006), "Protecting Victims of Domestic Violence in the Parenting Coordination Process," *Commission on Domestic Violence*

Quarterly Newsletter 2: 1–3, at http://www.abanet.org/domviol/enewsletter/vo12/
ProtectingVictimsofDVinPCprocess.pdf (retrieved September 1, 2007); Mary Lovik
(2004), *Update: Domestic Violence Benchbook,* 3rd ed. (Lansing: Michigan Judicial
Institute), at http://courts.michigan.gov/mji/resources/dvbook/dvbook.htm (retrieved
September 1, 2007).

64. Lovik (2004).

65. Chris S. O'Sullivan, Lori A. King, Kyla Levin-Russell, and Emily Horowitz
(2006), *Supervised and Unsupervised Parental Access in Domestic Violence Cases: Court
Orders and Consequences* (New York: Safe Horizon), 2.

66. Despite the prevalence and seriousness of the abuse, the authors of the study
speculated that "these pervasive experiences provided no useful information to the
court to determine which fathers might pose a current and ongoing danger." Ibid., 2.

67. The opportunity/snowball sample was not meant to be generalizable; one of
the selection criteria was that the women had been dissatisfied with the family court
processes or procedures.

68. Leslie Kaufman (2004), "Abuse Victims and the City Settle Lawsuit," *New
York Times,* December 18, B2, B6.

69. Mary Raines (2001), "Defending Motherhood: Battered Women Losing Their
Children to Our Child Protection System," *Children's Legal Rights Journal* 21(3): 17–24,
at 20.

70. Personal and confidential email communication with the author, March 2,
2007.

71. An undocumented woman cannot be deported for reporting her victimization. Yet, she faces other challenges such as language barriers, economic insecurity,
discrimination, and prejudice that may make it difficult for her to escape an abusive
situation.

Women who are lesbian, gay, bisexual, or transgender (LGBT) experience domestic violence, although no reliable estimates of the prevalence exist. Some studies have
found that somewhere between one-fifth and one-half of lesbians have been abused
by a woman partner at some point in their life. Battered LGBT women face unique
circumstances when trying to deal with domestic violence. For example, the perpetrator of violence may "out" or threaten to out a partner or will stress that she is isolated
and nobody will help because of her sexuality. A LGBT victim may feel more isolated
because of the lack of support among both advocates for battered women and those
for LGBT people. The sexism, homophobia, and other forms of social oppression that
LGBT women face may make it harder to get the practical support they need to escape
the abuse. If a woman is financially intertwined with her partner, she often has no legal process to make sure assets are evenly divided should she leave. A battered LGBT
woman who wants to access support services (e.g., a shelter or a crisis line) may feel
compelled to "pass" as a heterosexual in order to receive support. She may encounter
staff (and other battered women) who do not take abuse as seriously when it is committed by a woman. According to the National Coalition of Anti-Violence Programs,
many family courts only adjudicate domestic violence cases between married and/or
straight partners who have a child in common. In those jurisdictions, LGBT victims
must turn to the criminal court system for judicial relief. Gwat-Yong Lie and Sabrina

Gentlewarrior (1991), "Intimate Violence in Lesbian Relationships: Discussion of Survey Findings and Practice Implications," *Journal of Social Service Research* 15: 41–59; Michelle VanNatta (2005), "Constructing the Battered Woman," *Feminist Studies* 31(2): 416–443; Paul Cameron (2003), "Domestic Violence among Homosexual Partners," *Psychological Reports* 93: 410–416; Ken Moore and Rachel Baum (2001), *LGBT Domestic Violence in 2000* (New York: National Coalition of Anti-Violence Programs).

72. Browne (1995). See review of literature presented in Humphreys and Thiara (2003).

73. Raines (2001), 20.

74. Carole Echlin and Bina Osthoff (2000), "Child Protection Workers and Battered Women's Advocates Working Together to End Violence against Women and Children," *Journal of Aggression, Maltreatment, and Trauma* 46(3): 207–219.

75. Anonymous woman quoted in Jay G. Silverman, Cynthia M. Mesh, Carrie V. Cuthbert, et al. (2004), "Child Custody Determinations in Cases Involving Intimate Partner Violence: A Human Rights Analysis," *American Journal of Public Health* 94(6): 951–957, at 955.

76. For a description of the circumstances surrounding the case and the injustice that followed, see Beth Mandel (2005), "The White Fist of the Child Welfare System: Racism, Patriarchy, and the Presumptive Removal of Children from Victims of Domestic Violence in *Nicholson v. Williams*," *University of Cincinnati Law Review* 73: 1131–1162. See also Center for an Urban Future (2003), "Tough Decisions: Dealing with Domestic Violence," *Child Welfare Watch* 9: 1–16.

77. Mandel (2005), 1148.

78. Lyn Slater (2006), clinical associate professor, Fordham University Graduate School of Social Services and School of Law, email communication with the author, April 10, 2006.

79. Harvard School of Public Health (2004), *Researchers Say Massachusetts Family Courts Fail to Protect Battered Women and Their Children,* press release, May 27, at http://www.hsph.harvard.edu/press/releases/press05272004.html (retrieved September 1, 2007). See also Silverman et al. (2004). It is not only a woman's continuing relationship with a batterer that renders her questionable as an effective parent in the eyes of many judges and social workers. If a woman is in an intimate relationship with any man who is not the father of her children, her fitness to parent may be called into question by judges, social workers, and even her own attorney. She may be expected to abstain from relationships with all men in order to prove the centrality of children to her life. As Jennifer Reich observes in *Fixing Families,* this occurs even in child abuse and neglect cases where the mother is *not* battered or abused. Judges and attorneys often pressure the women to avoid relationships with men, considering the men in their lives as neither competent breadwinners nor fathers. "The presence of men not related to the child—most acutely those with a criminal history involving illegal drugs, violence, or driving under the influence—is seen as an indicator of likely maltreatment," Reich notes. "Although the state no longer determines [public assistance] benefits based on women's relationship with men, the presence of men does affect perceptions of risk." Jennifer Reich (2005), *Fixing Families: Parents, Power, and the Child Welfare System* (New York: Routledge), 164.

80. My friend Miki Akimoto deserves the credit for calling my attention to this point, as well as many others in this book.

81. In 2004, the Department of Justice's Office on Violence Against Women (OVW) awarded over $20 million to 15 communities across the country to establish comprehensive domestic violence victim service and support centers. The first center opened in Brooklyn, NY, a year later. The Family Justice Center features professionals from 37 community partners and 9 government agencies to provide necessary services to victims of domestic violence. For example, conceivably, a victim may meet with a prosecutor, access social services, begin long-term counseling, and meet with a clergy member in only one visit. As this is written, however, it is still too soon to tell whether the vision of comprehensive domestic violence service provision will be realized.

82. Susan J. Wells (1994), "Child Protective Services: Research for the Future," *Child Welfare* 73(5): 431–447.

83. News headlines are far more likely to report high-profile failures rather than the less exciting achievements of, say, reuniting families or reducing abuse.

84. Except, possibly, on rare occasions where the victim has been diagnosed with a mental illness that prevents her from being competent to make decisions in her best interest. See Erin L. Han (2003), "Mandatory Arrest and No-Drop Policies: Victim Empowerment in Domestic Violence Cases," *Boston College Third World Law Journal* 23(1): 159–191.

CONCLUSION

1. This point is an extension of one made in Lealle Ruhl (2002), "Dilemmas of the Will: Uncertainty, Reproduction, and the Rhetoric of Control," *Signs* 27(3): 641–663.

2. For example, Bryan Turner identifies three types of social identity based on effective entitlement: worker-citizens, warrior-citizens, and parent-citizens. Bryan Turner (2001), "The Erosion of Citizenship," *British Journal of Sociology* 52(2001): 189–209.

3. Dorothy E. Roberts (1996), "Welfare and the Problem of Black Citizenship," *Yale Law Journal* 105: 1563–1602, at 1566.

4. Jeffrey Reiman (2007), *The Rich Get Richer and the Poor Get Prison* (New York: Allyn and Bacon).

5. Nancy Rose (2000), "Scapegoating Poor Women: An Analysis of Welfare Reform," *Journal of Economic Issues* 34: 143–157, at 144.

6. Humphrey Taylor (2000), "The Public Tends to Blame the Poor, the Unemployed, and Those on Welfare for Their Problems," *Harris Poll,* May 3, at http://www.harrisinteractive.com/harris_poll/index.asp?PID=87 (retrieved January 21, 2008).

7. Miki Akimoto (2006), personal communication with the author.

8. Dana D. Dehart (2004), *Pathways to Prison: Impact of Victimization on the Lives of Incarcerated Women* (Columbia, SC: Center for Child and Family Studies). Interviews with incarcerated women shed light on "turning points" where intervention is most likely to be effective. For some women, finding out they were pregnant or landing a good job was an occasion to redouble their efforts to quit or reduce their drug use

or to leave a batterer. For others, having their children taken away precipitated a slide into increased drug use and criminal activity. In some cases, women identified incarceration and the support provided by some inmates and correctional staff as being instrumental in their rehabilitation. Recognizing that women's lives and circumstances are neither uniformly bleak nor fixed and unchanging suggests opportunities where support, when it is extended, may be most effective.

9. Barbara Katz Rothman (2005), *Weaving a Family: Untangling Race and Adoption* (Boston: Beacon), 36.

10. Stokely Carmichael and Charles V. Hamilton (1967), *Black Power: The Politics of Liberation in America* (New York: Vintage), 4.

11. Quoted in Diane Taylor (2006), "Women: The Pregnancy Police Are Watching You," *Guardian* (London), September 6.

12. Jennifer Reich (2005), Fixing Families: Parents, Power, and the Child Welfare System (New York: Routledge), 172.

13. Ibid.

14. Cynthia R. Daniels (1993), *At Women's Expense: State Power and the Politics of Fetal Rights* (Cambridge: Harvard University Press), 7.

15. Kay Johnson, Samuel F. Posner, Janis Biermann, et al. (2006), "Recommendations to Improve Preconception Health and Health Care: United States," *Morbidity and Mortality Weekly Report* 55(RR06): 1–23.

16. Jeanne Flavin and David Rosenthal (2003), "La Bodega de la Familia: Supporting Parolees' Reintegration within a Community Context," *Fordham Urban Law Journal* 30(5): 1603–1620.

17. Leslie Reagan (1997), *When Abortion Was a Crime: Women, Medicine, and Law in the United States, 1867–1973* (Berkeley: University of California Press).

Bibliography

Abel, Ernest L., and Michael Kruger. 2001. "Physician Attitudes Concerning Legal Coercion of Pregnant Alcohol and Drug Users." *American Journal of Obstetrics and Gynecology* 186: 768–772.

"Accessory to Firebomb Gets One Year." 2006. *Associated Press,* August 4.

Adalist-Estrin, Ann. 2003. *The Caregivers' Situation.* Palmyra, VA: Family and Corrections Network.

Agency for Healthcare Research and Quality (AHRQ). 2005. *Women's Health Care in the United States: Selected Findings from the 2004 National Healthcare Quality and Disparities Reports.* Publication No. 05-P021. Rockville, MD: AHRQ. At http://www.ahrq.gov/qual/nhqrwomen/nhqrwomen.htm (retrieved September 1, 2007).

Akimoto, Miki. 2006. Personal communication with the author.

Allina, Amy. 2002. "Cash for Birth Control: Discriminatory, Unethical, Ineffective and Bad Public Policy." *Network News* 27(1): 5–6.

"AMBER Alert Awareness Day 2007." 2007. At http://www.amberalert.gov/newsroom/AMBERCoorMessage2007.htm (retrieved September 1, 2007).

American Cancer Society. 2006. *Can Having an Abortion Cause or Contribute to Breast Cancer?* At http://www.cancer.org/docroot/CRI/content/CRI_2_6x_Can_Having_an_Abortion_Cause_or_Contribute_to_Breast_Cancer.asp (retrieved September 1, 2007).

American Civil Liberties Union (ACLU). 2004. *Public Funding for Abortion: Promoting Reproductive Freedom for Low-Income Women.* At http://www.aclu.org/ReproductiveRights/ReproductiveRights.cfm?ID=9039&c=146 (retrieved September 1, 2007).

American Correctional Association. 1990. *The Female Offender.* Lanham, MD: American Correctional Association.

American Psychiatric Association. 2000. *Diagnostic and Statistical Manual of Mental Disorders,* 4th ed., text revision. Washington, DC: American Psychiatric Association.

Amnesty International. 1999. *Not Part of My Sentence: Violations of the Human Rights of Women in Custody.* New York: Amnesty International.

———. 2006. *Abuse of Women in Custody: Sexual Misconduct and Shackling of Pregnant Women.* New York: Amnesty International. At http://www.amnestyusa.org/women/custody/abuseincustody.html (retrieved September 1, 2007).

Anderson, Michelle. 2003. "Marital Immunity, Intimate Relationships, and Improper Inferences: A New Law on Sexual Offenses by Intimates." *Hastings Law Journal* 54: 1463–1572.

Anton, Mike. 2003. "Forced Sterilization Once Seen as Path to a Better World," *Los Angeles Times,* July 16, A1.

"Appellate Court Rules Judge Overstepped Authority by Jailing Pregnant Woman." 2004. *Associated Press State and Local Wire,* June 15.

Arias, Elizabeth. 2006. "United States Life Tables, 2003." *National Vital Statistics Reports* 15(14): 1–40.

Arias, Ileana, and Phaedra Corso. 2005. "Average Cost per Person Victimized by an Intimate Partner of the Opposite Gender: A Comparison of Men and Women." *Violence and Victims* 20(4): 379–391.

Armas, Genaro. 2003. "Poverty Climbs, Incomes Slide." Washington, DC: Associated Press.

Arnold, Regina A. 1995. "Processes of Victimization and Criminalization of Black Women." Pp. 136–146 in *The Criminal Justice System and Women,* 2nd ed., ed. Barbara Raffel Price and Natalie J. Sokoloff. New York: McGraw-Hill.

Arria, Amelia M., Chris Derauf, Linda L. LaGasse, et al. 2006. "Methamphetamine and Other Substance Use during Pregnancy: Preliminary Estimates from the Infant Development, Environment, and Lifestyle (IDEAL) Study." *Maternal and Child Health Journal* 10(3): 293–302.

Arriola, Kimberly R. Jacob, Ronald L. Braithwaite, and Cassandra F. Newkirk. 2006. "At the Intersection between Poverty, Race, and HIV Infection: HIV-Related Services for Incarcerated Women." *Infectious Diseases in Corrections Report* 9(6–7): 1–7.

Assistant Inspector General for Evaluation and Inspections. 2005. Memorandum (OEI-02-03-00530), April 25. At http://opa.osophs.dhhs.gov/titlex/ OEI-02-03-00530.pdf (retrieved January 21, 2008).

Auer, Holly, and Charity Vogel. 2003. "Trapped by Pregnancy, Young Woman Turns Desperate: Unwanted Baby Placed in Dumpster." *Buffalo News,* October 27.

Baldwin, Katherine, and Jacquelyn Jones. 2000. *Health Issues Specific to Incarcerated Women: Information for State Maternal and Child Health Programs.* Washington, DC: Health Resources and Services Administration.

Balkin, Jack M. 2005. "*Roe v. Wade:* An Engine of Controversy." Pp. 3–27 in *What* Roe v. Wade *Should Have Said,* ed. Jack M. Balkin. New York: New York University Press.

Ballou, Brian R., and Raja Mishra. 2007. "Alleged Bid to Abort Leads to Baby's Death." *Boston Globe,* January 25.

Barak, Gregg, Jeanne Flavin, and Paul Leighton. 2001. *Class, Race, Gender, and Crime: Social Realities of Justice in America.* Los Angeles: Roxbury.

Barnard, Lisa, and Jeanne M. Flavin. 2007. *The Impact of Visiting: Fact Sheet and Bibliography.* New York: Fordham University Interdisciplinary Center for Child and Family Advocacy.

Bartlett, Linda A., Cynthia J. Berg, Holly B. Shulman, et al. 2004. "Risk Factors for Legal Induced Abortion-Related Mortality in the United States." *Obstetrics and Gynecology* 103(4): 729–737.

Beck, Laurie F., Christopher H. Johnson, Abrian Morrow, et al. 2003. *PRAMS 1999 Surveillance Report.* Atlanta: Division of Reproductive Health, Centers for Disease Control and Prevention.

Behrmann, Barbara. 2007. *Pregnant? In Labor? Your Rights Are under Attack.* At http://www.breastfeedingcafe.com/ReflectionsOnNAPWSummit.htm (retrieved January 28, 2008).

Benjet, Corina, Sandra T. Azar, and Regina Kuersten-Hogan. 2003. "Evaluating the Parental Fitness of Psychiatrically Diagnosed Individuals: Advocating a Functional-Contextual Analysis of Parenting." *Journal of Family Psychology* 17(2): 238–251.

Berenson, Abbey B., and Constance M. Wiemann. 1997. "Inadequate Weight Gain among Pregnant Adolescents: Risk Factors and Relationship to Infant Birth Weight." *American Journal of Obstetrics and Gynecology* 176(6): 1220–1224.

Bergen, Raquel. 2003. "Studying Wife Rape: Reflections on the Past, Present, and Future." *Violence against Women* 10(12): 1407–1416.

———. 2006. *Marital Rape: New Research and Directions.* Harrisburg, PA: VAWNet. At http://www.wcsap.org/advocacy/PDF/MaritalRapevawnet.pdf (retrieved September 1, 2007).

Berry, Phyllis E., and Helen M. Eigenberg. 2003. "Role Strain and Incarcerated Mothers: Understanding the Process of Mothering." *Women and Criminal Justice* 15(1): 101–119.

Bhargava, Shalini. 2004. "Challenging Punishment and Privatization: A Response to the Conviction of Regina McKnight." *Harvard Civil Rights–Civil Liberties Law Review* 32: 513–542.

Bischof, G., H. J. Rumpf, C. Meyer, et al. 2005. "Influence of Psychiatric Comorbidity in Alcohol-Dependent Subjects in a Representative Population Survey on Treatment Utilization and Natural Recovery." *Addiction* 100(3): 405–413.

Black, Edwin. 2003. *War against the Weak: Eugenics and America's Campaign to Create a Master Race.* New York: Four Walls Eight Windows.

Blackwell, Jeffrey. 2005. "Father, Son Prison Guards Charged in Alleged Sex Abuse." *Rochester (NY) Democrat and Chronicle,* March 31.

Bolling, Ian. 2003. "Infant Abandonment and Safe Haven Legislation." In *Report on Trends in the State Courts.* Williamsburg, VA: National Center for State Courts.

Bookwalter, Beth. 1998. "Note: Throwing the Bath Water Out with the Baby: Wrongful Exclusion of Expert Testimony on Neonaticide Syndrome." *Boston University Law Review* 78: 1185–1210.

Bosley, Barbara S., Christie Donner, Carolyn McLean, and Ellen Toomey-Hale, eds. 2002. *Parenting from Prison: A Resource Guide for Parents Incarcerated in Colorado.* Denver: Parenting from Prison Guide Committee.

Bosworth, Mary. 1999. *Engendering Resistance: Agency and Power in Women's Prisons.* London: Ashgate.

Boulos, Maissa, Alicia D'Addario, and Rachel Meeropol. 2005. *The Jailhouse Lawyer's Handbook.* New York: Center for Constitutional Rights and the National Lawyers Guild.

Boyd, Susan C. 1999. *Mothers and Illicit Drugs: Transcending the Myths.* Toronto: University of Toronto Press.

Breitbart, Vicki, Wendy Chavkin, and Paul Wise. 1994. "The Accessibility of Drug Treatment for Pregnant Women: A Survey of Programs in Five Cities." *American Journal of Public Health* 84: 1658–1661.

Brien, Peter M. 2005. *Improving Access to and Integrity of Criminal History Records.* NCJ 200581. Washington, DC: U.S. Department of Justice, Office of Justice Programs.

Britton, Dana. 2003. *At Work in the Iron Cage: The Prison as Gendered Organization.* New York: New York University Press.

Brown, T., M. Frederico, L. Hewitt, and R. Sheehan. 2000. "Revealing the Existence of Child Abuse in the Context of Marital Breakdown and Custody and Access Disputes." *Child Abuse and Neglect* 24(6): 849–859.

Browne, Angela. 1995. "Fear and the Perception of Alternatives: Asking 'Why Battered Women Don't Leave' Is the Wrong Question." Pp. 228–245 in *The Criminal Justice System and Women,* ed. Barbara Raffel Price and Natalie J. Sokoloff. New York: McGraw-Hill.

Bruch, Carol S. 2002. "Parental Alienation Syndrome and Alienated Children: Getting It Wrong in Child Custody Cases." *Child and Family Law Quarterly* 14(2): 381–400.

Bureau of Justice Statistics. 2005. *Profile of Jail Inmates, 2002.* Washington, DC: U.S. Department of Justice.

Burlingame, Phyllida. 2000. *Preventing Unfair Prosecution of Abortion Providers: An Investigation into Political Bias by the Medical Board of California.* San Francisco: ACLU of Northern California. At http://www.aclunc.org/news/press_releases/aclu_investigates_political_bias_by_the_medical_board_of_california.shtml?ht=burlingame%20burlingame (retrieved September 1, 2007).

Busch, Alisa, and Allison D. Redlich. 2007. "Patients' Perception of Possible Child Custody or Visitation Loss for Nonadherence to Psychiatric Treatment." *Psychiatric Services* 58(7): 999–1002.

Caldwell, Carol, Mack Jarvis, and Herbert Rosefield. 2001. "Issues Impacting Today's Geriatric Female Offenders." *Corrections Today* 63(5): 110–113.

Calhoun, Avery, and Heather Coleman. 2002. "Female Inmates' Perspectives on Sexual Abuse by Correctional Personnel." *Women and Criminal Justice* 13(2/3): 101–124.

Calman, Leslie, and Linda Tarr-Whelan. 2005. *Early Childhood Education for All: A Wise Investment.* New York: Family Initiative. At http://web.mit.edu/workplacecenter/docs/Full%20Report.pdf (retrieved September 1, 2007).

Cameron, Paul. 2003. "Domestic Violence among Homosexual Partners." *Psychological Reports* 93: 410–416.

Campaign to Promote Equitable Telephone Charges. 2007. *Current Status by State.* At http://www.etccampaign.com/etc/current_status.php (retrieved September 1, 2007).

Campbell, Jacquelyn. 1998. "Abuse during Pregnancy: Progress, Policy, and Potential." *American Journal of Public Health* 88(2): 185–187.

Campbell, Nancy D. 2006. "The Construction of Pregnant Drug-Using Women as Criminal Perpetrators." *Fordham Urban Law Journal* 33: 463–485.

Cantos, Arthur L., Leonard T. Gries, and Vikki Slis. 1997. "Behavioral Correlates of Parental Visiting during Family Foster Care." *Child Welfare* 76(2): 309–329.

Carey, Corinne. 2008. "Access to Reproductive Health Care in New York State Jail Facilities." New York: New York Civil Liberties Union.

Carmichael, Stokely, and Charles V. Hamilton. 1967. *Black Power: The Politics of Liberation in America.* New York: Vintage.

Carpenter, Laura M. 2005. *Virginity Lost: An Intimate Portrait of First Sexual Experiences*. New York: New York University Press.

Caruso, David L. 2004. "Court Cases Revive Debates about Rights of Mothers during Childbirth." *Boston Globe,* May 19.

Catalano, Shannon. 2006. *Intimate Partner Violence in the United States.* Washington, DC: U.S. Department of Justice, Bureau of Justice Statistics.

CEK Strategies. 2005. *CORI: Balancing Individual Rights and Public Access.* Boston: Boston Foundation and the Criminal Justice Institute. At http://www.tbf.org/up-loadedFIles/CORI%20Report.pdf (retrieved September 1, 2007).

Center for American Women in Politics. At www.cawp.rutgers.edu (retrieved September 1, 2007).

Center for an Urban Future. 2003. "Tough Decisions: Dealing with Domestic Violence." *Child Welfare Watch* 9: 1–16.

Center for Reproductive Rights. 2001. *Mandatory Parental Consent and Notification Laws.* New York: Center for Reproductive Rights. At http://www.reproductive rights.org/pub_fac_mandconsent.html (retrieved September 1, 2007).

———. 2003. Roe v. Wade *and the Right to Privacy,* 3rd ed. New York: Center for Reproductive Rights. At http://www.reproductiverights.org/pdf/roeprivacy.pdf (retrieved September 1, 2007).

———. 2006a. *The Federal Abortion Ban.* New York: Center for Reproductive Rights. At http://www.federalabortionban.org/press_statements/060221-court-review.asp (retrieved September 1, 2007).

———. 2006b. *The Teen Endangerment Act: Harming Women Who Seek Abortions.* New York: Center for Reproductive Rights. At http://www.crlp.org/pub_fac_ccpa.html (retrieved September 1, 2007).

———. n.d.. *Safe Pregnancy.* New York: Center for Reproductive Rights. At http://www. reproductiverights.org/ww_iss_mother.html (retrieved September 1, 2007).

Centers for Disease Control. 1997. *State Definitions and Reporting Requirements for Live Births, Fetal Deaths, and Induced Terminations of Pregnancy.* Hyattsville, MD: National Center for Health Statistics, Division of Vital Statistics.

Centers for Disease Control and Prevention. 2003a. *Cervical Cancer: Basic Facts on Screening and the Pap Test.* At http://www.cdc.gov/cancer/nbccedp/bccpdfs/cc_ba-sic.pdf (retrieved September 1, 2007).

———. 2003b. *Costs of Intimate Partner Violence against Women in the United States.* Atlanta: U.S. Department of Health and Human Services, Centers for Disease Control and Prevention, National Center for Injury Prevention and Control.

———. 2003c. "Pregnancy-Related Mortality Surveillance: United States, 1991–1999." *Morbidity and Mortality Weekly Report,* February 21.

———. 2005. *STD Surveillance 2005.* Atlanta: U.S. Department of Health and Human Services, Centers for Disease Control and Prevention.

———. 2006. "About Correctional Health." At http://www.cdc.gov/nchstp/od/cccwg/ WH_General.htm (retrieved October 12, 2006).

Central Ohio Crime Stoppers. At http://www.stopcrime.org/wanted.asp (retrieved January 18, 2008).

Chandler, Cynthia. 2003. "Death and Dying in America: The Prison Industrial Complex's Impact on Women's Health." *Berkeley Women's Law Journal* 18: 40–60.

Chang, Jeani, Cynthia J. Berg, Linda E. Saltzman, and Joy Herndon. 2005. "Homicide: A Leading Cause of Injury Deaths among Pregnant and Postpartum Women in the United States, 1991–1999." *Journal of Public Health* 95(3): 471–477.

Chaptman, Dennis. 2001. "High Court Limits Dad's Procreation." *Milwaukee Journal Sentinel,* July 11, A1.

Cherry, April. 2004. "Roe's Legacy: The Noncensual Medical Treatment of Pregnant Women and Implications for Female Citizenship." *University of Pennsylvania Journal of Constitutional Law* 6: 723–751.

———. 2007. "The Detention, Confinement, and Incarceration of Pregnant Women for the Benefit of Fetal Health." *Columbia Journal of Gender and Law* 16: 147–197.

Children's Defense Fund. 2004. *Basic Facts on Welfare.* Washington, DC: Children's Defense Fund. At http://www.childrensdefense.org/site/PageServer?pagename=fam ilyincome_welfare_basicfacts (retrieved September 1, 2007).

Children's Services Visiting Improvement Task Force. 2005. *Family Visiting Improvement Action Plan.* New York: Children's Services Task Force.

Child Welfare Information Gateway. 2004. *Grounds for Involuntary Termination of Parental Rights: Summary of State Laws.* Washington, DC: U.S. Department of Health and Human Services. At www.childwelfare.gov/systemwide/laws_policies/statutes/ groundterminall.pdf (retrieved September 1, 2007).

Citizens for Tax Justice and the Institute on Taxation and Economic Policy. 2004. *Corporate Income Taxes in the Bush Years.* At http://www.ctj.org/corpfed04an.pdf (retrieved September 1, 2007).

Clarridge, Christine. 2004. "Manslaughter Charges Filed in Infant's Death." *Seattle Times,* August 31, B4.

Claxton, Melvin, Ronald J. Hansen, and Norman Sinclair. 2005. "Guards Assault Female Inmates." *Detroit News,* May 22.

Clear, Todd R., and Dina R. Rose. 1999. *When Neighbors Go to Jail: Impact on Attitudes about Formal and Informal Social Control.* Washington, DC: U.S. Department of Justice.

Clear, Todd R., Dina R. Rose, and Judith A. Ryder. 2001. "Incarceration and the Community: The Problem of Removing and Returning Offenders." *Crime and Delinquency* 47(3): 335–351.

Clinton, Hillary Rodham. 2005. "Remarks by Senator Hillary Rodham Clinton to the NYS Family Planning Providers." January 24. At http://clinton.senate.gov/~clinton/ speeches/2005125A05.html (retrieved September 1, 2007).

Cnattingius, Sven, and Olof Stephansson. 2002. "The Epidemiology of Stillbirth." *Seminars in Perinatology* 26: 25–30.

Coleman, Chrisena. 2005. "Girl Faces Slay Rap in Newborn's Fall." *New York Daily News,* March 23, 7.

Collins, Patricia Hill. 1999. "Shifting the Center." Pp. 197–217 in *American Families: A Multicultural Reader,* ed. Stephanie Coontz. New York: Routledge.

Committee on the Judiciary. 2003. *Unborn Victims of Violence Act of 2003 or Laci and Conner's Law.* Hearing before the Subcommittee on the Constitution of the Committee on the Judiciary, House of Representatives, 108th Congress.

Congressional Budget Office. 2003. *Baby Boomers' Retirement Prospects: An Overview.* Washington, DC: Congressional Budget Office.

———. 2005. *Changes in Participation in Means-Tested Programs.* Washington, DC: Congressional Budget Office. At http://www.cbo.gov/showdoc. cfm?index=6302&sequence=0 (retrieved September 1, 2007).

———. 2007. *Estimated Funding for Operations in Iraq and the War on Terrorism.* Washington, DC: Congressional Budget Office. At http://www.cbo.gov/publications/ collections/iraq.cfm and http://www.cbo.gov/ftpdocs/77xx/doc7793/02-07-CostOf-War.pdf (retrieved September 1, 2007).

Connell, Michele. 2002. "The Postpartum Psychosis Defense and Feminism: More or Less Justice for Women?" *Case Western Reserve Law Review* 53: 143–153.

Connor, Tracy. 2005. "City's 30M Mea Culpa: Paying for Illegal Strip Searches." *New York Daily News,* July 13, 5.

Conova, Susan. 2006. "Do Babies Belong in Prison?" *In Vivo* 5(1): 1. At http://www. cpmc.columbia.edu/news/in-vivo/vol4_6_feb-mar_06/imprisoned_mother.html (retrieved September 1, 2007).

Contreras, Guillermo. 2000. "Defendant Told She Should Be Sterilized." *Albuquerque Journal,* October 12, A1.

Council of State Governments. 2006. *Homelessness and Prisoner Re-Entry.* New York: Council of State Governments Eastern Regional Conference. At http://www.csgeast. org/pdfs/Re-Entry/RPC_Homelessness%20one-pager_v8.pdf (retrieved September 1, 2007).

Craig, Gary. 2006. "Inmate Despair Hints at Abuse: Was She Raped? Lawyer Calls for New Inquiry into 3-Year-Old Suicide." *Rochester (NY) Democrat and Chronicle,* July 13.

Crary, David. 2003. "Love Locked Away: A Civil Rights Group Is Helping Imprisoned Mothers Keep Custody of Their Children." *Washington Post,* March 23, F1.

Crowder, Carla. 2003. "DYS Campus Superintendent, Psychologist on Leave in Probe." *Birmingham News,* March 14.

———. 2005a. "DYS Chalkville Abuse Charges Go Back to '94." *Birmingham News,* August 9.

———. 2005b. "Prison Medical Care Tied to Deaths." *Birmingham News,* April 21, 1A.

"Crusade against Quack Doctors." 1876. *New York Times,* October 5, 5.

Curl, Joseph. 2004. "Bush Signs Fetus-Protection Bill: Affirms 'Two Victims' in Crime on Pregnant Woman." *Washington Times,* April 2, A3.

Dailard, Cynthia. 2003. "HPV in the United States and Developing Nations." *Guttmacher Report* 6(3): 4–6.

Dallam, Stephanie J. 1999. "The Parental Alienation Syndrome: Is It Scientific?" Pp. 67–72 in *Expose: The Failure of Family Courts to Protect Children from Abuse in Custody Disputes,* ed. E. St. Charles and L. Crook. Los Gatos, CA: Our Children Our Children Charitable Foundation.

Daniels, Cynthia R. 1993. *At Women's Expense: State Power and the Politics of Fetal Rights.* Cambridge: Harvard University Press.

"Davenport Man Gets Probation for Breaking into Abortion Clinic." 2006. *Associated Press,* September 2.

Davis, Nanette. 1985. *From Crime to Choice: The Transformation of Abortion in America*. Westport, CT: Greenwood.

DeCarlo, Paul. 2005. "Experts Explain Roots of Infanticide." *Riverside Press Enterprise*, May 14, B1.

De Groot, Anne. 2005. Personal email communication with the author. July 27.

De Groot, Anne, and Susan Cu Uvin. 2005. "HIV Infection among Women in Prison: Considerations for Care." *Infectious Diseases in Corrections Report* 8(5–6): 1–4.

Dehart, Dana D. 2004. *Pathways to Prison: Impact of Victimization on the Lives of Incarcerated Women*. Columbia, SC: Center for Child and Family Studies.

Dekoning, Brian. 2005. "Jury Deciding Fate of Man Who Killed His Pregnant Girlfriend." *Manchester (NH) Union Leader*, June 22, A6.

"Del. Cosgrove: Don't Relax Just Yet." 2005. *Well-Timed Period.* January 8. At http://thewelltimedperiod.blogspot.com/2005/01/del-cosgrove-dont-relax-just-yet.html (retrieved September 1, 2007).

DeMartini, Alayna, and Penny Moore. 2004. "Police Not Naming Girl Who Left Her Baby in Alley." *Columbus Dispatch*, September 23, C1.

Denno, Deborah. 2003. "Who Is Andrea Yates? A Short Story about Insanity." *Duke Journal of Gender Law and Policy* 1: 1–139.

Department of HIV/AIDS and Department of Reproductive Health and Research. 2004. *Antiretroviral Drugs for Treating Pregnant Women and Preventing HIV Infection in Infants*. Geneva: World Health Organization.

Dietz, Patricia M., Roger W. Rochat, Betsy L. Thompson, et al. 1998. "Differences in the Risk of Homicide and Other Fatal Injuries between Postpartum Women and Other Women of Childbearing Age: Implications for Prevention." *American Journal of Public Health* 88: 641–643.

Dobson, Velma, and Bruce Sales. 2000. "The Science of Infanticide and Mental Illness." *Psychology, Public Policy and Law* 6: 1098–1112.

Drescher-Burke, K., J. Krall, and A. Penick. 2004. *Discarded Infants and Neonaticide: A Review of the Literature*. Berkeley, CA: National Abandoned Infants Assistance Resource Center.

"Dr. Hathaway's Crimes." 1883. *New York Times*, June 24, 1.

Driessen, Marguerite A. 2006. "Avoiding the Melissa Rowland Dilemma: Why Disobeying a Doctor Should Not Be a Crime." *Michigan State Journal of Medicine and Law* 10: 1–56.

Duck, Michael, and the Associated Press. 2005. "Murder Suspect Was Guilty in Valley Stabbing." *Allentown (PA) Morning Call*, July 25, A1.

Dugdale, Richard L. 1910. *The Jukes: A Study in Crime, Pauperism, Disease and Heredity*. New York: Putnam.

Durose, Matthew, Caroline Wolf Harlow, Patrick Langan, et al. 2005. *Family Violence Statistics*. NCJ 207846. Washington, DC: U.S. Department of Justice, Bureau of Justice Statistics.

Echlin, Carole, and Bina Osthoff. 2000. "Child Protection Workers and Battered Women's Advocates Working Together to End Violence against Women and Children." *Journal of Aggression, Maltreatment, and Trauma* 46(3): 207–219.

Edds, Kimberly. 2005. "Peterson Sentenced to Death by Injection." *Washington Post,* March 17, A10.

Edin, Kathryn, and Maria Kefalas. 2005. *Promises I Can Keep: Why Poor Women Put Motherhood before Marriage.* Los Angeles: University of California Press.

Edin, Kathryn, and Laura Lein. 1997. *Making Ends Meet: How Single Mothers Survive Welfare and Low-Wage Work.* New York: Russell Sage.

Edleson, Jeffrey, Lyungai F. Mbilinyi, and Sudha Shetty. 2003. *Parenting in the Context of Domestic Violence.* San Francisco: Judicial Council of California. At http://www. courtinfo.ca.gov/programs/cfcc/pdffiles/fullReport.pdf (retrieved January 21, 2008).

Ehrenreich, Barbara. 2000. "How 'Natural' Is Rape?" *Time Magazine,* January 31.

Eller, Alexandra Grosvenor, and Janice L. B. Byrne. 2006. "Stillbirth at Term." *Obstetrics and Gynecology* 108(2): 442–447.

English, Abigail, and Catherine Teare. 2001. "Statutory Rape Enforcement and Child Abuse Reporting: Effects on Health Care Access for Adolescents." *DePaul Law Review* 827(50): 838–863.

Enos, Sandra. 2001. *Mothering from the Inside: Parenting in a Women's Prison.* Albany: SUNY Press.

Evans, Kristina C. 2004. "Can a Leopard Change His Spots? Child Custody and Batterer's Intervention." *Duke Journal of Gender Law and Policy* 11: 121–139.

Evans, Murray. 2007. "Woman Enters Plea in Death of Baby." *Associated Press Wire Service,* September 21.

Faller, Kathleen Coulbourn, and Ellen DeVoe. 1995. "Allegations of Sexual Abuse in Divorce." *Journal of Child Sexual Abuse* 4(4): 1–25.

Fasbach, Laura. 2005. "Assembly OKs Birth Control Benefit Bill." *Bergen County (NJ) Record,* December 13, A1.

Fass, Mark. 2007. "Panel Rejects Court's Ban on Pregnancy." *New York Law Journal* 8(67): 1.

Federal Legislative Office of the National Right to Life Committee. 2006. *Constitutional Challenges to State Unborn Victims (Fetal Homicide) Laws.* December. At http://www.nrlc.org/Unborn_Victims/statechallenges.html (retrieved September 1, 2007).

Feminist Majority Foundation. 2008. *Washington State Refuses Abstinence-Only Programs.* At http://www.feminist.org/news/newsbyte/uswirestory.asp?id=11118 (retrieved July 18, 2008).

Fentiman, Linda C. 2006. "The New 'Fetal Protection': The Wrong Answer to the Crisis of Inadequate Health Care for Women and Children." *Denver University Law Review* 84: 537–599.

Fernandez, Elizabeth. 2000. "Jailed for Mistake in Abortion: Doctor Says He Was Singled Out." *Cleveland Plain Dealer,* September 24, 22A.

Ferraro, Kathleen J., and Angela M. Moe. 2003. "Mothering, Crime, and Incarceration." *Journal of Contemporary Ethnography* 32(1): 9–40.

Finer, Lawrence B., and Stanley K. Henshaw. 2006a. "Disparities in Rates of Unintended Pregnancy in the United States." *Perspectives on Sexual and Reproductive Health* 38(2): 90–96.

———. 2006b. *Estimates of U.S. Abortion Incidence: 2001–2003*. New York: Alan Guttmacher Institute. At http://www.guttmacher.org/pubs/2006/08/03/ab_incidence.
pdf (retrieved September 1, 2007).

Finer, Lawrence B., Lori F. Frohwirth, Lindsay A. Dauphinee, et al. 2006. "Timing of
Steps and Reasons for Delays in Obtaining Abortions in the United States." *Contraception* 74(4): 334–344.

Finkel, Norman, John Burke, and Leticia Chavez. 2000. "Commonsense Judgments of
Infanticide: Murder, Manslaughter, Madness, or Miscellaneous." *Psychology, Public
Policy and Law* 6: 1113–1137.

Finkelhor, David, Heather Hammer, and Andrea J. Sedlak. 2003. *Nonfamily Abducted
Children: National Estimates and Characteristics*. Washington, DC: Office of Juvenile Justice and Delinquency Prevention.

Flavin, Jeanne. 2001. "Of Punishment and Parenthood: Family-Based Social Control
and the Sentencing of Black Drug Offenders." *Gender & Society* 15(4): 609–631.

———. 2002. "A Glass Half Full? Harm Reduction among Pregnant Women Who Use
Cocaine." *Journal of Drug Issues* 32: 973–998.

———. 2007. "Slavery's Legacy in Contemporary Attempts to Regulate Black Women's
Reproduction." Pp. 95–114 in *Race, Gender, and Punishment: From Colonialism to
the War on Terror*, ed. Mary Bosworth and Jeanne Flavin. New Brunswick, NJ: Rutgers University Press.

Flavin, Jeanne, and David Rosenthal. 2003. "La Bodega de la Familia: Supporting Parolees' Reintegration within a Community Context." *Fordham Urban Law Journal*
30(5): 1603–1620.

"Florida: Illegal Abortion Clinic Busted." 2005. *Tampa Tribune*, January 6.

"Former AG's Case against Abortion Doctor Now Dead." 2007. *Kansas City Star*, February 14.

Fox, Bonnie, and Diana Worts. 1999. "Revisiting the Critique of Medicalized Childbirth: A Contribution to the Sociology of Birth." *Gender & Society* 13(3): 326–346.

Fox, James Alan, and Marianne Zawitz. 2004. *Homicide Trends in the United States*.
Washington, DC: U.S. Department of Justice, Bureau of Justice Statistics. At http://
www.ojp.usdoj.gov/bjs/pub/pdf/htius.pdf (retrieved September 1, 2007).

Frank, Deborah, Marilyn Augustyn, Wanda Knight, et al. 2001. "Growth, Development, and Behavior in Early Childhood Following Prenatal Cocaine Exposure."
Journal of the American Medical Association (JAMA) 285: 1613–1625.

Freeman, Richard B. 1996. *Why Do So Many Young American Men Commit Crimes
and What Might We Do about It?* Working Paper No. W5451. Cambridge, Mass.:
National Bureau of Economic Research. At http://papers.ssrn.com/so13/papers.
cfm?abstract_id=10140 (retrieved September 1, 2007).

Fretts, R. C. 2005. "Etiology and Prevention of Stillbirth." *American Journal of Obstetrics and Gynecology* 193: 1923–1935.

Frey, Hillary, and Miranda Kennedy. 2001. "Abortion on Trial: The Prosecution of Dr.
Pendergraft." *Nation*, June 18, 12–14.

Friedman, Ann. 2006. "Mail-Order Abortions." *Mother Jones*. November/December. At
http://www.motherjones.com/news/outfront/2006/11/mail_order_abortions.html
(retrieved September 1, 2007).

Friedman, Susan Hatters, Sarah McCue Horwitz, and Phillip J. Resnick. 2005. "Child Murder by Mothers: A Critical Analysis of the Current State of Knowledge and a Research Agenda." *American Journal of Psychiatry* 162(9): 1578–1587.

Frye, Victoria. 2001. "Examining Homicide's Contribution to Pregnancy-Associated Deaths." *Journal of the American Medical Association (JAMA)* 285(11): 1510–1511.

Futty, John 2004. "Baby's Death Shocks Somalis." *Columbus Dispatch*, September 9, B2.

Gardner, Richard A. 1998. *The Parental Alienation Syndrome*, 2nd ed. Creskill, NJ: Creative Therapeutics.

Genovese, Eugene. 1974. *Roll, Jordan, Roll: The World the Slaves Made*. New York: Vintage.

Gilbert, Dennis. 2006. *Hamilton College Hot Button Issues Poll: Guns, Gays, and Abortion*. At http://www.hamilton.edu/news/polls/HotButtonFinalReport.pdf (retrieved September 1, 2007).

Gilbert, William M., Thomas S. Nesbitt, and Beate Xen. 2003. "The Cost of Prematurity: Quantification by Gestational Age and Birth Weight." *Obstetrics and Gynecology* 102: 488–492.

Glaberson, William. 2006. "In Tiny Courts of New York, Abuses of Law and Power." *New York Times*, September 25, A1.

Glaze, Lauren, and Seri Pella. 2005. *Correctional Populations in the United States*. Washington, DC: U.S. Department of Justice, Bureau of Justice Statistics.

Goldenberg, R. L., R. Kirby, and J. F. Culhane. 2004. "Stillbirth: A Review." *Journal of Maternal-Fetal and Neonatal Medicine* 16: 79–94.

Goodman, Annekathryn. 2002. "Human Papillomavirus Infections in Incarcerated Women." *Infectious Diseases in Corrections Report* 5(1): 1–5.

Goodman, Walter. 1999. "Of Camera and Consequences at a Women's Prison." *New York Times*, November 2.

Goodnough, Abby, and Bruce Weber. 1997. "The Picture of Ordinary: Before Prom Night, a Suspect Was the Girl Next Door." *New York Times*, July 2, B1.

Gordon, Linda. 2002. *The Moral Property of Women: A History of Birth Control Politics in America*. Chicago: University of Illinois Press.

Greenfeld, Lawrence A., and Tracy L. Snell. 1999. *Women Offenders*. Washington, DC: U.S. Department of Justice, Bureau of Justice Statistics.

Greer, Germaine. 1985. *Sex and Destiny*. New York: Harper and Row.

Grella, Christine E., and Lisa Greenwell. 2006. "Correlates of Parental Status and Attitudes toward Parenting among Substance-Abusing Women Offenders." *Prison Journal* 86(1): 89–113.

Grendys, Jr., Edward C. 2004. "Pregnancy: Neoplastic Diseases." Pp. 1513–1520 in *Cecil Textbook of Medicine*, ed. Lee Goldman and Dennis Ausiello. Philadelphia: Saunders.

Grob, George. 2005. *Federal Efforts to Address Applicable Child Abuse and Sexual Abuse Reporting Requirements for Title X Grantees*. OEI-02-03-00530. April 25 memorandum. Washington, DC: Department of Health and Human Services, Assistant Inspector General for Evaluation and Inspections. At http://opa.osophs.dhhs.gov/titlex/OEI-02-03-00530.pdf (retrieved September 1, 2007).

"Guarding against Sexual Abuse." 2006. *Grand Rapids Press*, January 7, A10.

Guttmacher Institute. 2006a. *Parental Involvement in Minors' Abortions.* At http://www.guttmacher.org/statecenter/spibs/spib_PIMA.pdf (retrieved October 12, 2006).

———. 2006b. *U.S. Teenage Pregnancy Statistics: National and State Trends and Trends by Race and Ethnicity.* At http://www.guttmacher.org/pubs/2006/09/12/USTPstats.pdf (retrieved May 27, 2007).

———. 2007a. "Bans on 'Partial-Birth' Abortion." *State Policies in Brief.* At http://www.guttmacher.org/statecenter/spibs/spib_BPBA.pdf (retrieved November 1, 2007).

———. 2007b. "Infant Abandonment." *State Policies in Brief.* At http://www.guttmacher.org/statecenter/spibs/spib_IA.pdf (retrieved September 1, 2007).

———. 2007c. "Insurance Coverage of Contraceptives." *State Policies in Brief.* At http://www.guttmacher.org/statecenter/spibs/spib_ICC.pdf (retrieved November 1, 2007).

———. 2007d. "Mandatory Counseling and Waiting Periods for Abortion." *State Policies in Brief.* At http://www.guttmacher.org/statecenter/spibs/spib_MWPA.pdf (retrieved September 1, 2007).

———. 2007e. "Overview of Minors Consent Laws." *State Policies in Brief.* At http://www.guttmacher.org/statecenter/spibs/spib_OMCL.pdf (retrieved June 8, 2007).

———. 2007f. "Parental Involvement in Minors' Abortions." At http://www.guttmacher.org/statecenter/spibs/spib_PIMA.pdf (retrieved November 1, 2007).

———. 2007g. "Refusing to Provide Health Services." *State Policies in Brief.* At http://www.guttmacher.org/statecenter/spibs/spib_RPHS.pdf (retrieved September 1, 2007).

———. 2007h. "State Funding of Abortion under Medicaid." *State Policies in Brief.* At http://www.guttmacher.org/pubs/spib_SFAM.pdf (retrieved September 1, 2007).

———. 2007i. "Substance Abuse during Pregnancy." *State Policies in Brief.* At http://www.guttmacher.org/statecenter/spibs/spib_SADP.pdf (retrieved January 21, 2008).

Hallenborg, Mary Ann. 2004. *The New York Landlord's Law Book,* 2nd ed. New York: Nolo.

Hamilton, B. E., J. A. Martin, and S. J. Ventura. 2006. *Births: Preliminary Data for 2005.* Hyattsville, MD: National Center for Health Statistics. At http://www.cdc.gov/nchs/products/pubs/pubd/hestats/prelimbirths05/prelimbirths05.htm (retrieved January 21, 2008).

Hammer, Heather, David Finkelhor, and Andrea Sedlak. 2002. *Children Abducted by Family Members: National Estimates and Characteristics.* Washington, DC: Office of Juvenile Justice and Delinquency Prevention.

Han, Erin L. 2003. "Mandatory Arrest and No-Drop Policies: Victim Empowerment in Domestic Violence Cases." *Boston College Third World Law Journal* 23(1): 159–191.

Hanley, Robert. 1997. "Woman Indicted in Killing of Newborn Son at Prom." *New York Times,* September 18, B6.

Hanson, Eric. 2004. "A Matter of Conscience." *Houston Chronicle,* March 26, A1.

Harer, Miles D., and Neil P. Langan. 2001. "Gender Differences in Predictors of Prison Violence: Assessing the Predictive Validity of a Risk Classification System." *Crime and Delinquency* 47(4): 513–536.

Harlow, Caroline Wolf. 2003. *Education and Correctional Populations.* Washington, DC: U.S. Department of Justice, Bureau of Justice Statistics.

Harper, S., J. Lynch, S. Burris, and G. Davey Smith. 2007. "Trends in the Black-White Life Expectancy Gap in the United States, 1983–2003." *Journal of the American Medical Association (JAMA)* 21(11): 1224–1232.

Harris, B. 1994. "Biological and Hormonal Aspects of Postpartum Depressed Mood." *British Journal of Psychiatry* 164: 288–292.

Harris, Lynn. 2006. "Drugs While Pregnant: Dangerous vs. 'Endangerment'?" *Salon.* At www.salon.com/mwt/broadsheet/2006/09/06/drugs_as_endangerment/index.html (retrieved October 12, 2006).

Harris, Thomas. 1936. "Statutes Relating to Abortion, Appendix A." Pp. 453–475 in *Abortion, Spontaneous and Induced: Medical and Social Aspects,* by Frederick J. Taussig. St. Louis: Mosby.

Harrison, Paige, and Allen Beck. 2005. *Prisoners in 2004.* Washington, DC: U.S. Department of Justice, Bureau of Justice Statistics.

———. 2006a. *Prison and Jail Inmates at Midyear 2005.* Washington, DC: U.S. Department of Justice.

———. 2006b. *Prisoners in 2005.* Washington, DC: U.S. Department of Justice.

Hartney, Christopher. 2006. *U.S. Rates of Incarceration: A Global Perspective.* Washington, DC: National Council on Crime and Delinquency. At http://www.nccd-crc.org/nccd/pubs/2006nov_factsheet_incarceration.pdf (retrieved September 1, 2007).

Harvard School of Public Health. 2004. *Researchers Say Massachusetts Family Courts Fail to Protect Battered Women and Their Children.* Press Release. May 27. At http://www.hsph.harvard.edu/press/releases/press05272004.html (retrieved September 1, 2007).

Hasday, Jill. 2000. "Contest and Consent: A Legal History of Marital Rape." *California Law Review* 88: 1373–1505.

Hauser, Debra. 2004. *Five Years of Abstinence-Only-Until-Marriage Education: Assessing the Impact.* Washington, DC: Advocates for Youth. At http://www.advocatesforyouth.org/publications/stateevaluations.pdf.

Henshaw, Stanley K., and Lawrence B. Finer. 2003. "The Accessibility of Abortion Services in the United States, 2001." *Perspectives on Sexual and Reproductive Health* 35(1): 16–24.

Henshaw, Stanley K., and Kathryn Kost. 1992. "Parental Involvement in Minors' Abortion Decisions." *Family Planning Perspectives* 24: 196–209.

Hern, Warren M. 2003. "Did I Violate the Partial-Birth Abortion Ban? A Doctor Ponders a New Era of Prosecution." *Slate.* October 22. At http://www.slate.com/id/2090215/ (retrieved September 1, 2007).

Heslam, Jessica. 2002. "N.H. Police Save Newborn Dumped by Teen Mom." *Boston Herald,* August 23, 6.

Holmer, Evelyn. 2004/2005. "How *Ohio v. Talty* Provided for Future Bans on Procreation and the Consequences That Action Brings." *Journal of Law and Health* 19: 141–176.

Holmes, Melisa, Heidi Resnick, Dean Kilpatrick, and Connie Best. 1996. "Rape-Related Pregnancy: Estimates and Descriptive Characteristics from a National Sample of Women." *American Journal of Obstetrics and Gynecology* 175(2): 320–325.

Hooiveld, M. 2006. "Adverse Reproductive Outcomes among Male Painters with Occupational Exposure to Organic Solvents." *Occupational and Environmental Medicine* 63(8): 538–544.

Horon, Isabelle L. 2005. "Underreporting of Maternal Deaths on Death Certificates and the Magnitude of the Problem of Maternal Mortality." *American Journal of Public Health* 95(3): 478–482.

Horon, Isabelle L., and Diana Cheng. 2001. "Enhanced Surveillance for Pregnancy-Associated Mortality: Maryland, 1993–1998." *Journal of the American Medical Association (JAMA)* 285: 1455–1459.

Hoult, Jennifer. 2006. "The Evidentiary Admissibility of Parental Alienation Syndrome: Science, Law, and Policy." *Children's Legal Rights Journal* 26: 1–61

Hughes, Kristen. 2006. *Direct Expenditures by Criminal Justice Function, 1982–2004.* Washington, DC: U.S. Department of Justice, Bureau of Justice Statistics.

Hughes, Timothy A., Doris James Wilson, and Allen J. Beck. 2001. *Trends in State Parole 1990–2000.* Washington, DC: U.S. Department of Justice.

"Human Papillomavirus (HPV) 101." 2006. *Infectious Diseases in Corrections Report* 9(6–7): 8.

Human Rights Watch. 2002. *Ill-Equipped: U.S. Prisons and Offenders with Mental Illness.* New York: Human Rights Watch.

Human Rights Watch and ACLU. 2006. *Custody and Control: Conditions of Confinement in New York's Juvenile Prisons for Girls.* At http://hrw.org/reports/2006/uso906/ (retrieved September 1, 2007).

Humphreys, Cathy, and Ravi K. Thiara. 2003. "Neither Justice nor Protection: Women's Experiences of Post-Separation Violence." *Journal of Social Welfare and Family Law* 25(3): 195–214.

Humphries, Drew. 1999. *Crack Mothers: Pregnancy, Drugs, and the Media.* Columbus: Ohio State University Press.

Humphries, Drew, John Dawson, Valerie Cronin, et al. 1995. "Mothers and Children, Drugs and Crack: Reactions to Maternal Drug Dependency." Pp. 167–179 in *The Criminal Justice System and Women,* ed. Barbara Raffel Price and Natalie J. Sokoloff. New York: McGraw-Hill.

Hurley, Elizabeth. 2005. *More States Are Passing Fetal Homicide Laws.* Washington, DC: Concerned Women for America. At http://www.cwalac.org/article_202.shtml (retrieved October 12, 2006).

Jaffe, Peter, Nancy Lemon, and Samantha Poisson. 2003. *Child Custody and Domestic Violence.* Thousand Oaks, CA: Sage.

James, Denise, and Natalie E. Roche. 2006. "Therapeutic Abortion." *eMedicine.* At http://www.emedicine.com/med/topic3311.htm (retrieved September 1, 2007).

James, Doris J., and Lauren E. Glaze. 2006. *Mental Health Problems of Prison and Jail Inmates.* Washington, DC: U.S. Department of Justice.

Jayasinghe, Tiloma. 2007. Staff attorney, National Advocates for Pregnant Women. Personal communication with the author. September 4.

"Jersey City: Sentence in Baby's Death." 2007. *New York Times,* April 26.

Joffe, Carole. 1995. *Doctors of Conscience: The Struggle to Provide Abortion before and after* Roe v. Wade. Boston: Beacon.

———. 2007. "The Abortion Procedure Ban: Bush's Gift to His Base." *Dissent* (Fall): 57–61.

Johnson, Elizabeth I., and Jane Waldfogel. 2002. "Parental Incarceration: Recent Trends and Implications for Child Welfare." *Social Service Review* 76(3): 460–479.

Johnson, Kay, Samuel F. Posner, Janis Biermann, et al. 2006. "Recommendations to Improve Preconception Health and Health Care: United States." *Morbidity and Mortality Weekly Report* 55(RR06): 1–23.

Johnson, Michael. 1995. "Patriarchal Terrorism and Common Couple Violence: Two Forms of Violence against Women." *Journal of Marriage and the Family* 57: 283–294.

Johnson, Michael, and Kathleen Ferraro. 2000. "Research on Domestic Violence in the 1990s: Making Distinctions." *Journal of Marriage and the Family* 62: 948–963.

Johnston, Denise, and Katherine Gabel. 1995. "Incarcerated Parents." Pp. 3–20 in *Children of Incarcerated Parents,* ed. Katherine Gabel and Denise Johnston. New York: Lexington.

Jones, Rachel K., Mia R. S. Zolna, Stanley K. Henshaw, and Lawrence B. Finer. 2008. "Abortion in the United States: Incidence and Access to Services, 2005." *Perspectives on Sexual and Reproductive Health* 40: 6–16.

Jonsson, Patrik. 2007. "Ultrasound: Latest Tool in Battle over Abortion." *Christian Science Monitor,* May 15.

Kassebaum, Patricia. 1999. *Substance Abuse Treatment for Women Offenders: Guide to Promising Practices.* Rockland, MD: U.S. Department of Health and Human Services.

Katz, Michael. 2001. *The Price of Citizenship.* New York: Owl.

Kaufman, Leslie. 2004. "Abuse Victims and the City Settle Lawsuit." *New York Times,* December 18, B2, B6.

Kazura, Kerry. 2001. "Family Programming for Incarcerated Parents: A Needs Assessment among Inmates." *Journal of Offender Rehabilitation* 32: 67–83.

Keith, L., and J. J. Oleszczuk. 1999. "Iatrogenic Multiple Birth, Multiple Pregnancy and Assisted Reproductive Technologies." *International Journal of Gynecology and Obstetrics* 64: 11–25.

Kellman, Laurie. 2006. "Senate Set to Pass Parental Notification Requirement for Minors Seeking Abortions." *Associated Press,* July 25.

Kennedy, Miranda. 2000. "Partial Truth Abortion Coverage." *Fair and Accuracy in Reporting.* At www.fair.org (retrieved September 1, 2007).

Kertscher, Tom. 2004. "Punishment Varies in Newborn Deaths." *Milwaukee Journal Sentinel,* September 20, 1.

Kilbride, Howard W., Cheri A Castor, and Kathryn L Fuger. 2006. "School-Age Outcome of Children with Prenatal Cocaine Exposure Following Early Case Management." *Journal of Developmental and Behavioral Pediatrics* 27(3): 181–187.

King, Ryan S. 2006. *The Next Big Thing? Methamphetamine in the United States.* Washington, DC: Sentencing Project.

Kinzie, Susan. 2006. "Charges Rejected for Moms Who Bear Babies Exposed to Illegal Drugs." *Washington Post,* August 4, B6.

Kline, Wendy. 2001. *Building a Better Race: Gender, Sexuality, and Eugenics from the Turn of the Century to the Baby Boom.* Berkeley: University of California Press.

Klonoff-Cohen, Hillary, and Phung Lam-Kruglick. 2001. "Maternal and Paternal Recreational Drug Use and Sudden Infant Death Syndrome." *Archives of Pediatric and Adolescent Medicine* 155: 765–770.

Koehler, Robert C., and Tribune Media Services. n.d. "Secure Birth." *Common Wonders.* At http://commonwonders.com/archives/c01239.htm (retrieved September 1, 2007).

Koren, G., K. Graham, H. Shear, and T. Einarson. 1989. "Bias against the Null Hypothesis: The Reproductive Hazards of Cocaine." *Lancet* 2: 1440–1442.

Krisberg, Barry, and Carolyn Engel Temin. 2001. *The Plight of Children Whose Parents Are in Prison.* Oakland, CA: National Council on Crime and Delinquency.

Krupat, Tanya. 2007. Personal email communication with the author. June 26.

"Late Term Abortion Cases." 2001. *Associated Press State and Local Wire,* April 7.

Lawrence, Jane. 2000. "The Indian Health Service and the Sterilization of Native American Women." *American Indian Quarterly* 24: 400–419.

Layne, Linda L. 2003. *Motherhood Lost: A Feminist Account of Pregnancy Loss in America.* New York: Routledge.

Lee, Arlene F., Philip M. Genty, and Mim Laver. 2005. *The Impact of the Adoption and Safe Families Act on Children of Incarcerated Parents.* Washington, DC: Child Welfare League of America.

Lee, Henry K. 2003. "Vigil for Missing Modesto Mother-to-Be." *San Francisco Chronicle,* January 1, A17.

Lee, Jennifer. 2005. "After Her Baby Dies, Girl Only Wants School." *New York Times,* January 26, B8.

Lee, Susan J., Henry J. Pater Ralston, Eleanor A. Drey, et al. 2005. "Fetal Pain: A Systematic Multidisciplinary Review of the Evidence." *Journal of the American Medical Association (JAMA)* 294: 947–954.

Lefler, Dion. 2007. "New Judge Assigned to Hear Case against George Tiller." *Wichita Eagle,* August 22, n.p.

Legal Action Center. 2004. *After Prison: Roadblocks to Reentry.* New York: Legal Action Center. At http://www.lac.org/lac/upload/lacreport/LAC_PrintReport.pdf (retrieved September 1, 2007).

Leonard, Christina. 2004. "Inmates' Advocates Challenge Arpaio's Abortion Roadblocks." *Arizona Republic,* October 15, n.p.

Lerner, Sharon. 2002. "When Medicine Is Murder." *Village Voice,* April 2.

Lesli, Lourdes Medrano. 2003. "14-Year-Old Mom Charged in Her Newborn's Death." *Minneapolis Star Tribune,* October 7, B3.

Lester, Barry, Linda LaGasse, and Ronald Seifer. 1998. "Cocaine Exposure and Children: The Meaning of Subtle Effects." *Science* 282: 633–634.

Levin, Amy, and Linda Mills. 2003. "Fighting for Child Custody When Domestic Violence Is at Issue: Survey of State Laws." *Social Work* 48(4): 463–470.

Lewis, Pamela. 2004. "Behind the Glass Wall: Barriers That Incarcerated Parents Face Regarding the Care, Custody, and Control of Their Children." *Journal of the American Academy of Matrimonial Lawyers* 19: 97–115.

Liberto, Jennifer, and Rebecca Catalenello. 2007. "Legislators Want Pregnant Girls Reported." *St. Petersburg Times,* March 7.

Lie, Gwat-Yong, and Sabrina Gentlewarrior. 1991. "Intimate Violence in Lesbian Relationships: Discussion of Survey Findings and Practice Implications." *Journal of Social Service Research* 15: 41–59.

Lindbohm M. L., K. Hemminki, M. G. Bonhomme, et al. 1991. "Effects of Paternal Occupational Exposure on Spontaneous Abortions." *American Journal of Public Health* 81(8): 1029–1033.

Lipsky, Sherry, Victoria Holt, Thomas Easterling, and Cathy Critchlow. 2005. "Police-Reported Intimate Partner Violence during Pregnancy: Who Is at Risk?" *Violence and Victims* 20(1): 69–78.

Liptak, Adam. 2006. "Prisons Often Shackle Pregnant Inmates in Labor." *New York Times,* March 2, A16.

LIS, Inc. 2002. *Services for Families of Prison Inmates.* Longmont, CO: National Institute of Corrections.

———. 2006. *Interstate Transfer of Prison Inmates in the United States.* Longmont, CO: National Institute of Corrections

Lockie, Adrienne. 2005. "New York's Failure to Protect All Victims of Domestic Violence." *American Journal of Family Law* 18(4): 234–241.

Loe, Meika. 2005. *The Rise of Viagra: How the Little Blue Pill Changed Sex in America.* New York: New York University Press.

Lovik, Mary. 2004. *Update: Domestic Violence Benchbook,* 3rd ed. Lansing: Michigan Judicial Institute. At http://courts.michigan.gov/mji/resources/dvbook/dvbook.htm (retrieved September 1, 2007).

Luker, Kristin. 1984. *Abortion and the Politics of Motherhood.* Berkeley: University of California Press.

———. 1996. *Dubious Conceptions: The Politics of Teenage Pregnancy.* Cambridge: Harvard University Press.

———. 2006. *When Sex Goes to School.* New York: Norton.

Lutz, Lorrie L. 2005. *Relationship between Public Child Welfare Workers, Resource Families and Birth Families.* New York: National Resource Center for Family-Centered Practice and Permanency Planning.

Lynch, Robert G. 2005. "Early Childhood Investment Yields Big Payoff." *Policy Perspectives.* At http://www.wested.org/online_pubs/pp-05-02.pdf (retrieved September 1, 2007).

MacDorman, Marian F., Donna L. Hoyert, Joyce A. Martin, et al. 2007. "Fetal and Perinatal Mortality, United States, 2003." *National Vital Statistics Reports* 55(6): 1–20.

Macmillan, Ross, and Candace Kruttschnitt. 2005. *Patterns of Violence against Women: Risk Factors and Consequences—Final Report.* IJ CX-0011. Washington, DC: National Institute of Justice.

Magnusen, Debbe. 2000/2001. "From Dumpster to Delivery Room: Does Legalizing Baby Abandonment Really Solve the Problem?" *La Verne Law Review Journal of Juvenile Law* 22: 1–28.

Mallory, Caroline, and Phyllis Noerager Stern. 2000. "Awakening as a Change Process among Women at Risk for HIV Who Engage in Survival Sex." *Qualitative Health Research* 10(5): 581–594.

Maloney, Michelle, Rachel Wilgoren, Melissa Rothstein, and Shelly Inglis. 2005. "Special Issues of Women Prisoners." Pp. 246–248 in *A Jailhouse Lawyer's Manual,* 6th ed. New York: Columbia Human Rights Law Review.

Mandel, Beth. 2005. "The White Fist of the Child Welfare System: Racism, Patriarchy, and the Presumptive Removal of Children from Victims of Domestic Violence in *Nicholson v. Williams.*" *University of Cincinnati Law Review* 73: 1131–1162.

Mangino, Matthew T. 2005. "When a Murder Victim Is Pregnant." *Pennsylvania Law Weekly* 28(10): 8.

Mann, Judy. 2000. "N.Y. Suit Shows Fragility of Abortion Rights." *Washington Post*, March 29, C15.

"Man Pleads Guilty to Breaking into Iowa City Abortion Clinic." 2006. *Associated Press*, July 20.

Maple, Gabrielle. 2004. "Miscarriage Proof Frees Woman." *New Orleans Times-Picayune* August 18, 1.

Mapp, Susan C. 2002. "A Framework for Family Visiting for Children in Long-Term Foster Care." *Families in Society* 83(2): 175–182.

Marchevsky, Alejandra, and Jeanne Theoharis. 2006. *Not Working: Latina Immigrants, Low-Wage Jobs, and the Failure of Welfare Reform.* New York: New York University Press.

Marcus, Ruth. 2003. "'Partial Birth': Partial Truths." *Washington Post*, June 4, A27.

Martin, J. A., B. E. Hamilton, P. D. Sutton, et al. 2006. *Births: Final Data for 2004.* Hyattsville, MD: National Center for Health Statistics.

Martin, J. A., M. F. MacDorman, and T. J. Mathews. 1997. "Triplet Births: Trends and Outcomes, 1971–94." *Vital and Health Statistics* 55: 1–20.

Maruschak, Laura M. 2007. *HIV in Prisons, 2005.* Washington, DC: U.S. Department of Justice, Office of Justice Programs.

Maruschak, Laura, and Allen J. Beck. 2001. *Medical Problems of Inmates, 1997.* Washington, DC: U.S. Department of Justice, Bureau of Justice Statistics.

Marwick, Charles. 1998. "Physician Leadership on National Drug Policy Finds Addiction Treatment Works." *Journal of the American Medical Association (JAMA)* 279: 1149–1150.

May, Elaine Tyler. 1995. *Barren in the Promised Land: Childless Americans and the Pursuit of Happiness.* Cambridge: Harvard University Press.

Maynard, Rebecca. 2005. *First-Year Impacts of Four Title V, Section 510 Abstinence Education Programs.* Princeton, NJ: Mathematica Policy Research.

McCauley, A. P., and C. Salter. 1995. "Health Risks of Early Pregnancy." *Population Reports.* Baltimore: Johns Hopkins School of Public Health, Population Information Program. At http://www.infoforhealth.org/pr/j41/j41chap2_3.shtml#top (retrieved September 1, 2007).

MCC Drug Court (Missouri). n.d. *Mothers Choosing Change Drug Court Handbook for Participants.* On file with the author.

McFadden, Robert D. 1996. "Teen-Age Sweethearts Charged with Murdering Their Baby." *New York Times*, November 18, B1.

McFarlane, Judith, and Ann Malecha. 2005. *Sexual Assault among Intimates: Frequency, Consequences and Treatments.* Washington, DC: National Institute of Justice.

McMenamin, Jennifer. 2006. "The Roots of Child Abuse." *Baltimore Sun*, May 4.

McQueeney, Shannon M. 2005. "Recognizing Unborn Victims over Heightening Punishment for Crimes against Pregnant Women." *New England Journal on Criminal and Civil Confinement* 31: 461–483.

McWey, Lenore M., and Ann K. Mullis. 2004. "Improving the Lives of Children in Foster Care: The Impact of Supervised Visitation." *Family Relations* 53(3): 293–300.

McWey, Lenore, Tammy L. Henderson, and Susan N. Tice. 2006. "Mental Health Issues and the Foster Care System: An Examination of the Impact of the Adoption and Safe Families Act." *Journal of Marital and Family Therapy* 32(2): 195–214.

Melby, Todd. 2007. "A Flurry of Good News." *Contemporary Sexuality* 41(2): 1–3.

Mertens, Diana. 2001. "Pregnancy Outcomes of Inmates in a Large County Jail Setting." *Public Health Nursing* 18(1): 45–53.

Metraux, Stephen, and Dennis P. Culhane. 2004. "Homeless Shelter Use and Reincarceration Following Prison Release." *Criminology and Public Policy* 3(2): 139–160.

Meyer, Cheryl, and Michelle Oberman et al. 2001. *Mothers Who Kill Their Children: Understanding the Acts of Moms from Susan Smith to the "Prom Mom."* New York: New York University Press.

Michalsen, Venezia. 2007. "Going Straight for Her Children? Mothers' Desistance after Incarceration." Ph.D. diss., City University of New York.

Miller, Eleanor M. 1986. *Street Woman*. Philadelphia: Temple University Press.

Miller, Jonathan. 2006a. "Man Is Sentenced in Baby's Death." *New York Times,* December 14, B9.

———. 2006b. "Woman Admits She Threw Baby Down Air Shaft." *New York Times,* March 29, B6.

Miller, Neil. 2004. *Domestic Violence: A Review of State Legislation Defining Police and Prosecution Duties and Powers*. Alexandria, VA: Institute of Law and Justice. At http://www.ilj.org/publications/DV_Legislation-3.pdf (retrieved September 1, 2007).

Miltimore, Sarah. 2000. "Neonaticide: A Comparison Study of Cases Found in the United States with Cases Found in Britain and Canada." M.S. thesis, University of California at Irvine.

Minkoff, Howard, and Lynn M. Paltrow. 2006. "The Rights of 'Unborn Children' and the Value of Pregnant Women." *Hastings Center Report* 36(2): 26–28.

Mohr, James. 1978. *Abortion in America*. Oxford: Oxford University Press.

"Mom Finds Safe Haven for Infant." 2005. *Boston Herald,* March 19, 6.

Montgomery, Rick. 2006. "Regulating the Rights of the Unborn." *Kansas City Star,* July 9, A1.

Moore, Ken, and Rachel Baum. 2001. *LGBT Domestic Violence in 2000*. New York: National Coalition of Anti-Violence Programs.

Mother Child Community Corrections Project (MCCP). 2001. *Preliminary Mother Child Program Inventory*. Silver Spring, MD: MCCP. At http://www.nicic.org/pubs/2001/016737.pdf (retrieved October 17, 2007).

Moynihan, Daniel P. 1965. *The Negro Family: The Case for National Action*. Washington, DC: U.S. Department of Labor, Office of Planning and Research.

Mullings, Leith. 1997. *On Our Own Terms: Race, Class, and Gender in the Lives of African American Women*. New York: Routledge.

Mumola, Christopher J. 2000. *Incarcerated Parents and Their Children*. NCJ 216340. Washington, DC: U.S. Department of Justice, Bureau of Justice Statistics.

———. 2005. *Suicide and Homicide in State Prisons and Local Jails*. NCJ 210036. Washington, DC: U.S. Department of Justice, Bureau of Justice Statistics.

———. 2007. *Medical Causes of Death in State Prisons, 2001–2004*. NCJ 216340. Washington, DC: U.S. Department of Justice, Bureau of Justice Statistics.

Murphy, Sheigla, and Marsha Rosenbaum. 1999. *Pregnant Women on Drugs.* New Brunswick, NJ: Rutgers University Press.

Murr, Andrew, and Nadine Joseph. 2003. "A Husband in Trouble." *Newsweek,* April 28, 38.

Myers, Barbara J., Tina M. Smarsh, Kristine Amlund-Hagen, and Suzanne Kennon. 1999. "Children of Incarcerated Mothers." *Journal of Child and Family Studies* 8(1): 11–25.

Nahas, Brigitte M. 2001. "Drug Tests, Arrests, and Fetuses: A Comment on the U.S. Supreme Court's Narrow Opinion in *Ferguson v. City of Charleston.*" *Cardozo Women's Law Journal* 8: 105–142.

Nair, Prasanna, Maureen E. Schuler, Maureen M. Black, et al. 2003. "Cumulative Environmental Risk in Substance Abusing Women: Early Intervention, Parenting Stress, Child Abuse Potential and Child Development." *Child Abuse and Neglect* 27(9): 997–1017.

National Abortion Federation. 2006. *NAF Violence and Disruption Statistics.* At http://www.prochoice.org/pubs_research/publications/downloads/about_abortion/violence_statistics.pdf (retrieved October 12, 2006).

National Advocates for Pregnant Women. 2008. Data file shared with the author.

National Association of Social Workers. 2003. *Child Welfare Workforce.* At http://www.socialworkers.org/advocacy/updates/2003/082003_a.asp (retrieved September 1, 2007).

National Cancer Institute. 2003. *Summary Report: Early Reproductive Events and Breast Cancer Workshop.* At www.cancer.gov/cancerinfo/ere-workshop-report (retrieved September 1, 2007).

National Center for Health Statistics. 2005. *Health, United States, 2005.* Washington, DC: U.S. Government Printing Office. At http://www.cdc.gov/nchs/data/hus/hus05.pdf.

———. 2006. *Health, United States, 2006.* Hyattsville, MD: U.S. Government Printing Office.

National Center for State Courts and the National Criminal Justice Association. 2004. *Crossing Borders: Regional Meetings on Implementing Full Faith and Credit.* Washington, DC: Office on Violence against Women.

National Center for Victims of Crime. 2002. *Enforcement of Protective Orders.* NCJ 189190. Washington, DC: Office for Victims of Crime.

National Center on Addiction and Substance Abuse at Columbia University (CASA). 1999. *No Safe Haven: Children of Substance-Abusing Parents.* New York: CASA.

National Clearinghouse on Child Abuse and Neglect Information (NCCANI). 2002. *Current Trends in Child Maltreatment Reporting Laws.* Washington, DC: NCCANI.

———. 2003. *Reporting Child Maltreatment in Cases Involving Parental Substance Abuse.* At http://www.calib.com/nccanch/pubs/usermanuals/subabuse/report.cfm (retrieved October 12, 2006).

National Conference on State Legislatures. 2006. *Fetal Homicide.* At http://www.ncsl.org/public/help.htm (retrieved October 12, 2006).

———. 2007. *Fetal Homicide.* At http://www.ncsl.org/programs/health/fethom.htm (retrieved August 16, 2007).

National Organization for Women. 2005. *Supreme Court Ruling Leaves More Women Vulnerable to Domestic Violence.* Press release. June 28. At http://www.now.org/press/06–05/06–28.html (retrieved September 1, 2007).

National Right to Life Committee. *Unborn Victims of Violence.* At http://www.nrlc.org/Unborn_Victims/index.html (retrieved September 1, 2007).

Needell, B., D. Webster, S. Cuccaro-Alamin, et al. 2005. *Child Welfare Services Reports for California.* University of California at Berkeley, Center for Social Services Research. At http://cssr.berkeley.edu/ucb%5Fchildwelfare/ (retrieved September 1, 2007).

Nelson, Jennifer. 2003. *Women of Color and the Reproductive Rights Movement.* New York: New York University Press.

Neubeck, Kenneth, and Noel Cazenave. 2001. *Welfare Racism: Playing the Race Card against America's Poor.* New York: Routledge.

Newell, Jeff. 2000. "Court: No More Children for Mom." *Northwest Daily News,* February 25, B1.

New York Campaign for Telephone Justice. 2007. *Family Connections Bill Passes in New York State Legislature.* Press release. June 21. At http://www.telephonejustice.org/about/whats_new_content.asp?ID=41 (retrieved September 1, 2007).

New York Civil Liberties Union. 2000. "On Monday to Argue Court Order Prohibiting Former Inmate from Having Abortion Is Unconstitutional." *NYCLU News,* March 5, 2000, n.p. At http://www.nyclu.org/news2000.html (retrieved October 12, 2006).

———. 2004. "Legal Issues in Rochester Ruling." At http://www.nyclu.org/rrp_rochester_ruling_issues_062904.html (retrieved September 1, 2007).

New York State Department of Health, Office of Professional Misconduct and Physician Discipline. At http://www.health.state.ny.us/nysdoh/opmc/main.htm (retrieved September 1, 2007).

NIC/WCL (National Institute of Corrections/American University, Washington College of Law) Project on Addressing Prison Rape. 2006. *State Criminal Laws Prohibiting Sexual Abuse of Individuals in Custody.* Washington, DC: NIC/WCL Project on Addressing Prison Rape.

Nidus, David. 2002. Personal email communication with the author. October 21.

Nieves, Evelyn. 2005. "S.D. Makes Abortion Rare through Laws and Stigma: Out-of-State Doctors Come Weekly to 1 Clinic." *Washington Post,* December 27, A1.

Nossiff, Rosemary. 2007. "Gendered Citizenship: Women, Equality, and Abortion Policy." *New Political Science* 29(1): 61–76.

Notzon, F. C., Y. M. Korotkova, S. P. Ermakov, et al. 1999. "Maternal and Child Health Statistics: Russian Federation and United States, Selected Years, 1985–95." *Vital and Health Statistics.* Washington, DC: National Center for Health Statistics.

Nuckols, Christina. 2005. "Del. Cosgrove Pulls Bill after Internet Fuels Fiery Protest." *Norfolk Virgininian Pilot,* January 11, B1.

Oakley, Ann. 1984. *The Captured Womb: A History of the Medical Care of Pregnant Women.* Oxford: Basil Blackwell.

Oberman, Michelle. 2003. "Lady Madonna, Children at Your Feet: Tragedies at the Intersection of Motherhood, Mental Illness and the Law." *William and Mary Journal of Women and Law* 33: 35–67.

———. 2004. "Mothers Who Kill: Coming to Terms with Modern American Infanticide." *DePaul Journal of Health Care Law* 8: 3–107.

O'Brien, Charles P., and Thomas A. McLellan. 1996. "Myths about Addiction." *Lancet* 347(8996): 237–240.

O'Brien, Patricia. 2001. *Making It in the "Free World": Women in Transition from Prison.* Albany: SUNY Press.

———. 2002. *Reducing Barriers to Employment for Women Ex-offenders: Mapping the Road to Reintegration.* Chicago: SAFER Foundation Council of Advisors to Reduce Recidivism through Employment.

O'Connell, Patrick M. 2006. "Delicate Balancing Act: Local Case Highlights Problems in Court Rulings—Visitation Rights for Imprisoned Fathers." *South Bend Tribune,* April 30.

O'Connor, Julia S., Ann Shola Orloff, and Sheila Shaver. 1999. *States, Markets, Families: Gender, Liberalism and Social Policy in Australia, Canada, Great Britain and the United States.* Cambridge: Cambridge University Press.

Odem, Mary. 1995. *Delinquent Daughters: Protecting and Policing Adolescent Female Sexuality in the United States, 1885–1920.* Chapel Hill: University of North Carolina Press.

Office of Justice Programs. 2006. *Frequently Asked Questions on AMBER Alert.* At http://www.amberalert.gov/faqs.html (retrieved September 1, 2007).

Office of Management and Budget. 2006. *Budget of the United States Government.* Washington, DC.: Government Printing Office. At http://frwebgate5.access.gpo.gov/cgi-bin/waisgate.cgi?WAISdocID=008454473655+6+0+0&WAISaction=retrieve pp. 66, 72 (retrieved June 15, 2007).

Oransky, Ivan. 2003. "U.S. Congress Passes 'Partial-Birth Abortion' Ban." *Lancet* 363: 1464.

Ordover, Nancy. 2003. *American Eugenics: Race, Queer Anatomy, and the Science of Nationalism.* Minneapolis: University of Minnesota Press.

O'Sullivan, Chris S., Lori A. King, Kyla Levin-Russell, and Emily Horowitz. 2006. *Supervised and Unsupervised Parental Access in Domestic Violence Cases: Court Orders and Consequences.* New York: Safe Horizon.

Otto, R. K., and J. F. Edens. 2003. "Parenting Capacity." Pp. 229–30 in *Evaluating Competencies: Forensic Assessments and Instruments,* ed. T. Grisso, R. Borum, J. F. Edens, et al. New York: Kluwer Academic/Plenum.

Owen, Barbara. 1998. *"In the Mix": Struggle for Survival in a Women's Prison.* Albany: SUNY Press.

Pacenti, John. 2004. "Prenatal Care at Jail Criticized." *Palm Beach Post,* May 9, 1C.

Padawer, Ruth. 2006. "Lives after Death: Baby-Killing Drama Still Haunts Some of Those It Touched." *Bergen County (NJ) Record,* November 12, A1.

Paltrow, Lynn M. 1992. *Criminal Prosecutions against Pregnant Women: National Update and Overview.* New York: American Civil Liberties Union, Reproductive Freedom Project.

———. 1999. "Pregnant Drug Users, Fetal Persons, and the Threat to *Roe v. Wade.*" *Albany Law Review* 62: 999–1054.

———. 2001. "The War on Drugs and the War on Abortion." *Southern Law Review* 28(3): 201–253.

———. 2006. *Background Concerning* Ferguson et al. v. City of Charleston et al. At http://advocatesforpregnantwomen.org/issues/criminal_cases_and_issues/background_concerning_ferguson_et_al_v_city_of_charleston_et_al.php (retrieved September 1, 2007).

Petchesky, Rosalind Pollack. 1990. *Abortion and Woman's Choice: The State, Sexuality, and Reproductive Freedom*, 2nd ed. Boston: Northeastern University Press.

Pierre, Robert. 2004. "In Ohio, Supreme Court Considers Right to Procreate." *Washington Post*, May 11, A2.

Pilcher, C.D., H. Tien, J.J. Eron Jr., et al. 2004. "Brief but Efficient: Acute HIV Transmission and the Sexual Transmission of HIV." *Journal of Infectious Diseases* 189(10): 1785–1792.

Pollitt, Katha. 2004. "Pregnant and Dangerous." *Nation*, April 26.

Pollock, Joycelyn M. 2002. "Parenting Programs in Women's Prisons." *Women and Criminal Justice* 14(1): 131–154.

Pollock, Katie, with Lupe Hittle. 2003. *Baby Abandonment: The Role of Child Welfare Systems*. Washington, DC: Child Welfare League of America Press.

"Pregnant Woman Charged with Attempting to Abort Fetus." 2007. *Associated Press Wire Service*, April 11.

Project Cuddle. 2007. *No Baby Deserves to Die before Having a Chance to Live*. Los Angeles: Project Cuddle. At www.projectcuddle.org (retrieved September 1, 2007).

Project Prevention. "Statistics." At http://www.projectprevention.org/ (retrieved January 10, 2008).

Pursley-Crotteau, Suzanne, and Phyllis Noerager Stern. 1996. "Creating a New Life: Dimensions of Temperance in Prenatal Cocaine Crack Users." *Qualitative Health Research* 6(3): 350–367.

Radelet, Michael L., and Ronald L. Akers. 1996. "Deterrence and the Death Penalty: The Views of the Experts." *Journal of Criminal Law and Criminology* 87(1): 1–16.

Rafter, Nicole Hahn. 1992. *Partial Justice: Women, Prisons, and Social Control*. New Brunswick, NJ: Transaction.

———. 1997. *Creating Born Criminals*. Urbana: University of Illinois Press.

Raghavan, Ramesh, Laura Bogart, Marc Elliott, et al. 2004. "Sexual Victimization among a National Probability Sample of Adolescent Women." *Perspectives on Sexual and Reproductive Health* 36(6): 225–232.

Rai, Raj, and Lesley Regan. 2006. "Recurrent Miscarriage." *Lancet* 368: 601–611.

Raimon, Martha L. 2001. "Barriers to Achieving Justice for Incarcerated Parents." *Fordham University Law Review* 70: 421–426.

Raines, Mary. 2001. "Defending Motherhood: Battered Women Losing Their Children to Our Child Protection System." *Children's Legal Rights Journal* 21(3): 17–24.

Reagan, Leslie J. 1997. *When Abortion Was a Crime: Women, Medicine, and Law in the United States, 1867–1973*. Berkeley: University of California Press.

"Receiver Ordered for Prison Health System." 2005. *New York Times*, July 1.

Reeves, Jimmie L., and Richard Campbell. 1994. *Cracked Coverage: Television News, the Anti-Cocaine Crusade, and the Reagan Legacy*. Durham, NC: Duke University Press.

Reich, Jennifer. 2005. *Fixing Families: Parents, Power, and the Child Welfare System*. New York: Routledge.

Reiman, Jeffrey. 2007. *The Rich Get Richer and the Poor Get Prison.* New York: Allyn and Bacon.

Reinhold, Robert. 1980. "Virginia Hospital's Chief Traces 50 Years of Sterilizing the 'Retarded.'" *New York Times,* February 23, 6.

Rennison, Callie Marie. 2003. *Intimate Partner Violence, 1993–2001.* Washington, DC: U.S. Department of Justice, Bureau of Justice Statistics.

Rennison, Callie, and Mike Planty. 2003. "Nonlethal Intimate Partner Violence: Examining Race, Gender, and Income Patterns." *Violence and Victims* 18(4): 433–443.

Rhoden, Nancy K. 1986. "The Judge in the Delivery Room: The Emergence of Court-Ordered Cesareans." *California Law Review* 74: 1951–2030.

Rhor, Monica. 2006. "Orders Often Fail to Restrain Violence." *Orange County Register,* March 18.

Rich, Adrienne. 1984 [1977]. *Of Woman Born: Motherhood as Experience and Institution.* London: Virago.

Rich, Eric. 2006. "Bomb Suspect's Father Tipped Off Authorities." *Washington Post,* June 10, B1.

Richardson, Chinué Turner, and Cynthia Dailard. 2005. "Politicizing Statutory Rape Reporting Requirements: A Mounting Campaign?" *Guttmacher Report on Public Policy.* At www.guttmacher.org/pubs/tgr/08/3/gr080301.pdf (retrieved January 21, 2008).

Richardson, Chinué Turner, and Elizabeth Nash. 2006. "Misinformed Consent: The Medical Accuracy of State-Developed Abortion Counseling Materials." *Guttmacher Policy Review* 9(4): 6–11.

Richie, Beth E. 1996. *Compelled to Crime: The Gender Entrapment of Battered Black Women.* New York: Routledge.

Riger, Stephanie, and Susan Staggs. 2004. *The Impact of Intimate Partner Violence on Women's Labor Force Participation.* NIJ 207143. Washington, DC: National Institute of Justice. At http://www.ncjrs.gov/pdffiles1/nij/grants/207143.pdf (retrieved September 1, 2007).

Rivera, Jenny. 1997. "Domestic Violence against Latinas by Latino Males: An Analysis of Race, National Origin, and Gender Differentials." Pp. 259–266 in *Critical Race Feminism: A Reader,* ed. Adrien Katherine Wing. New York: New York University Press.

Roberts, Dorothy E. 1996. "Welfare and the Problem of Black Citizenship." *Yale Law Journal* 105: 1563–1602.

———. 1998. *Killing the Black Body: Race, Reproduction, and the Meaning of Liberty.* New York: Vintage.

———. 2002. *Shattered Bonds: The Color of Child Welfare.* New York: Basic Civitas.

"Robert Weiler Indicted on Charges of Possessing, Making Unregistered Destructive Device" (2006), *U.S. Federal News,* June 19, n.p.

Rose, Nancy. 2000. "Scapegoating Poor Women: An Analysis of Welfare Reform." *Journal of Economic Issues* 34: 143–157.

Rosenblatt, Roger. 1992. *Life Itself: Abortion in the American Mind.* New York: Random House.

Rosenfeld, Barry D. 1992. "Court-Ordered Treatment of Spouse Abuse." *Clinical Psychology Review* 12: 205–226.

Rosenthal, M. Sara. 2003. *The Gynecological Sourcebook*. New York: McGraw-Hill.

Rosing, Mark A., and Cheryl D. Archbald. 2000. "The Knowledge, Acceptability, and Use of Misoprostol for Self-Induced Medical Abortion in an Urban US Population." *Journal of the American Medical Women's Association* 55(3): 183–185.

Ross, Barbara. 2005. "Beau's Guilty of Killing His Girlfriend Refused Abortion." *New York Daily News*, April 8, A1.

Ross, Timothy, Ajay Khashu, and Mark Wamsley. 2004. *Hard Data on Hard Times: An Empirical Analysis of Maternal Incarceration, Foster Care, and Visitation*. New York: Vera Institute of Justice.

Roth, Rachel. 2000. *Making Women Pay: The Hidden Costs of Fetal Rights*. Ithaca, NY: Cornell University Press.

———. 2004a. "Do Prisoners Have Abortion Rights?" *Feminist Studies* 30(2): 353–381.

———. 2004b. "'No New Babies?' Gender Inequality and Reproductive Control in the Criminal Justice and Prison Systems." *Journal of Gender, Social Policy and the Law* 12(3): 391–425.

Roth, Rachel. 2004c. "Searching for the State: Who Governs Prisoners' Reproductive Rights?" *Social Politics: International Studies in Gender, State and Society* 11(3): 411–438.

Rothman, Barbara Katz. 1989. *Recreating Motherhood: Ideology and Technology in a Patriarchal Society*. New York: Norton.

———. 2005. *Weaving a Family: Untangling Race and Adoption*. Boston: Beacon.

Rubin, Paul. 2004. "No Choice Scenes from a 'Clown Show.'" *Phoenix New Times*, January 8.

Ruhl, Lealle. 2002. "Dilemmas of the Will: Uncertainty, Reproduction, and the Rhetoric of Control." *Signs* 27(3): 641–663.

Sabol, William J., Todd D. Minton, and Paige M. Harrison. 2007. *Prison and Jail Inmates at Midyear 2006*. Washington, DC: U.S. Department of Justice.

Sack, Emily J. 2004. "Domestic Violence across State Lines: The Full Faith and Credit Clause, Congressional Power, and Interstate Enforcement of Protection Orders." *Northwestern University Law Review* 98(3): 827–906.

Sage, Alexandria. 2004. "Woman Charged with Murder after Allegedly Refusing C-Section: She Denies She Feared Scars." *Associated Press*, March 12.

Saletan, William. 2003. *Bearing Right: How Conservatives Won the Abortion War*. Los Angeles: University of California Press.

Saltzman, Linda E., Christopher H. Johnson, Brenda Colley Gilbert, and Mary M. Goodwin. 2003. "Physical Abuse around the Time of Pregnancy: An Examination of Prevalence and Risk Factors in 16 States." *Maternal and Child Health Journal* 7(1): 31–43.

Sanger, Margaret. 1920. *Women and the New Race*. New York: Brentano's. At http://infomotions.com/etexts/gutenberg/dirs/etext05/7wmnr10.htm (retrieved January 20, 2008).

Santora, Marc. 2004. "Albany Court Reverses Rule on Stillbirths." *New York Times*, April 2.

Saulny, Susan. 2007. "Abortion Charges Filed against Kansas Clinic." *New York Times*, October 18, A26.

Schiller, Cassandra, and Pat Jackson Allen. 2005. "Follow-Up of Infants Prenatally Exposed to Cocaine." *Pediatric Nursing* 31(5): 427–436.

Schoen, Johanna. 2005. *Choice and Coercion: Birth Control, Sterilization, and Abortion in Public Health and Welfare.* Chapel Hill: University of North Carolina Press.

Schrock, Douglas P., and Irene Padavic. 2007. "Negotiating Hegemonic Masculinity in a Batterer Intervention Program." *Gender and Society* 21(5): 625–649.

SEICUS. 2005. *In Their Own Words: What Abstinence-Only-Until-Marriage Programs Say.* At http://www.siecus.org/policy/in_their_own_words.pdf (retrieved September 1, 2007).

Senate Judiciary Committee. 2005. *CS for Senate Bill No. 20. JUD,* April 21.Sentivan, Jennifer R. 2006. "Parent and Child: The Mother's Parental Rights Were Improperly Terminated under the Facts of This Case." *New Jersey Lawyer* 15(7): 22.

"Sex, Contraband to Private Prison for Women." 2005. *Casper Star Tribune,* February 25.

Shafer, Jack. 2006. "How Not to Report about Meth." *Slate.* March 21. At http://www.slate.com/id/2133898/ (retrieved January 28, 2008). See also "Why Does Drug Reporting Suck?" (August 10, 2005); "Methamphetamine Propaganda" (March 3, 2006); and "Pfft Goes the Methedemic" (July 1, 2006).

———. 2007. "About That Methedemic." *Slate.* January 31. At http://www.slate.com/id/2148739l (retrieved January 21, 2008).

Shane, Brian. 1999. "Restraining Order Loophole Enrages Committee Members." *Capital News Service.* November 30. At http://www.newsline.umd.edu/crimeold/spickna1112.htm (retrieved September 1, 2007).

Sharp, David. 2007. "Plea Deal Approved in Parental Abduction Case in Maine." *Associated Press,* October 12.

Shear, Beatrix. 1999. *Termination of Parental Rights.* Edison: Legal Services of New Jersey. At http://www.acwc.org/intranet/DV%20Toolkit/termparentrights.pdf (retrieved September 1, 2007).

Shilton, Mary K. 2000. *Resources for Mother-Child Community Corrections.* LaCrosse, WI: International Community Corrections Association.

Silverman, Jay G., Cynthia M. Mesh, Carrie V. Cuthbert, et al. 2004. "Child Custody Determinations in Cases Involving Intimate Partner Violence: A Human Rights Analysis." *American Journal of Public Health* 94(5): 951–957.

Silverstein, Helena. 2007. *Girls on the Stand: How Courts Fail Pregnant Minors.* New York: New York University Press.

Simon, Stephanie. 2006. "Kansas Judge Dismisses Abortion Charges." *Los Angeles Times,* December 23, A22.

Sinclair, Norman, Melvin Claxton, and Ronald J. Hansen. 2005a. "Michigan Faces Conflict of Interest." *Detroit News,* May 24.

———. 2005b. "Prisoner Complaints Unheeded." *Detroit News,* May 24.

Singer, Amy. 2002. "Investigation: Girls Sentenced to Abuse." *Marie Claire* (June).

Skolnik, Sam. 2004. "Woman Pleads Guilty in Death of Newborn." *Seattle Intelligencer,* September 14, B4.

Slater, Lyn. 2006. Personal email communication with the author. April 10.

Smith, Gordon C. S., Jill P. Pell, and Richard Dobbie. 2003. "Cesarean Section and Risk of Unexplained Stillbirth in Subsequent Pregnancy." *Lancet* 362: 1779–1784.

Smith, Leslie. 2004. "Sexual Abuse in Prison." Unpublished ms., Fordham University.

Smithey, Martha. 2001. "Maternal Infanticide and Modern Motherhood." *Women and Criminal Justice* 13(1): 65–83.

Snell, Tracy L. 1994. *Women in Prison*. Washington, DC: U.S. Department of Justice, Bureau of Justice Statistics.

Snyder, Howard N. 2000. *Sexual Assault of Young Children Reported to Law Enforcement*. Washington, DC: U.S. Department of Justice, Bureau of Justice Statistics.

Snyder, H., T. Finnegan, and W. Kang. 2006. "Easy Access to the FBI's Supplementary Homicide Reports: 1980–2003." Federal Bureau of Investigation. *Supplementary Homicide Reports* 1980–2003. Machine-readable data files. At http://ojjdp.ncjrs.org/ ojstatbb/ezashr/ (retrieved September 1, 2007).

Society of Adolescent Medicine. 2004. "Confidential Health Care for Adolescents: A Position Paper of the Society for Adolescent Medicine." *Journal of Adolescent Health* 35(5): 420–423.

Solinger, Rickie. 2001. *Beggars and Choosers: How the Politics of Choice Shapes Adoption, Abortion, and Welfare in the United States*. New York: Hill and Wang.

———. 2005. *Pregnancy and Power: A Short History of Reproductive Politics in America*. New York: New York University Press.

"Some Fear Popularity Is Weakening Amber Alerts." 2006. *New York Times*, March 19, A21.

Spinelli, Margaret G. 2001. "A Systematic Investigation of 16 Cases of Neonaticide." *American Journal of Psychiatry* 158: 811–813.

Stahly, Geraldine Butts. 1999. "Women with Children in Violent Relationships: The Choice of Leaving May Bring the Consequence of Custodial Challenge." *Journal of Aggression, Maltreatment and Trauma* 2(4): 239–251.

Stansell, Christine. 2007. "A Lost History of Abortion." *New Republic* 236(17): 12–14.

"State Fights Gun Lawsuit by Child-Killer's Ex-Wife." 2003. *Annapolis (MD) Capital*, July 16.

Steensma, C., J. F. Boivin, L. Blais, and E. Roy. 2005. "Cessation of Injecting Drug Use among Street-Based Youth." *Journal of Urban Health* 82(4): 622–637.

Stein, Theodore. 2000. "The Adoption and Safe Families Act: Creating a False Dichotomy between Parents' and Childrens' Rights." *Families in Society* 81: 586–592.

Stemp-Morlock, G. 2007. "Reproductive Health: Pesticides and Anencephaly." *Environmental Health Perspectives* 115(2): A78

Sterk, Claire E. 1999. *Fast Lives: Women Who Use Crack Cocaine*. Philadelphia: Temple University Press.

Sterngold, James, and Mark Martin. 2005. "Hard Time: California's Prisons in Crisis." *San Francisco Chronicle*, July 3, A1.

St. George, Donna. 2004a. "Many New or Expectant Mothers Die Violent Deaths." *Washington Post*, December 19, A1.

———. 2004b. "Violence Intersects Lives of Promise." *Washington Post*, December 20, A1.

Stoller, Nancy. 2001. *Improving Access to Health Care for California's Women Prisoners*. Santa Cruz: California Policy Research Center. At http://prisonerswithchildren.org/ pubs/stoller.pdf (retrieved September 1, 2007).

Strauss, Lilo, Joy Herndon, Jeani Chang, et al. 2005. *Abortion Surveillance: United States, 2002.* Atlanta: Centers for Disease Control and Prevention, National Center for Chronic Disease Prevention and Health Promotion, Division of Reproductive Health.

Strauss, Lilo T., Sonya B. Gamble, Wilda Y. Parker, et al., 2006. "Abortion Surveillance: United States, 2003." *Morbidity and Mortality Weekly Report* 55(S S11): 1–32.

Struckman-Johnson, Cindy, and David Struckman-Johnson. 2006. "A Comparison of Sexual Coercion Experiences Reported by Men and Women in Prison." *Journal of Interpersonal Violence* 21: 1591–1615.

Substance Abuse and Mental Health Services Administration. 2006a. *National Survey on Drug Use and Health, 2004 and 2005.* Rockville, MD: Office of Applied Studies, U.S. Department of Health and Human Services.

———. 2006b. *Results from the 2005 National Survey on Drug Use and Health: National Findings.* Rockville, MD: U.S Department of Health and Human Services, Office of Applied Studies.

Sullivan, Eileen, Milton Mino, and Katherine Nelson. 2002. *Families as a Resource in Recovery from Drug Abuse: An Evaluation of La Bodega de la Familia.* New York: Vera Institute of Justice.

Sullivan, John R. 2000. "Judge Temporarily Bars County Inmate from Having Abortion." *New York Times,* March 4, B2.

Sylvester, Ron. 2008. "Grand Jury Sworn in to Investigate Wichita Abortions." *Wichita Eagle,* January 8, n.p.

Task Force on Local Criminal Justice Response to Domestic Violence. 2005. *Keeping the Promise: Victim Safety and Batterer Accountability.* Sacramento, CA: Office of the Attorney General.

Taylor, Diane. 2006. "Women: The Pregnancy Police Are Watching You." *Guardian* (London), September 6.

Taylor, Humphrey. 2000. "The Public Tends to Blame the Poor, the Unemployed, and Those on Welfare for Their Problems." *Harris Poll,* May 3. At http://www.harrisinteractive.com/harris_poll/index.asp?PID=87 (retrieved January 21, 2008)

Termorshuizen, F., A. Krol, M. Prins, and E. J. C. van Ameijden. 2005. "Long-Term Outcome of Chronic Drug Use: The Amsterdam Cohort Study among Drug Users." *American Journal of Epidemiology* 161(3): 271–279.

Texas Department of Criminal Justice. 2006. *Women on Death Row.* At http://www.tdcj.state.tx.us/stat/womenondrow.htm (retrieved October 12, 2006).

Thorne, Barrie. 1992. "Feminism and the Family: Two Decades of Thought." Pp. 1–30 in *Rethinking the Family: Two Decades of Thought,* 2nd ed., ed. Barrie Thorne and M. Yalom. Boston: Northeastern University Press.

Thornton, Terry E., and Lynn Paltrow. 1991. "The Rights of Pregnant Patients: Carder Case Brings Bold Policy Initiatives." *HealthSpan* 8(5): n.p. At http://advocatesforpregnantwomen.org/articles/angela.htm (retrieved October 12, 2006).

Tough, Suzanne C., Christine Newburn-Cook, David W. Johnston, et al. 2002. "Delayed Childbearing and Its Impact on Population Rate Changes in Lower Birth Weight, Multiple Birth, and Preterm Delivery." *Pediatrics* 109(3): 399–403.

Trenholm, Christopher, Barbara Devaney, Ken Forson, et al. 2007. *Impacts of Four Title V, Section 510 Abstinence Education Programs*. Princeton, NJ: Mathematica Police Research.

Tribe, Lawrence H. 1990. *Abortion: The Clash of Absolutes*. New York: Norton.

Trocme, Nico, and Nicholas Bala. 2005. "False Allegations of Abuse and Neglect When Parents Separate." *Child Abuse and Neglect* 29(12): 1333–1345.

Troup-Leasure, Karyl, and Howard Snyder. 2005. *Statutory Rape Known to Law Enforcement*. Washington, DC: U.S. Department of Justice, Office of Justice Programs.

Turner, Bryan. 2001. "The Erosion of Citizenship." *British Journal of Sociology* 52(2001): 189–209.

"Two Infants Found in Trash, and a Darker Tale Unfolds." 2005. *New York Times*, September 17.

U.S. Cancer Statistics Working Group. 2006. United States Cancer Statistics: 2003 Incidence and *Mortality Web-Based Report*. Atlanta: U.S. Department of Health and Human Services, Centers for Disease Control and Prevention and National Cancer Institute. At www.cdc.gov/cancer/npcr/uscs (retrieved June 12, 2007).

U.S. Census Bureau. 2006. *Table 2: Annual Estimates of the Population by Selected Age Groups and Sex for the United States: April 1, 2000 to July 1, 2005*. NC-EST2005-02. Washington, DC: Population Division, U.S. Census Bureau.

U.S. Department of Health and Human Services. 2001. *Women and Smoking: A Report of the Surgeon General*. Atlanta: U.S. Department of Health and Human Services, Public Health Service, Centers for Disease Control and Prevention, National Center for Chronic Disease Prevention and Health Promotion, Office on Smoking and Health.

———. 2003. *Drug Use among Racial/Ethnic Minorities*. Bethesda, MD: National Institute on Drug Abuse.

U.S. Department of Health and Human Services. 2005. *Depression during and after Pregnancy*. At http://www.4woman.gov/faq/postpartum.htm (retrieved January 21, 2008).

———. 2006. *The AFCARS Report*. Washington, DC: Administration for Children and Families, Administration on Children, Youth and Families, Children's Bureau. At www.acf.hhs.gov/programs/cb and http://www.acf.hhs.gov/programs/cb/stats_research/afcars/tar/report13.htm (retrieved September 1, 2007).

U.S. Department of Health and Human Services, Administration on Children, Youth and Families. 2006. *Child Maltreatment 2004*. Washington, DC: U.S. Government Printing Office.

———. 2007. *Child Maltreatment 2005*. Washington, DC: U.S. Government Printing Office.

U.S. General Accounting Office. 1999. *Women in Prison: Issues and Challenges Confronting U.S. Correctional Systems*. Washington, DC: General Accounting Office.

———. 2002. *Violence against Women: Data on Pregnant Victims and Effectiveness of Prevention Strategies Are Limited*. Washington, DC: U.S. General Accounting Office.

———. 2003. *HHS Could Play a Greater Role in Helping Child Welfare Agencies Recruit and Retain Staff*. Washington, DC: U.S. General Accounting Office.

U.S. Government Printing Office. 2006. *Budget of the United States Government: Public Budget Database, Fiscal Year 2006.* At http://www.gpoaccess.gov/usbudget/fyo6/browse.html (retrieved September 1, 2007).

U.S. House of Representatives. 2006. *False and Misleading Health Information Provided by Federally Funded Pregnancy Resource Centers.* Washington, DC: Committee on Government Reform–Minority Staff. At http://www.democrats.reform.house.gov/Documents/20060717101140-30092.pdf (retrieved September 1, 2007).

U.S. Standard Certificate of Death. Rev. November 2003. At http://www.cdc.gov/nchs/data/dvs/DEATH11-03final-ACC.pdf (retrieved October 22, 2007).

Vallone, Doris, and Lori Hoffman. 2003. "Preventing the Tragedy of Neonaticide." *Holistic Nursing Practice* 17: 223–228.

VanNatta, Michelle. 2005. "Constructing the Battered Woman." *Feminist Studies* 31(2): 416–443.

Vaughn, Michael, and Leo Carroll. 1998. "Separate and Unequal: Prison versus Free-World Medical Care." *Justice Quarterly* 15(1): 3–41.

Ventura, Stephanie, Joyce C. Abma, William D. Mosher, and Stanley Henshaw. 2003. "Trends in Pregnancy Rates, 1976–1997, and New Rates for 1998–1999: United States." *National Vital Statistics Reports* 52(7): 1–15.

Vestal, Christine. 2007. *States Probe Limits of Abortion Policy.* June 11. At http://www.stateline.org/live/ViewPage.action?siteNodeId=136&languageId=1&contentId=121780 (retrieved September 13, 2007).

Vestal, Christine, and Elizabeth Wilkerson. 2006. *States Expand Fetal Homicide Laws.* At http://www.stateline.org/live/details/story?contentId=135873 (retrieved October 12, 2006).

Vintzileos, Anthony M., Cande V. Ananth, John C. Smulian, et al. 2002. "Prenatal Care and Black–White Fetal Death Disparity in the United States: Heterogeneity by High-Risk Conditions." *Obstetrics and Gynecology* 99: 483–489.

Von Zielbauer, Paul. 2005a. "As Health Care in Jails Goes Private, 10 Days Can Be a Death Sentence." *New York Times,* February 27.

———. 2005b. "Company's Troubled Answer for Prisoners with H.I.V." *New York Times,* August 1, A1.

———. 2005c. "In City's Jails, Missed Signals Open Way to Season Suicides." *New York Times,* February 28, A1.

———. 2005d. "Investigators Called Rikers Medical Contract Illegal, State Panel Says." *New York Times,* November 22, B1.

———, Paul. 2005e. "A Spotty Record of Health Care at Juvenile Sites in New York." *New York Times,* March 1, A1.

Walton, Val. 2002. "Most Sex Abuse Claims Dropped in DYS Lawsuit." *Birmingham News,* April 12.

Warren, Beth. 2005. "Calls, Emails Hammer DA on Sterilization Case." *Atlanta Journal-Constitution,* February 18, 20E.

Warren, Jenifer. 2005a. "The State: Rethinking Treatment of Female Prisoners." *Los Angeles Times,* June 19, A1.

———. 2005b. "U.S. to Seize State Prison Health System." *Los Angeles Times,* July 1, A1.

Wasow, Nina. 2006. "Planned Failure: California's Denial of Reunification Services to Parents with Mental Disabilities." *New York University Review of Law and Social Change* 31: 183–224.

Wayne, Alex. 2002. "Child's Parents Avoid Prison Term: A Superior Court Judge Says Christian Eddins' Parents Aren't Wholly to Blame for His Death." *Greensboro (NC) News and Record,* August 2, B1.

Weatherhead, K. 2003. "Cruel but Not Unusual Punishment: The Failure to Provide Adequate Medical Treatment to Women in the United States." *Health Matrix: Journal of Law and Medicine* 13(2): 429–472.

Weber, Ellen M. 2007. "Child Welfare Interventions for Drug-Dependent Pregnant Women: Limitations of a Non-Public Health Response." *University of Missouri UMKC Law Review* 75: 789–845.

Weir, James W. 1929. "West Virginia Aims at Crime Reduction." *New York Times,* May 12, E2.

Weiss, Harold B., Bruce A. Lawrence, and Ted R. Miller. 2004. "Pregnancy-Associated Assault Hospitalizations: Prevalence and Risk of Hospitalized Assaults against Women during Pregnancy." *Obstetrics and Gynecology* 100(4): 773–780.

Weissenstein, Michael. 2005. "NY Jails Ban Forced Exams for Women." *Associated Press,* July 14, n.p.

Welborn, Vickie. 2004. "Mother Pleads Guilty: Woman Negligent in Baby's Death Agrees to Sterilization." *Shreveport Times,* November 5, A1.

Wells, Susan J. 1994. "Child Protective Services: Research for the Future." *Child Welfare* 73(5): 431–447.

Whitlock, Craig. 1999. "Lapses in Gun Check Decried: Legislators Scold Md. Police Agencies." *Washington Post,* November 23.

Wilcox, Joyce. 2002. "The Face of Women's Health: Helen Rodriguez-Trias." *American Journal of Public Health* 92: 566–569.

Wilgoren, Jodi. 2005. "Kansas Prosecutor Demands Files on Late-Term Abortion Patients." *New York Times,* February 25.

"Woman Faces Charges for Performing Abortion on Self." 2005. *Columbia State,* May 1, B3.

Women in Prison Project. 2004. *Coalition for Women Prisoners: Proposals for Reform.* New York: Correctional Association of New York.

———. 2006a. *Bedford Hills Correctional Facility.* New York: Correctional Association of New York.

———. 2006b. *When "Free" Means Losing Your Mother: The Collision of Child Welfare and the Incarceration of Women in New York State.* New York: Correctional Association of New York

———. 2007. *Imprisonment and Families Fact Sheet.* New York: Correctional Association of New York.

Women's Advocacy Project. 2005. *Policy Recommendations: Making Family Reunification a Reality for Criminal Justice-Involved Women.* New York: Women's Prison Association. At http://66.29.139.159/pdf/Recommendations_2005.pdf (retrieved September 1, 2007).

Wood, Jennifer K. 2005. "In Whose Name? Crime Victim Policy and the Punishing Power of Protection." *NWSA (National Women's Study Association) Journal* 17(3): 1–17.

Wood, Michelle, Susie Gilligan, Patty Campos, and Daisy Kim. 2006. *2005 National Clinic Violence Survey.* Arlington, VA: Feminist Majority Foundation.

Workowski, Kimberly A., and Stuart M. Berman. 2006. "Sexually Transmitted Diseases Treatment Guidelines 2006." *Morbidity and Mortality Weekly Report* 51(RR-6): 1–94.

Wright, Alexi A., and Ingrid T. Katz. 2006. "*Roe* versus Reality: Abortion and Women's Health." *New England Journal of Medicine* 355: 1–9.

Young, Diane S., and Carrie Jefferson Smith. 2000. "When Moms Are Incarcerated: The Needs of Children, Mothers, and Caregivers." *Families in Society* 81(2): 130–141.

Zehnder, Christopher. 2003. "Not Medicine, but Social Control." *Los Angeles Mission.* At http://www.losangelesmission.com/ed/articles/2003/1103cz.htm (retrieved September 1, 2007).

Zernike, Kate. 2005. "A Drug Scourge Creates Its Own Form of Orphan." *New York Times,* July 11.

Ziegler, Michael. 2005. "No-More-Kids" Judge Orders Another Mom: Stop Procreating." *Rochester (NY) Democrat and Chronicle,* January 5.

Zitner, Aaron. 2003. "Abortion Foes Attack *Roe* on New Research: As Science Advances, Some Find Arenas in Which to Seek a Special Status Denied the Embryo and Fetus in the High Court's 1973 Ruling." *Los Angeles Times,* January 19, A1.

Zollo, Nina, and Robin Thompson. 2006. "Protecting Victims of Domestic Violence in the Parenting Coordination Process." *Commission on Domestic Violence Quarterly Newsletter* 2: 1–3. At http://www.abanet.org/domviol/enewsletter/vo12/ProtectingVictimsofDVinPCprocess.pdf (retrieved September 1, 2007).

COURT CASES

ACLU Fund of Michigan (2003), amicus brief filed in *Family Independence Agency v. Renee Gamez* (1999)

American College of Obstetricians and Gynecologists (2006), amicus brief filed in *Gonzales v. Carhart, et al.,* 550 U.S. _____ (2007), 05-380/1382

Amador v. Superintendents of the Department of Correctional Services (S.D.N.Y., Sept. 13, 2005)

Bradwell v. State, 83 U.S. 130 (1873)

Brown v. Beck, 481 F. Supp. 723 (S.D. Ga., 1980)

Buck v. Bell, 274 U.S. 200 (1927)

Department of Housing and Urban Development v. Rucker, consolidated with Oakland Hous. Auth. v. Rucker et al., 535 U.S. 125 (2002)

Doe v. Arpaio, et al., 214 Ariz. 237 (2007)

Doe v. Bolton, 410 U.S. 179; 93 S. Ct. 739 (1973)

Eisenstadt v. Baird, 405 U.S. 438; 92 S. Ct. 1029 (1972)

Estelle v. Gamble, 429 U.S. 97; 97 S. Ct. 285 (1976)

Ex parte Anonymous, 905 So. 2d 845 (2005)

Family Independence Agency v. Renee Gamez, Mich. App. LEXIS 2529 (2003) (unpublished opinion)

Ferguson v. City of Charleston, 532 U.S. 67; 121 S. Ct. 1281 (2001)

Gonzales v. Carhart, 127 S. Ct. 1610; 167 L. Ed. 2d 480 (2007)

Gonzales v. Carhart, et al., 550 U.S. ___ (2007)

Gonzales v. City of Castle Rock, 545 U.S. 748; 125 S. Ct. 2796; 366 F.3d 1093 (10th Cir. Colo., 2005)

Harris v. McRae, 448 U.S. 297 (1980)

In the Matter of the Adoption of A.M.B., 812 A.2d 659 (Pennsylvania Superior Court, Oct. 17, 2002)

Keevan v. Smith, 100 F.3d 644 (8th Cir., 1996)

Kidd v. Andrews, 340 F. Supp. 2d 333. U.S. Dist. (W.D.N.Y., 2004)

Klinger v. Department of Corrections, 107 F.3d. 609 (8th Cir., 1997)

Laube v. Haley, 242 F. Supp. 2d 1150 (M.D. Ala., 2003)

Maher v. Roe, 432 U.S. 464; 97 S. Ct. 2376 (1977) (Brennan, J., dissenting)

Matter of Bobbijean P., In re Bobbijean P., N.Y. Slip Op. 7173 (2007); N.Y. App. Div. (2004); No. NN 03626-03, N.Y. Slip Op. 50286(U) (2004) (Fam. Ct., Monroe County, Mar. 31, 2004)

Monmouth County Correctional Institutional Inmates v. Lanzaro, 834 F.2d 326 (1987)

National Abortion Federation v. Ashcroft, 330 F. Supp. 2d 436, LEXIS 17084 (S.D.N.Y., 2004)

Nicholson v. Scoppetta, 820 N.E. 2d 840 (N.Y., 2004)

N.J. Division of Youth and Family Services v. S.A., 382, N.J. Super. 525, 538 (App. Div. 2006)

Olmstead v. United States, 277 U.S. 438 (Brandeis, J., dissenting); 48 S. Ct. 564 (1928)

Pemberton v. Tallahassee Memorial Regional Medical Center, Inc., 66 F. Supp. 2d 1247 (N.D. Fla. 1999)

Physicians for Reproductive Health and Choice (2006), amicus brief filed in *Gonzales v. Carhart, et al.*, 550 U.S. ___ (2007)

Planned Parenthood Federation of America v. Ashcroft, 320 F. Supp. 2d 957 (N.D. Cal., 2004)

Planned Parenthood of Southeastern Pennsylvania v. Casey, 505 U.S. 833; 112 S. Ct. 2791 (1992)

Reinesto, 894 P. 2d 733 (1995)

Relf et al. v. Weinberger et al., Civil Action No. 73-1557, 565 F.2d 722 (Sept, 13, 1977)

Roe v. Crawford, 396 F. Supp. 2d 1041 (Western District of Missouri, 2005)

Roe v. Wade, 410 U.S. 113; 93 S. Ct. 705 (1973)

Skinner v. Oklahoma, 316 U.S. 535 (1942)

State v. McKnight, 352 S.C. 635 (2003)

State of New Jersey v. Ikerd, 69 N.J. Super. 610; 850 A.2d 516 (2004)

Stenberg v. Carhart, 530 U.S. 914; 120 S. Ct. 2597 (2000)

Thornburgh v. American College of Obstetricians, 476 U.S. 749, 106 S. Ct. 2169 (1986).

Thurman v. City of Torrington, 595 F. Supp. 1521 (1984)

Victoria W. v. Larpenter, 369 F.3d 475; 205 F. Supp. 2d 580 (Eastern District of Louisiana, 2004)

Ward v. State, 184 S.W. 3d 874 (Tex. App., 2006)

Webster v. Reproductive Health Services, Inc., 492 U.S. 490 (1989) (Blackmun, J., dissenting)

Whitner v. South Carolina, 492 S.E. 2d 777 (S.C., 1997)

Women Prisoners v. District of Columbia, 93 F.3rd 910 (1996)

LAWS AND LEGISLATION

Adoption and Safe Families Act (ASFA) of 1997, Pub. L. No. 105-89, 111 Stat. 2115 (codified as amended in scattered sections of 42 U.S.C.) (1997)

Child Abuse Prevention and Treatment Act (CAPTA), 42 U.S.C. § 5106a; 42 U.S.C.S. § 1983; Keeping Children and Families Safe Act of 2003, Pub. L. No. 108-36

Child Interstate Abortion Notification Act (CIANA), H. R. 748; S. 8, 396, 403 (2006)

Elliott-Larsen Civil Rights Act, MCLS §§ 37.2101 et seq.

Freedom of Access to Clinic Entrances (FACE) Act, 18 U.S.C.S. § 248 (2005)

Hyde Amendment, Pub. L. No. 94-439, 42 C.F.R. § 441.200 (1987)

Motherhood Protection Act, S. 2219, 108th Cong. (2004) (introduced by Sen. Feinstein (D-CA)) and the Motherhood Protection Act of 2003, H. R. 2246, 108th Cong. (2003) (introduced by Rep. Lofgren (D-CA))

Offenses against the Person and Reputation, Murder, Manslaughter and Infanticide, R.S.C. 1985, c. C-46, s. 233 (Canada)

Oklahoma Habitual Criminal Sterilization Act, Okla Stat Ann § 57 171-95 (1935)

Partial Birth Abortion Ban Act, 18 U.S.C. § 1531 (2000 ed., Supp. IV)

Personal Responsibility and Work Opportunity Reconciliation Act (PWORA) of 1996, Pub. L. No. 104-193, 110 Stat. 2105 (1996)

Prison Litigation Reform Act (PLRA) of 1996, 42 U.S.C. § 1997e(a) (2000)

Prison Rape Elimination Act of 2003, Pub. L. No. 109-79, 42 U.S.C. §§ 15601–15609 (enacted Sept. 4, 2003)

Sexual Abuse of a Minor or a Ward, 18 U.S.C. § 2243 (2006)

Title VII of the Civil Rights Act of 1964, 42 U.S.C. § 2000e (1994)

Title V of the Social Security Act, 42 U.S.C.S. 710(b)(2) (2005)

Unborn Child Pain Awareness Act, S. 51, § 2902(b); 109th Cong. (2005), 151 Cong. Rec. S512 (daily ed. Jan. 24, 2005)

Unborn Victims of Violence Act (UVVA), Pub. L. No. 108-212, 18 U.S.C. 1841 & 10 U.S.C. 919a (2004)

Violence Against Women Act (VAWA), 42 U.S.C. 13981 (1994)

Women's Health and Human Life Protection Act, S.D. Codified Laws §§22-17-7 to -12 (2006)

Acknowledgments

I've amassed a lot of intellectual and social debt in recent years that cannot be repaid, much less adequately recognized, in a page or two. But I'll try. My first thanks go to Ilene Kalish, my editor at NYU Press, her colleagues Despina Papazoglou Gimbel, Cynthia Garver, and Gabrielle Begue. Ilene "got" this book from the beginning; her careful editing ensured that others would stand a better chance of getting it, too. I'm proud to join the ranks of authors whose books Ilene has fostered and shaped.

Reviewers Jennifer Reich and Helen Eigenberg gave this manuscript a thorough and critical reading, providing pages of astute and helpful comments. The book has been transformed as a result. Pierre Diaz read most of the entire manuscript, twice, and raised several sensitive questions in the kindest way. Tanya Krupat of the Osborne Association and Fordham colleagues Jenny Brooks-Klinger, Evelyn Bush, and Ayala Fader helpfully commented on individual chapters. My thinking about reproductive rights (and the cause in general) has been aided and altered by knowing Lynn Paltrow and the women of National Advocates for Pregnant Women, especially Cheryl Howard, and Tiloma Jayasinghe. (Proceeds from this book will be shared with NAPW). I also leaned heavily on the ideas and scholarship of Dorothy Roberts, Rachel Roth, Nicole Rafter, Rickie Solinger, and researchers at the Guttmacher Institute. All mistakes and missteps are, of course, my own.

Graduate students Ed Gallagher, Brian McKernan, Lisa Barnard, and Ming Shi undertook several tedious but important tasks with competence and good humor. Thanks are in order to Jim McCabe and his capable and accommodating staff at Walsh Library. Fordham University also provided me with well-timed and much-appreciated research support and course relief.

Friends who provided a sounding board for the issues raised in this book include Sandra Baxter, Dick Bennett, Jim Lynch, as well as Liz Agosto, Lisa Barnard, Hugo Benavides, Mary Bosworth, and Candace McCoy,

Holly Catania, Erica Chito Childs, Mary Beth Combs, Ed Gallagher, Greta Gilbertson, Iesha Haywood, Linda Ireland, Jacki Johnson, Mary Kenny, Aileen Leonard, Laura Logan, Eileen Markey and Jarrett Murphy, Venezia Michalsen, Kerry Mullins, Stacy Torres, and my sisters, Karin and Elaine. I am also grateful to Rosa Giglio and Paula Genova, Doyle McCarthy, Mary Powers, Orlando and Phyllis Rodriguez, Amy Desautels, Stephanie Laudone, and my colleagues and graduate students in the Department of Sociology and Anthropology; as well as friends Kathy Ashby, Mary Boyce, Jennifer Nye, Ellen Unruh, Bruce Berg, Jacque Helvey Moore and Rosie Winkel; and Andrea Arroyo, Felipe "Feggo" Galindo, Catherine Friedl, Pat Friesen, Adrienne Navon, and the inimitable Pamela Roberts. My life is decidedly richer for having these people in it.

I couldn't ask for better champions than four women: Nicola Pitchford and Jeanne Kalosieh remain warmly regarded and regular sources of distraction and support. Miki Akimoto critiqued an early draft of the manuscript, a noteworthy feat in itself. Our longstanding friendship grounds me and sustains me. As much as I marvel at Maria Fernandez Gold's unparalleled organizational skills, I admire her warmth and her devotion to daughters everywhere (not just her own) even more. To the staff of Memorial Sloan-Kettering Cancer Center I owe a debt of life and health.

My parents and a rural farm upbringing ensured that I (like my siblings) was raised with the values of "pitching in," getting along, and doing what one thinks is right. If there are two more hard-working and rock solid people than Harold and Leona Flavin, I haven't met them. Two of my aunts, Sr. Edwardine Flavin, CSJ, and Sr. Loretta Jasper, CSJ, belong to a small convent that was involved in the immigrant sanctuary movement of the 1980s. I credit both of them with being lifelong role models and advocates for social justice. Today, they, along with my parents, are the family members I most count on for a grounded perspective on the way the world is and how it ought to be.

Finally, one of the hardest parts of writing this book has been knowing that there are people in my life whose opinions I value who will not just disagree with some of what I've said but may be offended by it. I write secure in the knowledge, though, that we share a commitment to bettering women's lives and a belief in the need to address the inequalities that define our society. And for that, I am very grateful.

New York City, July 2008

Index

nicotine. *See* substance use
no-procreation orders, 5, 24, 29–30,
  37–38, 41, 48, 192n11, 202–203n70;
  challenges to, 202–203n70; 204n87;
  rationalizations for, 42–46. *See also*
  eugenics movement; sterilization

Paltrow, Lynn, 95, 187, 223n5
parental alienation syndrome, 172–175,
  251n53, 256n45
parental notification, 62–65, 77, 79,
  211n89. *See also* abortion; contraceptives; teen pregnancy
patriarchy, 3–4, 7, 165, 166, 170,
  174–175, 180–181, 185, 189
Peterson, Laci and Connor, 98–99. *See
  also* fetal homicide laws
*Planned Parenthood of Southeastern
  Pennsylvania v. Casey,* 40, 61
pregnancy, 66–67, 74, 95–118, 119–163,
  194n13; continuous nature of conception and, 192n14, 193n10; criminalization of, 108–118; crisis pregnancy
  centers, 62; incidence, 52, 79, 124;
  outcomes, 49, 52, 97, 105–108, 111,
  125, 226n33; rape-related, 78; unintended, 52, 74–79, 90, 216n18. *See
  also* abortion; birth; pregnant women;
  teen pregnancy
pregnancy and childbirth, 124–127,
  237n48, 237n50; turning points,
  260–261n8; victimization of, 129,
  130–133, 212–213n105, 240n96,
  250n124
pregnant women: and HIV/AIDS,
  238n56; incarceration, 66–67,
  124–127, 237n48, 238n50; killing of,
  97–98, 224n16, 224n18, 224–225n20;
  policing of, 108–118, 185; prenatal care, 61, 82, 98, 113, 116, 124,
  125–126, 220n46, 238n55; relationship to fetus, 96, 102; substance use,
  103–105, 108–118, 229n76; violence
  against, 95, 97–98, 99–103, 216n18,
  223–224n10, 224n11, 224n18. *See also*

infant abandonment and neonaticide;
  pregnancy; teen pregnancy; violence
prison and jail: correctional staff misconduct, 130–133, 212–213n10, 240n96;
  geographic remoteness, 122, 146,
  156; medical care, 119–130, 133–135,
  234n3, 236n28, 236n30, 236–237n39;
  privatization, 123, 131, 236–237n39;
  reproductive health care of, 65–69,
  119–130, 133–135; 234n3, 239n75,
  241n111. *See also* Federal Bureau of
  Prisons; incarceration
prison and jail, by state: Alabama, 65–66,
  121–123, 212–213n105; Arizona,
  66–67, 126; California, 34, 119–120,
  125, 133, 200n31, 234n3, 249n98,
  201n36, 202n53; Colorado, 131; District of Columbia, 127; Florida, 121,
  129; Illinois 119, 126–127, Louisiana
  206n7; Maryland, 129; Michigan,
  132–133; Missouri, 148; New Jersey, 34, 68, 129; New York, 51–52,
  128, 129, 130–131, 133, 143, 146,
  147, 148, 199–201n21, 236–237n39,
  239n76, 240n96; North Carolina
  202n53; Pennsylvania, 68, 246n64;
  Virginia, 202n53; Washington 126.
  See also Federal Bureau of Prisons;
  incarceration
Prison Litigation Reform Act (PLRA),
  134
Prison Rape Elimination Act (PREA),
  131–132
Privacy. *See* rights
Project Prevention, 29, 47–48, 204n95,
  204–205n96. *See also* eugenics mve-
  ment; sterilization
public assistance, 16, 19, 20, 36, 42–45,
  142, 150, 160, 179–180, 184; federal
  budget, 44, 120; Medicaid, 18–21,
  29, 61, 112; Personal Responsibility
  and Work Opportunity Reconciliation Act, 42, 203n72; Temporary
  Assistance to Needy Families, 45,
  150, 184

About the Author

JEANNE FLAVIN is Associate Professor in the Sociology and Anthropology Department at Fordham University in the Bronx, New York. She also serves on the board of National Advocates for Pregnant Women. Jeanne is the recipient of a 2008–2009 Fulbright award.

LaVergne, TN USA
16 August 2009
154909LV00001B/4/P

9 780814 727546